DISCOVER NEW ENGLAND

Eric and Ruth Bailey

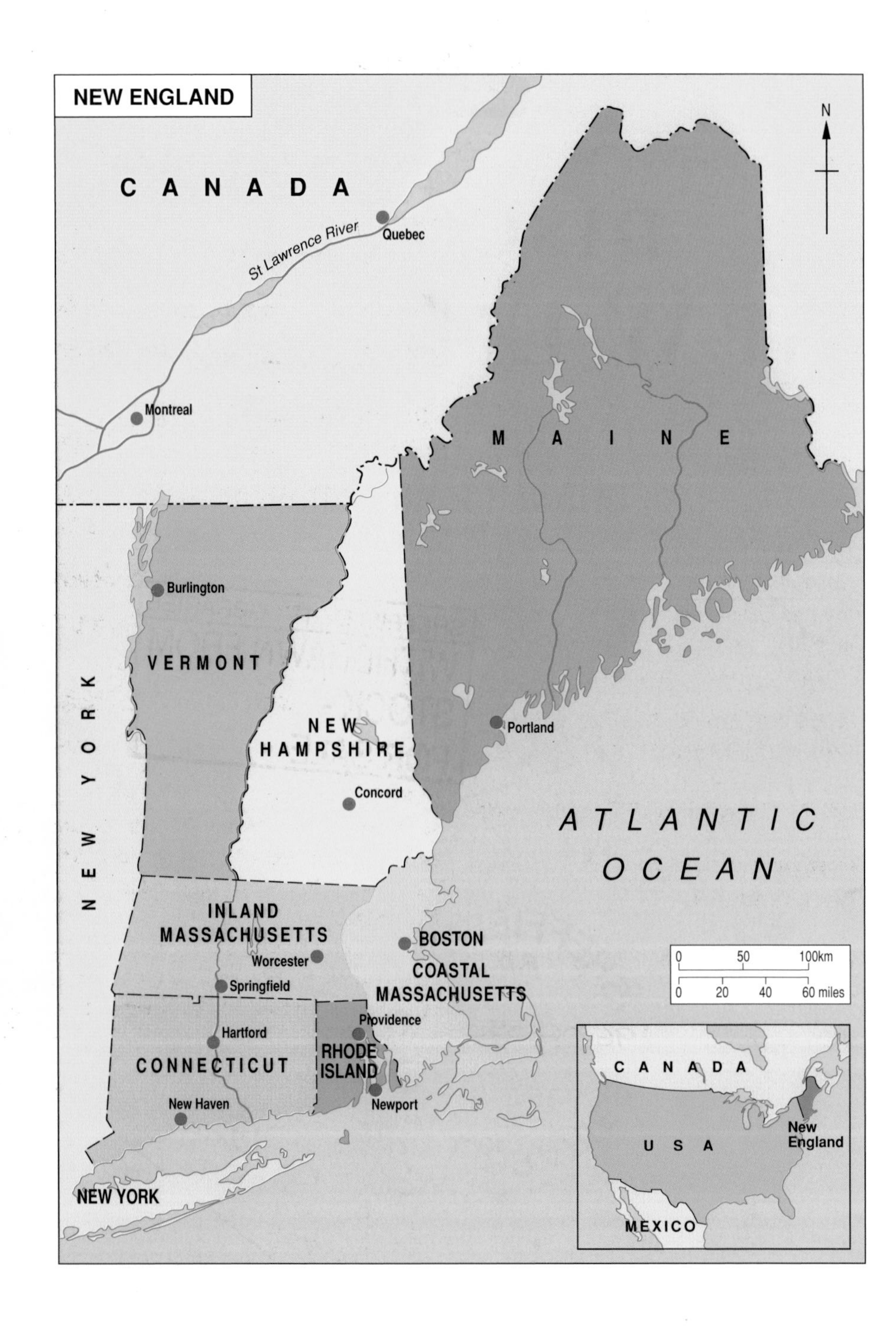

NEW ENGLAND
N
CANADA
St Lawrence River
Quebec
Montreal
MAINE
Burlington
VERMONT
NEW YORK
NEW HAMPSHIRE
Portland
Concord
ATLANTIC OCEAN
INLAND MASSACHUSETTS
BOSTON
Worcester
COASTAL MASSACHUSETTS
Springfield
0 50 100km
0 20 40 60 miles
Providence
Hartford
RHODE ISLAND
CONNECTICUT
Newport
New Haven
NEW YORK
CANADA
USA
New England
MEXICO

Contents

A Place for all Seasons

Although certain images stand out in most people's minds as typically New England, each of the six states that make up the region – Connecticut, Maine, Massachusetts, New Hampshire, Rhode Island and Vermont – has characteristics that make it different from the rest. The differences add up to a wonderful range of holiday opportunities to suit all tastes throughout the year.

A Brief Tour

The region is compact and covers a mere 66,068 square miles (172,518 km^2), slightly less than the area covered by the state of Washington alone. No place is more than a comfortable day's drive from any other. It is bounded on the north by the Canadian provinces of Quebec and New Brunswick, and on the south by the Atlantic Ocean and Long Island Sound. To the east lie New Brunswick and the Atlantic Ocean, and to the west is New York State.

The massive Basilica at the world headquarters of the First Church of Christ, Scientist, in Boston seats up to 5,000 people.

Massachusetts is the most populous of the New England states, with a total of just over six million people. Boston, the state's capital and the largest city in the region, is also the principal gateway, with Logan International Airport, an important shipping port, and major road and rail connections. Few visitors will fail to be delighted with Boston, a surprisingly compact and intimate city that is steeped in history. To take full advantage of its delights, it is best traversed on foot rather than by car.

Coastal Massachusetts offers a wide range of historic and scenic options to the north and south of Boston. Gloucester, Salem, Rockport and Marblehead are favourite attractions on the North Shore. To the south, Cape Cod, with its beaches and dunes, is a famed centre for summer

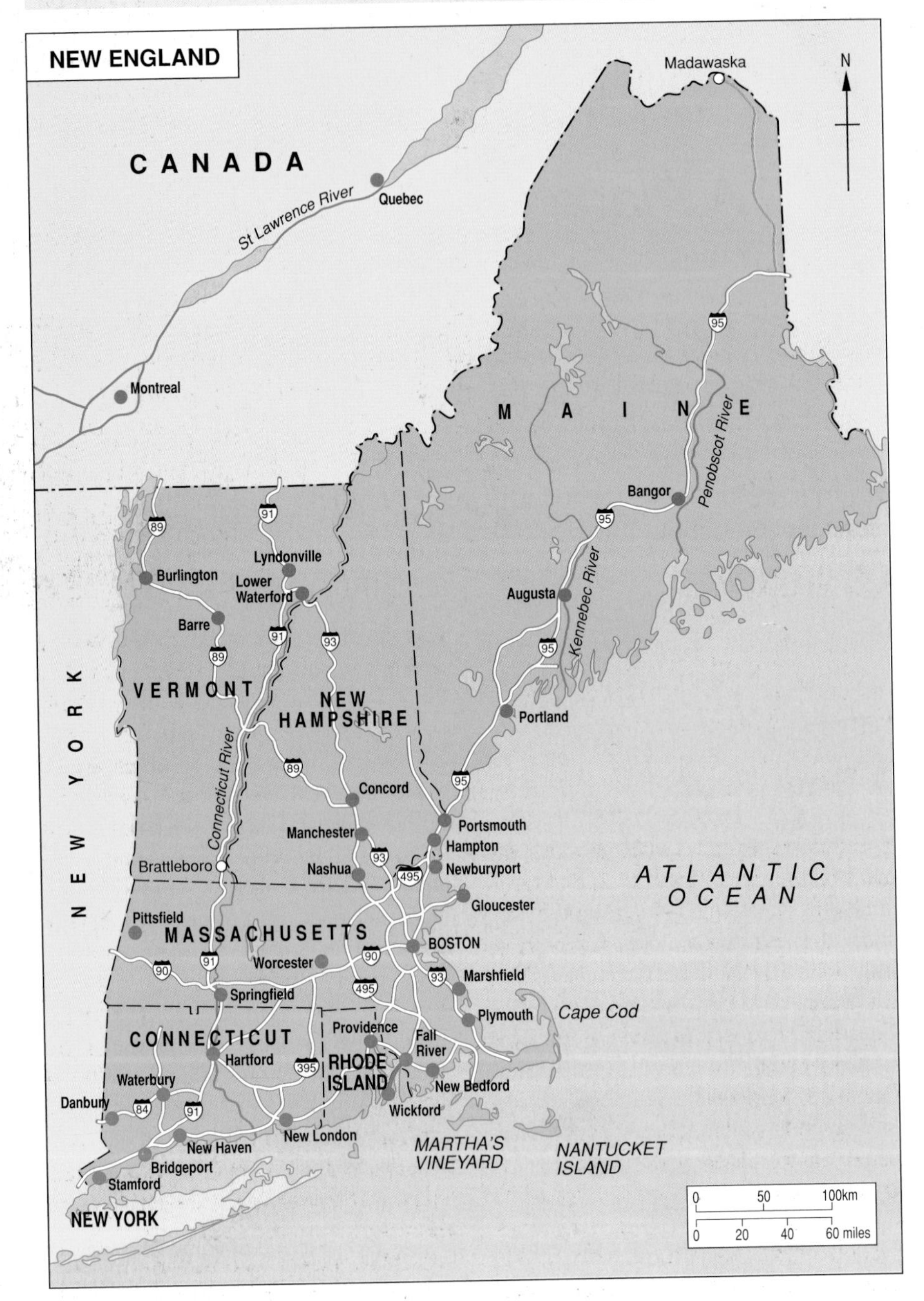

holidays, as are the islands of Martha's Vineyard and Nantucket. Plymouth boasts many traces of the Puritan settlers, while New Bedford recalls the days of whaling.

Inland Massachusetts, stretching westwards to the border of New York State, is

Shelburne Falls is one of the many natural attractions you will find in Massachusetts.

a predominantly rural area, although the industrial centre of Worcester is New England's second largest city. Another city with an important manufacturing heritage is Springfield, famous for the rifle which was made there. Pioneer Valley, along the Connecticut River, and the Berkshires offer stunning views and a variety of touring experiences.

You are never far from the sea in tiny Rhode Island. The smallest state in the Union, it covers little more than 1,000 square miles (2,560km^2) and measures only 48 miles (77km) from north to south. The capital, Providence, has a delightful historic district with many restored houses from the 18th and 19th centuries. Newport, an internationally renowned yachting centre, boasts fine 18th-century streets and lanes and is equally proud of the extravagant summer 'cottages' built for the likes of the Astors and Vanderbilts, that are now major tourist attractions.

Much of south-eastern Connecticut serves as a dormitory or weekend retreat for people who work in New York City, but the state is no dreary suburb. It is a 5,000-square-mile (12,800km^2) patchwork of farmland, forests, hills and mountains. The state capital is Hartford, an important centre for the insurance industry. New Haven, on the coast, is best known as the home of historic Yale University, but the city also earns its keep from the less rarefied pursuits of commerce and industry. The coast between New Haven and Rhode Island is strung with attractive clapboard villages and picturesque harbours.

Rural Vermont, backyard America at its pastoral best, is New England's only landlocked state, although it has an impressive coastline along the lovely eastern shore of Lake Champlain. With its old-fashioned

Locally produced foods and crafts are a strong feature of rural Vermont.

red barns, covered bridges and maple sugar-houses, the state is a favourite with visitors at all times of the year.

New Hampshire bears the stamp of frontier territory, an impression strengthened by the dramatic declaration, 'Live Free Or Die', carried on the licence plates of residents' cars. It has only 18 miles (29km) of coast along a wedge of land pinched between north-east Massachusetts and south-east Maine. Nevertheless, there are excellent sandy beaches, and good bathing, fishing, boating and dining facilities. The Seacoast Region's principal city, Portsmouth, played an important role in the Revolutionary War.

Inland New Hampshire has a wealth of rugged beauty, and the sound of white water cascading over rocks is never far away. Lakes Sunapee and Winnepesaukee are a joy for watersports enthusiasts, and the White Mountains are a source of enjoyment for skiers in the winter and walkers and climbers in the summer. The Monadnock Region, taking its name from the 3,165ft (965m) Grand Monadnock, America's most climbed mountain, has winding country roads, rolling farmland, village greens and white steepled churches.

Independently-minded New Hampshire imposes no sales tax, so its extensive shopping malls and factory retail outlets, to say nothing of its state-run liquor stores, draw shoppers from throughout the region.

Known as 'the Pine Tree State', Maine covers an area of 38,000 square miles (98,420km^2), making it bigger than all the other five New England states combined. Much of it is a wilderness of forests and lakes, the home of black bears, moose and deer, and anyone in search of solitude really can get away from it all. Along its rocky 3,500-mile (5,600km) coast are some 2,000 islands. Maine's capital is Augusta, but its largest city is Portland, a centre of commerce, industry and maritime interests.

Getting There

By Air

Boston's Logan International Airport is New England's major gateway, served by carriers from throughout the United States and abroad. Logan Airport is only 3 miles (4.8km) from downtown Boston, whose citizens like to point out that theirs is closer to Europe than any other US airport. It has five terminals, labelled A to E, and has excellent transportation services, including a water shuttle link to and from Rowes Wharf. Direct services from Britain are provided by American Airlines, British Airways, Northwest Airlines, TWA and Virgin Atlantic. Transatlantic flights take about seven hours. Services from other parts of Europe are provided by Aer Lingus, Air France, Alitalia Airlines, El Al Airlines, Lufthansa German Airlines, Olympic Airlines, Sabena Belgian World Airlines, Swissair, and TAP Air Portugal. New York's JFK and Newark Airports give travellers a wider choice of airlines and routes, but changing to a domestic service increases the total journey time.

Other important airports in New England are Bradley International Airport at Windsor Locks, just north of Hartford, Connecticut, and Theodore Francis Green State Airport, near Providence, Rhode Island. Major US carriers also fly into Worcester, Massachusetts; Manchester, New Hampshire; Burlington, Vermont; and Bangor and Portland, Maine.

By Land

Amtrak has frequent train services from Washington and New York to Boston, with stops at New Haven and New London, Connecticut, and at Westerly and Providence, Rhode Island. *The Montrealer* calls at Connecticut, Massachusetts and Vermont on its overnight journey from Washington to Montreal. The Lake Shore Limited runs from Chicago to Boston. Regional services are provided by the Massachusetts Bay Transportation Authority, linking Boston with stops on the north and south shores. The only

New England caters for all tastes – this is Storyland at Glen, in New Hampshire's White Mountains region.

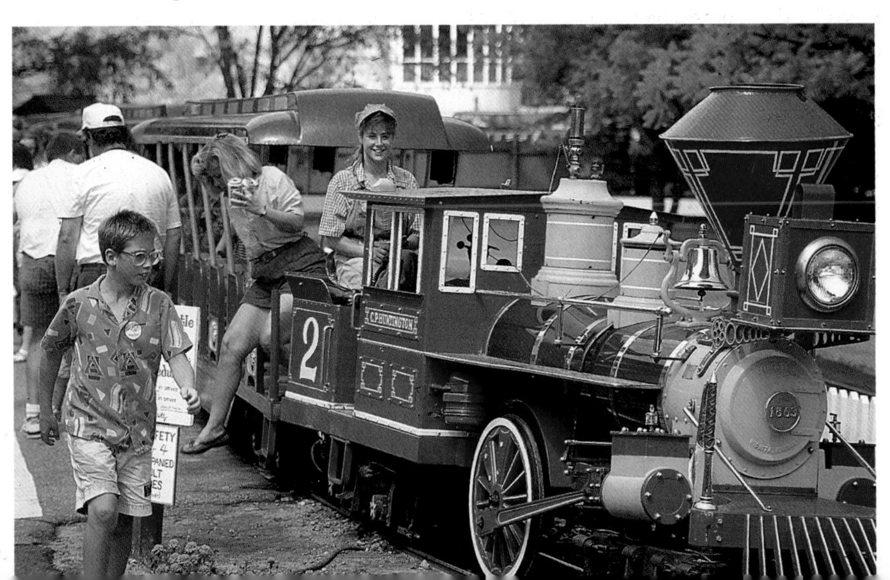

passenger rail service in Maine comes from Canada's VIA Rail, whose route from Montreal to Halifax, Nova Scotia, crosses the northern part of the state.

New England has a network of good roads, with Interstate highways 84, 89, 90, 91, 93 and 95 providing fast routes through all six states. Excellent road maps are provided free by each of the states at roadside information centres. The major international car rental agencies have locations at airports and cities throughout the region.

Bus services to Boston from cities throughout the US and Canada are provided by Greyhound Lines, and Peter Pan Bus Lines has services from New York, New Hampshire and Cape Cod.

By Sea

Boston's Black Falcon terminal is in South Boston, just a few minutes' drive from the Massachusetts Turnpike, the superhighway that links Boston to western Massachusetts, New York and cities in the Great Lakes states. The terminal is a year-round facility which can simultaneously accommodate a 1,200-passenger vessel and a 600-passenger vessel, turning Boston into a world-class cruise port. Passengers embark and disembark across a modern enclosed gangway joining ship and terminal. A mezzanine floor has lounge and seating areas, snack bar and ticketing areas. Passenger drop-off areas and long-term parking are inside the terminal.

Passports and Visas

British visitors to the United States need a full ten-year passport valid for at least the duration of the intended stay. The one-year British Visitors' Passport – the kind obtained at a post office – is not acceptable. For many other nationalities, passports must be valid for at least six months beyond the intended period of stay.

Citizens of the European Union, New Zealand, Switzerland and Japan no longer need visas to enter the US. To be eligible for visa-free entry, travellers must hold an unexpired national or European Union passport and be travelling for business, pleasure or transit purposes only. Their stay in the US must not exceed 90 days, and they must hold a return or onward ticket issued by an air or sea carrier acceptable to the American immigration authorities.

Initial entry by land from Canada or Mexico without a visa is precluded, although travellers who have entered the US visa-free may, within the 90-day admission period make side trips to Mexico, Canada, the Caribbean islands and Bermuda, and return without a visa by any mode of transport. Canadian citizens and citizens of British Commonwealth countries and Ireland who have 'landed immigrant' status in Canada or Bermuda do not need visas.

Travel for purposes other than short business trips or tourist visits often requires special documentation. Information can be obtained from the US Embassy or Consulate General in your country, and visa application forms – one for each traveller, including children and infants – can be sent to you.

Alternatively, write to Visa Branch, United States Embassy, 5 Upper Grosvenor Street, London W1A 2JB (tel. 0171 499 9000). Other US Embassies are at: United States Consulate General, Queen House, 14 Queen Street, Belfast

BT1 6EQ; 27 Boulevard du Regent, B1000, Brussels, Belgium (Tel. 02-513 3830); Moonah Place, Canberra, ACT 2600, Australia (Tel. 06-270 5000); PO Box 1190, 29 Fitzherbert Terrace, Thorndon, Wellington, New Zealand (Tel. 04-722068); Thibault House, 877 Pretorius Street, Pretoria, South Africa (Tel. 012-3421048).

Visa applications – with passport-sized stamped addressed envelopes, and your passport – should be mailed as early as possible, at least 14 days before departure. Personal applications are only possible in an emergency. Time can be saved with a postal application by personally delivering your application form and passport to the Embassy. If travel plans do not allow enough time for a postal application, travellers may use a travel agent or special courier service through whom an application can be completed in 24 hours, although a charge will be made.

If you do need a visa and are likely to make repeated visits to the United States, apply for a 'multiple entry, indefinite period' visa. This will remain valid even when the passport in which it is stamped expires, so make sure you have the old passport with you when you travel on the new one.

Visitors to the United States have to complete a landing card. It is not the world's best-designed questionnaire. Our tip is to fill it in from the bottom, and all will fall neatly into place. Part of the card will be stapled into your passport by the immigration officer. Don't lose this – it should be collected as you leave the US.

In Britain, tourism information on each of the states, and on the region as a whole, is available from the United States Travel and Tourism Administration, PO Box 1EN, London W1A 1EN (Tel. 0171-495 4336).

Customs Regulations

US Customs regulations allow travellers to import personal effects – clothing, personal jewellery, hunting, fishing and photographic equipment – a litre of alcoholic beverages (wine, beer or liquor), 200 cigarettes, or 50 cigars or 2kg (4.4 lbs) of tobacco. Non-residents may also take in articles worth up to $100 as gifts for other persons. Meat, meat products, seeds, plants, fruit – and of course illegal drugs – are forbidden.

When to Go

Conversation is unlikely to flag in New England because however fascinating current events or the latest scandal may be, there's always the weather to talk about.

New England's climate is generally cool and humid, but the great variations found within the region, and the weather changes that frequently occur within a very short time span, are legendary.

Northern Maine has only 90 to 100 frost-free days each year. Winters there are long and cold with deep snow, and the summer is short, cool and humid. New Hampshire's Presidential Range has a climate which is almost subarctic, but other parts of New England remain relatively warm. Spring, frequently wet and cool, brings the notorious and mercifully short 'Mud Season' to the north. Low pressure areas bring frequent changes to the summer weather.

Rainfall averages 40 to 50 inches (1,000 to 1,300mm) a year in the east and south and 30 to 40 inches (750 to 1,000mm) elsewhere. The Fall is unanimously regarded as the best season, with crisp, cool nights, bright sunny days and, of course, those wonderful colours.

Despite the changeable nature of its climate, New England is a year-round destination, though it's worth remembering that many attractions do not open until May or early June, and some open only at weekends until well into the high season, so it is wise to check in advance if possible before going too far out of your way.

Fog shrouds the skyscrapers on Boston's Waterfront. New England's capricious weather is always a topic for conversation.

City dwellers, especially those in Boston, head for the beaches at the first hint of warm weather, but there is no serious swimming or other waterborne activity until summer truly arrives, which tends to be around the end of May. Even then, visitors can expect to have the beaches to themselves on weekdays until July when the holiday season gets into full swing.

New England's fabulous Fall starts in the north in mid-September, and works its way southwards until the end of October when the leaves are finally gone. This gives 'leaf-peepers', as they are rather coyly named, an extended opportunity to catch the glorious spectacle at its best. Autumn is the most popular tourist season – and, of course, the most expensive. Accommodation is difficult to find in many places, and should always be booked well in advance.

In the north, snow will be on the ground as early as the last week in November, remaining until mid-April,

'Leaf-peepers' can keep up with the glorious Fall foliage from mid-September to the end of October.

but farther south it is unlikely to be seen much before Christmas. Skiing is a well organized activity, with centres ranging from the simple to the sophisticated in every state except Rhode Island. Many places use snow-making equipment to extend the season artificially.

Clothing

Bearing in mind the region's changeable climate, the best advice at any time is to be prepared for the worst. In the summer make sure you have an umbrella or raincoat, and even a sweater for the evening, as it can become disconcertingly cool once the sun goes down. In the winter you'll need a good topcoat, gloves, waterproof footwear and warm socks. If you go whale-watching, take some warm clothing even on a warm day – there can be a big difference in temperature once you're out at sea.

Casual wear is accepted in most places, but shops and restaurants – even the most casual eating places – will not serve barefooted people in swimsuits. Jacket and tie is the standard dress code in the more upmarket restaurants in Boston and some of the other larger cities, and in some hotel dining rooms.

Driving

Driving is the most convenient way to get around the region, but traffic can be heavy on popular routes – to the beaches during the summer and to the forest colours in the Fall, for example – and rush hours in Boston are a nightmare. Driving standards and manners are gen-

Travelling by car is by far the most convenient way to get around New England, especially in a classic such as this.

erally good, although Bostonians tend to sound their horns impatiently at the slightest delay, even when the lights are on red. Driving is on the right.

Maximum speed limits vary from state to state – 55mph (88kph) in some, 65mph (104kph) in others – and they are rigidly enforced. Limits in small towns may be as low as 20mph (32kph), and locals will tell you to look out for the police, who have little else to do but catch offenders. The wearing of seat belts is a legal requirement only in Connecticut, Massachusetts and Rhode Island.

Nothing could be easier than collecting a rented car at an airport in New England, as long as you've remembered your driving licence and have a major credit card (drivers under 25 are charged extra). After the briefest of formalities, the keys are handed over. If you have any misgivings or queries – where the light switches are, for instance, how the air-conditioning works, or even how to get to your hotel – just ask. People will be only too pleased to help.

DRIVING TIPS

Before setting out on a trip, it's a good idea to take a look at a map and get some idea of the general direction you'll be heading in, and to make a note of highway numbers. Highway signs generally include both: 'Interstate 84 East', or 'US Highway 7 South'. Even numbers always indicate a highway that runs east/west, odd numbers one that runs north/south. Road numbers are usually abbreviated thus: I-4 E (Interstate 4 East), US 19 S (US Highway 19 South), SR 528 (State Road 528), CR 1234 (County Road 1234). Usually, though, people simply refer to 'Route so-and-so'.

Those used to driving on the left may find difficulty at first in readily spotting signs, traffic lights and street names. Traffic lights are often slung in the centre of intersections (crossroads), sometimes quite high, but the sequence is the same as elsewhere. A single flashing yellow or red light means proceed with caution. Unless there is a sign to the contrary, you can filter right on a red traffic light, but take great care, since vehicles coming from the left still have right of way.

Health

Sunburn is not unknown in New England because the light is intensified by all that sea, sand, snow and sky, so take an appropriate sunscreen in your personal health kit. You should also take an insect repellent with you, since blackflies and greenhead flies can be troublesome in the mountains and on the seashore.

Many supermarkets have well-stocked sections selling a variety of non-prescription medicines and preparations and offer advice on ailments and treatments. However, drugstores may be few and far between in rural areas, and will almost certainly be closed on Sundays.

Medical attention can be very costly in the United States, so make sure you have adequate insurance lined up in advance. Adequate these days means at least $2 million cover for medical expenses. On the plus side, spectacles ('eyeglasses') are much cheaper than they are in western Europe, and opticians can usually supply a new pair overnight, frequently within the hour, so if you wear glasses it makes sense to take a copy of your prescription with you. Even if you don't lose your present pair, you can still treat yourself to some new ones.

Money Matters

The United States has moved further than most countries towards use of credit cards as the main means of paying for goods and services. Most large shops, restaurants, hotels and car rental firms in New England will accept credit cards, especially VISA, MasterCard and American Express. Personal cheques are anathema, and travellers' cheques are good only if they are in US dollars. Although travellers' cheques are widely accepted, a surprising number of establishments are reluctant to honour them. An internationally accepted credit card, validated for use in automatic teller machines (ATMs), enables you to obtain cash as and when you need it – on a daily basis, if you like. This is convenient but the cost of obtaining cash from credit cards must be weighed against the cost of buying and cashing travellers' cheques. By obtaining cash with credit cards, security is improved because you only need to carry relatively small amounts of cash. However, the list of places where you can use your card may not be up to date. On some occasions the card that did nicely in some banks' machines last year has been politely but firmly rejected this year. If your card is rejected do not persist in trying to obtain money with it as after three attempts the machine will eat the card. Instead, abandon the attempt and try another company's machine. Remember that your card will have to be validated for ATM use before you leave home.

US bank notes come in denominations of $1, $2 (rare), $5, $10, $20, $50 and $100. They are all the same size and the same shade of green, but each bears the portrait of a different American president. Coins are one cent (a penny), five cents (nickel), ten cents (dime), 25 cents (quarter), 50 cents and, occasionally, $1.

Security

New England does not have the crime problems that bedevil life in some other parts of the United States. The citizens of many small towns will tell you that the local police force exists solely to keep an eye out for traffic offenders, and even Boston has a comfortably safe feel to it, although certain areas are best avoided at night.

However, all that is not to say that petty criminals – muggers, pickpockets, sneak thieves – do not exist, and at all times it pays to exercise commonsense security. Valuables should be deposited in hotel safes when you go out for the day, and precious items should never be left in a hotel room. Never leave cameras, camcorders or anything else of value in view in a parked car. Lock everything you don't take with you out of sight, preferably in the boot.

The first security precaution should be taken before you leave home: make sure you are adequately insured against loss, damage or theft.

Accommodation

Whether you stay in a quiet country inn, a bed-and-breakfast home or a city hotel belonging to an international chain, you will find high accommodation standards throughout New England. Hotels and

motels are more usually found in and around major cities and popular holiday centres. Many of the larger resort hotels and inns with restaurants will offer the Modified American Plan (MAP) where rates include breakfast and dinner. At peak times MAP may be mandatory in some establishments.

The region's accommodation strength, however, lies in the variety of its small inns and B & B facilities, most often family-owned and run, and with no two rooms alike. Some historic inns have been in business since before the Revolution, others have been transformed from old

The good life – New England style. This is a speciality from Cape Cod.

farmhouses, mansions and sea captains' homes. Furnishings are generally of a very high standard, and it is not unusual to sleep in a room filled – and sometimes seemingly over-filled – with valuable antiques. Almost always there will be a good view.

Other accommodation options are small seaside cottages, country cabins, and camping facilities ranging from wilderness sites to locations with dining, shopping and laundry amenities. Many excellent campsites are located in state parks throughout the region. Sites operated by Kampgrounds of America (KOA), which has locations all over North America, are to be found in each of the six New England states. KOA facilities are excellent for family camping, often with electricity and water hook-ups for camper trucks or recreational vehicles as well as tent pitches and log cabins for rent.

There is a list of recommended hotels and B & Bs on page 338.

Food and Drink

New England offers an enormous diversity of ethnic cuisines, thanks to the many thousands of immigrants who have settled in the region over the past three and a half centuries. And because many New England towns are small and restaurants tend to be located downtown, you don't have to work hard to find something that interests you. A walk along Main Street or the waterfront could well lead you from menu to menu originating from China, Russia, France, Thailand, Vietnam, Spain, Portugal, Italy....

Exotic ethnic dishes, however, are only part of the story. New England has its own wonderful cuisine. The region is best known, of course, for its seafood: succulent Maine lobster, clams – baked, steamed or served as chowder – crab and scallops. Tasty dishes – often quite inexpensive – are created with freshly-caught schrod, cod and bluefish as the main ingredients. A favourite way to dine out is to sit on the rough wooden benches of a seaside clambake 'shack', tucking into a selection of seafood eaten off picnic plates.

Other specialities have evolved from the imaginative treatment of game birds, rabbit, venison, beef, lamb and pork. The ubiquitous cranberry is used to create a spectrum of sauces, chutneys and preserves. Boston is known as 'Beantown', but beans are baked in pits by purists all over the region. In Connecticut, 'the Nutmeg State', they proudly serve chilled spinach soup with nutmeg and cream.

In Rhode Island they've been feuding for generations over the jonnycake, on the face of it a simple cornmeal flapjack. They argue over its origins: was it a 'journey cake' introduced by the Pilgrims and carried by travellers, or a 'Shawnee cake' made by Indians? They argue over its spelling – 'jonnycake' or 'johnnycake'? Should it be made thick or thin? With boiling water or cold milk? There's even a state law defining the kind of corn that must be used in a genuine Rhode Island Jo(h)nnycake, as well as a Society for the Propagation of the Jonnycake (sic). Tradition in Rhode Island maintains a vigilant and spirited defence of the state dish. But whichever way the argument runs, jonnycakes taste good with a hearty New England breakfast. The thick variety may also turn up with stews, in place of dumplings.

Silent advice – mailboxes and newspaper vending machines near a Boston rapid transit station.

Drinks and Beverages

After all that fuss in Boston Harbour in 1773 (see page 36), afternoon tea is making a comeback in New England. All over the region, people of all ages are beginning to set the middle of the afternoon aside for a genteel meal of tiny sandwiches, pastries and rich fruit cake with an accompaniment of Earl Grey tea.

Wine-making is not a big business in New England, and there are probably not much more than a dozen wineries, mostly in the south. One of the largest is Vinland Wine Cellars which produces a range of seven wines at Middletown, Rhode Island. Vinland, of course, is the place in North America where legend says Leif Ericsson found grapes growing wild in AD 1000. The Middletown winery, at 909 East Main Road (Route 138 on Aquidneck Island), offers free tastings and tours, and has its own vineyards on the shores of Narragansett Bay.

An increasing number of small privately owned breweries is now to be found throughout the region, and the beer they brew is similar to the 'real ale' favoured in Britain. Unlike many internationally known American lager-type beers, these real ales are intended to be served at cellar temperature rather than chilled. The Commonwealth Brewing Company, in Boston, brews a dozen or so varieties of beer in the basement of a restaurant that serves inexpensive meals.

Cider, a non-alcoholic drink unless labelled 'hard cider', has long been a traditional beverage, and is brewed in all six states of New England. It is often mixed with rum to make a potent and warming punch and is also used to lend piquancy to sauces.

Tips and Gratuities

You can expect to tip anyone who performs any kind of personal service: waiters and waitresses, bellhops, airport baggage handlers and taxi drivers especially. Give 15 to 20 percent to waiters and taxi drivers, a dollar upwards to bellhops and baggage handlers, depending on the amount of luggage toted. It is also usual to tip a dollar or so to the person who returns your car from valet parking.

Post and Telephone Services

Stamps can be bought at hotel receptions, and for straightforward holiday correspondence – postcards and airmail letters – staff are usually familiar with the rates. There is usually a mail box somewhere in the lobby. Post offices are often located near other public buildings – the court room, mayor's office, sheriff's office and the like – and they can also be found in shopping malls.

Telephone calls can be expensive if made from hotel bedrooms because hotels can impose a hefty surcharge on top of the normal charge. However, there are usually plenty of public payphone cubicles in hotel reception areas.

British visitors will find that the easiest way to phone home is to dial 1-800-4455667. This connects you directly with a British Telecom operator in London through whom you can make a transfer charge call or use a British Telecom chargecard. Whether you go through an American or British operator, it might be cheaper to make a collect call (ie, transfer the charge).

Travellers from other parts of the world should check with their national telecommunications organization before leaving home to see if there is a similar direct-line operation. Other options available to all travellers are international charge cards – such as the AT&T Calling Card – and various types of prepaid telephone vouchers. Your travel agent should have details.

Shopping

Some people travel to New England simply for the shopping, especially in the big factory outlet malls. Designer clothing, jewellery, leatherware, shoes, sportswear, brand name luxury goods, glassware and luggage are offered at huge reductions, and you can certainly spend your money in comfort, with huge car parks and in many cases covered walkways leading from store to store.

Some of the best locations for outlet shopping are along Route 1, especially at Kittery and Wells, in Maine; at North Conway, New Hampshire; and at the

Fall River and New Bedford, Massachusetts. Discount outlets specializing in the kind of clothing found in smart boutiques are found in all six states. In Boston few bargain-hunters will want to miss Filene's Basement, on Washington Street. If price is no object, try the city's Faneuil Hall Marketplace, where three elegant but busy arcades house more than 160 shops as well as stalls, food stands and restaurants.

Flea markets, farmers' markets, produce stalls and pick-your-own fruit farms are very much a part of life's rich pattern in New England, along with antique shops, craft centres and bazaars. The region's compactness means you rarely have far to travel to find somewhere to tempt purse or credit card. New Hampshire has no sales tax, and its state-run liquor stores attract buyers from neighbouring states and even from Canada. Tourists from abroad will probably find liquor cheaper in New Hampshire than in the airport duty-free shop.

Language

It doesn't take long on your first visit to realize the truth in that old saw about Britain and the United States being two nations divided by a common tongue. The two peoples do use English in different ways.

Restaurants and food shops are the places where British visitors will notice the main differences. Jelly, for example, is jam. It is usually served with peanut butter and biscuits. American biscuits are similar to British scones. What the British call biscuits are cookies to an American. Zucchini is courgette. Ask for eggplant and you will get aubergine.

A SHORT GLOSSARY OF USEFUL WORDS

British	**American**
Food	
Chips	**French fries**
Grill	**Broil**
Pancakes	**Crepes**
Runner beans	**String beans**
Swede	**Rutabaga**
Tomato sauce	**Ketchup**
Driving	
Car bonnet	**Hood**
Car boot	**Trunk**
Car park	**Parking lot**
Car park, multi-storey	**Parking garage**
Dual carriageway	**Divided highway**
Give way	**Yield**
Lay-by	**Rest area**
Lorry	**Truck**
Pavement	**Sidewalk**
Petrol	**Gasoline ('gas')**
Windscreen	**Windshield**
Clothing	
Plimsolls/trainers	**Sneakers**
Pullover/cardigan	**Sweater**
Trousers	**Pants**
Waistcoat	**Vest**
Miscellaneous	
Autumn	**Fall**
Biro	**Ballpoint**
Chemist	**Drugstore**
Cheque	**Check**
Cloakroom	**Washroom**
Face flannel	**Washcloth**
Football	**Soccer**
Hair slide	**Barette**
Perspex	**Lucite**
Queue	**Line**
Restaurant bill	**Check**
Spectacles	**Eyeglasses**
Toilet	**Rest room**
Torch	**Flashlight**
Transfer charge call	**Collect call**

WHAT IS MAN THAT THOU ART MINDFUL OF HIM
EMERSON HALL

THE REGION, ITS HISTORY AND ITS PEOPLE

A Background of Colour, Characters and Drama

New England's indefinable mixture of qualities – its beauty, its character, its people – can alter your life. Many have gone there for a vacation, discovered a sudden and lasting change in themselves, and returned to spend the rest of their life there, with never a moment's regret. Visit the region for the first time and within a week you will know whether you have fallen victim to its enchantment. This is Outdoorsville on a big scale, and at every season.

The Fall is unbelievably beautiful – and also very busy. In winter, in the northern states, the cold grips relentlessly, and everyone, from tots to grandparents, dons skis, skates or snowshoes and revels in the arctic conditions.

The winter lasts a long time. People who service the tourism trade take a breather in the 'Mud Season', that period in late April and early May when the snow should have stopped falling, and started melting, swelling the rivers which gush down the mountainsides. Before that, usually in early February, the sap starts to rise in the maple trees, and suddenly the moment is right to tap the trunks and process the world's premier maple syrup.

Most of New England is forest, mountain and lake country, where the motor touring holiday comes into its own. Excellent roads mean that Boston and major cities are never more than two or three hours' drive away. Boston itself is one of the world's most beautiful and exhilarating cities to visit.

The true New Englander is found in the small rural communities – a rugged individualistic soul whose offer of the hand of friendship may not be immediate, but will undoubtedly be sincere.

Emerson Hall, Harvard – black students were admitted to the university as early as the 1860s.

Connecticut's Dinosaur State Park tells the story of the region's pre-historic days.

The Shape of the Land

Geographically, New England is regarded as an upland region or dissected plateau, but the region owes its diverse terrain, and its beauty, to the ravages of prehistoric climatic extremes, especially flooding and glaciation. These shaped five basic belts in a more-or-less north-south orientation: the New England coastal district; the New England hilly belt; the White Mountains; the Connecticut River Valley lowland; and the Green Mountains.

Two old structural basins which are important features of the New England coast are the Boston Basin in Massachusetts and Rhode Island's Narragansett Basin. The unmistakable recurved spit of Cape Cod is a moraine, while glacial deposits form the basic make-up of Nantucket Island and Martha's Vineyard. The rugged, rocky

range in the region. Mount Washington, in New Hampshire's Presidential Range, is the highest peak in both the region and north-eastern North America with an altitude of 6,288ft (1,917m).

Dinosaur tracks have been found in the Connecticut River Lowland, a long, narrow depression which consists mainly of Triassic sandstone with some shale and conglomerate.

The Green Mountains cover an area 250 miles (400km) long and up to 50 miles (80km) wide, extending from the St Lawrence River Valley in Quebec to north-western Connecticut, but they are most prominent in Vermont, averaging 3,000ft (900m). The highest peak in the range, at 4,393ft (1,339m), is Mount Mansfield.

Small rivers and streams abound in New England. The region's most important rivers – the Androscoggin, Kennebec, Penobscot and Saco in Maine, and the Merrimack, which flows through New Hampshire and Massachusetts – empty into the Atlantic Ocean. The Thames, Connecticut and Housatonic river systems flow into Long Island Sound.

shores of the north are a drowned coast, reminiscent in some places of the fiords found elsewhere in the world.

The New England hilly belt is a low dissected plateau of hard crystalline rock covered by glacial deposits. The most prominent of the isolated residual peaks found in this area are Wachusett Mountain in Massachusetts and New Hampshire's Mount Manadnock.

Extending from Mount Katahdin in Maine, through most of New Hampshire and south west into Massachusetts, the White Mountains form the most important

People

A New Englander is a citizen of one of the six states – Rhode Island, Vermont, Maine, Connecticut, Massachusetts and New Hampshire – as well as of the United States. In addition, New Englanders feel they have an added identity, and the region as a whole has a character of nationhood. This is the land of independence, where colonists first stood up to the British motherland and fought for self-rule. New England is an entity in itself – geographically, historically, socially and spiritually.

Fun and games on Boston Common, playground and melting pot for New England's varied ethnic groups.

There are differences between the peoples of New England – differences each state is proud of. The people of Maine, rugged, laconic, take life as it comes; New Hampshire's individualists scorn the taxman and proclaim independence with every breath of mountain air; Vermonters reflect quietly on their rural environment – then whoop it up wildly when they get the chance! In Massachusetts, the mask of the stolid Bostonian slips when Saturday comes and the bars of Quincy Market beckon. Rhode Islanders, very conscious of the fact that their 'Ocean State' is the smallest in the Union, are closely associated with sailing and the sea. The good folk of Connecticut enjoy their neat villages and picturesque fishing harbours, make money quietly, and ignore the fact that Manhattan is barely 40 miles (64km) from their western border.

These, of course, are the popular archetypal images. New Englanders are more complex and varied than that, as we can see by looking at the different racial groups in more detail.

Native Americans

The first Puritans to settle in New England found the land already inhabited by a people who had arrived there at least 2,000 years earlier. They were tribes of the Algonquins, a nation which still thrives in eastern Canada and the north-east United States. Things went well at first, and the Indians – Mohegans, Pequots, Narragansetts and Wampanoags – helped the early settlers to survive their first New World winter and passed on such skills as fishing, farming the land's strange produce and canoe making and handling.

The white men repaid them with death. The first Native American casualties were the result of infectious European diseases to which they had no resistance. Later, it was religious zeal and greed for land that decimated the native populations. First the English waged war against the Pequots. Next came the Wampanoags whose chief, King Philip, was executed at Plymouth. The Narragansetts, who had allied themselves with the English in the war against the Pequots, were reduced from about 5,000 to less than 100 by 1676. Old rivalries which had kept the tribes in a state of constant warfare since long before the discovery of America prevented the tribes from getting together against a common enemy, and divided they fell.

Dispossessed, scattered and demoralized, the Indians went into decline, and for two centuries were so insignificant they were scarcely noticed as part of the New England population. But from the 1960s a new consciousness began to stir among them and lawsuits were taken out to re-establish tribal lands. Today, about one third of the region's 21,000 or so Indians live on nine reservations.

Spurred by the success of court action, a new dynamism is sweeping the surviving tribes, established principally in Cape Cod, Martha's Vineyard, Rhode Island and Southern Connecticut. There are about 700 Penobscot Indians in Maine.

The Pequots of Southern Connecticut have set themselves up in business on an awesome scale. Skilfully using the white man's legal system, they have beaten a state ban on gambling and established Foxwoods, a gigantic casino and resort complex that offers an alternative to Las Vegas. Foxwoods, which will continue to expand for some years to come, has brought a new prosperity to the Pequots and pours at least $100 million a year into the state coffers. Other tribes in other parts of New England have taken note of the Pequots' success and are expected to follow suit.

Settler Stock

Even in New England, few people today can trace their ancestry back to the region's earliest settlers, and bar-room claims that someone's forbears came over on the *Mayflower* can be taken with a very large pinch of salt. The Puritans did make a lasting impression on New England society and their principles steered the

Plymouth Rock, where the Pilgrims came ashore to found their first settlement, is still a place of pilgrimage.

course of social development for some two centuries, but long before the Revolution their dominance was being diluted by immigrants of other or no religious persuasion. For a long time many of the region's most powerful families – those self-appointed aristocrats who came to be known as the 'Boston Brahmins' – were certainly descended from early arrivals, if not from the Pilgrim Fathers themselves. Unlike Europe's hereditary aristocracy, however, the Brahmins' position was based entirely on commercial success, and those who failed in business – as many did – lost their status. There are still some Brahmins who can claim pre-Revolution descendancy, but not many.

There is justifiable pride in family history in New England's humbler social strata, among the descendants of later immigrants from places other than England. A New Hampshire farmer will tell you that his Irish great-grandfather was one of the first white men to set eyes on the Old Man of the Mountains. Everywhere you will hear vivid tales of pioneer endeavour and achievement: of the discovery of mountain passes; of homesteads being carved from the wilderness; of railroads being laid, towns founded, factories built, and so on.

The Blacks

The first black New Englanders arrived in Boston from the West Indies to serve white settlers as 'perpetual servants', an elegant euphemism for slaves. As elsewhere in America, slavery was a fact of life, though blacks in New England were generally treated better and had more rights than those in the South. They also had a wider choice of occupations. In the South they worked either as domestic servants or field labourers. In New England they worked in the docks, on whaling vessels, in construction and in almost every other industry.

The greatest concentration of African Americans has always been found in Boston. In the 1750s it was as high as 10 percent of a total population of 50,000, but as white 'Tories' (supporters of the British crown) fled during the Revolution (see page 34) – taking their slaves with them – the black population dropped dramatically, to less than 2 percent in Boston by 1860.

Massachusetts abolished slavery in 1783, and schools were desegregated in 1855. Many runaways fled to Boston, settling first in North End then moving on to Beacon Hill. The anti-slavery movement became very active and the 'underground railroad' brought other runaway slaves to freedom in the city.

African Americans have always played their part during key moments in American history. Colonel George Middleton of Boston led an all-black company during the War of Independence. In the Civil War the 54th Regiment, the first black force raised in the North, was recruited entirely in Massachusetts.

Before 1861 black students were being admitted to Harvard, and Connecticut and Vermont had joined Massachusetts in extending suffrage to African Americans. Although the blacks in these states enjoyed greater freedom than their brethren elsewhere, they nonetheless remained low in the social structure, and there were few to be found in such professions as medicine and the law. This situation has improved greatly in the second half of the 20th century.

On the face of it, New England's blacks appear to have had a relatively tranquil, if still repressed, history. But there have been times of great violence, especially in New Haven and Hartford, Connecticut, and in Boston in the 1960s and 1970s when riots broke out over the issue of school buses. There was a poignant irony about the situation in Boston, where schools had been desegregated nearly 120 years earlier.

Today, the greatest concentrations of African Americans in New England are to be found in Greater Boston (about 270,000) and in Connecticut (217,000). (See page 82 for the Black Heritage Trail.)

The Irish

When the Great Potato Famine of 1845 decimated Ireland's population, thousands of people were driven abroad in search of a new life. Many of them found their way to America, and a great number – no one knows the exact figure – landed in Boston. They were not welcomed. The city's Protestants, firmly entrenched after two centuries of religious monopoly, did not relish the idea of a huge influx of Catholics. The hostility was reciprocated. The Irish felt they had already suffered enough from Protestant oppression, and Bostonian attitudes were a little too English for comfort.

Nevertheless, the Irish flourished and became increasingly active in politics. Hugh O'Brien became Boston's first foreign-born mayor when he was elected in 1884, and in 1918 the state's first Irish Catholic governor took office. Joseph Kennedy, father of the late President John F. Kennedy, was a successful banker and financier and so became the first Irishman to become a Brahmin.

The bulk of Boston's Irish community, now centred mainly in South Boston and Charlestown and representing about 22 percent of the city's population, is engaged in blue collar employment. More than most other ethnic groups, the Irish have set themselves apart from the rest and retained their original identity.

The Jews

The first Jews to settle in New England arrived not all that long after the first Puritans, establishing a community in Newport, Rhode Island, in 1658. Descendants of the Sephardic Jews who were expelled from Spain in the 15th century, they arrived from Holland but were prevented from settling in Massachusetts because of the Puritans' intolerance of anyone not adhering strictly to their ideals. Rhode Island, however, had been founded by religious dissenters and had a more liberal attitude, although the Jews were not permitted to vote until the Revolution. Newport's Jewish community flourished, and its Touro Synagogue, built in 1763, is the oldest in the US.

It was not until the closing years of the 19th century, by which time attitudes in Massachusetts had been relaxed somewhat, that Jewish immigrants, mostly from Eastern Europe, began to arrive in great numbers. By 1920 10 percent of Boston's population was Jewish, and Jews continue to play a significant role in society throughout the region.

Italians

The Italians are among the most recent arrivals in New England, settling mainly from southern Italy and Sicily in waves of immigration during the first three decades of this century. Rhode Island and Massachusetts were the choice of many Italians, and prominent communities continue to flourish in both states. Today, Boston's North End is known as 'Little Italy' and there is a dominant Italian presence in East Boston. The Italians have been especially successful in such fields as the construction industry, jewellery manufacturing, property and the law.

Other Ethnic Groups

Portuguese immigrants who arrived in the mid-19th century to work on whaling vessels settled mainly in southern Massachusetts, and their communities can still be found in New Bedford and Fall River. With the decline of whaling, many of these people turned instead to the textile industry for employment.

The beginning of this century saw an influx of Arabic-speaking Christians who had fled from the Turks in Syria and the Lebanon. Many settled in Rhode Island, where they continue to flourish.

Chinese immigrants settled mainly in Boston, which today has the third largest Chinese community in the United States.

French-Canadians began arriving in the region in the mid-1800s to work in the textile and lumber industries. The community is concentrated in Massachusetts, New Hampshire and Maine. Staunchly Catholic, insistently speaking French as a first language, and keeping strong links with Quebec, its members have probably travelled the shortest distance of all along New England's assimilation route.

History

History is the very stuff of New England, and there isn't a state – scarcely a county, you may be thinking before long – that doesn't have a reconstructed this or a re-enacted that. Historical markers dot the landscape like flags on a pitch and putt course, and the presence of the past is felt as keenly on the Freedom Trail in Boston, or on the waterfront in Mystic, Connecticut, as it is on the elegant village green at Woodstock, Vermont, or along New Hampshire's Kancamagus Pass, where it takes little imagination for you to see a buckskin-clad pioneer paddling a birch bark canoe along the Swift River.

The story of European settlement in North America begins in New England, of course, but the region's history goes back much further than 1620 when the first Puritan colonists were put ashore from the *Mayflower* at Plymouth Rock in Massachusetts. Although there is little evidence of prehistory, some people believe that 4,000 years ago there was a civilization similar to that of the Celts, and to support their belief they point to Mystery Hill, near North Salem, New Hampshire. The hill is also known as America's Stonehenge, because strange rock structures and chambers seem to indicate an ancient astronomical site.

Ancient legends suggest that European voyagers may have strayed across the Atlantic long, long ago. Ireland's St Brendan is said to have braved the ocean in a leather sailing vessel, and the Norse saga of Leif Ericsson and his landing in Vinland is well known. Long before Christopher Columbus's official discovery of the continent, the area was settled by native Americans – the 'Indians', as early explorers erroneously called them. Tribes of the Algonquin nation had been hunting the forests, fishing the streams, lakes and the sea, and producing crops of cereals, pumpkins and tobacco for a good 500 years before navigators from Holland, Portugal, Italy and England began sailing along the coast.

Five years after the epic voyage by Columbus, John Cabot inched along the coasts of Massachusetts and Maine, looking for the fabled Northwest Passage – a

Pilgrims' Memorial at Provincetown, Cape Cod, marks the site of the Puritans' first landfall in the New World.

short cut to the East, it was believed. He failed in his task, but laid claim to most of North America on behalf of the king of England, Henry VII. Similar claims were made some 30 years later by Miguel Corte Real for Portugal and Giovanni da Verrazano for Italy. Dutchman Adriaen Block and the English Captain John Smith were busy producing charts and maps in 1614. Exploring on behalf of a group of London merchants, Smith was captivated by the territory and named it New England.

The Puritans

Captain Smith's glowing write-up of New England attracted the attention of the Puritans, a strict Protestant sect whose religious beliefs did not square with the rest of Anglican England. The New World, they felt, would give them the chance to develop their own community along their own lines. They persuaded the Plymouth Company to underwrite a settlement, and in the late summer of 1620 the *Mayflower* cast off with 102 Puritans aboard. It was a monstrously uncomfortable voyage, and most of the passengers remained below decks throughout its two months' duration for fear of being washed overboard. Their first whiff of fresh air came in November when land was sighted at what is now Provincetown, Cape Cod. But they felt that area's sandy soil was unsuitable for farming, and after searching along the coast, they landed at Plymouth Rock on 21 December.

New England proved to be an unwelcoming place during that first savage winter. Debilitated by their long voyage and with no harvest to sustain them, the Pilgrims fell victim to scurvy and pneumonia, and nearly half the group died. They might all have perished had it not been for the support given by friendly Indians. At last, it was springtime, the weather warmed and the settlement was able to start planting crops. When they gathered in the first harvest in the autumn of 1621 the Pilgrims and Indians joined together for three days of feasting – America's first Thanksgiving Festival.

More Puritans bravely crossed the Atlantic. In the Great Migration of 1630 about 1,000 were landed from 11 ships at Salem. The attraction of a large natural harbour drew many of them to the south, and Boston began to develop as the major settlement. The Pilgrims' abhorrence of idleness and luxury served them very well in the establishment of fledgling communities where there was a great deal to be done and few to do it. Villages then began to grow up farther afield – in Connecticut, Rhode Island and New Hampshire – and fur-trading posts were set up in Maine.

The colonists' success encouraged others to make the voyage west, and by 1636 the population of New England had been increased by a further 12,000 immigrants. In addition to their virtues of industriousness and thrift, the Puritans held education in high regard. Public schools and institutions of higher education were established; Harvard University was founded as a college for the training of ministers in 1636.

The Puritans' blind spot, ironically, was religion. Although they were refugees themselves originally, they offered no refuge to those holding other beliefs. Indeed, followers of other faiths received harsh treatment in the New World. In 1651, a Baptist from Rhode Island was flogged in Boston. Quakers escaping from persecution in England were arrested on ships in Boston Harbor before they had a chance to set foot ashore. Three Quakers, one of them a woman, were hanged in Massachusetts in 1659.

Rhode Island became a haven for the dissidents, much to the disgust of the Puritans who scornfully dubbed it 'Rogues' Island'. By the end of the 1660s, French Huguenots, Quakers and New England's first Jews were settled in the little liberal colony.

THE WITCH HUNTS

In Massachusetts, Puritan zeal turned life for many into a nightmare. Witches were said to be abroad and many accusations were made. Trials were held at Charlestown in 1648 and Boston in 1655, but Salem is the place that springs most readily to mind when people think of witches in New England.

Salem today is a pleasant town with red brick sidewalks and tree-shaded streets, and it is difficult to imagine the chill fear that must have stalked the place in 1692 when neighbour accused neighbour in a witch hunt hysteria which led to the execution of 20 women and the imprisonment of a further 150.

The Indians

The Puritans also turned on their old friends, the Indians. Within 50 years of the *Mayflower*'s arrival, about a quarter of the native population had officially accepted the faith of the Pilgrim Fathers as a result of vigorous missionary work. Still the Puritans were not content. They wanted the Indians to abandon their old ways totally, and also wanted their land.

A series of skirmishes led to all-out war between the settlers and Chief Metacomet, known to the colonists as King Philip. Defending his territory, Metacomet led raids against the settlers during 1675 and 1676, but was betrayed and captured soon after losing the 'Great Swamp Fight' near Kingston, Rhode Island, in which hundreds of Indian women and children were killed. The chief was beheaded and quartered. For 20 years his head was displayed on a gibbet at Plymouth.

The Revolution

The beginning of the 18th century saw the Puritans already losing their grip on the colonies. England's preoccupation with its own internal affairs during its Civil War and the rule of Oliver Cromwell had left the New World pretty much to its own devices. Then the restored monarchy, scenting the whiff of revenue, began to take a keen interest in what was happening across the ocean. To weaken the Puritans' political power, suffrage was extended to all property-holders, whatever their religion. At the same time, legislation was introduced to force the colonies to trade exclusively with the motherland.

Members of New England's newly-enfranchised merchant class continued to trade with anyone they wished. Shipbuilding and fishing – to say nothing of the 'triangle' trade in slaves, sugar and rum – brought prosperity, and the politics of independence began to flourish as new people and new ideas flooded in. Britain tried to crack down on the colonies with a succession of stinging taxes. The 1764 Revenue Act, imposing duties on silk, sugar and wine, was steadfastly ignored. A year later the Stamp Act, taxing newspapers and legal documents, caused such an outrage that every stamp agent in New England resigned, and the Act was repealed.

Next came the Townshend Acts, which levied heavy duties on paper, lead, glass and tea. There was another outcry – and this time British troops broke up rioting in Boston. Demonstrations and clashes between citizens and soldiers were frequent, and by a strange irony on the day the Townshend Acts were repealed – 5 March 1770 – five colonists

Samuel Adams, the leader of the Sons of Liberty, is interred in Boston's Old Granary Burying Ground.

died when troops fired into a crowd in what was later to become known as the Boston Massacre.

Revolution was brewing, but another 16 months of martial law, when resented British troops were billeted in private homes, were to pass before the Battle of Lexington was started with 'the shot heard round the world'. The colonists had been stockpiling weapons and ammunition and preparing to form their own army. The military governor of Massachusetts, General Thomas Gage, sent 800 Redcoats to Concord, 20 miles (32km) west of

A TEA PARTY

The British Parliament continued to impose a tax on tea, the colonists' most popular beverage. Samuel Adams, leader of an active group of political agitators called the Sons of Liberty, addressed a spirited protest meeting, and with the cry 'No taxation without representation!' ringing in their ears, 50 men disguised as Indians boarded three tea ships in Boston Harbor on 16 December 1773, and tossed their cargoes overboard. This incident became known as the 'Boston Tea Party'.

Paul Revere rode out to warn: 'The British are coming!' at the start of the Revolutionary War.

General George Washington, immortalized in this Boston statue, led the Americans to victory over the British.

Boston, when he heard of an arms cache there.

Robert Newman, sexton of Boston's Christ Church, kept an eye on the British column from the church belfry. He had two lanterns, and had been instructed to show one if the troops advanced by land, two if they used the Charles River. Newman lit two lanterns, and Paul Revere, one of the Sons of Liberty, rode off to warn people 'The British are coming!'

The troops were met on the green at Lexington by 70 'Minutemen' – armed volunteers ready to fight at any time. It was a short but bloody confrontation which ended with eight Minutemen dead and ten wounded. The Redcoats marched on to Concord, destroyed the weapons stored there, and headed back towards Boston. This time, the rebels were hidden along the route, and their musket fire killed 73 of the troops and wounded a further 200.

Lifted by their daring defiance, the rebels' spirits were boosted again at the Battle of Bunker Hill – which was actually fought on nearby Breed's Hill – on 17 June 1775. Short of ammunition and forced to retreat, the Minutemen technically lost the fight, but they had proved they could hold their own against the trained British army, which had suffered nearly 1,500 casualties.

The colonies rallied together and on 4 July 1776 adopted the Declaration of Independence. General George Washington

took command of the Americans, and after six more years of war, the British were defeated.

A short-lived slump followed the war, but New England buoyantly entered the 19th century. There was a further slight setback during the War of 1812, when Britain and America were at loggerheads over Canada and a complex set of other issues, but a vigorous shipbuilding industry, together with technical improvements in the production of cotton and wool, brought more prosperity. New technologies followed in the wake of the Industrial Revolution, and as the railways advanced, the wilderness areas in northern New Hampshire, Vermont and Maine were opened up to pioneers. The climate and soil, however, prevented the establishment of agriculture on a grand scale – the emergent Midwest had the advantage in that respect – so New England farmers concentrated on specialist crops such as apples, potatoes, cranberries, maple syrup and Christmas trees.

With few mineral resources in the region, other than granite and marble, industrial development was also restricted, but the New Englanders were a resourceful and imaginative people and trade flourished in the wake of seaborne commerce and whaling. Factories producing textiles, shoes, clocks and hardware began to supply the needs of a growing consumer society, and the Yankee pedlar invented foot-in-the-door salesmanship as he carpet-bagged his way across the nation.

Marble is one of the few mineral resources in New England. This early photograph was taken at Proctor, Vermont.

Mass immigration brought thousands of newcomers from Europe. Many had escaped from famine, exploitation and tyranny, and liberal idealism began to spread, challenging the established attitudes of the entrenched conservative Protestants. There were campaigns for temperance, the reform of prisons and insane asylums, and an end to child labour. The abolition of slavery became the biggest single issue, and the New England states supported the Unionist cause in the American Civil War (1861-1865). There was a cultural renaissance too, and the region became a magnet for writers, artists and philosophers as figures such as Nathaniel Hawthorne, Herman Melville, Henry David Thoreau, Oliver Wendell Holmes, Julia Ward Howe and Ralph Waldo Emerson achieved international acclaim.

The Economy

New England's economy has fallen and risen dramatically since the start of the 20th century. The region suffered badly during the Depression, and nearly 150,000 textile workers alone lost their jobs between 1929 and 1950. Many thousands of people lost their homes. There was a further setback in the 1970s when manufacturing industries were hit by competition from foreign importers.

Recent years have seen an improvement due to tourism and the development of high-tech industries. Among the major enterprises are those involved in missile, space and aviation technology, computers and scientific equipment. Massachusetts and Connecticut share one of the largest pools of capital in the United States, and new businesses are growing in southern New Hampshire, Rhode Island and Vermont.

Just the Essentials

On a first-time visit to New England you may be overwhelmed by the wealth of choice you have, wherever you start. The major landmarks and places to visit are proposed here to help you establish priorities.

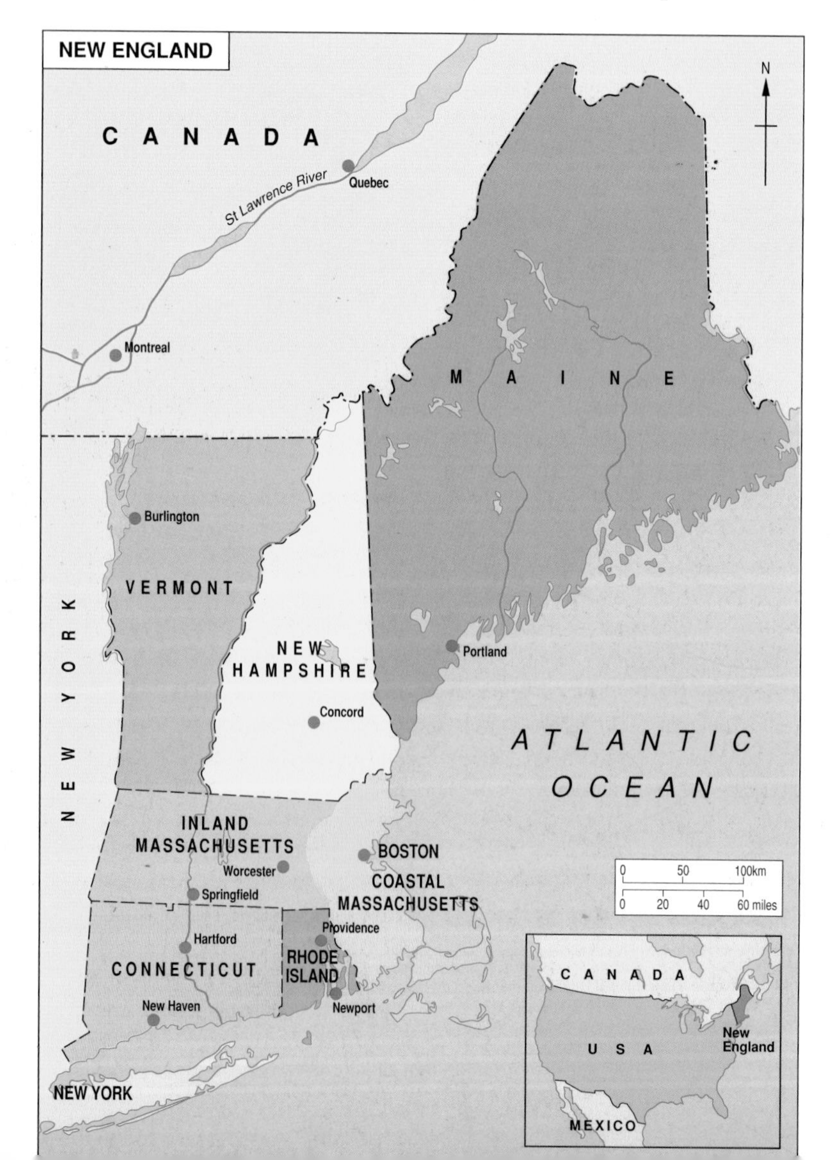

Connecticut

Stamford: Whitney Museum of American Art
Bridgeport: Barnum Museum
New Haven: Yale University
New London: US Coast Guard Museum; Monte Cristo Cottage, Eugene O'Neill's boyhood home
Mystic Seaport

Maine

York: National Historic District
Kennebunkport: Dock Square, Town Green and Cape Porpoise
Portland: restored old port area
Mount Desert Island: Acadia National Park
Bar Harbor: Abbe Museum, focusing on the Abnaki Indians
Augusta: Maine State Museum

Boston

Faneuil Hall Marketplace: great for shopping, people-watching
Old South Meeting House: a hotbed of protest during the run-up to the American Revolution
The Old State House: Boston's oldest public building
Old North Church: revered Revolutionary monument
Beacon Hill: quaint streets and old mansions
USS Constitution: world's oldest floating warship
Museum of Science: with hands-on exhibits
Bunker Hill Memorial, Charlestown
Harvard University, Cambridge

Inland Massachusetts

Concord and Lexington: flashpoints in the Revolutionary War
Old Sturbridge Village: re-creation of 19th-century rural community
Historic Deerfield: preserved colonial town
Mount Greylock: viewpoint overlooking five states
Pittsfield: Hancock Shaker Village
Stockbridge: Norman Rockwell Museum

Coastal Massachusetts

Marblehead: delightful old houses, winding lanes and lovely harbour
Salem: Peabody and Essex Museum, collections include New England architecture; Salem Witch Museum
Plum Island: Parker River National Wildlife Refuge
Plymouth: Plimoth Plantation – 'living' museum locked into the 17th century
New Bedford: Whaling Museum

New Hampshire

Portsmouth: Strawbery Banke – huge open-air museum on waterfront
North Salem: America's Stonehenge
Concord: State House; Christa McAuliffe Planetarium
Canterbury Shaker Village: situated in former Shaker community
Gorham: Mount Washington (by cog railway or car)
North Conway: Factory outlets

Rhode Island

Providence: Rhode Island State House; The Arcade, America's first indoor shopping mall; Benefit Street, 'a mile of history'
Newport: Museum of Yachting; International Tennis Hall of Fame; The 'Cottages', summer homes of the incredibly rich; informative walking tour of the city's major sights

Vermont

Bennington: museum featuring Revolutionary and Civil War
Quechee Gorge: awesome work of nature
Woodstock: Billings Farm and Museum
Vergennes: Lake Champlain Maritime Museum
Shelburne Museum: 40 buildings housing 80,000 exhibits
Waterbury: Ben and Jerry's Ice Cream Factory

Going Places with Something Special in Mind

Travellers with special interests can supplement or scrap the standard itineraries, pursuing instead the angles that most appeal to them. New England offers an incredible number of attractions, and it can be quite a problem knowing where to start. For visitors with special interests, this selection may help you to choose your favourites from the large menu available.

The American Revolution

1 MINUTEMAN NATIONAL HISTORIC PARK
Between Lexington and Concord, Massachusetts, this is situated at the centre of a number of sites connected with the start of the Revolutionary War.

2 FAIRFIELD VILLAGE
Fairfield, Connecticut. This village was settled in 1639 and almost entirely destroyed during a raid in July 1779. Four of the surviving houses still stand, and more than 100 Revolutionary soldiers are buried in Old Burying Ground. There is also an 18th-century farmhouse with furnishings from the Revolutionary era and a museum of 18th-20th century artefacts. A wildlife sanctuary offers walks and exhibits.

The windmill at Eastham is a landmark for cyclists on the Cape Cod Rail Trail.

3 BLACK ROCK AND NATHAN HALE FORTS
New Haven, Connecticut. Reconstructed defences from the Revolutionary and Civil Wars. Both provide stunning views of New Haven harbour.

4 FORT GRISWOLD BATTLEFIELD STATE PARK
Groton, Connecticut. The site of a 1781 killing of American defenders by British troops in a 40-minute battle. There is a

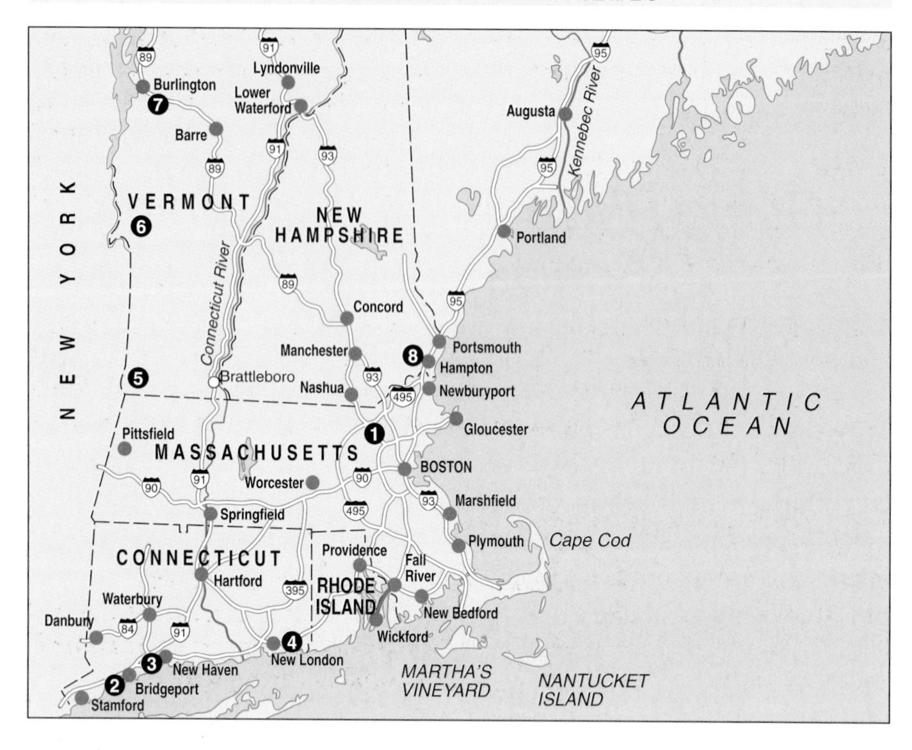

Revolution in America as the fight for independence gradually unfolds.

museum and monument, with historic displays in summer months.

5 BENNINGTON MUSEUM
Bennington, Vermont. Exhibits in this museum relate to the Revolutionary and Civil Wars. The items include documents, toys, tools, decorative arts and furniture. The town is dominated by the Bennington Battle Memorial, a monolith commemorating the battle of 16 August 1777.

6 HUBBARDTON BATTLEFIELD
East Hubbardton, Vermont. The site of a Revolutionary battle on 7 July 1777. The museum is open in summer.

7 ETHAN ALLEN HOMESTEAD
Burlington, Vermont. This restored farmhouse home of a Revolutionary hero illustrates frontier life in the 18th century.

8 AMERICAN INDEPENDENCE MUSEUM
Exeter, New Hampshire. A new museum which features rare documents and military items relating to the Revolution.

Art Museums

1 PEABODY AND ESSEX MUSEUM
Salem, Massachusetts. A prestigious historical foundation featuring 200 years of New England architecture in restored

buildings. There are also paintings and collections of decorative art, artefacts and furniture.

2 WORCESTER ART MUSEUM

Worcester, Massachusetts. New England's third largest art museum which houses a fine collection of American paintings.

3 MUSEUM OF FINE ARTS

Springfield, Massachusetts. This collection includes works by Gauguin, Degas, Monet and Renoir, with 15 centuries covered in 20 galleries.

4 STERLING AND FRANCINE CLARK ART INSTITUTE

Williamstown, Massachusetts. A famous art collection which includes works by Renoir, Corot, Degas, Monet and Toulouse-Lautrec.

5 NORMAN ROCKWELL MUSEUM

Stockbridge, Massachusetts. The world's largest collection of work by the famous *Saturday Evening Post* illustrator housed in larger premises opened in April 1993. Rockwell lived in Stockbridge from 1953 until his death in 1978.

6 BEAUPORT MUSEUM

Gloucester, Massachusetts. Twenty-six rooms furnished with American and European decorative arts in a house that grew and grew with its owner's art collection.

A variety of art collections and even architecture to appeal to all tastes in a cultural trip around the region.

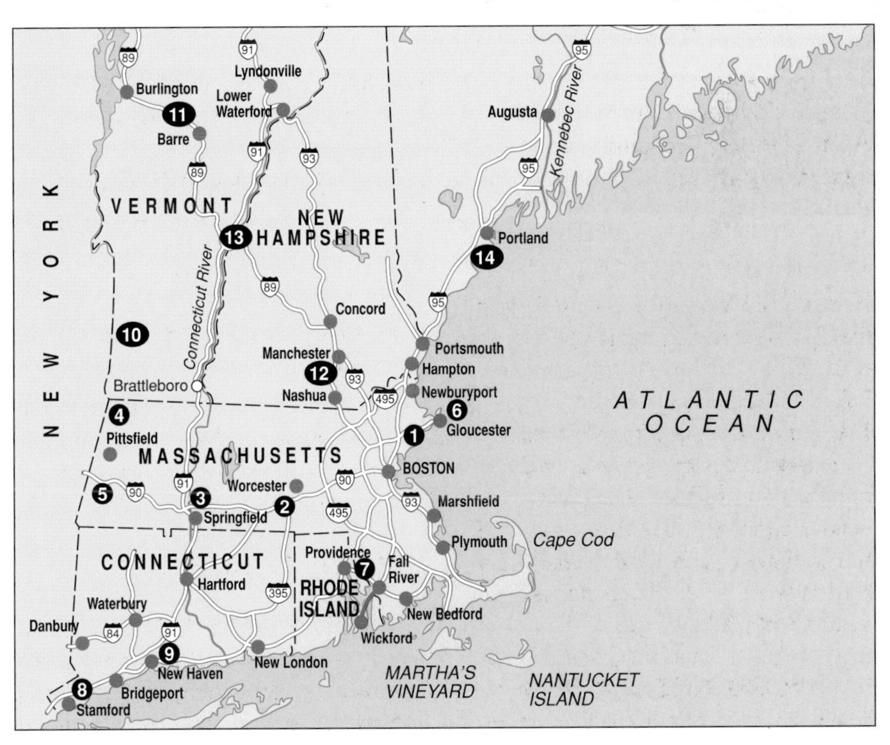

7 RISD MUSEUM OF ART
Providence, Rhode Island. A comprehensive range of collections, including French Impressionist works, Paul Revere silver, porcelain and antiquities maintained by the Rhode Island School of Design.

8 WHITNEY MUSEUM OF AMERICAN ART
Stamford, Connecticut. A branch of New York's prestigious institution which has permanent displays of sculpture and folk art, regularly changing exhibitions and special events.

9 CENTER FOR BRITISH ART
New Haven, Connecticut. A Yale University institution featuring British works in all media dating from Elizabethan times.

10 NORMAN ROCKWELL EXHIBITION
Arlington, Vermont. Hundreds of Rockwell's *Saturday Evening Post* covers and other work displayed in the artist's home town.

11 T.W. WOOD ART GALLERY
Montpelier, Vermont. A gallery founded in 1895 by Thomas Waterman Wood, one of America's leading portrait painters at the time. Many of his works are exhibited, and there are temporary exhibits of work by contemporary artists, with the accent on Vermont painters and sculptors.

12 CURRIER GALLERY OF ART
Manchester, New Hampshire. Seven centuries of paintings and sculptures are on show here. Transport is provided to visit the 1950 Zimmerman House designed by Frank Lloyd Wright.

13 HOOD MUSEUM OF ART
Dartmouth College, New Hampshire. Ten galleries of exhibits house collections from ancient art to Picasso.

14 PORTLAND MUSEUM OF ART
Portland, Maine. 18th- and 19th-century sculptures, furniture and paintings displayed.

A number of major museums in Boston are detailed in the Boston chapter.

Bargain Hunting

1 FILENE'S BASEMENT
Boston. An Aladdin's Cave of bargains and a continuous Dutch auction on selected items in this famous downtown store.

2 FALL RIVER OUTLETS
Fall River, Massachusetts. Follow the signs marked with a heart from Route 24, Exit 2, to find the bargain clothing, leather goods, jewellery, and so on, on sale in huge converted old textile mills.

3 DIRECT SELL SHOE FACTORY OUTLET
Bennington, Vermont. Up to 50 percent discount on men's and women's styles in leather.

4 OUTLET CENTER
South Burlington, Vermont. Two dozen stores offering goods at direct-sell prices.

5 JOHNSON WOOLEN MILLS FACTORY STORE
Johnson, Vermont. Sweaters, ties, hats, scarves, mittens and other clothing in wool and other natural fibres at bargain prices.

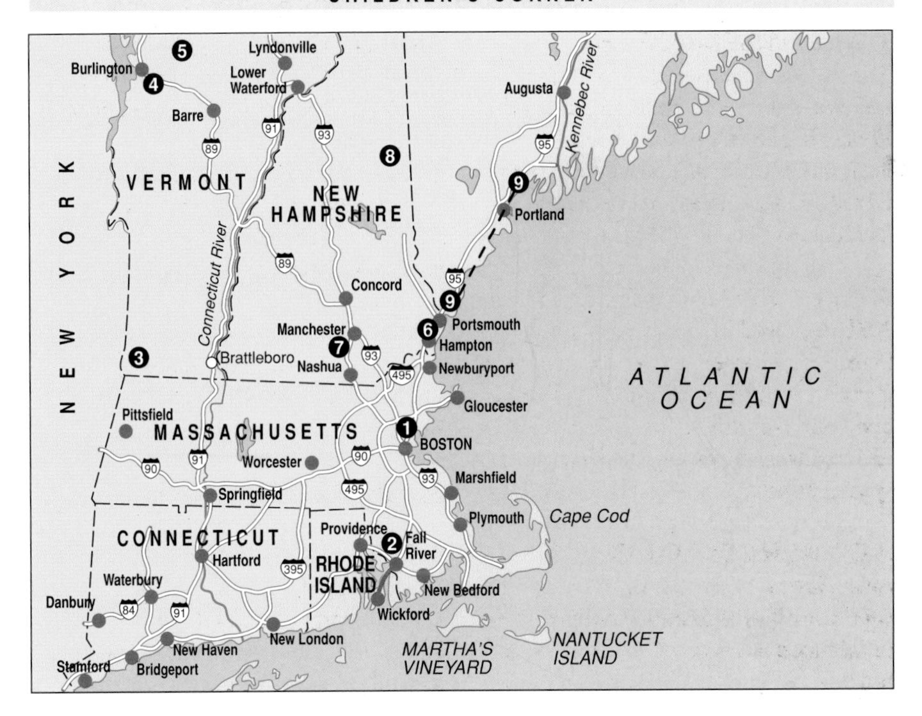

6 NORTH HAMPTON OUTLETS
North Hampton, New Hampshire. More than 30 stores offering a wide range of discounted goods.

7 MALL OF NEW HAMPSHIRE
Manchester, New Hampshire. About 100 stalls and stores, including Filene's, offering clothes, gifts, jewellery, housewares. There is no sales tax in New Hampshire!

8 NORTH CONWAY & CONWAY VILLAGE OUTLETS
North Conway, New Hampshire. Goods of all types with prices reduced by as much as 75 percent.

9 ROUTE 1 OUTLETS
Between Kittery and Freeport, Maine. Many factory outlets are grouped together in malls about an hour's drive from Boston. The famous 'We Never Close' L.L. Bean store is at Freeport. Other outlets can be found throughout Maine.

Paradise for shoppers and bargain hunters.

Children's Corner

1 THE CHILDREN'S MUSEUM
Boston. Visitors are encouraged to handle, scramble over, climb on and jump on and off exhibits. They can blow huge bubbles and visit a traditional Japanese home.

2 THE COMPUTER MUSEUM
Boston. More hands-on experience for the kids, who can walk through a giant computer and fly a jetliner into a volcano.

3 WILLOWS PARK
Salem, Massachusetts. A public pier, beaches, games and children's rides.

4 CHILDREN'S MUSEUM OF RHODE ISLAND
Pawtucket, Rhode Island. No holds barred in this treasure house of high-tech challenges. A taste of yesteryear in Great-grandma's Kitchen and a room-sized map to roll around on.

5 ROCKY POINT AMUSEMENT PARK
Warwick Neck, Rhode Island. New England's largest amusement park, with more than 100 rides.

6 ROGER WILLIAMS PARK AND ZOO
Providence, Rhode Island. Sea lions, penguins, polar bears, wolves and animals from Africa, plus more approachable species in the International Farm. Lots to do and see.

7 BEARDSLEY ZOOLOGICAL GARDENS
Bridgeport, Connecticut. A special children's zoo in a New England farm setting with pony rides and a picnic area. Main exhibits range from North American mammals to rainforest species.

8 CONNECTICUT CHILDREN'S MUSEUM
New Haven, Connecticut. Children under seven are encouraged in discovery and use

Challenges as well as a great deal of fun for children of all ages.

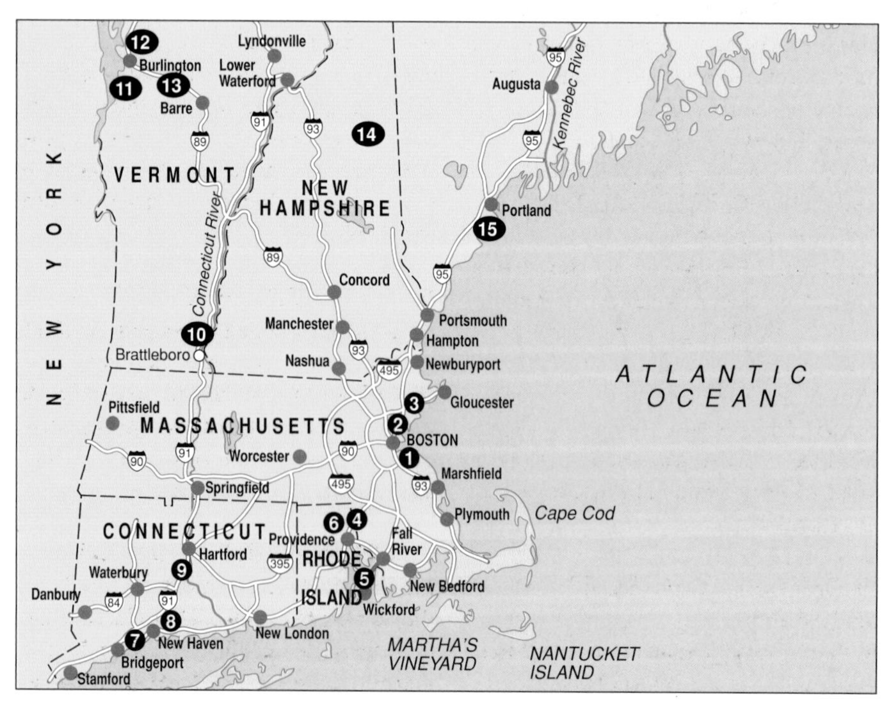

of imagination. There is an extensive play village. Adults must accompany children.

9 ROCKY HILL DINOSAUR PARK
Ten miles (16km) south of Hartford, Connecticut. The state's own *Jurassic Park*, where visitors can make plaster casts of dinosaur footprints. It has nature trails, and picnic areas.

10 SANTA'S LAND
Putney, Vermont. It's Christmas all year round here, and children can chat with Santa Claus, visit the Elves' Home, and take a ride on a train or carousel.

11 VERMONT TEDDY BEAR COMPANY
Shelburne, Vermont. Factory tours are conducted daily, year-round, to see the creation of hand-made, huggable teddies.

12 THE DISCOVERY MUSEUM
Essex Junction, Vermont. A hands-on museum for children, with nature, history, science and art exhibits. It also has a nature trail, park, picnic area.

13 BEN AND JERRY'S ICE CREAM FACTORY
Waterbury, Vermont. The state's most popular attraction where everyone – grown-ups and kids – comes away with sticky fingers.

14 STORY LAND
Glen, New Hampshire. A child-sized world of fairy tale characters, rides and adventures.

15 CHILDREN'S MUSEUM OF MAINE
Portland, Maine. Art and science exhibits with a built-in element of play.

Literary Figures

1 HENRY WADSWORTH LONGFELLOW HOUSE
Cambridge, Massachusetts. Longfellow lived at 105 Brattle Street for 45 years until his death in 1882. The poet wrote many of his best-known works here, including *The Song of Hiawatha*.

2 EMERSON HOUSE
Concord, Massachusetts. The great naturalist and writer spent the last 47 years of his life at the house at 28 Cambridge Turnpike. Other writers who lived in Concord were Nathaniel Hawthorne, Louisa M. Alcott and Henry David Thoreau.

3 EMILY DICKINSON'S HOME
Amherst, Massachusetts. The house in which the poet lived and wrote some 1,800 poems is at 280 Main Street.

4 ARROWHEAD
Pittsfield, Massachusetts. Herman Melville's home from 1850 to 1863, where he wrote most of *Moby Dick*. Some people say he was inspired by the whale-like bulk of Mount Greylock, which the house overlooks.

5 THE HAWTHORNE COTTAGE
Lenox, Massachusetts. A reconstruction of the cottage in which Nathaniel Hawthorne wrote *The House of the Seven Gables*. It is part of the Tanglewood Estate, summertime home of the Boston Symphony Orchestra.

6 ANN BRADSTREET'S HOME
Ipswich, Massachusetts. The New World's first woman poet produced some of her work at 33 High Street, including *The Tenth Muse Lately Sprung Up in*

America, first published in England in 1650. The house is now privately owned.

7 WHITTIER'S HOME

Amesbury, near Salisbury, Massachusetts. John Greenleaf Whittier, the abolitionist, lived at 56 Friend Street for 56 years, writing his articles and poems.

8 MONTE CRISTO COTTAGE

New London, Connecticut. The boyhood home of Eugene O'Neill. Memorabilia and multimedia presentation provide an insight into the great playwright's family relationships.

9 MARK TWAIN AND HARRIET BEECHER STOWE HOMES

Hartford, Connecticut. Mark Twain's home is a riot of turrets and balconies, with interiors by Louis Comfort Tiffany. Mrs Stowe's old abode is a simpler cottage.

10 ROBERT FROST FARMHOUSE

Londonderry, New Hampshire. The revered poet lived here for ten years in the early 1900s. The white clapboard building is a National Historic Landmark.

11 FROST PLACE

Franconia, New Hampshire. Robert Frost's home from 1915 to 1920, during which time he received the Pulitzer Prize. His desk and signed first editions are displayed, and the farmhouse is now a cultural centre with a poet-in-residence.

12 LONGFELLOW'S BOYHOOD HOME

Congress Street, Portland, Maine. The house was built by Longfellow's grandfather in 1785. Some of the furniture the poet lived with is still in place.

Memories of great literary and cultural figures.

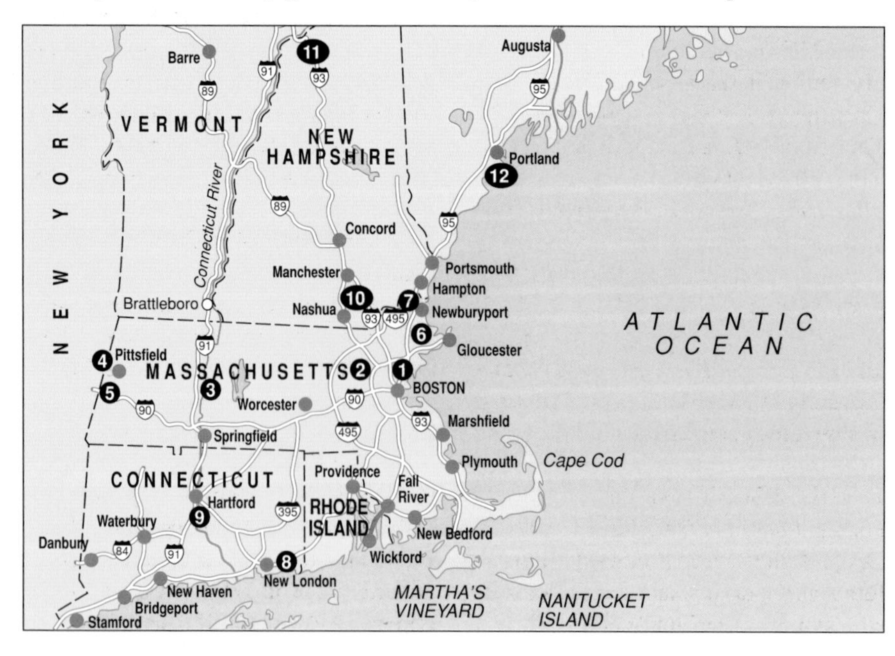

Living Museums

1 LOWELL NATIONAL HISTORIC PARK

Lowell, Massachusetts. Costumed gatekeepers and wives 'drawn back' from the 19th century set the tone in this complex of mills, canals and worker housing.

2 OLD STURBRIDGE VILLAGE

Fifteen miles (24km) west of Worcester, Massachusetts. Authentic re-creation of a 19th-century rural community.

3 HISTORIC DEERFIELD

This village at the eastern end of the Mohawk Trail, Massachusetts, has one of New England's best-preserved colonial streets with a dozen homes open to the public.

4 PIONEER VILLAGE

Salem, Massachusetts. A re-creation of the original settlement founded by Roger Conant and a group of fishermen in 1626.

5 PLIMOTH PLANTATION

Plymouth, Massachusetts. The ultimate time-trip, to the Plymouth Colony in 1627. This reconstruction is so convincingly done – by people as well as buildings – that visitors really feel they have gone back in time.

6 BILLINGS FARM AND MUSEUM

Woodstock, Vermont. One of America's leading agricultural museums and a working farm featuring the lifestyle and skills of a hundred years ago.

7 STRAWBERY BANKE

Portsmouth, New Hampshire. A workshop, artisans' galleries and more than 40 furnished historic homes on a waterfront site, with costumed guides.

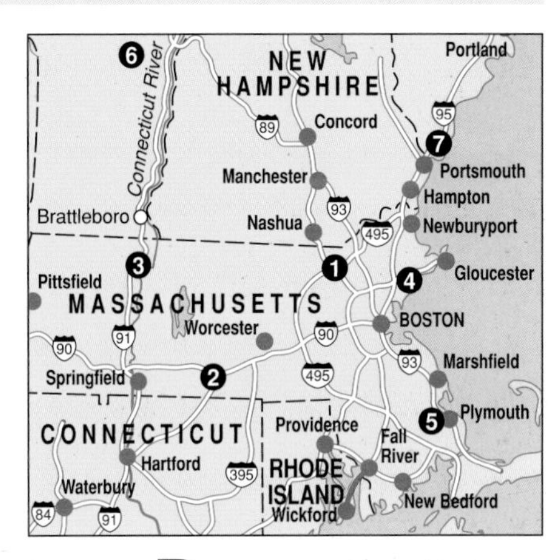

Re-creations and reconstructions of lives and times gone by.

Maritime Museums

1 SALEM MARITIME NATIONAL HISTORIC SITE

Salem, Massachusetts. 18th- and 19th-century buildings restored along the old waterfront include the Custom House in which Nathaniel Hawthorne once worked. Orientation centre, with audio-visual presentation, is the base for guided tours.

2 ESSEX SHIPBUILDING MUSEUM

Essex, Massachusetts. A museum crammed with artefacts and pictures illustrating 300 years of the town's former industry.

3 MAYFLOWER II

Plymouth, Massachusetts. A full-size replica of the ship that brought the Pilgrim Fathers to the New World. The vessel is crewed by costumed interpreters locked impressively into the 17th century.

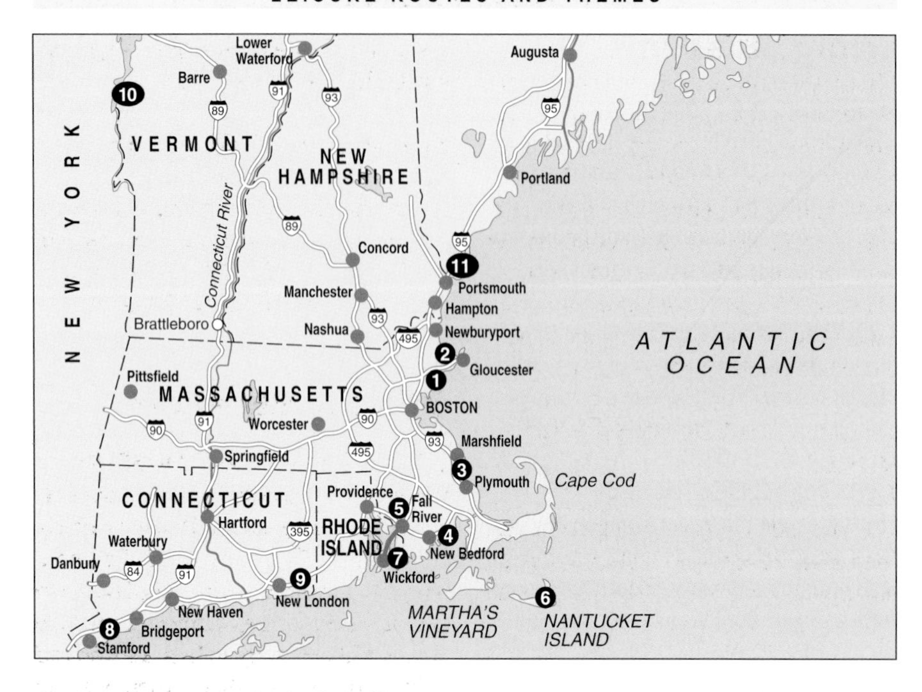

Museums devoted to the maritime history of New England.

4 NEW BEDFORD WHALING MUSEUM

New Bedford, Massachusetts. America's largest whaling museum, founded in 1902, has a large collection of tools, figureheads, scrimshaw, ships' logbooks (one listing Herman Melville) and paintings. The centrepiece of the museum is the half-scale model of the *Lagoda*, a fully-rigged whaling ship.

5 BATTLESHIP COVE

Fall River, Massachusetts. The battleship *USS Massachusetts* is the focal point in this floating museum of wartime vessels. Nearby, the Marine Museum features the days of sail and steam, and includes more than 150 model ships.

6 NANTUCKET WHALING MUSEUM

Nantucket Town, Massachusetts. Housed in an 1846 candle factory, this superb collection of scrimshaw and whaling artefacts, including a whale skeleton, is located on the tiny island that led the world in the pursuit of whales.

7 NAVAL WAR COLLEGE MUSEUM

Newport, Rhode Island. The story of the US Navy in Narragansett, and the art and science of naval warfare.

8 SONO MARITIME CENTER

South Norwalk, Connecticut. You can board an oyster sloop, a steam tender and other vessels, and there are demonstrations, exhibitions, an IMAX theatre and a huge aquarium.

9 MYSTIC SEAPORT
Mystic, Connecticut. You will need a couple of days to get the most out of this restored 19th-century village and whaling harbour. The area includes a whaling ship, boatbuilding demonstrations, a planetarium, a smokehouse for preserving fish, art galleries, collections of scrimshaw, maritime instruments and artefacts, shops with a maritime theme, and even a sailors' tavern and a children's play museum.

10 LAKE CHAMPLAIN MARITIME MUSEUM
Basin Harbor, near Vergennes, Vermont. The cultural, military, commercial and technological history of Lake Champlain displayed in six exhibition buildings, with a working 18th-century-style forge and boatbuilding demonstrations.

11 PORT OF PORTSMOUTH MARITIME MUSEUM
Portsmouth, New Hampshire. A major exhibit is the submarine *USS Albacore*, in service from 1953 to 1972. There is also a visitor centre and memorial garden.

Unusual sites and collections of offbeat memorabilia.

Offbeat Museums

1 HIGGINS ARMORY MUSEUM
Worcester, Massachusetts. A huge collection of medieval and Renaissance armour, as well as some of the more peaceful arts of the period, displayed in a Gothic castle setting. Attractions include demonstrations, story-telling, a sound and light show, and a gallery where visitors can try on the armour and items of medieval clothing.

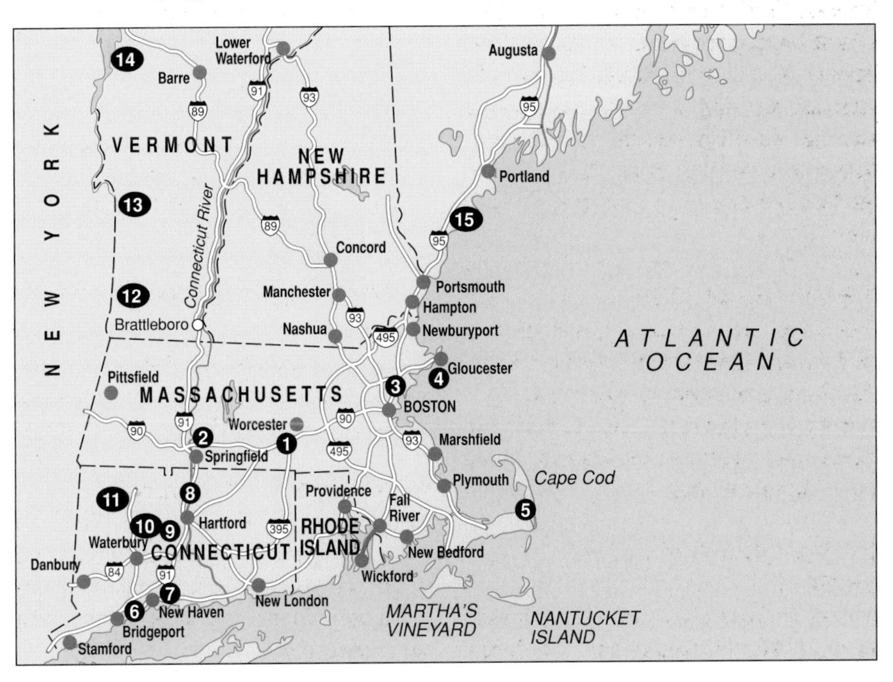

2 BASKETBALL HALL OF FAME

Springfield, Massachusetts. Test your skills from a moving sidewalk. Video presentations, demonstrations and exhibits in the city where the game was invented.

3 SAUGUS IRON WORKS

Saugus, Massachusetts, 7 miles (11km) north of Boston. The imposing site of one of New England's earliest industrial enterprises, founded in the 1640s, with a reconstructed blast furnace, forge, mill and blacksmith's shop.

4 HAMMOND CASTLE

Gloucester, Massachusetts. An enormous and bizarre castle built by an electronics pioneer. It overlooks the rock that wrecked Longfellow's *Hesperus* and houses an eccentric collection of antiquities, art and an outsize organ.

5 NEW ENGLAND FIRE AND HISTORY MUSEUM

Brewster, Cape Cod, Massachusetts. One of the largest collections in the US of early fire engines and fire-fighting equipment.

6 BARNUM MUSEUM

Bridgeport, Connecticut. Lots of circus items and permanent exhibits associated with Phineas T. Barnum, General Tom Thumb and Jenny Lind, 'the Swedish Nightingale'.

7 SHORE LINE TROLLEY MUSEUM

East Haven, Connecticut. About 100 classic trolleys are on show in this National Historic Site. Trolley rides are available.

8 NEW ENGLAND AIR MUSEUM

Bradley International Airport, Windsor Locks, Connecticut. The largest indoor display of military, civil and private aircraft in the north-eastern US. Visitors can 'fly' a jet plane simulator.

9 AMERICAN CLOCK AND WATCH MUSEUM

Bristol, Connecticut. More than 3,000 timepieces of all shapes and sizes, and a tour of clock-making history are offered in an 1801 house with a sundial garden.

10 LOCK MUSEUM OF AMERICA

Terryville, Connecticut. Some 22,000 locks and allied artefacts displayed.

11 KEROSENE LAMP MUSEUM

Winchester Center, Connecticut. A private collection of more than 500 lamps used between 1852 and 1880.

12 AMERICAN MUSEUM OF FLY FISHING

Manchester, Vermont. Fly fishing through the ages in a state that thrives on the art.

13 VERMONT MARBLE EXHIBIT

Proctor, Vermont. The world's largest marble museum, with historical displays and a Hall of Presidents carved in pure white marble. Proctor is the centre of Vermont's marble industry.

14 SHELBURNE MUSEUM

Shelburne, Vermont. You'll need a full day, at least, to take in the 80,000 exhibits on show in 40 buildings covering a variety of themes. Don't miss the *Ticonderoga*, a sidewheel steamship.

15 SEASHORE TROLLEY MUSEUM

Cape Arundel, Maine. A collection of over 100 veteran trolleys and repair shops. Visitors can take a ride as trolleys are 'exercised' along the tracks.

Science Museums

1 NEW ENGLAND SCIENCE CENTER

Worcester, Massachusetts. A planetarium, observatory, nature trail and science exhibit in a 60-acre (25-hectare) site.

2 MARIA MITCHELL SCIENCE CENTER

Nantucket, Massachusetts. Natural science exhibits, an aquarium and observatory at the birthplace of the astronomer who discovered a comet in 1849 and became the first woman member of the American Academy of Arts and Sciences.

3 BRIDGEPORT'S DISCOVERY MUSEUM

Bridgeport, Connecticut. About 100 hands-on exhibits, a planetarium and computer-simulated space missions. Also there are art galleries containing extensive collections.

4 SCIENCE MUSEUM OF CONNECTICUT

West Hartford, Connecticut. Planetarium, mini-zoo, marine life touch tank, computer lab and children's discovery room.

5 THE YANKEE SCIENCE AND NATURE CENTER

Seabrook, New Hampshire. Hands-on energy, science and nature study centre.

6 CHRISTA McAULIFFE PLANETARIUM

Concord, New Hampshire. Dedicated to the New Hampshire teacher who died in the *Challenger* space shuttle explosion.

See also pp. 61-103 for details of Boston Museums.

Science museums, some with hands-on exhibitions to enjoy.

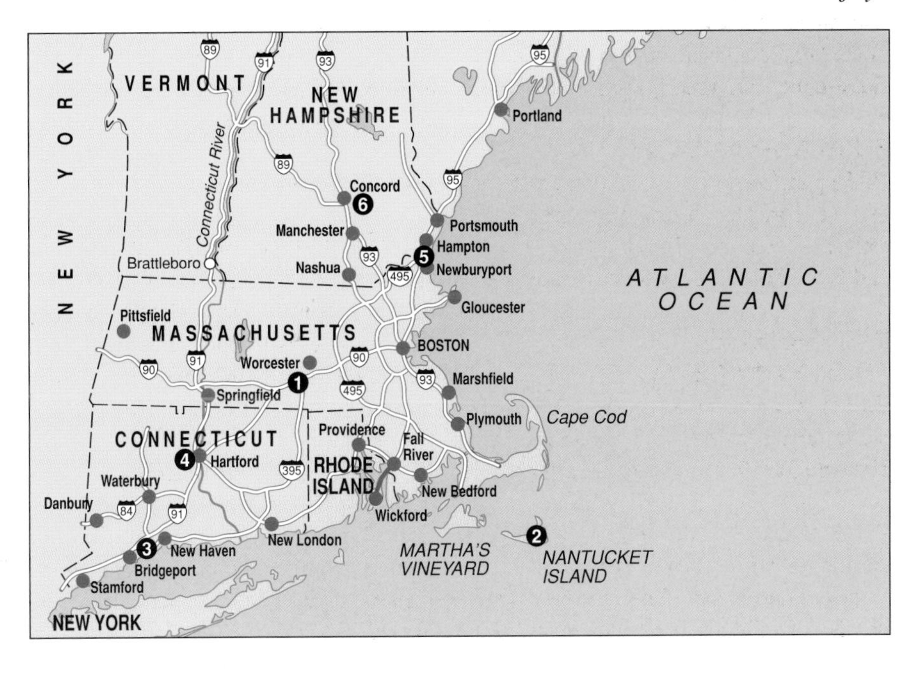

Traditional Crafts

1 HANCOCK SHAKER VILLAGE
Pittsfield, Massachusetts. Displays of Shaker crafts in 20 original buildings erected by a community founded in 1790.

2 STAMFORD MUSEUM AND NATURE CENTER
Stamford, Connecticut. A working farm with demonstrations of 19th-century farming methods, bee-keeping and cookery, plus wildlife trails and picnic areas.

3 VERMONT CRAFT CENTER
Traditional and contemporary work by Vermont craftspeople is displayed in galleries at Burlington, Manchester Village and Middlebury.

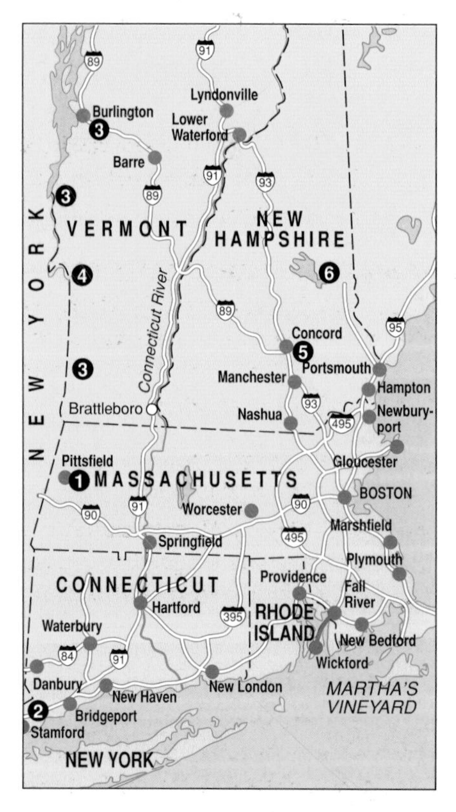

4 NEW ENGLAND MAPLE MUSEUM AND MAPLE MARKET
Pittsford, Vermont. The story of maple sugaring from sap to syrup. Demonstrations, slide shows and old photographs.

5 CANTERBURY SHAKER VILLAGE
Canterbury, New Hampshire. Visitors can take a guided tour and buy crafts, including beautifully simple furniture, brooms, boxes and baskets.

6 HAMPSHIRE PEWTER COMPANY
Wolfeboro, New Hampshire. Craftsmen employ colonial techniques to create ornaments and candlesticks. The workshop is open to the public.

Wildlife

1 MOUNT AUBURN CEMETERY
Cambridge, Massachusetts. Nearly 400 species of tree mean that many birds – and birdwatchers – flock to this cemetery in which burials still take place.

2 PLUM ISLAND
Reached by causeway from Newburyport, Massachusetts. The island is the site of the Parker River National Wildlife Refuge, a superb birdwatching area where more than 300 species have been recorded. Deer, woodchuck and turtles may also be seen.

3 CAPE COD MUSEUM OF NATURAL HISTORY
Brewster, Massachusetts. This has nature

Traditional crafts to see.

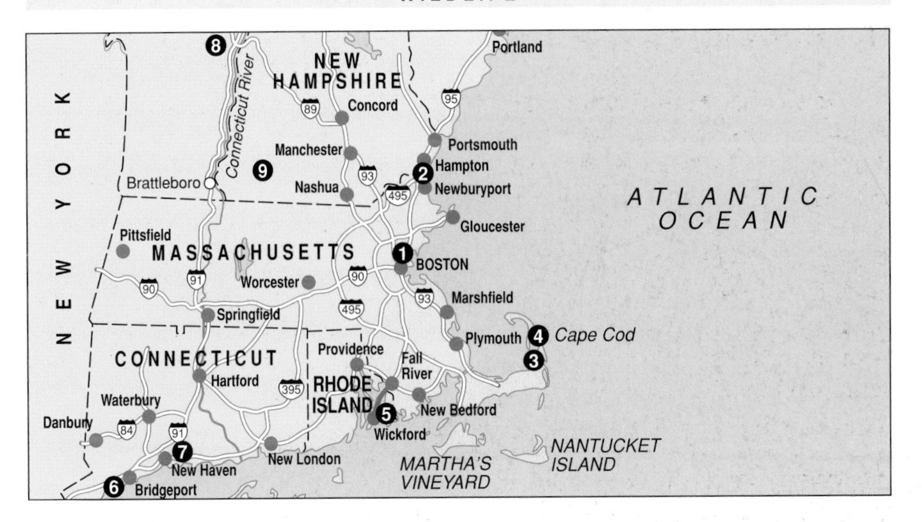

trails, exhibits, films and a working beehive which visitors can observe.

4 CAPE COD NATIONAL SEASHORE

North of Orleans, Cape Cod, Massachusetts. Vast expanses of beach, dunes, marshes, swamps and scrubland, with trails for hikers, cyclists and horse riders.

5 NORMAN BIRD SANCTUARY

Middletown, Rhode Island. More than 260 species have been recorded in this 450-acre (182-hectare) sanctuary of trails, streams and rock ledges. There are guided walks on Sundays.

6 FAIRFIELD NATURE CENTER

Fairfield, Connecticut. Walks for the blind, disabled and elderly are among the 6 miles (10km) of trails in this wildlife sanctuary maintained by Connecticut Audubon Society.

7 PEABODY MUSEUM OF NATURAL HISTORY

Yale University, New Haven, Connecticut. Everything from Connecticut's present wildlife back to dinosaur fossils is featured in one of America's oldest natural history museums.

Refuges and reserves to give protection to wildlife and enjoyment to visitors.

8 VERMONT RAPTOR CENTER

Woodstock, Vermont. Nearly 30 species of New England hawks, owls and eagles are kept here, all injured birds that cannot be released into the wild.

9 WAPACK NATIONAL WILDLIFE REFUGE

Monadnock Region, New Hampshire. A hawk migration area and good birdwatching opportunities in mixed habitats.

The beautifully decorated Romanesque Trinity church in Copley Square, Boston (see next page).

A City for Strollers

Boston comes as a surprise to most people visiting the city for the first time. It is an astonishingly compact place – even the airport, a major international gateway, is only 3 miles (5km) from the downtown area. With the exception of a mini-Manhattan down by the Waterfront, it is a generally low-rise city. Major highways cross at its very heart, making it an easy place both to enter and leave – its horrendous rush-hour traffic jams permitting.

The best way to explore Boston is on foot, although three trolley companies provide excellent orientation tours covering the major sights, and the 'T' – the city's rapid transit system – enables you to travel around cheaply and in relative comfort.

Greater Boston consists of around 100 towns and three million people in an area of 1,100 square miles (2,848km^2), but the city itself, the part with almost everything everyone wants to see, is spilt over a peninsula measuring no more than 2 miles (3.2km) from north to south or east to west. This tiny spit of land encompasses ten separate districts, each with its own unique character; each unmistakably Boston. Beyond Boston Proper, as its residents like to describe it, lie another nine communities, including Charlestown, which is one year older than Boston.

The Charles River, named after England's King Charles I, is a year-round sports amenity for Bostonians.

A Brief Boston History

Boston was founded in 1630 when 150 Puritans led by John Winthrop crossed the Charles River to settle on the hilly Shawmut peninsula. A meeting of the new settlement's freemen decided to name it after their home town in Lincolnshire, England. Within ten years Boston's population had grown to 1,200. Life for those early settlers was severe. To the burdens of

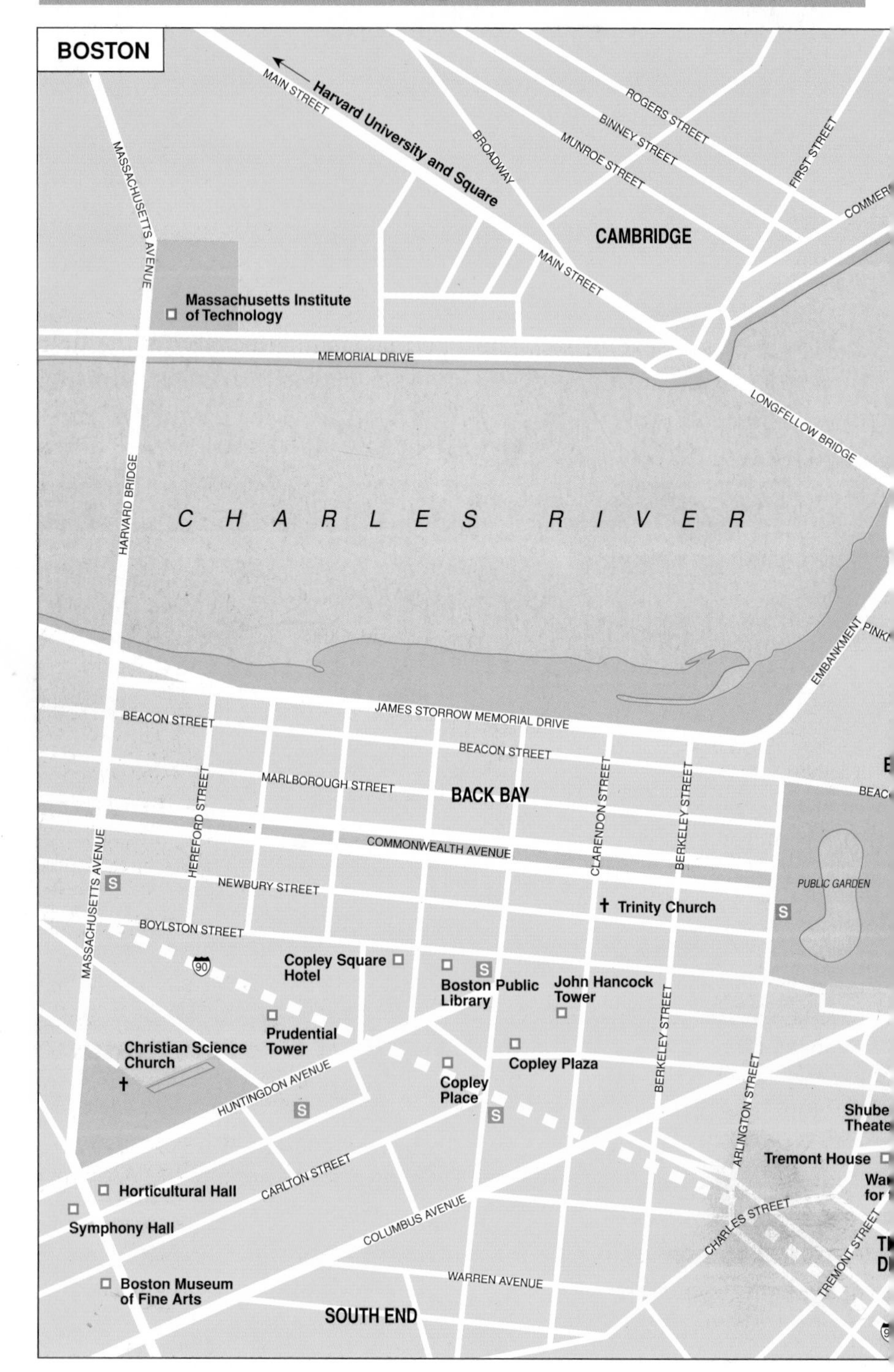
BOSTON
Harvard University and Square
MAIN STREET
ROGERS STREET
BINNEY STREET
MUNROE STREET
BROADWAY
FIRST STREET
CAMBRIDGE
MAIN STREET
MASSACHUSETTS AVENUE
Massachusetts Institute of Technology
MEMORIAL DRIVE
LONGFELLOW BRIDGE
HARVARD BRIDGE
C H A R L E S R I V E R
EMBANKMENT
JAMES STORROW MEMORIAL DRIVE
BEACON STREET
BEACON STREET
MARLBOROUGH STREET
BACK BAY
HEREFORD STREET
CLARENDON STREET
BERKELEY STREET
COMMONWEALTH AVENUE
NEWBURY STREET
PUBLIC GARDEN
Trinity Church
BOYLSTON STREET
MASSACHUSETTS AVENUE
90
Copley Square Hotel
Boston Public Library
John Hancock Tower
Prudential Tower
Christian Science Church
HUNTINGDON AVENUE
Copley Place
Copley Plaza
BERKELEY STREET
ARLINGTON STREET
Tremont House
CARLTON STREET
Horticultural Hall
Symphony Hall
COLUMBUS AVENUE
CHARLES STREET
TREMONT STREET
WARREN AVENUE
Boston Museum of Fine Arts
SOUTH END

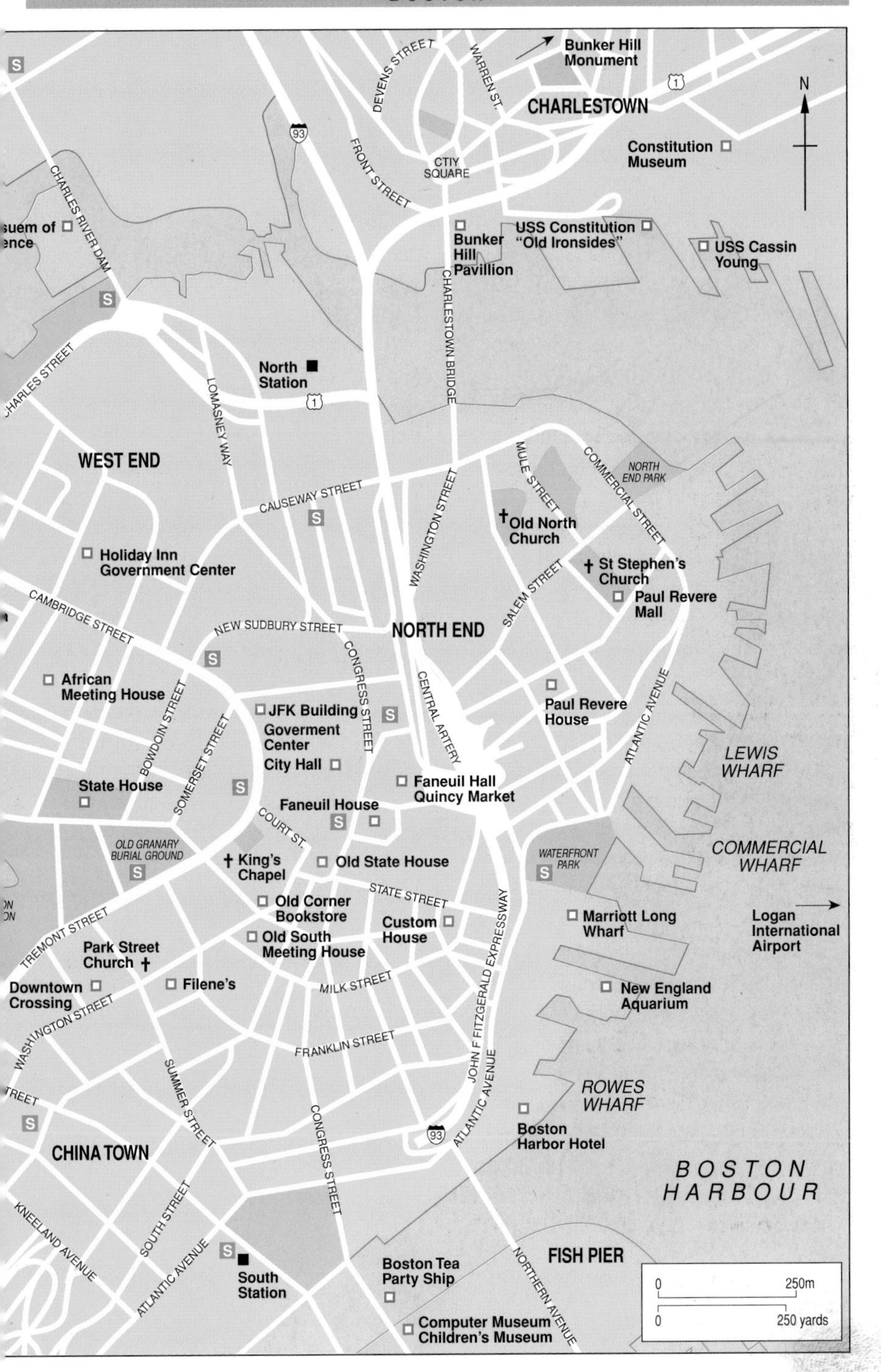

Bunker Hill Monument
CHARLESTOWN
N
Constitution Museum
DEVENS STREET
WARREN ST.
FRONT STREET
CTIY SQUARE
USS Constitution "Old Ironsides"
USS Cassin Young
Bunker Hill Pavillion
CHARLES RIVER DAM
CHARLES STREET
North Station
LOMASNEY WAY
CHARLESTOWN BRIDGE
WEST END
CAUSEWAY STREET
MULE STREET
COMMERCIAL STREET
NORTH END PARK
Old North Church
WASHINGTON STREET
Holiday Inn Government Center
St Stephen's Church
Paul Revere Mall
SALEM STREET
CAMBRIDGE STREET
NEW SUDBURY STREET
NORTH END
CONGRESS STREET
African Meeting House
JFK Building
Goverment Center
CENTRAL ARTERY
Paul Revere House
ATLANTIC AVENUE
BOWDOIN STREET
SOMERSET STREET
City Hall
LEWIS WHARF
State House
Faneuil Hall Quincy Market
Faneuil House
COURT ST.
OLD GRANARY BURIAL GROUND
King's Chapel
Old State House
WATERFRONT PARK
COMMERCIAL WHARF
STATE STREET
Old Corner Bookstore
Custom House
Marriott Long Wharf
Logan International Airport
TREMONT STREET
Old South Meeting House
Park Street Church
Downtown Crossing
Filene's
MILK STREET
JOHN F FITZGERALD EXPRESSWAY
New England Aquarium
WASHINGTON STREET
FRANKLIN STREET
SUMMER STREET
ROWES WHARF
Boston Harbor Hotel
CONGRESS STREET
ATLANTIC AVENUE
CHINA TOWN
BOSTON HARBOUR
KNEELAND AVENUE
SOUTH STREET
ATLANTIC AVENUE
South Station
Boston Tea Party Ship
NORTHERN AVENUE
FISH PIER
Computer Museum Children's Museum
0
250m
0
250 yards

establishing civilization in a generally hostile, wilderness environment were added the disciplines of a strict and intolerant religious regime. However, each new wave of immigrants brought people with more relaxed attitudes, and Boston became more liberal as it became more of a city.

By the early 1700s shipbuilding and cod fishing were the city's major industries, and its port dominated both domestic and international trade. Although it followed a generally prosperous course, Boston was hit badly by the effects of wars involving England, France and the Indians – wars which were fought elsewhere, but nevertheless drained it of people and resources. Then came the struggles over taxes imposed by the English Crown and the dramatic events that led to the War of Independence. Thanks to the swift departure of British troops at the start of the war, Boston escaped the worst of the bitter conflict, and when peace returned quickly got back to business.

As the city prospered once more, so the members of its merchant class – the Brahmins, as they came to be known – entrenched themselves as its aristocracy, snootily proclaiming the virtues of thrift and modesty as they built themselves grand homes and shifted the focus of fashion from North End to Beacon Hill. By the mid-1800s Boston was being regarded as the Athens of America, a place of fine architecture and fine ideals.

Although its seafaring character has largely gone, Boston today remains a bustling, cosmopolitan city, with the ambience of a European rather than a North American port. Thus, the streets in the Downtown, Waterfront and North End districts follow the plodding routes of cattle raised in the days of the Puritans. Those in the more modern Back Bay area may be laid out along a strict gridiron pattern, but tables and chairs nevertheless spill across the sidewalks from cafes and restaurants.

Bostonians show a lack of reserve more commonly found in Mediterranean lands. They converse at full volume, gesturing vigorously, and there is an eruption of impatience and a cacophony of car horns whenever traffic is halted for more than a few seconds.

Boston is a city of colour. Bright flowers and shrubs embellish the green of Boston Common and the neighbouring Public Garden; Faneuil Hall Market vibrates with the hues of balloons, stalls, flags and casual clothing. And at twilight the city's buildings – brick, granite, clapboard or glass – glow with a rosy warmth.

Central Boston

The city has a precisely marked centre point, though it isn't precisely the centre of anywhere, except perhaps the map of the rapid transit system. Downtown Crossing is a huge bronze disc set in the sidewalk at the intersection of Washington and Summer Streets. Thanks to the nearby Downtown Crossing subway station, it is an easy place to reach from all parts of the city and a good place from which to get your bearings. It is also a great place for shopping bargains.

Shopping Attractions

Boston's most famous bargains can be found in 'Effbee's', the short form for **Filene's Basement**. Filene's is a large traditional department store, but there is nothing traditional about its basement, which is a frenzied Aladdin's Cave of bargains in as wide a range of goods as can be imagined. A major feature of Effbee's is a

THE FREEDOM TRAIL

The best, but not necessarily the quickest, way to find your feet in Boston, and get a good flavour of the city at the same time, is to follow the Freedom Trail. This is a 3-mile (4.8km) route linking 16 historic sites from colonial and Revolutionary times. It is clearly marked on the sidewalk, either with red bricks or a painted red line.

The trail begins at the Visitor Information Center, near Park Street subway station on Boston Common. It winds through the downtown financial and shopping district to Faneuil Hall and Quincy Market, through the North End and across the Charles River into Charlestown. Maps and literature are available at the Boston Common Visitor Center, the Prudential Visitor Center on the west side of Prudential Plaza, and the National Park Service at 15 State Street.

Officially designated as a National Recreational Trail, the route climbs across the north-east corner of Boston Common to the **State House**, with its distinctive gold dome, then doubles back to Tremont Street and the graceful Park Street Church.

Next comes the **Old Granary Burying Ground** in which Paul Revere, John Hancock, Samuel Adams and all those who signed the Declaration of Independence are buried. Peter Faneuil and the parents of Benjamin Franklin are also buried here. The trail then crosses the road to **King's Chapel**, built in 1754 and the church in which British troops and Royal officials worshipped.

School Street takes you past Benjamin Franklin's statue and the site of the first public school in the US to the **Old Corner Bookstore**, a flourishing literary centre in the mid-19th century. The works of Henry Wadsworth Longfellow, Harriet Beecher Stowe, Nathaniel Hawthorne and Ralph Waldo Emerson were first published here.

The **Old South Meeting House**, close to the Old Corner Bookstore, was built in 1729 as a Puritan house of worship. The flames of revolution were fanned during political meetings and it was from here that Samuel Adams signalled the start of the Boston Tea Party. There is a charge for admission.

The **Old State House**, dwarfed by surrounding skyscrapers, is the oldest public building in the city, built in 1713. Here, the Declaration of Independence was first read to the people of Boston. A charge is made for visiting the Old State House. Nearby, a circle of cobblestones on State Street marks the site of the Boston Massacre of 5 March 1770, when five patriots were killed in a clash with Redcoats.

Faneuil Hall – the 'Cradle of Liberty' – was built in 1742 by the merchant Peter Faneuil and served as an open forum meeting place and market for more than 240 years.

Colourful **Quincy Market,** with its dozens of stalls, eating places, bars and exciting street entertainment, may divert walkers from the Freedom Trail, which continues to the **Paul Revere House** at 19 North Square, North End. There is an admission charge to visit the house, which is Boston's oldest building, dating from around 1680.

Two lanterns hung in the belfry of **Old North Church** signalled the start of the American Revolution by warning patriots that the British were advancing on Concord by sea. The man who hung them there, Sexton Robert Newman, is buried in nearby Copp's Hill Burying Ground, which served as a vantage point for the British when they were preparing for the Battle of Bunker Hill.

Across the river, the trail leads next to the **Charlestown Navy Yard** and the *USS Constitution* – 'Old Ironsides'. Launched in 1797 and undefeated in 44 major engagements with the British fleet in the War of 1812, the frigate is the world's oldest commissioned warship still afloat. Admission is free, but there are often long queues waiting for the guided tour.

The Freedom Trail ends at the **Bunker Hill Monument**, the 220ft- (68m-) obelisk built to honour the patriots who died on 17 June 1775 in the first battle of the American Revolution.

The State House, with its distinctive gold dome, is undiminished by Boston's high-rise buildings.

continuous Dutch auction in which selected items become progressively cheaper and cheaper until somebody's nerve breaks. Here you can buy a quality suitcase at half price or less to take home all those other things you simply couldn't resist.

Nearby is another classic department store – the original, in fact: Jordan Marsh. The store had its beginnings in 1851 when it was opened by Eben Dyer Jordan, a young entrepreneur from Maine. A good few dollars have been rung up on the Jordan Marsh tills since Eben made his first sale – two cents' worth of silk ribbon.

Downtown Crossing marks Boston's major shopping quarter. Here there are stores selling all kinds of goods. Many are relatively small establishments, and there's a village store standard of personal service even in the latest high-tech photographic and computer shops. The whole area is closed to traffic, and there are usually lots of vendors selling pretzels, hot dogs and flowers, while trinkets, souvenirs and postcards are sold from kerbside stalls.

Tourist Sites

North of Downtown Crossing are some of the city's major historical sites. A mere stroll away, on the corner of Washington and Milk Streets, is the **Old South Meeting House**, one of the most important locations for events before and leading up to the American Revolution. The original meeting house, an oak and cedar-board structure, was built in 1663 and stood until 1727. Benjamin Franklin, born in a house nearby on Milk Street, was baptised in the old building on 6 January 1706.

The present building, dating from 1729, followed the style of Sir Christopher Wren, architect of London's most graceful churches. It was the setting for many a fiery protest meeting during the run-up to the Revolution, and it was from here that Samuel Adams encouraged his Sons of Liberty to stage the Boston Tea Party.

The **Globe Corner Bookstore**, a favourite with Bostonians and visitors alike, stands on the corner of Washington and School Streets. The red brick building,with its Dutch-style roof, has had a varied history since it was built in 1712. It replaced an earlier structure which was destroyed in Boston's great fire of 1711. After serving as an apothecary's shop, general store and a private home, it became a book store and publishing house in 1828. Its printing press was literally driven by horsepower – by teams of draught horses – and by the mid-1850s the store had become a meeting place for Boston's literary lions.

At the end of Washington Street, where it intersects with State Street, stands the oldest public building in Boston, the **Old State House**, built in 1713. This was where the Declaration of Independence was first read to the citizens of Boston. Now housing a museum of the city's history, the Old State House stands on the site of the original Town House, built in 1658 and burned down in the fire of 1711. The present structure, which still bears the lion and the unicorn of the British royal coat of arms, was itself gutted in another blaze in December 1747.

Next to Old State House, a circle of cobblestones in State Street marks the spot

The flames of revolution were fanned at meetings in the Old South Meeting House.

where five Bostonians – one of them Crispus Attucks, a black man – were killed in the Boston Massacre on the night of 5 March 1770. Opposite the Old State House, the National Park Service Visitor Center at 15 State Street (Tel. 242-5642) is a goldmine of information about Boston in particular and New England in general. The centre has a comprehensive book shop as well as public telephones and toilets, and is the starting point for guided walks along the Freedom Trail.

Turning left on to Court Street and left again on to Tremont Street brings you to more historical landmarks. King's Chapel, on the corner of Tremont and School Streets, dates from 1754 and was Boston's first Anglican church. Here, British troops and officials worshipped, though not without a great deal of opposition by the local Puritans.

Attempting to crack down on the Puritans in the mid-1680s, Britain's King James II had sent a clergyman to establish the Church of England in Boston, a move which did not go down well with the locals. Backed by the colonial governor, Sir Edmund Andros, the Rev Robert Ratcliffe commandeered the Old South Meeting House, which he used as a church until the original King's Chapel was built of wood in 1689. The citizens of Boston felt no warmer towards the Anglicans when the present chapel was dedicated. A large crowd of them hurled abuse, rubbish and even animal corpses at those taking part in the ceremony.

King's Chapel Burying Ground, on Tremont Street, was Boston's first cemetery and was used from 1630 to 1796. It contains the remains of John Winthrop, first Governor of the Bay Colony.

A few yards' detour into School Street brings you to the site of America's first public (free) school, the Boston Latin School founded in 1635 and still going strong in the city's Roxbury neighbourhood. The site is marked on the sidewalk in front of the fussy granite architecture of Old City Hall. Here is another first: the first portrait statue in the US, erected in bronze to commemorate Benjamin Franklin, shown with a half smile.

Continuing south on Tremont Street takes you past the **Old Granary Burying Ground**, final resting place of many Revolutionary heroes, including John Hancock, Samuel Adams, Paul Revere and Peter Faneuil. Next to it is Park Street Church, where the song '*America*' was first sung on Independence Day, 1831. During the War of 1812, the church was known as Brimstone Corner because its cellar was packed with gunpowder.

Downtown Boston

The area most people regard as Downtown Boston extends to the east of Downtown Crossing, taking in the Financial District and the immensely popular Faneuil Hall Market.

The Financial District

This area is encompassed by Atlantic Avenue between South Station and Long Wharf, with its northern and western edges marked by State Street and Federal Street respectively. This is high-rise Boston. Although the skyscrapers are rather more generously spaced out than those in Manhattan, they are no less grand, and their architects have been lavish in the use of glass, steel and marble.

Doyen of the tall buildings is **Custom House Tower**, at McKinley Square, on the intersection of State and India Streets. Now reaching a height of nearly 500ft (152m), it was a lot shorter when it first opened in 1847. For 66 years the stately dome and granite columns of the original Greek Revival building designed by Ammi B. Young dominated the Boston skyline, the subject of a controversy between those who thought it a thing of beauty and those who could not stand it. In 1913 architects Peabody and Stearns were commissioned to give the building a more contemporary look. Two years later Custom House Tower had an extra 30 floors, carved scrolls and mythical beasts, and an ornate clock with four faces which for many years told different times.

All those who signed the Declaration of Independence lie in the Old Granary Burying Ground.

BOSTON COMMON

The open land facing Park Street Church is the north-eastern end of Boston Common, the city's 50-acre (21 hectare) five-sided playground. The oldest public park in the United States, the area was set aside as common grazing land for sheep and cattle as early as 1640. It soon became a focal point for social, military and political gatherings.

Troops have been mustered and drilled on the common, and from the branches of its Great Elm, which stood until 1876, criminals and religious and political dissenters – including the Quaker Mary Dyer – were hanged. Up to 2,000 British troops were camped here during the American Revolution, and a number of Redcoats who were killed at the Battle of Bunker Hill were buried in the Central Burying Ground on the common's Boylston Street edge.

More recently, the common has been the setting for such innocent pursuits as walking and jogging, eating ice cream, sunbathing, sledging and snowballing. Senior members of Boston's Chinese community can be seen practising the graceful choreographed exercises of t'ai chi, while open air evangelists practise their oratory on the seemingly deaf ears of passers-by.

The Information Center run by Boston Convention and Visitors Bureau is located on the common, next to the Park Street subway station. The station was the first of its kind to be opened in the US and is now a Historic Landmark.

The **Soldiers and Sailors Monument** on Telegraph Hill, on the western side of the Common, is 70ft (21.5m) high. It commemorates those who died fighting for the Unionist cause in the American Civil War.

Another area of parkland stands at the common's western edge, across Charles Street. This is the 24-acre (8-hectare) Public Garden, an attractive rectangle of greenery, shrubs and flower beds surrounding the Lagoon, where visitors can take genteel trips on elegant swan boats pedal-operated by young men and women.

Some 80 years on, the building is dwarfed by more modern structures, but the rows about its style continue.

Close to the Custom House Tower, in the New England Telephone Company Building at 185 Franklin Street, the **Alexander Graham Bell Garret** is open to the public. This is a reconstruction of the attic in nearby Court Street from which the inventor transmitted the first speech sounds over wire on 3 June 1875. Although the garret is not the actual location, the equipment has been reassembled from Bell's original laboratory.

Faneuil Hall Marketplace

North of Custom House Tower, on the opposite side of State Street, is **Faneuil Hall Marketplace**, one of the liveliest, most colourful 6.5 acres (2.7 hectares) of urban revitalization you will find anywhere in the world. In fact, the rescue and restoration of the area has served as a model and inspiration for urban restoration worldwide, including London's Covent Garden.

Many newcomers to Boston think of the area as Quincy Market, but this is only one of three markets on the site. The others are North Market and South Market, and all three are housed in long elegant buildings of classical proportions. Quincy, the one in the middle, has Doric colonnades as well as a dome and a rotunda.

The building that gives its name to the area is **Faneuil Hall**, also known as 'the Cradle of Liberty'. It was built and donated to the city in 1742 by Peter Faneuil, a wealthy young merchant who had made his fortune in the 'triangle trade' (see

p. 72). The area on which it stands was a marketplace then, though rather more down-to-earth than some of the chic craft and jewellery stalls of today. Dock Square, as it was known earlier, was a raucous bedlam of rough trade where the produce of land and sea was exchanged. Merchant out-shouted merchant, and the pungent odours of fish and farm animals competed. Faneuil Hall, slightly aloof from it all then as it is now, became the stage on which the early Revolutionary moves were enacted by the likes of Samuel Adams and Paul Revere. Today, it still serves as a forum for debate, a marketplace for ideas.

Architects in Boston have been lavish in the use of glass, steel and marble.

Quincy and its neighbouring markets are the focal points for a wide paved area positively teeming with fun. Street entertainment here is superb: Andean Indians playing pan pipes and competing with a college all-male choir; a young comedian from Britain vying with a Yankee conjuror. There are harpists, zither-players, bagpipers, folk dancers, clog dancers, tap dancers....

Faneuil Hall Marketplace was almost lost forever. After 125 years of trade in meat and vegetables – the present buildings date from 1826 – the area had fallen into decay and in the 1950s faced demolition. Luckily, America's throwaway society had just been succeeded by the conservationists. Many other cities now have reason to be grateful to Boston's progressive thinkers.

Now claimed as America's premier marketplace, the three buildings between

The Quincy Marketplace is one of three elegant buildings in the lively Faneuil Hall marketplace complex.

them house more than 125 shops and 21 restaurants, including Durgin Park, a resident business for more than 160 years. Outdoors, a colourful flower market and stalls selling balloons, ice cream, T-shirts, rugs and knick-knacks add to the overall vibrancy that attracts more than 14 million visitors a year.

Other Downtown Attractions

The **Union Oyster House** – also known as Ye Olde Oyster House – on Union Street, just north of Faneuil Hall, is one of Boston's oldest buildings. It is certainly mentioned in a plan dated 1708, though some people believe it may go back to the street's origin in 1636. Between 1771 and 1775 the *Massachusetts Spy* newspaper was published in the building, which later became the headquarters of Ebenezer Hancock, the Continental Army's paymaster. Brother of the Revolutionary John Hancock, Ebenezer lived in the nearby house on Salt Lane which has survived to become the city's oldest brick-built house, dating from 1660. Its original owner was William Courser, Boston's first town crier.

At the corner of Salt Lane and Marshall Street stands the **Boston Stone**. The stone ball and companion trough were brought to Boston from England in 1700 to ground pigment for paint, but the ball later served as a zero point from which all distances from Boston were measured.

The drabness of Blackstone Street, which runs parallel to the John F. Fitzgerald Expressway, disappears on Fridays and Saturdays when dozens of stalls are set up and it becomes the Haymarket, where traders and customers bargain vigorously in the exchange of fruit, vegetables and meat, including such exotic delicacies as tripe, squid, octopus and sheeps' heads.

Bounded by Congress, Court, Cambridge and New Sudbury Streets, Government Center has a station on the T's blue and green lines and is surrounded by City Hall Plaza, which comes to life when concerts are staged there. The multi-level, wide-open brick plaza is deemed an eyesore by many, and Bostonians either love or hate the aggressively geometrical New City Hall at its centre. Not long ago this was Scollay Square, an area of burlesque theatres, night clubs, fortune tellers and sleazy bars, but demolition squads put an end to it all in the early 1960s.

BAY VILLAGE

Adjoining theatreland is Bay Village, a tiny neighbourhood of narrow streets with brick townhouses and gas lamps. Lying between Tremont Street and Columbus Avenue, with the Massachusetts Turnpike marking its southern boundary and Boston Common to the north, the village dates from the 1820s and originally housed the artisans who serviced residents in more affluent parts of the city, which now include the village itself. Bay Street, at the end of Fayette Street, notches up two points in Boston's book of records. It is the city's shortest street, and its only house is the city's smallest.

Chinatown

Walking south from Downtown Crossing along Washington Street takes you to Boston's Chinatown, the third largest Chinese community in the United States. The largest, of course, is in San Francisco, but where, trolley tour guides like to ask their passengers, is the second? New York? Chicago? Few people come up with the right answer, which is Honolulu.

Avery Street marks the start of the once-notorious area known as the Combat Zone. Vice ran rife among the zone's topless bars, clubs and sex dens. Now cleaned up after a loud and indignant public outcry, it is being embraced by Chinatown, whose eastern frontier is marked by a pair of stone dragons and an oriental arch that acts as a gateway across Atlantic Avenue opposite South Station.

Chinatown's main artery is Beach Street, and the whole area is full of small, colourful shops with exotic window displays and intriguing scents. In the evenings especially, when the crowds turn out from the nearby theatre district, the streets and restaurants are packed. The **China Trade Center** at Washington and Boylston Streets contains many ethnic restaurants and shops. This is the place to buy those colourful silks, jade, porcelain, herbs and spices. The top festivals in the area are Chinese New Year, in February, and the August Moon Festival.

Turning right on Kneeland Street, at the southern end of Chinatown, leads to Stuart Street and then on to the intersection with Tremont Street. This is at the heart of the **Midtown Cultural District**, where houses such as the Charles Playhouse and the Wilbur, Schubert and Colonial theatres stage drama, comedy, ballet, opera, Broadway spectaculars and performances by the city's homegrown talent.

The Waterfront

There was a time when the Waterfront was Boston. Strung along the western shore of the inner harbour, between Fort Point Channel and the mouth of the Charles River, were a dozen or so wharfs, some large even by today's supertanker standards. Here there were scenes of ant-heap activity as men, horses and carts toiled and wheeled almost constantly to load and unload the graceful schooners and clippers that came and went during the port's busiest period at the rate of 15 vessels a day, year round.

The warehouses, shipping offices and counting houses swarmed with clerks, longshoremen, ship owners, master mariners and seamen. Cargo arrived from all over the world, much of it merely to be processed and repacked for trade elsewhere. Tea came and went. In the infamous 'triangle trade', on which the fortunes of many powerful Bostonians were based, sugar and molasses from the Caribbean were made into rum, which was then exchanged for African slaves, who in turn were swopped for more sugar and molasses.

The tempo began to slow down from the 1850s on, and the construction of Atlantic Avenue in 1878 placed a barrier between the wharfs and the city, a process which was reinforced in the 1950s with the building of the John F. Fitzgerald Expressway. The old warehouses, now deserted, began to crumble and the bustle of the past gave way to the scurrying of rats. Then with the restoration of the Faneuil Hall Marketplace, Bostonians again saw the Waterfront as both an amenity and an asset. The desirable condominiums, the expensive hotels and restaurants, the marinas and museums, may all be a far cry from those busy days of sail, but they have brought back some of the activity – albeit at a more leisurely pace – and there is once more an atmosphere of hope rather than hopelessness.

Boston is still a major port, with more than two dozen steamship lines carrying general cargo between Boston and 175 ports throughout the world. New England's major international gateway, the port annually handles more than 25 million tons of cargo, worth around $7 billion. Its 23 private terminals process bulk products, such as petroleum, natural gas, cement, scrap metal and salt. High-value general cargo, mostly containerized, including machinery, photographic and computer equipment and consumer goods, is handled by three public terminals owned and operated by the Massachusetts Port Authority (Massport).

Supported entirely by revenues from its own facilities, Massport was created by the State legislature in 1956. In addition to the three public terminals, it owns and operates Logan International Airport, the Black Falcon cruise-ship terminal, the Tobin Memorial Bridge (carrying US Highway 1 across the Mystic River), the Boston Fish Pier, and World Trade Center Boston on Commonwealth Pier, South Boston.

South Boston

Few people using the Black Falcon cruise-ship terminal would care to be reminded that its name honours the memory of 12 longshoremen who died when the cargo vessel *Black Falcon*, carrying a cargo of chemicals, caught fire and blew up on the site in November 1953.

Boston Fish Pier and World Trade Center Boston are on adjoining locations on South Boston's waterfront. The fish pier was built in 1915 to serve the city's fishing industry and has recently undergone a $19 million modernization programme. **World Trade Center Boston**, located on the site of a former cruise-ship

LUNCH ON THE LINE

A railway station may not seem to be the best place for a rendezvous or a break from the office, but many Bostonians find the South Station is ideal for such purposes. South Station, the Amtrak terminus, has an elegant, curved beaux art façade, dating from 1898. After a period of outrageous dilapidation, the station has been splendidly restored. Its concourse now sparkles with marble floors and brass railings, and there are relaxed cafes and restaurants. Bright kiosks sell flowers, confectionery, chocolates, ice cream and yoghurt, perfume, newspapers and magazines. Jazz concerts are held in the concourse during summer months, and many office workers take their lunch break there.

terminal, has 1 million square feet (93,000m²) of office and exhibition space, a conference centre and docking facilities.

For sightseers, as good a link as any with the past, and a bit of fun for all the family, can be found at the brig *Beaver II*, boarded from a jetty in the middle of the Congress Street Bridge. The bridge provides a link with South Boston across the Fort Point Channel. Each of the tour trolleys stops somewhere near the bridge, or you can take the T's red line to South Station, just one stop from Downtown Crossing. The walk from South Station to Congress Street Bridge takes about 5 minutes.

Beaver II is better known as the Boston Tea Party Ship. It isn't the original, of course. But the brig, launched in Denmark

Beaver II, *a replica of the 1773 Boston Tea Party ship, is the setting for a tongue-in-cheek presentation of an historic event.*

in 1908, is similar to the smallest of the three ships which were boarded on a December evening in 1773 by Samuel Adams's rebellious tax dodgers disguised as Indians. A small museum alongside the brig illustrates the background to the Boston Tea Party, but the fun part is the not-too-serious re-enactment on board *Beaver II*, especially if one or two unrepentant Britons are in the audience. Everyone – visitors and all – takes part in the charade, and everyone gets the chance to throw a tea chest overboard in protest. It's on a rope to prevent the harbour from becoming cluttered.

The actual site of the Tea Party was Griffins Wharf, about 300 yards (275m) north of the bridge on the western shore. The wharf no longer exists, but its location is marked by a plaque on the wall of a building at the end of Pearl Street.

The Wharfs of South Boston

The elegant Boston Harbor Hotel, with its awesome six-storey arch, stands on Rowe's Wharf, site of the South Battery which was built in 1666. Later, the battery became a busy dock. Today, it is a terminal for the ferries that ply between Boston and Logan Airport, and for some harbour cruise vessels.

Northward again, the twin 40-storey towers on India Wharf are the work of the internationally acclaimed architect I.M. Pei, and next comes Central Wharf and the **New England Aquarium**. This is set in a splendid plaza with a giant red mobile, *Echo of the Waves*, rotating and undulating with the breezes that blow across the harbour.

The aquarium features more than 2,000 aquatic creatures in its giant transparent Ocean Tank, which contains 200,000 gallons (757,000 litres) of salt water and is as deep as a four-storey building is tall. Sharks, moray eels, giant turtles and fish of all shapes, sizes and hues swim among its man-made coral reef. A winding ramp enables visitors to ascend the tank's exterior, viewing the various creatures encountered at different depths. Six times

A LOT OF BOTTLE

A 40ft- (12.2m-) high milk bottle at the South Boston end of the Congress Street Bridge will certainly beckon curious sightseers. Bostonians will tell you that the wooden bottle could hold 50,000 gallons (189,300 litres) of milk topped with 860 gallons (3,250 litres) of cream, but all it has ever held is people, food and kitchen equipment, for the strange building is a novel diner put up in the whimsical 1930s. The giant bottle acts as a landmark for two interesting museums: the Children's Museum and the Computer Museum, both located at 300 Congress Street.

'Don't touch' is an expression never heard in the **Children's Museum**, where visitors are encouraged to handle, scramble over and climb on the exhibits. They can blow giant bubbles, visit a Japanese home from Kyoto (Boston's twin city), read the weather forecast on television, and shop in a scaled-down supermarket. At the Recycle Room children can buy waste material of all kinds to turn into something else when they get home.

The **Computer Museum**, the first of its kind, is entirely devoted to the history of information technology, and there are more hands-on experience for younger visitors. They can walk through the innards of a model computer the size of a two-storey building, jump on the keys of its 25ft- (8m-) long keyboard, fly an airliner into a volcano and scrawl on a wall without the fear of a ticking-off.

There are admission charges payable at both museums.

Indian home-building techniques are displayed in the Children's Museum in Boston.

a day scuba divers enter the tank to feed its inhabitants.

The Tidal Pool is a sophisticated 'touch tank' where children are encouraged to make friends with hermit crabs, starfish, sea urchins and clams.

Next to the aquarium is the *Discovery*, a floating pavilion in the style of a Mississippi sternwheeler, where sea lions entertain and educate in daily shows. Central Wharf is also the starting point for cruises aboard *Voyager*, the aquarium's whale-watching vessel. A marine biologist accompanies each trip to talk about the habits and habitat of whales and other creatures encountered.

Long Wharf, dominated now by the red brick splendour of the Boston Marriott Long Wharf Hotel – which offers some of the best harbour views available to the public – adjoins Central Wharf. Built in 1710, it originally reached some 2,000ft (610m) into the harbour, but since then it has been diminished by reclamation and redevelopment. Nevertheless, it remains impressive, especially when you consider that the hotel sitting so snugly along its length, has no fewer than 400 guest rooms, two 200-seat restaurants, a 220-seat waterfront lounge and a ballroom in which a reception can be staged for a thousand people.

The old wharf has witnessed some historic moments. The *Columbia Rediviva*, the first American ship to take part in the China trade and the first to circumnavigate the world, berthed here in 1790 after a voyage that covered 50,000 miles (80,000km) and lasted a month short of three years. In 1819 the first missionaries embarked here on their way to take Christianity to Hawaii, and 76 years later, in 1895, the eccentric

More than 2,000 aquatic creatures are on show at the New England Aquarium on Boston Waterfront.

Joshua Slocum set sail aboard his vessel *Spray* on the first solo voyage round the world. He was gone for 38 months. Today, Long Wharf is the departure point for harbour cruises and for ferries to the Charlestown Navy Yard, the Harbor Islands and Provincetown, Cape Cod.

Between Long Wharf and neighbouring Commercial Wharf is the small but welcome area of greenery known as **Christopher Columbus Park**. Wedged between the wharfs and Atlantic Avenue, the park embraces a children's playground and the Rose Kennedy Rose Garden. It has a cobblestoned frontage on to the water embellished with bollards and lengths of chain – all very nautical. The condominiums on Commercial Wharf are housed in the old warehouse where sails were made for the *USS Constitution*, the world's oldest commissioned warship still afloat, now moored in the Navy Yard at Charlestown.

THE HARBOR ISLANDS

Thirty islands contained within Boston Harbor's 50 square miles (130km^2) provide visitors and residents alike with the opportunity to get away from it all for a little while at least. Each of the islands has something different to offer, and eight of them constitute the Boston Harbor Islands State Park (office at 349 Lincoln Street, Hingham, Tel. 617 740-1605).

George's Island, a 45-minute ferry ride from Long Wharf, is the park's headquarters. The chief attraction here is Fort Warren, a National Historic Landmark. Built between 1833 and 1869, the fort housed Confederate prisoners during the Civil War and remains almost intact. It is said to be haunted. During the summer months there is a water taxi service from George's to other islands in the park.

Peddocks Island also has a 19th-century fort, and its 188 acres (76 hectares) contain a wildlife sanctuary, old cottages, woodlands, salt marshes, rocky beaches and open fields. **Lovells Island** (yet another fort here) has long beaches, dunes and rock pools, and is the only island from which swimming is permitted. According to legend, pirate treasure is buried here.

The remoter islands are Gallops, Bumpkin and Grape Islands and Great and Little Brewster. From rugged Great Brewster (accessible only to those with their own boat) there are superb views of Boston's inner harbour and the Atlantic Ocean. Little Brewster has the only lighthouse in the US which is still manned by the US Coastguard. Known as the **Boston Light**, it is a National Historic Landmark, built in 1782 after the original had been blown up by the British when they left Boston in 1776.

Camping is allowed on Lovells and Peddocks Islands (permits are obtainable from the Metropolitan District Commission, 98 Taylor Street, Dorset; Tel. 617 727-5359), and on Bumpkin and Grape Islands (for permits call the State Park on 617 727-7676). Fishing is allowed from rocky shores and public piers on all the islands except Peddocks. The best catches are cod, flounder, haddock, striped bass and pollack.

Most of the Harbor Islands have always been exploited to some extent by man. Indians fished from them and raised crops long before the first settlers arrived. During the 18th century they attracted city dwellers in search of fresh air, as well as the pleasures of illegal gambling and barefist boxing tournaments.

Five islands – Deer, Castle, Hog, Long and Moon – are connected to the mainland by bridges or causeways, and another three will certainly be visited by the bulk of visitors to Boston, especially those arriving from abroad. Apple, Bird and Governor's Islands were joined together to form Logan International Airport.

Lewis Wharf, home of the Boston Sailing Club, is believed by some to be the actual setting of Edgar Alan Poe's horror story, *The Fall of the House of Usher*. Certainly there was an Usher House on the wharf, and when it was demolished in 1880 two skeletons were found in the basement, locked in an embrace – enough evidence to spark speculation that they were the remains of the seaman and young woman of the novel.

The North End

Boston's oldest residential neighbourhood, now identified as the city's Little Italy, the North End has always been a place apart. This was where the Puritans first settled when they crossed the Charles River and found a place that for all its marshy remoteness was at least free of wolves, rattlesnakes and mosquitoes. Soon it was a true island, isolated from the rest of the Shawmut Peninsula by a canal. It remains an island in the cultural sense, and is now cut off from the rest of Boston by the John F. Fitzgerald Expressway, which follows the route of the old canal.

The North End has undergone a number of ethnic metamorphoses in its time. After the Puritans, it became a fashionable area with some very wealthy Tory families occupying fine houses. The Revolution put them to flight, and as the focus of fashion turned to Beacon Hill, the North End became a working class neighbourhood housing shipbuilding workers and their families. The Potato Famine of 1846 brought a flood of Irish immigrants who dominated the area until the late 1880s, when East European Jews started to arrive. The Italians, many of them originating in Sicily and the southern provinces, have been established since the 1920s. Now there are signs that the North End may be undergoing yet another change as gentrification and rising rents force old residents out and draw newer, wealthier ones in.

However, the Italian influence is still strong enough to maintain the illusion at times that this is Naples rather than Boston. The staples here are home-made pizzas and pastas, and the narrow, lively streets are filled with the scents of olive oil, freshly-baked bread and espresso coffee. And since almost every day is a saint's day, there are lots of festivals.

Two of the most important sites on the Freedom Trail are in the North End – Paul Revere's House and Old North Church – but the neighbourhood is very much worth a tour on its own account. Its main artery is Hanover Street, and it is here that tourists will find themselves first if they follow the Freedom Trail from downtown Boston.

Hanover Street Environs

Hanover is a busy street lined with restaurants and cafes from end to end. A right turn into Parmentier Street, followed by a left into North Square, brings you to the **Paul Revere House**, built in 1676. Revere bought the house in 1770. At that time it had three floors, but 20th-century pedants removed the top storey to restore the house to its 17th-century condition. Although the building cannot be as Revere would have known it, there are pieces of furniture which belonged to the family, and a bedroom has been covered with a reproduction of wallpaper made in Boston at the end of the 18th century. There is a display of silverware, some made by Revere himself, and a 931lb (423kg) bell cast by the craftsman.

Number 19 North Square is better known as Paul Revere House – he lived here from 1770 to 1800.

Back on Hanover Street, and about 150 yards (135m) farther on from Parmentier, you come to St Stephen's Church, with its slender white steeple. Built in 1804, it is the only one to survive of five Boston churches designed by Charles Bullfinch, mastermind of the city's Federalist architecture. St Stephen's began as a Congregationalist Meeting House, then became a Unitarian church in 1813. It was acquired by the Roman Catholics in 1862. Apart from its sectarian switches, the

THE MAN WHO WAS GOOD AT EVERYTHING

One of history's most famous despatch riders, Paul Revere was born in Boston on 1 January 1735, the son of a couple who had emigrated from the Channel Islands. Apollos de Revoire was a gifted craftsman in gold and silver, and young Paul soon showed that he had inherited his father's talent. He acquired the family business on his father's death and before long was regarded as the best silversmith in the colony.

Revere was one of those people who was apparently good at everything. An explosives expert, he served as an artillery officer in the French and Indian wars, in which he also proved himself to be an excellent horseman. He was a skilled artist, engineer and inventor. He made false teeth and produced the copper sheathing for the *USS Constitution*. He cast bells, and rang them in Old North Church. He ran a gunpowder mill and ran messages as a despatch rider for the Sons of Liberty. He was a persuasive orator and politician. He married twice, fathering eight children each time.

The opportunity for Revere to carve himself a lasting niche in American history came on the night of 18 April 1775 when he rode from Boston to Buckman's Tavern, Lexington, to warn Samuel Adams and John Hancock that the British were coming to arrest them and seize a rebel ammunition store at Concord. As 800 Redcoats fought with a handful of Minutemen, Revere was arrested. Amazingly, the British released him after a few hours of questioning.

The Revolutionary War over and independence gained, Revere settled back into a busy life. He died in 1818, aged 83, and is buried in Boston's Old Granary Burial Ground on Tremont Street.

church has also been physically moved. In 1870 it was moved 12ft (3.69 metres) back and raised 6ft (1.8m) when Hanover Street was widened. In 1965 it was restored to its original level and appearance.

Opposite St Stephen's is a lively brick-paved square dominated by a splendid statue of the Great Despatch Rider himself. This is the **Paul Revere Mall**, known to North Enders as the Prado. The figure was cast in 1940 from a work modelled in 1885 by Cyrus Dallin. Bronze murals on the left illustrate the history of Boston.

Christ Church, better known, perhaps, as Old North, is reached through a small gate at the far end of the mall. Built in 1723 for Boston's second Anglican parish, Old North is the oldest church in the city and is a revered monument to the American revolutionary movement. With its 191ft (58.7m) steeple and a commanding view of Boston and the Charles River, the church was a natural lookout post, and from here the sexton Robert Newman hung the two lanterns that set Paul Revere off on his historic ride to Lexington. Later, it is said, the British Governor, General Thomas Gage, used the same vantage point to watch his troops take a hammering at the Battle of Bunker Hill. Hurricanes have twice blown the steeple down, in 1804 and 1854.

MYSTERIOUS FLIGHT

An historic marker in a small public garden just outside Old North Church records that a man named John Childs flew three times from the church steeple on 13 September 1757, firing a pistol during one flight. The marker says Childs 'had given public notice of his intention' and was watched by 'a great number of spectators'. There is no record of how he performed his remarkable feat.

The peal of bells hanging in the belfry at Old North is America's first. The eight bells were cast in England, weigh a total of 7,272lbs (3,305kg) and were first rung in 1745. They are tolled on the death of every President, a tradition since George Washington died in 1799. Paul Revere joined the church bellringers at the age of 15 and later became their captain.

Old North is very much as it was in colonial days, with boxed pews designed to contain warmth during the winter months. There are said to be 1,100 bodies in the church's 37 crypts. A small museum next to the church contains a **Vinegar Bible** sent to Old North as a gift from King George II in 1733. Vinegar Bibles are so called because a typographical error changes the Parable of the Vineyard to the Parable of the Vinegar.

Hull Street, opposite the front of Old North, leads to **Copp's Hill Burying Ground**, one of the oldest in Boston, dating from around 1660. Robert Newman is buried here. The cemetery's north-west corner contains the remains of about 1,000 black people, a reminder that Boston's first black community was located at the foot of Copp's Hill.

Beacon Hill

Boston's image of quaintness, of narrow cobblestoned streets, dignified old town houses and mansions, gas lamps and red brick sidewalks is encapsulated in Beacon Hill, a neighbourhood bounded by Cambridge Street to the north, Beacon Street to the south, Bowdoin Street to the east and the Charles River to the west. The area was developed in the late 18th and early 19th centuries to the designs of the

THE BLACK HERITAGE TRAIL

The part played by black people in the history of Boston is marked by the city's Black Heritage Trail, a walking tour of the north slope of Beacon Hill. Slavery was declared illegal in Massachusetts in 1783, and many slaves from elsewhere in the US fled to Boston. Free blacks first settled in North End, but moved to Beacon Hill around 1800.

The trail begins in Smith Court, off Joy Street. Here are typical brick residences occupied by black Bostonians during the 19th century. At one time, all the houses in the court were occupied by black families. Also in Smith Court, at Number 8, is the **African Meeting House**, dedicated in 1806, and the oldest black church building still standing in the United States. Its first worshippers dubbed it 'the haven from the loft' because they had been banished to the upper floor when attending services at Old North Church. Many fiercely anti-slavery meetings were held here, including the inaugural meeting of the New England Anti-Slavery Society, founded in 1832 by William Lloyd Garrison.

On the corner of Smith Court and Joy Street is the Abiel Smith School, built in 1834 as a grammar school for black pupils from all over the city. It had been built after a long campaign by the black community, but opponents who felt its existence encouraged segregationist sentiments soon led a boycott against it. The school was closed in 1855 when segregation was outlawed in the state. The building now houses the Museum of Afro-American History.

Coburn's Gaming House, at the corner of Phillips and Irving Streets, was established by John P. Coburn in 1844 for 'the upper ten who had acquired a taste for gambling'. The house was designed by Asher Benjamin, a Boston architect whose work influenced the façade of the African Meeting House.

At No. 66 Phillips Street is the **Lewis and Harriet Hayden House**, an important stop on the 'underground railroad' along which fugitive slaves were shunted to freedom. Harriet Beecher Stowe, author of *Uncle Tom's Cabin,* found the Haydens harbouring 13 slaves when she visited the house in 1853. Lewis Hayden was elected to the State Legislature in 1873. In her will, Harriet Hayden established a scholarship fund for 'needy and worthy colored students in the Harvard Medical School'.

The **Charles Street Meeting House**, at Mount Vernon and Charles Streets, was the last black institution to leave Beacon Hill. As the Tremont Temple, it was known as 'the first integrated church in America', but it was built in 1807 for the segregationist Third Baptist Church which expelled the abolitionist Timothy Gilbert when he invited black friends to worship with him. The African Methodist Episcopalian Church took over the building in 1876 and remained until 1939.

The stately brick residence at **86 Pinckney Street** was the home of John J. Smith, a black statesman who was three times appointed to the Massachusetts House of Representatives and served on the Boston Common Council. His hairdressing shop in Boston was a centre of black abolitionist activity and a meeting place for runaway slaves. During the Civil War he served in Washington as a recruiting officer for the all-black Fifth Cavalry.

Phillips School, on the corner of Pinckney and Anderson Streets, became one of the first interracial schools in Boston when it first accepted black students in 1855.

The **George Middleton Home** at 5 Pinckney Street is the oldest existing home on Beacon Hill to be built by a black person. A colonel in the Revolutionary War – he led the all-black company, 'Bucks of America' – Middleton built the house in 1797.

The trail ends opposite the State House, beside the entrance to Boston Common, where a bronze plaque framed in marble serves as a memorial to Robert Gould Shaw and the 54th Regiment. The first black regiment raised in the North, the 54th was recruited in Massachusetts and led by Shaw who volunteered for the command. He and many of his men died in battle.

influential architect, Charles Bullfinch, and settled by the city's powerful Brahmins. Today, its character has changed. Many of the mansions and larger town houses have been converted into apartment buildings and former servants' cottages have been gentrified. The Hill remains a desirable address.

The area was originally 60ft (18.5m) higher than it is today, and its three peaks provided its first name, Tremont. It acquired its present name when the early citizens of Boston erected a mast with a bucket of tar on the tallest peak to serve as a warning signal in the event of attack.

Pinckney Street has associations with the black liberation movement of the 19th century.

The Hill was developed just a little too late for it to have played any kind of role in the dramatic events that shaped independent America. There were no stirring meetings held here, no defiant gatherings. Paul Revere did pass this way – but only at the speed of his herd of cows, on their way to graze on Boston Common. The sound of musket fire had died away long before the first substantial homes began to appear in the area, and by then the red coats of the British army had gone forever. Nevertheless, the Hill is entitled to a place in the city's history, and is well worth a visit because of the people who subsequently lived there and the stamp they left on the face of Boston.

Beacon Hill's topography neatly divides the neighbourhood into three sub-sections. The really posh end, the South Slope, borders on Boston Common and extends to Pinckney Street; its western boundary is

Beacon Hill, originally settled by Boston's elite, the powerful Brahmins, is still a desirable address.

Charles Street, and at its south eastern edge, dominating the whole area, is the State House, whose gold dome seems to symbolize the power and wealth of Boston's Brahmins. The North Slope has the same ring it would have if the area were a vineyard: good, but not quite so good. It runs from Pinckney Street to Cambridge Street. The third sub-section, built on landfill between Charles Street and the Charles River, has been bluntly named the Flat Side.

The South Slope

The most dominant building on the South Slope – indeed, it is one of the most dominant in the city – is the **Massachusetts State House**, designed by Charles Bullfinch and completed in 1803. Distinguished by its golden dome, the State House manages to get itself into most Boston panoramas, peeping from behind other buildings like a mischievous child in a school photograph. The dome was originally intended to be covered in white shingles, but Paul Revere, getting in on yet another act, sheathed it in copper. The gold leaf was applied in 1861. During World War II it was painted black to make it less of a target in the event of an air raid.

Most tourists doing the Freedom Trail stop in front of State House, take their pictures, and then move on. The inside is well worth a visit, and there are free guided tours from 10am to 4pm, Monday to Friday. The most notable rooms are the Senate Chamber, the House of Representatives, the Reception Room and Doric Hall. The seals of the original 13 colonies are depicted in a stained-glass skylight, and there are murals of the American Revolution. The 'black lace' iron railings on each side of the main staircase are unique; the moulds were broken immediately after the railings were cast. Among other State House sights not to be missed are the hundreds of flags which have fluttered during campaigns in American wars, and the Sacred Cod, a wooden fish hung in the House of Representatives in 1784 as a tribute to the Massachusetts fishing industry.

A stroll along Beacon Street will take you past the oldest and grandest of The Hill's residences. Some of the purple panes for which the South Slope is renowned are to be seen in the windows of **King's Chapel Parish House** at No. 63 Beacon Street. The panes date from the early 19th century and their tint is the result of an unusual chemical reaction. More distinguished homes, many designed by Bullfinch, are to be found on **Chestnut Street**, which connects with a network of delightful old lanes. The houses here were the homes of the coachmen, cooks and maidservants who worked in the larger houses. Acorn Street, a block north of Chestnut Street, between West Cedar and Willow Streets, has all the classic features: Federal brick townhouses, shutters, window boxes and gas lamps.

Travelling uphill along Willow Street takes you across the rather grand Mount Vernon Street to the even grander **Louisburg Square**, where Nos 8 to 22, on the west side, are regarded as perhaps the finest terraced houses in the United States. The writer Louisa M. Alcott and the singer Jenny Lind, 'the Swedish Nightingale', both had homes here.

The North Slope

Pinckney Street, at the far end of Louisburg Square, marks the start of the North Slope. This part of Beacon Hill is a shade jauntier, a degree or two closer to bohemianism, than its neighbour to the south. The presence of a university campus and even a few shops and cafes add a touch of everyday liveliness.

The North Slope was certainly lively in its early days. The area began to be developed around 1725, and its character was determined more by the demands of the sailors whose vessels moored in the Charles River than the attitudes of Boston's Puritans. For a century or so its taverns and brothels pleased one side and plagued the other. The moralists won the day, however, and a crackdown started in the 1820s.

Although a faint whiff of seediness remains, the North Slope today is eminently respectable and there are some charming little lanes and alleys running from Revere and Phillips Streets. Two notable buildings at the western end of Cambridge Street are the Old West Church and the first Harrison Gray Otis house.

Built of dignified red brick, the **Old West Church** was designed by Asher Benjamin, another influential Federalist architect, and built in 1806 to replace a church which the British destroyed in 1775 when they thought – probably correctly – that its steeple was being used as a signal post by the rebels. The present building is used as a Methodist church. Next door at No. 141 Cambridge Street is

the first **Harrison Gray Otis House** – there are two others, the second at No. 85 Mount Vernon Street and the third at 45 Beacon Street, both on the South Slope. This one was designed by Bullfinch for his friend Otis, who was a prominent lawyer and also a member of Congress. Its interior is richly decorated with neoclassical motifs and relief borders, and there are imported carpets, wallpaper, curtains and gilt-framed mirrors. The house is now the headquarters of the Society for the Preservation of New England Antiquities and it is open to the public from noon to 5pm, Tuesday to Friday, and from 10am to 5pm on Saturday. There is an admission charge.

The Flat Side

Much of the missing top 60ft (18.5m) from Beacon Hill was used to fill in the marshland on which the Flat Side was built. Although the area does boast some architectural niceties, its chief attraction is Charles Street, a casual shopping centre which has boutiques, antique shops and good bookstores, as well as a number of cafes and restaurants. A major attraction for television comedy fans is the Bull and Finch – the exterior of the bar is featured in the internationally popular series, *Cheers*. In here you can buy a *Cheers* T-shirt, a *Cheers* mug, a *Cheers* cap – and even a drink! The bar is near the corner of Brimmer and Beacon Streets, but there are *Cheers* retail stores at other locations in Boston.

Back Bay

West of Boston Common, the city suddenly seems to straighten its shoulders and pull itself together. There are no curving lanes and meandering alleyways in Back Bay. Here, the streets are marshalled into the angular pattern of the gridiron, though their tree-lined width and boulevard proportions give more than a hint of Paris, especially in the summer months when the sidewalks are taken over by the chairs and tables of restaurants and cafes.

Back Bay was originally beneath the waters of the Charles River, until in 1814 a developer named Uriah Cotting hit on the progressive idea of using the river's tidal currents to power 80 or so industrial mills. A dam was built across the bay, but Cotting did not live to see it completed – which was just as well because his scheme did not work. The dam failed to provide enough power for the mills, and to make matters worse it turned the bay into a stagnant, noisome quagmire in which raw sewage festered. The work of infilling the bay began in 1856 and continued for a further 30 years, by which time the city's land area had been extended by 450 acres (182 hectares).

Development of the area was disciplined and restrained, and right from the start it was decided that 40 percent of the new land should be set aside as an 'Emerald Necklace' of parks and open spaces. Streets were to be wide, straight and stately. Most of the work was completed by the turn of the century, and Back Bay today presents what is probably the richest mix of graceful Victorian townhouses and brownstone residences in North America. There are also some stunning examples of contemporary architecture.

Taking Boylston Street as the dividing line, Back Bay falls into two distinctive parts. The area to the north is largely residential, though Boylston and Newbury Streets are noted shopping thoroughfares. Moving westward from Public Garden, the cross streets are named alphabetically from Arlington to Hereford. Massachusetts Avenue (everyone calls its 'Massav') marks the western boundary.

Tree-shaded Commonwealth Avenue (what else but 'Commav'?) is about 100 yards (90m) wide with half a dozen or so statues spaced out down its centre. It was designed to serve as Boston's Champs Elysées, and there is certainly a Parisian influence in the varied architecture of some of its buildings, most noticeably, perhaps, at No.160, formerly the Hotel Vendôme, whose guests included several American Presidents.

Francophiles will not want to miss the French Library at **53 Marlborough Street**, a Back Bay townhouse dating from 1867. The library was founded by a Free French group after World War II. It has a Louis XV-style theatre in which films and concerts are held, and there are also lectures, art exhibitions and cookery demonstrations. A special celebration takes place on Bastille Day (14 July).

The **Gibson House**, an Italian Renaissance Revival house at 137 Beacon Street, is a museum dedicated to Boston's Back Bay Victorians. Black walnut panelling and gold-embossed faux leather decorate the walls and there are authentic paintings and photographs, as well as china, porcelain, Turkish ottomans and 18th-century furniture. The house is open Wednesday to Sunday from May to October and at weekends in the winter. There is an admission charge.

The **First Baptist Church**, which is located on the corner of Commonwealth Avenue and Clarendon Street, was designed in the Romanesque style by Henry Hobson Richardson and has a frieze which was modelled by Frederic Bartholdi, who also sculpted the *Statue of Liberty*. Emerson, Hawthorne, Longfellow and Sumner are said to be portrayed among the faces carved on the frieze. Other buildings, such as the **Burrage** and **Ames Mansions**, at Nos. 314 and 355 respectively, are outrageously Gothic –

turreted, towered, and glowering with vaulted doorways and windows.

The area from Boylston Street to the southern end of Back Bay, marked more or less by the line of the Massachusetts Turnpike, presents a more public face with four major open space developments – Copley Square, Copley Place, the Prudential Center and the Christian Science Headquarters – and the emphasis is on shops, department stores, offices and hotels.

Copley Square

About halfway along Boylston Street, Copley Square lies at the heart of Back Bay and is regarded as one of the major plazas in the United States. It is not especially attractive, but with a range of architectural styles that swing from one extreme to the other there is certainly plenty to look at.

The most striking of Copley Square's contrasts is between Trinity Church and the John Hancock Tower. No two buildings could be quite so different, and it is likely that your first observation of the church will be as a distorted reflection on the walls of the skyscraper.

Trinity Church marks the pinnacle of Henry Hobson Richardson's work in the Romanesque style, and its interior is a treasure house of carved woodwork, stained-glass windows and frescoes by John LaFarge. The **John Hancock Tower** is a huge rhomboid mirror soaring 60 storeys to a height of 790ft (243m), the work of I.M. Pei. The tower's shape creates a curious optical illusion that from some angles makes it appear to be only two-dimensional. In its early days, the building was renowned for the fact that its windows kept falling out into the square below and on to the neighbouring Copley Plaza Hotel. The fault was the result of

BOSTON'S GRANDE DAME – 'THE COSTLY PLEASURE'

The whole of one side of Copley Square is taken up by an enterprise which cynics believed had no chance of success when it was opened more than 80 years ago. Today, the **Copley Plaza Hotel** is as much a part of Boston as the Tea Party Ship.

Designed by Henry Janeway Hardenbergh, who also built its sister establishment, the New York Plaza, and the Willard, right next to the White House in Washington, DC, the Copley Plaza was thought to be 'too far uptown for good business' when it opened on 19 August 1912. The management obviously had greater confidence: the opening ceremony was attended by more than 1,000 guests headed by the then Mayor of Boston, John F. Fitzgerald, grandfather of President John F. Kennedy. Other celebrities included captains of industry and stars of the stage and silent movie screen. The press dubbed it 'the four million dollar opening'.

Since then the Copley Plaza has served royalty from Greece, Thailand, Ethiopia, Saudi Arabia, Iran, Belgium, Denmark and the United Kingdom, and every President since William Howard Taft has been a guest there. More couples have been married in the hotel's Oval Room than in Trinity Church next door. The Oval Room was the scene of popular tea dances during the 1930s, when debutantes and their escorts listened to Rudy Valli crooning through his megaphone and nicknamed the hotel 'the Costly Pleasure'.

The Copley Plaza's Ballroom, a Boston legend, has been the setting for moments of history and some spectacular parties. On one occasion 1,000 people jostled to shake the hand of JFK; on another King Saud gave a dinner for 55 guests amid a $25,000 garden scene in which the food was served on a gold service flown in from California. The opulent ballroom is still the setting for Waltz Evenings in the fall and winter.

unusual wind forces acting on the structure and has long since been corrected.

Spectacular views of Boston and the surrounding areas can be seen from the observatory on the tower's top floor. Boston 1775, an exhibit featuring an audio-visual presentation and a miniature colonial Boston, takes visitors back to the time when the city was seething with revolution. In another presentation, Skyline Boston, an architectural historian narrates a colourful account of the changes that transformed the city from a small peninsular town to an international metropolis. The observatory is open daily from 9am to 10pm (Sunday noon-10pm) and there is an admission charge.

Boston Public Library, opposite Trinity Church, is a stolid Renaissance Revival building that could be either a palace or an opera house. It was designed by Charles Follen McKim and completed in 1895, with an extension added in 1971. Inside, the Bates Hall reading room, all oak, sandstone and marble, is quite medieval in its proportions and atmosphere. A more tranquil place to enjoy a quiet read is probably the cloistered courtyard at the building's centre. Art lovers will doubtless want to visit the John Singer Sargent Gallery which features a collection of striking murals.

New Old South Church, on the Boylston Street edge of Copley Square, is in Gothic style. The present tower was recycled from the original which began tilting like the Leaning Tower of Pisa and had to be dismantled in 1931.

Copley Place

This 9-acre (3.75-hectare) development was built in the mid-1980s and tucked into a triangular site south of Copley Square, between Huntington Avenue and Stuart Street. A layer cake of glass, gleaming metal and subtle lighting, with a waterfall tumbling over rocks in its central atrium, the mall has more than 100 shops, among them such purse-twitching names as Bally of Switzerland, Gucci, Tiffany and Nieman-Marcus. There are also 13 restaurants, a cinema and two major hotels – a Marriott and a Westin.

The Prudential Center

A footbridge enclosed in glass connects Copley Place with the Prudential Center, a similar development dating from the early 1960s. Saks Fifth Avenue and Lord & Taylor are the biggest names in the Pru's shopping mall, which has recently undergone a massive renovation and

Boston Public Library, stolidly palatial, was completed in 1895 and extended in 1971.

extension. The Skywalk, on the 50th floor of the Prudential Tower, presents a 360-degree viewpoint of Boston. On a clear day, it is claimed, you can see as far away as New Hampshire and Vermont. The Skywalk is open daily from 10am to 10pm (there is an admission charge).

The Prudential Center adjoins the Hynes Convention Center, which has five exhibition halls, three ballrooms and 38 meeting rooms on three levels. Opposite the Hynes Center, at 955 Boylston Street, is the Institute of Contemporary Art in which a constantly changing programme of exhibitions is staged.

The tower of New Old South Church was recycled from the original which was dismantled in 1931 after tilting dangerously.

The Christian Science Headquarters

At the corner of Huntington and Massachusetts Avenues, the disciplined angles of the Pru and the Hynes Center give way to a softer, rounder type of architecture, a basilica that would be more at home perhaps in Rome or Istanbul. This is part of the complex that constitutes the world headquarters of the First Church of Christ, Scientist, founded in the 19th century by Mary Baker Eddy. The basilica seats up to 5,000 people on three levels, houses the largest pipe organ in the western world and is an annexe to the considerably more modest Mother Church next door.

The Mother Church was opened in 1894 after Mary Baker Eddy and 15 followers had moved to Boston from Lynn, outside the city. Today there are more than 2,600 Christian Science churches worldwide. The headquarters complex, set out behind a 670ft- (206m-) long pool, includes the church's Publishing Society Building, a five-storey Sunday school and a 28-storey administrative building. The publishing society's publications – headed by the internationally respected daily newspaper, *The Christian Science Monitor* – and its radio and television stations reach a weekly audience of more than nine million people. There are free tours of the Mother Church and the Publishing Society Building. A popular attraction is the Mapparium, a stained glass world globe, 30ft (9m) in diameter. Visitors can step

inside the globe which illustrates fascinating data about the world.

Just across Massachusetts Avenue, situated opposite the Christian Scientists' Sunday school, is the Symphony Hall, the home of the Boston Symphony Orchestra (October–April) and the Boston Pops (May and June). Opened at the turn of the century, the hall is noted for its wonderful acoustics. It is said that nowhere among its 2,500 seats is there a 'dead spot', and the hall remains a favourite with musicians and concertgoers.

Copley Place has more than 100 shops, including some internationally famous names.

The Fenway

Frederick Law Olmsted, the man who created New York's Central Park, had the fenlands of England in mind when he landscaped this area as part of Boston's Emerald Necklace of parklands and wide boulevards. Beyond Massachusetts Avenue, The Fenway is bordered by the Charles River and traversed by the Muddy River, and although Olmsted's intention to create a kind of American East Anglia may be less obvious than it was last century, the district still has a good share of open space. The Fenway Victory Gardens – opened to commemorate the ending of World War II – and the City Rose Garden are both popular havens of tranquillity and colour. Less tranquil, but still popular, especially between April and early October, is Fenway Park, home of the Boston Red Sox and smallest of America's major baseball stadiums. It was opened in 1912.

The area's major attractions, however, are the **Museum of Fine Arts** (MFA) and the Isabella Stewart Gardner Museum. Founded in 1870, the MFA has one of the world's finest, most comprehensive art

collections, and is especially noted for its collection of Asian art. The museum also has works by every prominent American painter of the 18th and 19th centuries, and its Department of American Decorative Arts and Sculpture displays furniture, folk art, glass, ceramics, pewter and silver, including the 'Liberty Bowl' and other works by Paul Revere. There is also an extensive collection of Egyptian antiquities, obtained from archaeological digs in Egypt over the past century. The MFA is at 465 Huntington Avenue (Tel. 617 267-9300), and is open daily except Monday. There is an admission charge, but entry is free on Wednesday, 4–9.45pm.

Nearby (280 The Fenway, Tel. 617 566-1401), the **Isabella Stewart Gardner Museum** is housed in a Venetian-style palace surrounding a splendid courtyard. Mrs Gardner began her superb collection, which includes works by Bellini, Botticelli, Matisse, Titian and Whistler, in the late 1900s when she travelled to Europe after the death of her only child. The palace was built to house the collection and was opened to the public in 1903 when Mrs Gardner took up residence there, remaining until her death in 1924. An admission fee is charged.

Outer Boston

Charlestown

Although it is separated from Boston proper by the Charles River, Charlestown is very much a part of the downtown scene, from the visitor's point of view, at least. Bostonians themselves may regard it as a northern suburb, but it can easily be reached on foot, as thousands of people do when they cross the Charlestown Bridge and follow the Freedom Trail. You can also get there by taking the short ferry ride from Long Wharf to the *USS Constitution* or by taking the T's Orange Line to Community College (four stops from Downtown Crossing).

As a community, Charlestown is senior to Boston. It was settled in 1629, a year earlier than the founding of Boston. Its first inhabitants were ten Puritan families. They were joined early in 1630 by a further 750 Puritans led by John Winthrop, soon to become the new colony's first governor. Disease, bad water and poor conditions caused Winthrop and many of his followers to cross the river and start a settlement on the other side.

The perseverance of the few who remained was rewarded for a time. The little community thrived, prospering as the New World's fourth largest port by the end of the 17th century. Today, however, there is little left that was built before the start of the 19th century. The British blasted the place with artillery fire during the Battle of Bunker Hill, and razed what was left as they pulled out of the area in 1776. That said, however, Charlestown is still an interesting and attractive place to visit, with pleasant tree-lined streets and an ambience rich with echoes of the past.

Central Sights

Charlestown Bridge leads directly into **City Square**, the town's focal point, and from here all the major points of interest are within strolling distance. On the north-

USS Constitution, *launched in Boston in 1797, is the world's oldest commissioned warship still afloat.*

west side of the square are three reminders of Charlestown's connection with Harvard University. John Harvard Mall, Harvard Square and Harvard Street honour the man whose bequest of books and money on his death in 1638, at the age of 27, helped place the struggling Newtowne College on a firm footing. A granite memorial to John Harvard stands in the mall.

The **Bunker Hill Pavilion** on Water Street houses Charlestown's tourist information centre where an audio-visual presentation, The Whites of Their Eyes, tells the story of the Battle of Bunker Hill. The pavilion is outside the Navy Yard, home of the world's oldest commissioned warship still afloat. The *USS Constitution* – 'Old Ironsides' – was launched in Boston in 1797 and remained undefeated in a succession of 44 major encounters against the Royal Navy during the War of 1812. The frigate earned her nickname during a 30-minute battle in which *HMS Guerrière* was destroyed on 19 August 1812, when it was noticed that the British cannonballs merely bounced off the *Constitution*'s hull of stout live oak from Georgia.

After surviving all those battles at sea, Old Ironsides almost became a wreck in her home port. In 1830 there was a plan to scrap the vessel, but Oliver Wendell Holmes, then a student at Harvard, wrote a stirring poem that stirred up a national outcry when it was widely published, and the ship was saved. Another threat came in 1911 when she was about to be used for target practice. This time it was the Massachusetts Society of the Daughters of 1812 who saved the day. In the 1920s Boston schoolchildren contributed their pocket money to help pay for urgently needed restoration. Since then, the *Constitution* has undergone extensive

refurbishment, and less than 10 percent of her original timbers remain. These days, however, the old warship makes only one voyage a year. Every Independence Day she is towed into Boston Harbor where she fires a celebratory broadside before being returned to her berth in the Navy-Yard for another 12 months.

Old Ironsides' dockmate is the *USS Cassin Young*, a World War II destroyer which saw action at Iwo Jima and Okinawa. Both vessels are open to the public. The nearby Constitution Museum provides a further insight into the old frigate's history, with details of how she was built, as well as information about her equipment and captains. Established in 1800, the Navy Yard remained active until as late as 1974. Several of its facilities remain open, including the quarter-mile-(0.4km-) long ropewalk, where every strand of rope used by the US Navy was made until 1955.

The **Bunker Hill Monument** actually stands on Breed's Hill, which is where the historic battle took place on 17 June 1775. Bunker Hill, about 300 yards (275m) to the north, was where the American forces entrenched after falling back. The monument itself was dedicated in 1843, some 18 years after the 50th anniversary of the battle, when the original cornerstone was laid. A small museum displays a diorama of the battle, and visitors can pant their way up the 294 steps to the top of the monument. There is a bronze statue of Colonel William Prescott, commander of the American forces at the battle, located between the obelisk and the main gate of the monument park.

Cambridge

Although it contains two of the nation's leading centres of higher learning, Cambridge is rather more than Boston in a cap and gown. Founded in 1630, the same year as Boston, Cambridge was originally known as New Towne and was the colony's first capital. In 1638, however, it

The Bunker Hill Monument honours patriots who died in the first major battle of the American Revolution.

was renamed after the English university city. Yet this is no musty Academia – the city is a lively place with plenty of good shopping, dining and entertainment. Cambridge is a city of squares, and each has its own distinctive character. **Harvard Square**, an outdoor festival marketplace with lots of buskers and cafes, has three shopping arcades and contains what is said to be the greatest concentration of bookstores in the US. Massachusetts Avenue, between Central Square to the east and Porter Square to the north, is also a good place for shopping.

Many of Greater Boston's best restaurants are to be found in Cambridge, and these range from budget to haute cuisine as well as covering the ethnic spectrum from African to Japanese, Thai to Spanish, Greek to Mexican and all shades in between. The city's entertainment scene is particularly vibrant, presenting everything from coffee-house jazz to heavy drama. Its American Repertory Theatre (64 Brattle Street) is internationally acclaimed. There are laughs to be had in the numerous neighbourhood pubs and clubs throughout the area.

THE CHARLES RIVER BASIN

You do not have far to travel in Boston before you come up against water, for the city is wedged on a peninsula between Boston Harbor and the Charles River. The river was named in honour of England's King Charles I, and the basin, extending some 9 miles (14km) upstream and ranging from 200–2,000 yards (185–1850m) wide, makes a significant contribution to the unique character of Greater Boston. During the summer months it is used extensively by watersports enthusiasts, and its surface is alive with craft propelled by sail, oar, paddle and petrol. Rowing crews from Harvard and other Boston colleges train here. During winter months its frozen surface frequently becomes a gigantic skating rink.

The river was first bridged in 1786. Eleven years earlier, Paul Revere had had to row across before starting his historic ride to Lexington. The present **Charlestown Bridge** has a span of 1,053ft (321m) and is 423ft (130m) wide. The Charles River Information Center is located on the New Charles River Dam, just upstream from the Charlestown Bridge. A short audio-visual presentation explains the workings of the basin's flood control system, and an observation window allows visitors to look out on the three locks which enable vessels to pass between the basin and Boston Harbor.

A mile (1.6 km) or so farther upstream, on the older dam, are the **Museum of Science and the Hayden Planetarium** (admission fees charged). World-renowned, the museum has hundreds of exhibits, many offering hands-on experience. In the Mugar Omni Theater images are projected on to a domed screen 76ft (23.2m) high. Laser shows are a feature of the planetarium.

Longfellow Bridge, another half mile (0.8km) upstream, was built in 1900 and is known as the Salt and Pepper Bridge because of the four cruet-like towers on its central span. On the Cambridge side of the bridge the Lechmere Canal runs into a basin in front of the Cambridge-Side Galleria, a recently completed shopping mall. On the Boston side, on The Esplanade upstream of the bridge, is the **Hatch Memorial Shell** where the Boston Pops and other free concerts take place during the summer.

Harvard Bridge carries Massachusetts Avenue from Boston to Cambridge, just beyond the widest part of the river basin. On the northern bank is the **Massachusetts Institute of Technology**. Busy at all times with strollers and joggers, Harvard Bridge presents a superb view to the east, with the Downtown skyscrapers acting as a backdrop to Back Bay, Beacon Hill and the ubiquitous State House.

Boston University, also with a namesake bridge, is the next educational establishment to come into view, then the extensive buildings of **Harvard University** spill across the banks on both sides of the river.

The T's Red Line reaches Cambridge at Kendall Square, three stops from Downtown Crossing, then goes on to follow the course of Massachusetts Avenue from Central to Porter, which is good because Cambridge is no place for the car. Driving is difficult and parking almost impossible. Public transport is effective, with bus routes criss-crossing the city, but most visitors will find the best way to get around is on foot. Start at Harvard Square, where the Cambridge Discovery information booth is located and from where the Old Town Trolley and guided walking tours begin.

Maps are available at the booth and walking-tour leaflets cover different aspects of the city, including Revolutionary Cambridge. Guided tours of the oldest parts of Cambridge are conducted by entertaining and well-informed high school students.

The Education Industry

Education has been a major industry in New England since the days of the Puritans. Among the region's many universities and colleges – Massachusetts alone has about 120 – are Harvard and Yale, America's most prestigious universities.

Harvard University is located in Cambridge, Massachusetts, originally known as New Towne, but renamed by settlers who had been educated at the university in England.

The country's first college, Harvard was founded by the Puritans in 1636, six years after the establishment of the Bay Colony. It was founded as a training institution for ministers and was first known as New Towne College. It was named Harvard in 1638 in honour of John Harvard, the minister who left a library and a donation to the school. Right from the start, the college was a symbol of the settlers' determination to be independent of Britain, especially in educational and religious affairs, and an early act of defiance was the granting of degrees, which legally Harvard was not empowered to do. In 1640 the college established the country's first printing press.

The establishment in the 19th century of schools of dentistry, divinity and law, as well as its graduate school of arts and sciences, placed Harvard among the world's leading universities. Its reputation was enhanced even further between 1869 and 1909 when Charles William Eliot was the president of Harvard. During this time academic standards were raised, and students were permitted to choose their own courses. Eliot also played an influential role in the establishment of Radcliffe College

Harvard University's Widener Library houses some three million books.

The Massachusetts Institute of Technology has some 10,000 students, half of them graduates.

for women. Now coeducational and fully integrated with Harvard, Radcliffe was founded in 1879 to enable Harvard professors to teach women. Its name honours Lady Anne Radcliffe Mowlson, a British benefactor who donated £100 to establish Harvard's first scholarship in the 17th century.

The Massachusetts Institute of Technology (MIT) is sited close to Harvard University in Cambridge, Massachusetts. The school's charter was awarded in 1861, but the opening was delayed by the Civil War. Studies began in 1865 when six professors and 15 students met in a room in Copley Square. MIT moved to its present site in 1916, and now has some 10,000 students, half of them graduates.

Yale was founded in 1701 as a collegiate school at Branford, a village some eight miles (13 km) east of New Haven, Connecticut, and moved to its present home in 1716. Its name honours Elihu Yale, a merchant who donated a collection of books to be sold to raise funds for the school in 1718. The college achieved university status in 1887, and now has 11,000 students.

New Hampshire's Dartmouth College now dominates the town of Hanover, but it was actually founded at Lebanon, Connecticut, in 1755, when it was known as Moor's Indian Charity School. In those days, it provided education for native Americans. It moved to its present site in 1769 after receiving a grant of 3,300 acres (1,335 hectares) and a generous cash donation from England's second Earl of Dartmouth.

Brown University, in Providence, Rhode Island, is the seventh oldest university in the United States. It was founded in 1764. University Hall was used during the Revolution as a barracks and hospital for American troops.

Main Attractions

North of Harvard Square is **Cambridge Common**, where George Washington took command of the Colonial Army on 3 July 1775. Washington is said to have stood beneath an elm tree as the new army marched before him in review, but historians laugh this off as a local legend. Either way, the local authority regarded it with enough respect to fell the Washington Elm in favour of a road improvement scheme in 1923. A flagpole and three cannons abandoned by the British on St Patrick's Day, 1776 – the day the Redcoats left Boston – mark the spot today.

Beside the common, on Garden Street, stands **Christ Church**, the oldest place of worship in the city. Designed by Peter Harrison, architect of the King's Chapel, Boston, Christ Church was completed in 1761. When mounting revolutionary feelings drove most of its Tory congregation away in 1774 the church became a barracks for the Patriots, who melted down the organ pipes for bullets. The church was re-opened on New Year's Eve 1775, with George Washington and his wife, Martha, among the worshippers.

The Washingtons at that time lived at 105 Brattle Street, a short walk south west from the church. The house is now rather better known as the **Henry Wadsworth Longfellow House**, home of America's best-known poet of the 19th century. The house was built in 1759 and abandoned when the Tories fled in 1774. Longfellow lived there from 1837 until his death in 1882, and the house is furnished virtually the same today as it was in his time. Among the memorabilia is an inkstand given to him by the English poet Samuel Taylor Coleridge and a chair presented by Cambridge schoolchildren and made from the spreading chestnut tree under which *The Village Blacksmith* toiled. The blacksmith of the poem, Dexter Pratt, lived at 56 Brattle Street and his tree shared the fate of Washington's Elm – cut down for street-widening in 1870.

As a professor of modern languages at Harvard, Longfellow first rented rooms in the house. He married Fanny Appleton in 1843 and her father, a wealthy resident of Beacon Hill, bought the house for them as a wedding gift. Longfellow wrote many of his best-known works here, including *The Song of Hiawatha* which brought him fame and wealth. Tragically, Fanny Longfellow died in the house in 1861 after her dress caught fire. The house, now open to the public (admission charge) was maintained by the Longfellow family until 1973, but is now run by the US National Park Service.

Brattle Street has the finest of Cambridge's 18th- and 19th- century houses, mainly privately owned, and was known in Revolutionary times as Tory Row.

Harvard University

Harvard has expanded greatly since its foundation, and its buildings are now to be found on both banks of the Charles River, but the most historic are in Harvard Yard, on the east side of Harvard Square. **Wadsworth Hall**, the yellow clapboard building closest to the square, was built in 1762 and was the residence of the university's presidents until 1849. **Massachusetts Hall** is the oldest building in the Yard. It was built as a dormitory in 1720, and like its neighbour, Harvard Hall, built in 1764, housed troops of Washington's Continental Army in 1775 and 1776.

The **statue of John Harvard** in front of University Hall is known as the Statue of the Three Lies. Firstly, no portrait could be found of the college's benefactor so the

The seat of Harvard University, Cambridge has many dignified streets.

sculptor, Daniel Chester French, chose an undergraduate of 1884 as his model. Secondly, the inscription incorrectly describes John Harvard as the founder; and thirdly, it is two years out in the date it gives for the founding of the college.

On the south side of Harvard Yard is the colonnaded **Widener Library**. Completed in 1915, this is the university's main library and commemorates Harry Widener, a graduate of 1907 who died when the *Titanic* went down. The Widener is the world's largest university library, with some three million books on 50 miles (80km) of shelving. There are dioramas depicting Harvard Square as it was in 1667, 1775 and 1936. The library also displays a copy of the *Gutenberg Bible* and a Shakespeare first folio published in 1623.

The university maintains eight museums in Cambridge (there are others in Boston, Washington DC, and Florence, Italy). The famous **Fogg Art Museum**, on Quincy Street, east of Harvard Yard, houses collections of European, Far Eastern and American works of art from the Middle Ages to the present time. The **Busch-Reisinger Museum**, entered

Henry Wadsworth Longfellow lived and worked at 105 Brattle Street, Cambridge, for 45 years. The house is furnished virtually as it was in his time.

through the Fogg, has an important collection of Expressionist masterpieces by artists of the calibre of Beckmann and Klee. A common entrance fee covers both the Fogg and Busch-Reisinger, as well as the **Arthur M. Sackler Museum** across the street at 485 Broadway. The Sackler contains collections from ancient Greece, Egypt, Rome and the Near and Far East. Its collection of ancient Chinese jades and ceramics is said to be the world's finest.

Harvard University Museums of Natural History, on Oxford Street, are four museums in one, with exhibits on botany, minerals, zoology and archaeology. The **Peabody Museum of Archaeology and Ethnology** houses extensive anthropological collections, with the emphasis on the cultures of North, Central and South America. The **Botanical Museum** includes the celebrated display of hand-made glass flowers – replicas of some 850 species – used for teaching botany. The **Museum of Comparative Zoology** displays everything from hummingbirds to whale skeletons; and the **Mineralogical and Geological Museum** has a collection ranging from precious stones to rocks from outer space.

Harvard students run the university information office in the Holyoke Center at 1350 Massachusetts Avenue and also conduct a free 60-minute tour of Harvard Yard daily, Monday–Saturday.

Massachusetts Institute of Technology

A mile and a half (2.4km) from Harvard Square, down by the Charles River, the campus of the **Massachusetts Institute of Technology** is split by Massachusetts Avenue. The East Campus is where students devote themselves to 'tooling' – their word for studying tomorrow's science and engineering; the West Campus is where they relax. The **MIT Museum** traces the institute's achievements since its foundation. Two other MIT museums open to the public are the **Hart Nautical Museum**, featuring model craft from sailing vessels to atomic age warships, and the **List Visual Arts Center**, which stages temporary shows of contemporary art. There are also outstanding examples of contemporary architecture, notably the Kresge Auditorium and Chapel designed by Eero Saarinen, the Finnish architect.

MIT's information office is at Building 7, 77 Massachusetts Avenue (Tel. 617 253-4795) Free tours of the campus are conducted Monday–Friday at 10am and 2pm.

SIGHTINGS IN THE CEMETERY

Birdwatchers in the Cambridge area flock to the **Mount Auburn Cemetery,** about a mile (1.6km) south west of Harvard Square, along Mount Auburn Street (Route 16). More than 235 species have been sighted in the cemetery, which is said to be one of the best places for observing the spring migration of warblers.

The birds are attracted to the cemetery by its 2,500 trees – 380 species in all, and many of them rare. The graves of Henry Wadsworth Longfellow, Oliver Wendell Holmes, Charles Bullfinch and Mary Baker Eddy, and many other less illustrious mortals, are shaded by weeping dogwood, White Russian mulberry, cherry, star magnolia and many other trees. A map of the graves is available at the main gate, and walks and lectures are conducted by the Friends of Mount Auburn Cemetery (Tel. 617 864-9646).

Consecrated in 1831, Mount Auburn was the first garden cemetery in the US. Burials still take place there.

Culture in the Countryside

Some people argue that the real Massachusetts doesn't start until you're west of I-495, about 30 miles (48km) out of downtown Boston. Within the Interstate's wide arc, every town and village seems to be looking inwards towards Greater Boston. Beyond it there is a region with its own identity, an area where each community, no matter how urban, regards itself as part of the countryside, rather than part of a metropolis. Within that outer ring there are some appealing places for tourists.

Lexington and Concord

North west of Cambridge's Harvard Square, Massachusetts Avenue travels through the suburbs to historic Lexington and Concord. This is the route Paul Revere rode on the night of 18 April 1775, followed a few hours later by 700 Redcoats. The British had set out to seize an arms cache, but soon found themselves involved in a full-scale war.

The Redcoats had left Boston in a mood of confidence, believing their raid, which they thought had been kept a secret, would catch the rebels by surprise. Thanks to the riders Paul Revere and William Dawes, the Americans were prepared for battle, though only 77 Minutemen were there to meet the Britons when they arrived at Lexington Green. But there were hundreds more at Concord, and the Redcoats, reinforced by a further 1,000 troops, had to run a gauntlet of 3,500 colonial snipers as they retreated to Boston. At the end of the day, 247 Redcoats had been killed or wounded against a total of 89 on the American side. The Battle of Lexington is re-created annually on Patriots' Day, the third Monday in April.

The fiercest fighting during the retreat was at Arlington, and bullet holes can still be seen in the **Jason Russell House** at 7 Jason Street. Here a dozen Patriots,

Tranquil today, Lexington Green was the setting for the outbreak of the Revolutionary War.

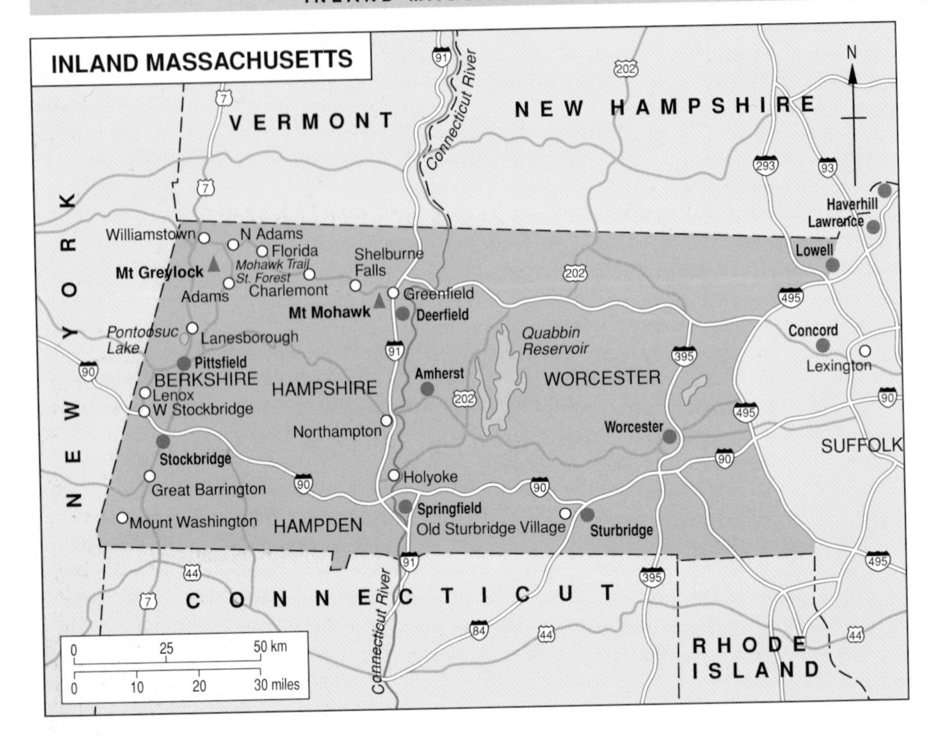

A typical New England home, near Lexington Green.

Ralph Waldo Emerson wrote his first book, Nature, *in The Old Manse at Concord (opposite).*

The reconstructed North Bridge near Concord commemorates 'the shot heard around the world'.

including Jason Russell who owned the house, were killed by Redcoats. The restored house, dating from 1680, is now owned by the Arlington Historical Society and there is an admission charge for visitors.

Lexington

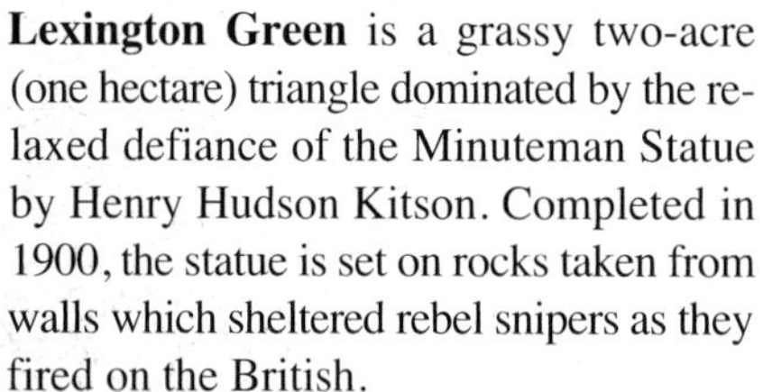

Lexington Green is a grassy two-acre (one hectare) triangle dominated by the relaxed defiance of the Minuteman Statue by Henry Hudson Kitson. Completed in 1900, the statue is set on rocks taken from walls which sheltered rebel snipers as they fired on the British.

Facing the Green on the right is the **Buckman Tavern**, built in 1690, where the Minutemen first gathered when they heard that the British were on their way. The tavern has displays of 18th-century weaponry, cooking equipment and furniture – and a bullet hole in one of its doors. **Munroe Tavern**, which the Redcoats used as a field headquarters, has a bullet hole in its ceiling. The tavern, at 1332 Massachusetts Avenue, has been maintained as it was in the 1770s.

About 500 yards (460m) north of the Green, on Hancock Street, is the **Hancock-Clarke House**, dating from 1698. This is where John Hancock and Samuel Adams were awakened by Paul Revere. Maintained by the Lexington Historical Society, the house has a number of exhibits relating to the battles, and displays the drum which was beaten to summon the Minutemen to the conflict.

A combination ticket covers admission to the two taverns and the Hancock-Clarke House.

Route 2-A between Lexington and Concord is known as Battle Road and more or less follows the route of 1775. For 5 miles (8km) the road is within the 750-acre

(305-hectare) **Minuteman National Historical Park**. The Battle Road Visitor Center shows a 20-minute film outlining the events that led up to the start of the Revolutionary War. Near the car park a section of the old road has been restored to its 18th-century condition. Farther along the road, the spot where Paul Revere was held by Redcoats is marked by a boulder.

Concord

Concord has two strings to its bow of fame, one historic, the other literary. This was where the second confrontation took place between British and American troops, on 19 April 1775, and where in the first half of the 19th century three of America's leading writers – Ralph Waldo Emerson, Nathaniel Hawthorne and Henry David Thoreau – settled and worked. Louisa May Alcott also lived in the town.

Monument Square, the centre of Concord, is where a British soldier accidentally set fire to a building while burning captured supplies. The Minutemen, gathered on the opposite side of the Concord River, thought the Redcoats were burning the town down and vowed to defend Concord 'or die in the attempt'. At **North Bridge**, about a mile (1.6km) north along Monument Road, they encountered a British detachment. Someone fired 'the shot heard round the world', and in the ensuing exchange of fire each side suffered the loss of two men. Two hours later the British began their retreat. The original North Bridge lasted no longer than 1793, and a commemorative bridge was built in 1875. The present structure dates from 1956. At the western end of the bridge is Daniel Chester French's famous statue of a Minuteman.

Close to the bridge is **The Old Manse**, where Ralph Waldo Emerson lived in 1834 and 1835. His first book, *Nature*, was written there. The manse was built around 1770 by Emerson's grandfather, the Reverend William Emerson, who witnessed the battle for North Bridge from here and later died of fever while serving as a chaplain in the Continental Army. Nathaniel Hawthorne and his wife Sophia, who was a painter, moved into the house on their wedding day, 9 July 1842, and stayed until 1846. The restored manse is open to the public (an admission fee is payable).

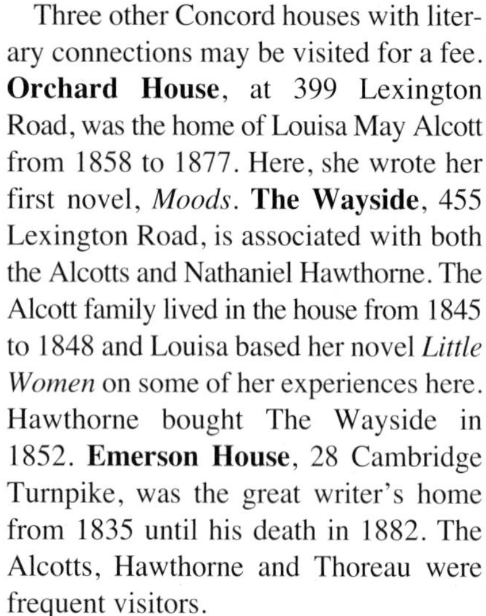

Three other Concord houses with literary connections may be visited for a fee. **Orchard House**, at 399 Lexington Road, was the home of Louisa May Alcott from 1858 to 1877. Here, she wrote her first novel, *Moods*. **The Wayside**, 455 Lexington Road, is associated with both the Alcotts and Nathaniel Hawthorne. The Alcott family lived in the house from 1845 to 1848 and Louisa based her novel *Little Women* on some of her experiences here. Hawthorne bought The Wayside in 1852. **Emerson House**, 28 Cambridge Turnpike, was the great writer's home from 1835 until his death in 1882. The Alcotts, Hawthorne and Thoreau were frequent visitors.

Concord Museum, 200 Lexington Road, houses Emerson's reconstructed library and a display of the simple furniture Thoreau made for his retreat at Walden Pond. A replica of Thoreáu's cabin stands in the grounds of the Thoreau Lyceum at 156 Belknap Street. Walden Pond itself, where Thoreau practised self-sufficiency from 1845 to 1847, is about a mile and a half (2.5km) south of Concord, on Walden Street, in a state park whose popularity would have given Thoreau much food for thought but little tranquillity.

Concord's literary giants are all buried in the town's **Sleepy Hollow Cemetery** on Bedford Street, along with the sculptor Daniel Chester French.

Merrimack River Valley

Power from the waters of the Merrimack River created an industrial corridor along the north-eastern border of Massachusetts in the first half of the 19th century, with factories replacing occupations which had

Walden Pond, where Henry David Thoreau practised self-sufficiency, is now a popular state park.

been followed since the days of the earliest European settlers.

Haverhill

Less than a 30-minute drive from the coast today, Haverhill was settled in the 1640s as a frontier village and its earliest industries were farming and fishing. By the early 19th century it had become an important shipbuilding centre and port, but as ships became too large to navigate the river, the town turned to manufacturing. By the end of the century it had gained international prominence as a shoe-making centre.

Today, Haverhill's development can be traced in such areas as the **Rocks Village Historic District**, **Bradford Common**, and in the **Washington Street Shoe District**, said to be the finest Queen Anne-style industrial street in the US. The town's Victorian residential heritage is to be seen in the **Highlands Neighbourhood**, while collections of locally made shoes, archaeological material and fire-fighting equipment are displayed in the **Buttonwoods Museum**. Maintained by the Haverhill Historical Society, the museum is located at 240 Water Street, in a house built by a merchant in 1814.

Haverhill's major attraction is the **Whittier Homestead** (admission fee payable), birthplace of the Quaker poet and abolitionist, John Greenleaf Whittier. He was born here on 17 December 1807 and remained until he was 29. The old farmhouse, at 305 Whittier Road, off Route 110, has been restored and furnished to this period.

Lawrence

Lawrence was settled in 1655 as Bodwell's Falls. Its history as a major textile centre began in 1845 when the first mills were built. Lawrence became a symbol of all that was wrong with the new societies of the Industrial Revolution: workers, including women and children, toiled long hours for little pay and were housed in appalling conditions. In 1860 a jerry-built factory collapsed, killing 88 workers. Finally, in 1912, a two-month strike succeeded in winning better conditions and pay, not only for the textile workers of Lawrence, but also for those throughout New England.

The city's story is told at the **Lawrence Heritage State Park** at 1 Jackson Street, and there are industrial exhibits and videos in the 1847 boarding house now used as a visitors' centre. There are tours of old mills and canals and of the Great Stone Dam built on the Merrimack by immigrant labour between 1845 and 1848. The **Immigrant City Archives**, 6 Essex Street, has photographs, recordings and printed material on the history of Lawrence. The **Hibernian Cultural Center**, 9 Appleton Street, has extensive material on the city's Irish heritage.

Lowell

Every inch the ideal Industrial Revolution city, Lowell was founded in the 1820s by a group of Boston entrepreneurs who had both a vision and a conscience. Led by Francis Cabot Lowell, they were determined that the degradation they had seen in the slums of Britain's industrial cities would not be repeated here. The new factories were light, spacious and airy; workers were provided with clean dormitory accommodation, and for their off-duty time were provided with educational and recreational opportunities. Women were also encouraged to join the workforce – but were paid only half the wages that the men received!

The dream was too good to last. As the textile mills grew busier and bigger, more labour was needed. More immigrants were brought in, housing became inadequate and Lowell plunged into the very situation its founders had tried so hard to prevent. By the 1920s the city was struggling in the face of vigorous competition from mills in the South, and the Depression only made things worse.

Today, thanks to energetic restoration of its mills and canals in the 1970s and 1980s, Lowell is enjoying a renaissance, and much of the city is now part of the **Lowell National Historical Park**, which includes mills, more than 5 miles (8km) of canals, worker housing, and 19th-century commercial buildings. An extensive industrial museum is housed in a huge cotton and woollen mill, and there are guided tours by barge, trolley and on foot. Costumed gatekeepers and their wives, 'drawn back' from the mid-19th century, jolly things along with a touch of authenticity.

The best place to start in Lowell is the park's Visitor Center, located in the 1828 Market Mills, at 246 Market Street, where you can obtain information, maps and literature and see a multi-slide audio-visual presentation. Most of the 'action' takes place at **Boott Cotton Mills** in John Street, an old industrial complex now housing a museum and other exhibits. Named after Kirk Boott, who supervised the construction and operation of the canals and mills of Lowell during its early development, the complex was built on land bordered by the Merrimack River and the Eastern Canal. The canal, 8ft (2.44m)

deep and 2,037ft (621m) long, was dug in 1835–6 to supply water power and provide a means of transport for the mills.

The Boott Cotton Mills Museum (admission fee) has a 1920s weave room with 88 working power looms giving a dramatic representation of what working life must have been like when the mills were in operation – bearing in mind that under real conditions the noise, heat and humidity would have been much greater, and the air would have been filled with cotton dust. The museum also features the growth and decline of Lowell's mills, textile production from bale to bolt of cloth and historic machinery.

The museum contains a gallery of artefacts, paintings and photographs, a performing arts centre and the New England Folklife Center which features traditional arts, crafts and industries in a variety of exhibits, gallery tours and demonstrations. A specially designed foodways area allows the public to view demonstrations of the cuisines of New England.

Central and Western Massachusetts

From Boston, the quickest way to reach the rolling hills, the meandering streams and rivers, the fields and forests of real Massachusetts is to to take I-90 – the Massachusetts Turnpike – which cuts across the state for about 140 miles (225km) from Boston to the New York state line. The first worthwhile stop on this route is another city: Worcester, pronounced 'Wooster', the way the English say it.

Worcester

Forty miles (64km) west of Boston, at the geographic centre of the region, Worcester is New England's second largest city, with a population of around 162,000 – but it has a lot of firsts to its credit. The nation's first newspaper, the *Massachusetts Spy*, was published here, and the American Antiquarian Society – the first national historical society in the country – was founded here in 1812. The Valentine card was invented in Worcester, and so was the birth-control pill.

Worcester has thrived on the output of its factories – paper, textiles, wire, nails and machinery – yet it is the only major industrial city in the US not located on a river, lake or coast. The development difficulties this would have posed were overcome in the 1820s when a group of investors financed the digging of the Blackstone Canal to Providence, Rhode Island, which is some 40 miles (64km) away. A railway replaced the canal in 1848.

The city's story is told through collections of factory goods, clothing, furniture, art, photographs and household items in the **Worcester Historical Museum** (admission fee) at 30 Elm Street. The American Antiquarian Society's headquarters, at 185 Salisbury Street, holds the country's largest single collection of printed source material in a research library specializing in American history, literature and culture up to 1877. There is limited access to the library, but changing exhibits are open to the public, and there are free tours of the building available every Wednesday at 2pm.

One of the few 18th-century residences to survive the city's industrialization is the **Salisbury Mansion**, built in 1772 by Stephen Salisbury, a local merchant and philanthropist. The mansion (admission fee) has been restored with furnishings from the 1830s. Nearby, at 55 Salisbury

Street, the **Worcester Art Museum** spans 15 centuries of human creativity. The third largest art museum in New England, it houses one of the region's finest collections of American paintings, including *The Peaceable Kingdom* by the Quaker Edward Hicks, and works by Samuel F.B. Morse, Mary Cassatt, and James Abbott McNeill Whistler.

On the city's northern edge, the **Higgins Armory Museum** (admission fee) at 100 Barber Avenue, houses what is claimed to be the largest display of medieval and Renaissance armour in the western hemisphere. Housed in a Gothic castle setting, the collection also features weaponry, tapestries, stained glass and paintings. There are demonstrations, story-telling, a sound and light show, and a gallery in which visitors can try on armour and medieval clothing. The museum is reached from I-190 (exit 1) and Route 12 North. There is also a public bus service from downtown Worcester.

Another fun place for the family is the **New England Science Center** (admission fee), east of the downtown area on Harrington Way. The 60-acre (25-hectare) site includes science exhibits, a zoo, observatory, planetarium, nature trail and a narrow-gauge railway.

VILLAGE LIFE

About 15 miles (24km) west of Worcester, you can experience life in an early 19th-century rural New England community at **Old Sturbridge Village**, an authentic re-creation set on some 200 acres (81 hectares) of land, with country roads, a sawmill, shops, banks, meeting houses, homes and a farm. The village encompasses some 40 historical buildings moved from other locations in New England. These include the 1704 Fenno House and an 1832 Greek Revival Baptist church.

First opened in 1946, the village is a non-profit educational institution and is the largest living history museum in the north-eastern US. Visitors can chat with costumed interpreters as they go about their 19th-century business. There are demonstrations by a blacksmith, cooper, printer, potter and other artisans – all doing real work with real materials. Rural activities change with the seasons, and special events and celebrations, such as an 1830s Fourth of July and a traditional Thanksgiving, take place at the appropriate times.

Admission charges to the village cover two consecutive open days, and overnight accommodation is available in the Old Sturbridge Village Lodges and Oliver Wight House. Visitors can dine in a tavern and there are picnic areas.

Pioneer Valley

The Pioneer Valley is a section of the Connecticut River Valley that reaches north to the boundary with New Hampshire and Vermont and on to the Canadian border. The larger towns in the south of the valley, including Springfield and Holyoke, are heavily industrial, but further north the valley is pleasantly rural, and is a great educational centre, with five major colleges and several exclusive prep schools. The ambience is so relaxed that it's known as 'Happy Valley'. The valley is followed by both I-91 and Route 5.

Springfield

The not-so-happy pursuit of war brought international renown to the city of Springfield, at the southern end, of the valley. Founded in 1636, and thus the oldest settlement in western Massachusetts, the city produced firearms for the US Army from 1794 until 1968. Its famous armoury opened on a site chosen by George Washington. The Springfield Rifle was renowned for its accuracy and reliability during World War I, and the M-1 won a similar reputation when it became the US Army's standard issue weapon in World War II. The story of the city's arms industry is told at the **Springfield Armory National Historic Site**, in a former armoury building off Federal Street. The museum contains one of the most extensive collections of firearms in the world. There is no charge for admission.

Springfield's cultural centre is **The Quadrangle**, which houses four museums displaying rather more conventional collections. The **Connecticut Valley Historical Museum** covers three-and-a-half centuries of history with exhibits of furniture, household items, craft displays and folk art. The **Museum of Fine Arts** contains works by Gauguin, Degas, Monet and Renoir, and covers 15 centuries in its 20 galleries. Oriental arms and armour, as well as American paintings and sculpture are featured at the **George Walter Vincent Smith Art Museum**. The **Springfield Science Museum** contains a planetarium, Native American displays and dinosaur exhibits.

Basketball was invented in Springfield by Dr James Naismith in 1891, and is celebrated in the **Naismith Memorial Basketball Hall of Fame** (admission fee) at 1150 West Columbus Avenue. There are video shows, demonstrations and exhibits, and you can test your Harlem Globetrotter skills from a moving sidewalk.

Holyoke

Some 10 miles (16km) north of Springfield, Holyoke honours the game of volleyball, invented here by a YMCA physical education instructor in 1895. There is no charge for visiting the one-room **Volleyball Hall of Fame** at 44 Dwight Street. Also accessible without charge is the nearby **Holyoke Heritage State Park**, in which the story of the city's industrial development is colourfully chronicled. At one time Holyoke had more than two dozen paper mills and was known as 'Paper City', but has recently suffered an economic decline. Four-and-a-half miles (7km) of canals dug in the 19th century still channel water through the city. There are audio-visual presentations, exhibits and walking tours of the old mills and workers' housing. On some weekends visitors can ride in vintage cars on the 5-mile (8km) Heritage Park Railroad (fare charged).

Next door to the heritage park is the **Children's Museum** (open daily except Monday), situated in a converted mill. It is full of toys, hands-on exhibits and games for the youngest members of the family. There is an admission charge.

Further north

A few miles north of Holyoke on Route 116 is South Hadley, the site of Mount Holyoke College, founded in 1837 as the first university in the US for women. The poet Emily Dickinson studied here; she was born in **Amherst**, north of Hadley on Route 116. The house in which she was born in 1830 – and where she died 56 years later – is at 280 Main Street. An admission fee is charged, but access is limited and appointments are required for tours. The bulk of the poet's personal effects and furniture is at Harvard University, but the room in which she wrote some 1,800 poems has been re-created.

With a population of around 30,000, **Northampton** is the last place of any significant size in the Pioneer Valley.

ON THE WARPATH

Heading west, Route 2 at the northern end of Pioneer Valley follows the old Mohawk Trail for 63 miles (100km) from Millers Falls to the New York State line. The trail was first used as a warpath when the Pocumtuck Indians of the Connecticut River Valley blazed it in 1663 to attack the Mohawks near present-day Troy, New York. As things turned out, the exercise brought the Pocumtucks nothing but the worst of bad luck.

Dutch settlers living in the Hudson Valley negotiated an end to the Indian war, but a Mohawk prince, travelling along the trail to ratify the Dutch treaty, was ambushed and murdered. The Mohawks repaid the treachery by slaughtering the Pocumtucks to a man.

Later the trail served as a route for pioneer settlers travelling between the Massachusetts Bay Colony and Dutch settlements in the Hudson Valley, and in post-Revolutionary America it became a 'Shunpike' – the first toll-free interstate highway.

The present automobile highway – the New Mohawk Trail – was opened in 1914. It traverses some of the most stunning scenery in Massachusetts, and passes through a number of attractive small towns.

Northwards from here, the valley becomes ever more rural in character. Northampton is a lively, cosmopolitan city, thanks largely to the 3,000 or so students at the **Smith College** for women, with good restaurants, art galleries, boutiques and some restored historic buildings, many of them still in private occupation.

Calvin Coolidge, 30th President of the United States, spent most of his life in Northampton, where he practised law. A collection of memorabilia is displayed in the **Coolidge Room** at the Forbes Library, 20 West Street. Three restored homes are maintained by the city's Historical Society and are open to the public. The **Isaac Damon House** (admission fee) was built in 1813 by a prominent New England architect and features a parlour of 1820. The **Shepherd House**, 66 Bridge Street, depicts life at the turn of the century, and the **Parson House**, 58 Bridge Street, stages changing exhibitions of furniture, textiles, decorative arts and artefacts.

The Mohawk Trail

The highway passes through a region which has 15 state forests, abundant rivers and streams for trout-fishing, canoeing and white-water rafting, campsites and marinas. In the winter a wonderland for skiers, snowmobilers and snowshoe walkers; in the Fall, there are the spectacular colours of the leaves – and bumper-to-bumper traffic along the Trail.

Deerfield

On Route 5 just south of the intersection with Route 2, this town got off to a bad start. The town was settled in 1669, but for decades remained a lonely outpost surrounded by hostile wilderness. In September 1675 the settlement was raided by Indians, and 64 of its men died. Worse was to come in February 1704, when the French led an attack by 350 Indians. In five hours, 49 settlers were killed and half the town burned down. The 112 survivors were marched 350 miles to Canada, and in the bleak winter conditions, 20 of the prisoners died.

Today, Deerfield is a peaceful place, one of New England's best-preserved colonial towns, genteel and even a little precious. It preens itself rather as 'Historic Deerfield', and much of **The Street** – its coyly-named main thoroughfare – serves as a museum.

One of the restored homes that may be visited at Historic Deerfield.

A dozen 18th-century homes are open to the public, some exhibiting antique furnishings, needlework, household items and decorative art, others displaying collections of silverware – including works by Paul Revere – pewter, ceramics and textiles. The **Memorial Hall Museum**, on Memorial Street, contains collections of Indian artefacts, quilts, musical instruments and photographs. The exhibit most visitors want to see, however, is a door with a hole chopped through its centre and the scars of a severe battering, a relic of the 1704 massacre.

There is a degree of regimentation in the way visitors must tour Deerfield. Its museums may be visited only on a guided tour, and walking tours of the village start at the north end of The Street. Tickets may be purchased at the information centre in the Hall Tavern, and are valid for a week.

Further along the Trail

The Mohawk Trail proper is reached at the town of Greenfield, the most northerly frontier post before the Canadian border some 170 miles (270km) away when it was incorporated in 1753. A winding 10 miles (16km) or so to the west, the trail reaches Shelburne Falls, the first of a series of picturesque villages set in increasingly hilly surrounds.

Shelburne Falls' greatest claim to industrial fame is that here Linus Yale made the first of his locks, but major activities in the area today are dairy and fruit farming, and in the spring there is a great deal of maple sugaring, with many sugarhouses open to the public.

Two sightseeing oddities here are the Bridge of Flowers and the Salmon Falls glacial potholes. The 400ft (123m) long bridge crosses the Deerfield River in five spans and was built in 1908 to carry trolley tracks between Shelburne and neighbouring Buckland. When the bridge was abandoned in 1928, the local Women's Club decided to turn it into a botanical walk rather than let it fall into dereliction. The potholes, about 50 of them, are just downstream of the bridge. Varying from the size of a soup plate to about 40ft (12m) in diameter, they were formed by glacial

The lovely Bridge of Flowers at Shelburne Falls was created by members of the local Women's Club.

action during the last Ice Age. In summer months the largest potholes are used as swimming pools.

Just east of the town of Charlemont, overlooking the Deerfield River, stands the statue of a Native American, arms raised in supplication to the Great Spirit. This is *Hail to the Sunrise*, a monument erected in 1932 in memory of the five Indian nations who lived along the Mohawk Trail. The statue weighs 900lbs (409kg), and the adjacent pool contains 100 inscribed stones from tribes and councils throughout the US.

From the tiny village of Florida, the trail climbs to its highest point, the Whitcomb Summit, at an altitude of 1,773ft (540m). Then comes a steep descent with hairpin bends to the once thriving industrial town and railroad centre of North Adams.

The **Western Heritage State Park**, located in the old freight yard at North Adams, features the town in its heyday and tells the story of the Hoosac Tunnel, built in 1875 to connect a railway line from the northern Berkshire region to eastern Massachusetts. Nitroglycerine was used for the first time in blasting the 5-mile (8km) tunnel, which is said to be haunted by the ghosts of the 200 men who

Hail to the Sunrise *commemorates the five Indian nations who lived along the Mohawk Trail.*

died during its construction. The tunnel is on Route 2 near Florida.

North Adams also boasts a unique attraction: the only solid marble natural bridge in North America. It was formed by melting glaciers millions of years ago. The bridge is located in **Natural Bridge State Park**, just north of the town on Route 8.

From North Adams there's a choice of routes to the central and southern Berkshires. You can head south on Route 8, or you can travel west on the Mohawk Trail for another 5 miles (8km) or so to reach Williamstown, then take Route 7 south. Either way, you'll end up in Pittsfield.

Route 8 passes through the Victorian Industrial town of Adams, a riverside town in the valley between Mount Greylock, the highest point in the state, and the Hoosacs. Its streets are lined with the factory buildings, industrial chimneys and mill housing that reflect its 19th-century prosperity. Some 70 Victorian homes constitute the **Adams National Register Historic District**. Mount Greylock can be reached from Adams by hiking the Cheshire Harbor Trail. The local chamber of commerce sponsors the annual Mount Greylock Ramble when about 1,000 hikers climb the mountain on Columbus Day (9 October).

Aficionados of vintage Americana will doubtless be pleased to find the Miss Adams Diner, near the statue of William McKinley on the town's delightfully old-fashioned Park Street. The diner is a restored original, built in 1949, with lots of chrome and a green and white tiled floor. The food is as traditional as the décor.

North America's only solid marble natural bridge is to be found near the town of North Adams.

The Berkshires

Small towns, villages and large swathes of hilly countryside traced with hiking trails provide a range of attractions and activities for the tourist.

Williamstown

The northernmost town in the Berkshires is proud of its colonial cultural attractions and activities, many of them associated with Williams College, whose dignified buildings line the main street. Established in 1753 as a plantation called West Hoosuck, the town was renamed in 1765 after Colonel Ephraim Williams Jr, who left enough money to set up a free school on the condition that West Hoosuck became Williamstown.

The 500-seat, air-conditioned Adams Memorial Theatre provides facilities for Williams College productions in the winter and for the professional Williamstown Theatre in the summer, when the Williamstown Theatre Festival draws cosmopolitan audiences to showcase productions with performances by international stars.

The town also has two fine art galleries, neither of which charges an admission fee. The **Williams College Museum of Art** features modern, contemporary and American works, while the **Sterling and Francine Clark Art Institute** has a famous collection of paintings by such masters as Renoir, Corot, Degas, Monet and Toulouse-Lautrec, as well as works by Italian, Flemish, Dutch and French Old Masters. The Institute also houses prints, and drawings from the 10th to the 15th centuries, and has an outstanding collection of English, Continental and American silver from the 16th to the 19th centuries.

Heading South

Route 7 south of Williamstown heads deep into the Berkshires, the Massachusetts equivalent of The Hamptons on Long Island, with lots of neat lawns and suave living. There are plenty of places to visit and things to see without feeling you have to fight back the desire to gape!

From just north of the attractive village of Lanesborough, on the edge of Pontoosuc Lake, you can drive to the 3,491ft (1,064m) summit of **Mount Greylock**, and on a good day gaze out across 100 miles (160km) and five states. The summit is surrounded by a 10,000-acre (4,047-hectare) state reservation, which has 45 miles (72km) of trails and is popular with hikers and cross-country skiers. Camping, cycling, fishing, horseback riding and hunting are also available.

About 20 miles (32km) south of Williamstown, **Pittsfield** is a busy paper milling town, but there are some interesting Victorian buildings in its **Park Square Historic District**. The **Berkshire Museum**, at 39 South Street, is a bit of a hotch-potch, but its 18 galleries include a collection of paintings by artists of the Hudson River School, early American portraits and historical displays. Children will enjoy the museum's aquarium and animal exhibits.

The **Gothic Revival Berkshire Athenaeum**, 1 Wendell Avenue, houses the public library, and its **Herman Melville Memorial Room** displays a collection of the author's books, correspondence and other memorabilia.

Arrowhead, Melville's home from 1850 to 1863, is on the southern outskirts of Pittsfield, at 780 Holmes Road. This was where he wrote most of *Moby Dick*, and some people say he was inspired to write the book because he thought Mount Greylock, viewed from Arrowhead, looked like a huge white whale. Whatever the truth, the book did him little good in his own lifetime. By the time it was published, the popularity he had enjoyed earlier had begun to wane, and he began to suffer financial problems. Melville sold Arrowhead to his brother in 1863 and returned to New York City, where he worked as a customs inspector. He was almost forgotten when he died in 1891. Arrowhead is open to the public (admission fee). Behind the old farmhouse is the red

STYLE OF THE SHAKERS

Pittsfield's major attraction is the **Hancock Shaker Village** (admission fee), 5 miles (8km) west of the town on Route 20. The Shakers were an odd New England sect which sprang up in 1774, keeping themselves to themselves in self-contained communities devoted to a simple, self-sufficient life. They were named 'Shakers' because of their animated singing and dancing during worship.

The Hancock community was founded in 1790 and reached its peak in the 1840s with about 250 members. They worked together in farming, producing herbal medicines and furniture-making. Antique Shaker furniture is sought after by collectors for its simple, yet graceful design.

Hancock was closed as a religious community in 1960, and opened as a museum a year later. Twenty of the original brick and wooden buildings remain, and there are displays of Shaker crafts – baking, box-making, spinning and weaving – as well as programmes of lively Shaker hymn music. From time to time, Shaker-style dinners are served by candle-light. Workshops on gardening and herb-growing are held throughout the year.

The Shakers were noted for their ingenuity in functional design, and a favourite with visitors to Hancock is the Round Stone Barn, dating from 1826, in which one person standing in the middle could feed 54 cows at once.

Hancock Shaker Village is not accessible from the town of Hancock to the north on Route 43.

barn in which Melville and his friend Nathaniel Hawthorne used to chat.

Lenox

This town is in the heart of the area known as 'Inland Newport'. Like Rhode Island's famous yachting centre, this part of the

These music lovers meet each year under the same tree at the Tanglewood Music Festival at Lenox.

Berkshires became fashionable in the 19th century when the cream of New York society built the opulent and sometimes grossly overblown mansions which, with peculiar modesty, they called their summer 'cottages'.

About 20 of the hundred or so stately homes which once graced Lenox have survived, of which the best known is **The Mount**, summer home of the novelist and design specialist Edith Wharton from 1902 to 1911. Built in Georgian Revival style to the author's own principle of symmetrical design, the white mansion has marble floors and fireplaces, elaborately moulded ceilings and 50 acres (20 hectares) of lovely grounds. The Mount (admission fee) is on Plunkett Street.

Another famous residence has been reconstructed in Lenox – the **Hawthorne Cottage**, and this time the word is rather more honestly used. The house in which the writer Nathaniel Hawthorne and his family lived for 18 months from 1850 was described by his wife Sophia as 'the little red shanty'. Hawthorne wrote *The House of the Seven Gables* during his stay at the cottage, which burned down in the 1890s.

The Hawthorne Cottage (free entry) is on Hawthorne Street and is part of **Tanglewood**, the 200-acre (83-hectare) estate which is the summertime home of the Boston Symphony Orchestra. Each season thousands of music-lovers picnic on the lawns at concerts featuring international singers and soloists.

The **old train station** at Lenox, built in 1902, has been restored as a railway museum. It is also the terminus of the Berkshire Scenic Railway which during the summer operates a vintage train to the neighbouring communities of Lee and Stockbridge. Passengers can buy an open ticket which allows them to alight and re-board at will. The station is on Willow Creek Road.

Stockbridge

Prosperous, picturesque, urbane, Stockbridge has become the universal image of both a New England and Middle American small town, thanks to Norman Rockwell, who immortalized it in his paintings and on the covers of the *Saturday Evening Post*. Its Main Street is familiar, tree-shaded, lined with small shops and dominated by the rambling wooden mass of the Red Lion Inn. Rockwell lived in Stockbridge from 1953 until his death in 1978, and the world's largest collection of originals of his work is held in the **Norman Rockwell Museum** (admission fee) which moved into new, larger premises at 9 Glendale Road, off Route 183, in 1993.

Other famous Stockbridge residents have been the writers Norman Mailer and Robert Sherwood and the sculptor Daniel Chester French, who lived at Chesterwood (admission fee) on Williamsville Road for 34 years until his death in 1931. Among the works displayed in his studio are the clay and plaster models he made when working on the Lincoln Memorial for Washington DC. The house is furnished with European and American antiques and a collection of sculptures. The 130-acre (52-hectare) grounds include Italianate gardens and woodlands with trails designed by French.

The 108-room Red Lion Inn, on Main Street, was built soon after the original

The studio at Stockbridge where the artist and illustrator Norman Rockwell worked from 1953 until his death in 1978.

burned down in 1896. The first Red Lion was built in 1773 on a staging post between Boston and Albany, New York. The present inn has grown considerably over the years and now spills into a number of annexes. Guest rooms and restaurants are furnished with antiques.

Five miles (8km) or so south of Stockbridge, just before the busy little town of Great Barrington, is **Monument Mountain** where legend has it that an Indian girl hurled herself to her death for unrequited love. The mountain was also the scene of a dramatic literary encounter in the summer of 1850 when Nathaniel Hawthorne and Herman Melville met for the first time as members of a climbing party. A sudden thunderstorm broke and the climbers drank champagne and recited poetry as rain fell and lightning crackled.

Two other natural attractions can be reached from Great Barrington. **Bartholomew's Cobble** is a National Natural Landmark, a knob of quartzite and limestone in a wooded setting with 6 miles (9.6km) of trails and many unusual ferns and rock plants. There is a small museum (admission fee) displaying animal and plant specimens and Indian relics. Bartholomew's Cobble is on Route 7A, about 11 miles (18km) south of Great Barrington.

Bash Bish Falls, 16 miles (26km) south west of the town, on the New York State line, is another place where a beautiful Indian maiden is said to have hurled herself to death – this time over an 80ft (24m) waterfall. The falls are in a state forest on the slopes of Mount Washington.

Beaches, Islands and Historic Places

Massachusetts, also known as the Bay State, has a magnificent weather-beaten coast that curves and curls for some 170 miles (276km) from New Hampshire to Rhode Island, swirls into the shape of a muscleman's bicep-flexing arm to form Cape Cod, and breaks up into the islands of Nantucket and Martha's Vineyard. It is an area of great contrasts: wonderful beaches, historic towns, picturesque harbours and industrial heritage. Here are the facts of Pilgrim landfalls and Puritan witch hunts, and the fictions of Herman Melville and Nathaniel Hawthorne.

The state's extensive coastal area can be divided into three very distinctive regions. Between Boston and the New Hampshire border lie the North Shore and Merrimack Valley. Below Boston, the South Shore tumbles down to Rhode Island. Cape Cod and the islands reach out to embrace a corner of theAtlantic Ocean.

Widows' walks, which were used by sea captains' wives to scan the horizon for their husbands' returning ships, can still be found on many of the old homes at Martha's Vineyard.

The North Shore

The most striking thing about the North Shore area is its compactness. Less than an hour after leaving Boston by car you could be crossing the state line into New Hampshire, having traversed the North Shore from end to end, but to do so would be a shame because the area is perfect for touring and rich in sightseeing opportunities. Disregarding Interstates 93 and 95, the best major highways to use are Routes 1 and 1A, with 127, 128 and 133 as interlinking roads.

The first few miles north out of Boston are as tacky as you will find in seaside suburbs anywhere in the world, with ribbon development, gas stations, used car lots and indeterminate workshops. Traffic can be heavy, especially at weekends

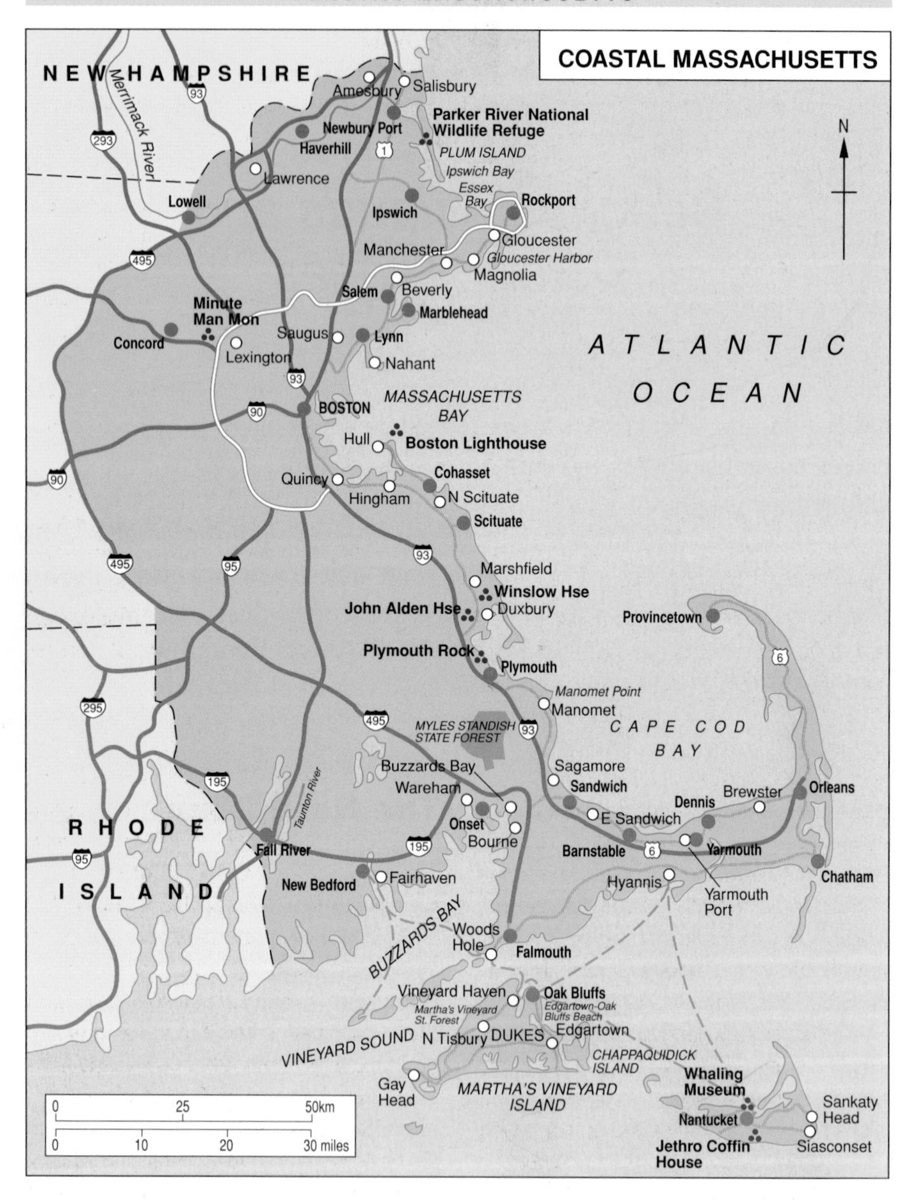

when Bostonians head for the nearby beaches, which are extensive and sandy.

Saugus

Seven miles (11km) out of Boston on Route 1, is **Saugus**, settled in 1630 and site of an early New World industrial enterprise. The **Saugus Iron Works**, now a National Historic Site, was established in the 1640s by John Winthrop Jr, son of the Bay Colony's governor, to supply nails and other artefacts which had previously been shipped from England at great cost. Deposits of iron ore had been found in the area, there was plenty of wood to use as fuel, and the Saugus River provided both water and power. There are guided tours of the reconstructed blast furnace, forge, slitting mill and blacksmith's shop, and of the Iron Works House, built as a home for the owner in 1646. A museum displays artefacts found on the site and demonstrates 17th-century technology. The iron works, at 244 Central Street, Saugus, is clearly signposted. Access is free.

Lynn

Collectors of historical sideshoots should visit **Lynn**, just beyond Saugus on Route 107. Founded in 1629, it is New England's third oldest community and was once the world's largest shoe manufacturing centre. A **museum** (admission fee), run by the Lynn Historical Society in a 19th-century house at 125 Green Street, features the shoemaker's craft in exhibits of tools, clothes and photographs. Pride of place goes to a medallion 5ft (1.5m) in diameter made entirely of miniature shoe soles. It was made for the 1893 Chicago Exposition and the 234 soles – each one different – represented each of Lynn's manufacturers and dealers at that time. The museum is the starting point of a walking tour of some of the old shoe factories.

An early shoemaker's workshop is featured at **Lynn Visitor Centre**, on the corner of Union and Washington Streets, which also houses exhibits depicting three centuries of the city's industrial history. **Lynn Heritage State Park**, at 154 Lynnway (Route 1A) is a 4.5-acre (1.8-hectare) waterfront site providing public access to Lynn Harbor. There is a scenic boardwalk, and concerts and other special events are staged in the park. Paddle boats may be rented, and there are water taxis to the Boston Harbor Islands.

Nahant

A causeway connects Lynn with **Nahant**, a sandy peninsula dropping to the south. Nahant was a fashionable seaside resort in the 19th century, with grand hotels and seaside cottages owned by the rich and famous, and its beaches are still acclaimed. Harriet Beecher Stowe spent her summers at 298 Nahant Road, and Henry Wadsworth Longfellow wrote part of *Hiawatha* in a boarding house at the corner of Willow and Wharf Streets. Lawn tennis was played for the first time in the US in Nahant in 1874.

Back on the mainland, Atlantic Avenue (Route 129) peels to the right from Route 1A and follows the coast to Marblehead. Not that you will be all that aware of the coast, which is mostly hidden behind hills, trees and the shrubbery of smart homes.

Marblehead

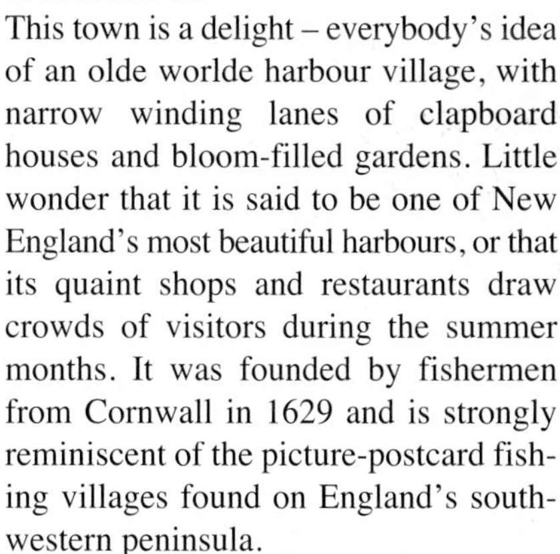

This town is a delight – everybody's idea of an olde worlde harbour village, with narrow winding lanes of clapboard houses and bloom-filled gardens. Little wonder that it is said to be one of New England's most beautiful harbours, or that its quaint shops and restaurants draw crowds of visitors during the summer months. It was founded by fishermen from Cornwall in 1629 and is strongly reminiscent of the picture-postcard fishing villages found on England's southwestern peninsula.

In the old days Marblehead made its living from fishing, shipbuilding and maritime trade. Today its main waterborne activity is yachting. During the Revolutionary War, the town had the distinction of providing the first American warship. This was the *Hannah*, owned by General John Glover, who rented it to the Continental Congress. Washington sent the

Hannah to sea to intercept British supplies. Marblehead seamen served valiantly during the struggle for independence. Led by Glover, they prevented Washington's army from being wiped out after the Battle of Long Island by ferrying them from Brooklyn to Manhattan, and they rowed through ice floes at night on the Delaware River so that Washington's force could attack Trenton. Marblehead paid a heavy price for independence: by the end of the conflict more than 450 of its womenfolk had been widowed.

The town's common, **Washington Square**, is surrounded by mansions built by master mariners and merchants. Here also is **Abbot Hall**, the Victorian town hall with its landmark clock tower. Inside is the famous painting **The Spirit of '76** by Archibald Willard. Access is free, but the hall is closed at weekends and on holidays. The **Jeremiah Lee Mansion** at 161 Washington Street is said to be one of America's finest pre-Revolutionary houses. It was built in 1768 and contains 16 rooms. Its timber exterior was cut to look like stone. There is a wealth of elegant period furnishings and paintings, and there are exhibits illustrating the town's history. There are guided tours during the summer months (admission fee).

Salem

Immortalized by the hysteria that led to the dreadful witch trials of 1692, Salem is a surprisingly jolly place today, with friendly tree-lined streets and brick-paved pedestrian malls. The witchcraft theme, not surprisingly, is a little overdone, but Salem has plenty of alternative attractions. For those hell-bent on the town's wicked past, it is possible to visit it without realizing that it also played an important role in New England's maritime history, and has some of the finest Georgian and post-Revolutionary houses in the US. More than two dozen museums and historic houses are open to the public, as well as other sites. A red line painted on the sidewalks traces a 1.7-mile (2.7km) heritage trail through the town, and the hour-long narrated Salem Trolley tours link all the

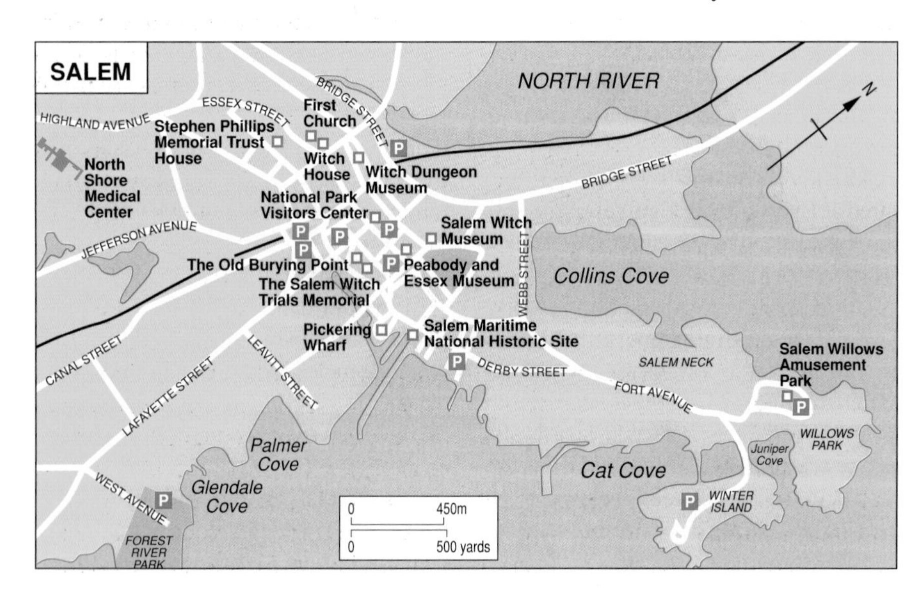

major attractions. Information and brochures are available at the National Park Visitors Center, Museum Place.

Salem's first settlers were a group of fishermen led by Roger Conant who arrived from Cape Ann, some 20 miles (32km) to the north east, in 1626. They rightly decided that the cove at their new site would make a fine harbour, and the town prospered so much from maritime trade that by 1770 it was one of one of the most active ports in America, trading with Britain, France, the Netherlands, Spain and the West Indies. After the War of Independence, trade was extended to the Far East, where American goods were exchanged for tea, coffee, and valuable silk and spices. By the beginning of the 19th century so many of the town's ships visited Asian ports that some traders there believed Salem was a country.

The town's nautical heritage is brought to life at the **Salem Maritime National Historic Site**, covering 9 acres (3.65 hectares) along the old waterfront. Entrance to the site is free, and there is an audio-visual presentation at the Orientation Center at 174 Derby Street, from where guided tours also start. Visitors can get a taste of the old days by strolling down the 2,000ft (610m) long Derby Wharf, and by paying a visit to the Custom House, the Derby House and a warehouse displaying examples of cargoes and ships' stores from the 19th century. The Derby House is a brick-built mansion named after the man who built it, Elias Derby, a successful merchant who also turned his hand to running a fleet of privateers during the Revolution.

The **Custom House** with its red bricks and white portico is a proud monument to Salem's maritime past. It was built in 1819, and the writer Nathaniel Hawthorne worked here from 1846 to 1849 – his office and the desk he used have been preserved. The Custom House is described in the opening of Hawthorne's *The Scarlet Letter*. At the eastern end of the Maritime National Historic Site, at 54 Turner Street, is the **House of the Seven Gables** which inspired Hawthorne's classic novel. The house, restored to its appearance in Hawthorne's time, was the home of a cousin of the writer, who frequently visited it. Guided tours (admission fee) begin with an audio-visual presentation, and include the **Retire Becket House**, a shipbuilder's home erected in 1655, the 1682 **Hathaway House**, and the **Hawthorne Birthplace**, which has been restored to the mid-18th century. The birthplace originally stood in Union Street.

Salem's grandest attraction is in the centre of town, a few blocks inland, although the maritime link is maintained. This is the **Peabody and Essex Museum** in East India Square (admission fee), the oldest museum in continuous operation in the US. In 1799 a group of Salem sea captains decided to pool their more exotic souvenirs and founded the East India Marine Society as 'a museum of natural and artificial curiosities'. Its first permanent home, the granite East India Marine Hall, built in 1824, is now part of a complex of seven buildings and more than 30 galleries housing more than 300,000 items.

The Peabody has four major collections. The maritime history section includes scrimshaw, figureheads, navigational instruments, paintings, model ships, and even a full-size reconstruction of the elegant stateroom on an ocean-going yacht of 1816. The Asian Export Art Collection – the world's largest – includes objects in silver, gold, ivory and porcelain, furniture and paintings, and covers the period from

1500 to 1940. The Pacific Island Collection comprises works of art and artefacts from Indonesia, Melanesia, Micronesia and Polynesia. The fourth major collection displays exhibits relating to New England's natural history.

Across the street, displays in two elegant Italian Revival style buildings focus on 200 years of New England architecture. A research library is situated in the John Tucker Daland House. Built in 1852, this building is the work of the Boston architect Gridley J.F. Bryant. A portrait gallery and a collection of paintings, decorative arts, artefacts and furniture are to be found in the 1857 Plummer Hall. Three restored houses situated in the surrounding landscaped grounds illustrate colonial, Georgian and Federal styles.

The oldest home in Salem, the **John Ward House**, was completed in 1685 and restored to its 17th-century appearance in 1912. Its original owner worked in leather and the house is modestly furnished. An annexe houses an 18th-century weaving room and an early 19th-century apothecary's shop.

The oldest part of the **Crowninshield-Bentley House** was built by Captain John Crowninshield in 1727. The Reverend William Bentley, who rented rooms in the house from 1791 to 1819, was a dedicated diarist who left an invaluable chronicle of life in late 18th- and early 19th-century Salem. The house was restored in 1960. The **Gardner-Pingree House** was designed for the wealthy merchant John Gardner by Samuel McIntire, the leading architect of Salem's Federal period and the man responsible for the town's most graceful homes. The Gardner-Pingree House, acclaimed as McIntire's masterpiece, was completed in 1805 and reflects life at the top of 19th-century Salem society. Gardner ran into business difficulties in 1815 and had to sell up. In 1834 the house was bought by David Pingree, and it remained in the Pingree family for a hundred years.

Few visitors interested in architecture will want to miss the **Chestnut Street** area, a National Historic Landmark at the western end of downtown Salem. The district includes Summer and Flint Streets and Chestnut Street itself, first laid out in 1796 and considered one of the most beautiful streets in the US. The only building in the district open to the public is the early 19th-century Stephen Phillips Memorial Trust House at 34 Chestnut Street (admission fee). Inside are furnishings from the homes of Salem sea captains and some of the treasures they brought back from overseas. Visitors can also look round an exhibition of antique carriages and cars.

Returning downtown, it's worth diverting to Charter Street to visit **Old Burying Point**, Salem's oldest cemetery, which dates from 1637. Among those buried here are Judge John Hawthorne, who presided over the witchcraft trials and was an ancestor of Nathaniel Hawthorne, the architect Samuel McIntire, and one of the first settlers, Richard More, who at the age of 12 arrived at Plymouth aboard the *Mayflower*.

Essex Street, the town's artery, contains a number of historic buildings, but the most famous is the gabled **Witch House** on the corner of North Street. This was the home of Jonathan Corwin, one of the witch trial judges, who questioned some 200 suspected witches in the house. At last we are moving into the area of Salem's dark past.

At its opposite end Essex Street intersects with Hawthorne Boulevard, and a

WITCHCRAFT HYSTERIA

Twentieth-century Salem enjoys a permanent Halloween atmosphere, with children prowling the streets in witch masks and tall hats, but in 1692 there was nothing even remotely festive about the awful events that gave the town its infamy.

Superstition ruled the lives of many people in the unenlightened 17th century, and witchcraft was widely held to be the cause of any unexplained mishap or illness. Salem was not the only place where hysteria broke out – there were grim trials elsewhere in New England, and in Europe – but the town earned its place in history for the extent of accusation and the number of executions.

The hysteria began when a group of young girls, including the daughter of a local minister, began to suffer convulsions after listening to tales of the supernatural told by Tituba, a West Indian slave. Under questioning, the girls accused Tituba, as well as Sarah Good and Sarah Osborne, of bewitching them.

Bolstered by ignorance – and considerable political exploitation by the Puritan establishment – the hysteria spread. Hundreds were accused and hauled in for interrogation. Nineteen suspected witches were hanged and an 80-year-old man was ordered to be crushed to death with heavy stones. Sense was restored only when the womenfolk of leading citizens – including the governor's wife herself – were accused of being witches.

The furore actually began in neighbouring Danvers, where there is a memorial in Hobart Street to the witch hunt victims. Among those was 70-year-old Rebecca Nurse whose reconstructed homestead at 149 Pine Street is now open to the public (entrance fee). The site features a 'first period' saltbox house and a graveyard with the tombstones of two of those executed.

Danvers Archival Center, 15 Sylvan Street, contains an extensive collection of printed items connected with the witchcraft trials, and the Danvers Historical Society stages changing exhibitions on local history at **Tapley Memorial Hall**, 13 Page Street.

left turn here leads straight to the **Salem Witch Museum** on Washington Square North. The museum (admission fee) is located in a grim-looking stone church built around 1840, but before you go inside take a closer look at the statue in front. You will see that it is not a witch, as you probably thought at first, but the likeness of Roger Conant, the founder of Salem, looking very sinister with tall hat and flowing cape and holding what looks suspiciously like a broomstick. The museum shows a 30-minute sound and light presentation dramatizing the events of the witch hunt. It speaks volumes for the popularity of the museum and the universal interest in its subject that its narration, which is historically accurate rather than sensationalized, is simultaneously translated into Japanese, French, German, Italian and Spanish.

Professional actors present a witch trial dramatization based on 1692 transcripts at the **Witch Dungeon Museum** at 16 Lynde Street, and audiences take part in a re-enactment of the trial of Bridget Bishop in the Old Town Hall on Derby Square. There are charges for both performances.

Pioneer Village is a re-creation of the original settlement founded by Roger Conant. Authentically costumed colonists walk and work among the small thatched houses, showing off their gardens, crafts and animals. The village (entrance fee) is located in Forest River Park, on the coast

Witchcraft hysteria is re-created realistically in the Salem Witch Museum.

The parlour in the House of the Seven Gables, which inspired Nathaniel Hawthorne's classic novel.

about a mile (1.6km) south of downtown Salem, just off Route 114. The park has beaches, picnic areas and a salt water swimming pool. Those requiring a change of pace as well as fresh air may decide to head for **Willows Park**, about the same distance east on Salem Neck and reached by way of Essex or Derby Streets and Fort Avenue. Willows (free admission and parking) has a public pier, beaches, amusement games, children's rides, food and refreshments, and is a stop on the Salem Trolley route.

Salem is well equipped to cater for its many visitors. There is ample parking, rail connection with Boston, and accommodation ranging from bed-and-breakfast to inns and international standard hotels. For the hungry (and thirsty) there is everything from sandwich shops to pubs, grills and full-blown restaurants. The Lyceum Bar and Grill, at 43 Church Street, is in an attractive Federal-style brick building which was formerly a lecture hall. Hawthorne, Emerson and Thoreau were frequently seen there.

Cape Ann

East of Salem, down on the coast, Route 127 is the scenic route to Cape Ann, whose residents are proud of its fishing heritage. The cape was named in honour of the mother of Charles I, king of England, and its picturesque towns and quaint harbours have always been the focus of considerable maritime activity. In the early days its fishing fleet helped feed settlers in Boston and other communities inland. By the early 18th century its ships were to be found anywhere between the Caribbean and the English Channel.

Beverley

Many places in the area bear the names of towns and cities in England. Beverley, settled in 1626, is known as the birthplace of the American Navy – the schooner *Hannah* engaged *HMS Nautilus* off the town on 10 October 1775 – and has four major historic houses within its boundaries.

Exercise Conant House, 634 Cabot Street, was built around 1666 by the son of Roger Conant. **Balch House**, 448 Cabot Street, believed to be the oldest wooden frame house in the US, was built in 1636. David Balch died in the house

The setting sun outlines pleasure craft plying their trade at Cape Ann.

after being 'tormented by witches' during the Salem hysteria. Another home connected with the witch hunts is the **John Hale House** at 39 Hale Street. John Hale was Beverley's first minister and his testimony led to the hanging of Bridget Bishop as a witch. He helped calm things down when his own wife was accused. The **John Cabot House**, 117 Cabot Street, is a Federal mansion built in 1781 by a wealthy merchant and privateer. It now serves as the headquarters and museum of the Beverley Historical Society. Combination tickets permit viewing of the Balch, Hale and Cabot houses.

Manchester-by-the-Sea

Incorporated in 1645, this town has some qualities rather more endearing than those found in the streets of its namesake in north-west England. Picturesque and fashionable, the Massachusetts resort has a popular yacht harbour and is famous for its Singing Beach, where a strange musical sound is produced when you walk across the hard sandy surface.

Gloucester

Gloucester is the oldest seaport in the US. The harbour was named Le Beauport by Samuel de Champlain when he anchored there in 1604, and it was first settled in 1623. After more than 370 years, fishing is still the major industry and the fleet is a colourful sight. Rudyard Kipling immortalized the Gloucester fleet in his novel *Captains Courageous*, and the heroism and dedication of its crews are acknowledged by the Fisherman Statue on Stacey Boulevard. Depicting a stalwart man at the wheel, the statue was commissioned from Leonard Craske by the citizens of Gloucester in 1923 to mark the port's 300th anniversary.

Trawlers apart, the harbour bustles with sightseeing cruisers, deep-sea game-fishing craft and whale-watching vessels. The arts and crafts of the area are featured by the **Cape Ann Historical Association** at 27 Pleasant Street (admission fee). In addition to model ships. furniture, Paul Revere silver, fishing equipment, China trade artefacts and photographs, there is a collection of marine paintings which includes works by the 19th-century Gloucester-born Fitz Hugh Lane.

Artists have long sought inspiration in the Gloucester area and the **Rocky Neck Art Colony**, at East Gloucester, is the oldest working art colony in the US. It has restaurants, shops and galleries exhibiting paintings and other works in all media. There are also exhibits and demonstrations at the North Shore Arts Association, 197 East Main Street, Gloucester.

The Beauport Museum, 75 Eastern Point Boulevard (admission fee) is an unusual house built between 1907 and 1934 by Henry Davis Sleeper, an interior decorator who collected American art and antiquities. Sleeper added rooms to the house as his collection grew, and by 1934 there were 40. Today, 26 of them, furnished with American and European decorative arts, are open to the public.

A rather more bizarre museum is to be found at 80 Hesperus Avenue, overlooking the Atlantic Ocean and the rock that was the setting for Longfellow's poem *The Wreck of the Hesperus*. The enormous **Hammond Castle** (admission fee) was built between 1926 and 1929 by John Hays Hammond Jr, the pioneer scientist in the fields of radio, television and radar.

Hammond lived and worked at the castle, which included a gallery for his art collection, a Roman bath, secret passages and an organ with 8,200 pipes housed in the Great Hall, 100ft (30m) long and 60ft (18m) high. There is a collection of Roman tombstones, a Renaissance dining room and Gothic and early American bedrooms. George Gershwin, Cole Porter, Noel Coward, and Ethel and Lionel Barrymore were among those who stayed at the castle as guests of Hammond and his wife. The Barrymores could not resist the temptation to present cameo performances of Shakespeare in the Great Hall.

Rockport

Route 127 continues across Cape Ann to Rockport, just a 10-minute drive from Gloucester. Rockport owes its name to the quarries which once shipped granite all over the world, but it remained a sleepy fishing village until it was discovered by artists soon after the Civil War. Although the town is now a busy resort, the beautiful seascapes, the harbour and the cliffs which attracted those 19th-century painters are still there, keeping contemporary artists and photographers busy. **Bearskin Neck**, a narrow peninsula lined with shops, galleries and restaurants housed in old cottages, is the main attraction for tourists. At its far end is Motif #1, an old fishermen's shack which has been a favourite subject for painters for a long time.

North of Rockport, at the very tip of the cape, **Halibut Point State Park** tells the story of the area's granite-exporting days. The park is set in an old quarry, and an audio-visual presentation in the visitor centre relates how local paving blocks were sent to Boston, New York, Philadelphia, and even as far afield as Havana. Halibut Point granite was used in the Custom House at Boston, the Brooklyn Bridge and New York City's Holland

Granite quarries gave Rockport its name, but as this typical cottage testifies, lobster fishing is still a major activity.

Tunnel. A self-guided trail leads through the old quarry workings and emerges on a stunning viewpoint overlooking the Atlantic Ocean. The park is also a good location for birdwatching.

Beyond Halibut Point, Route 127 follows the cape into Ipswich Bay, where the tiny village of **Annisquam** has maintained a low profile for more than three centuries. The shingled and saltbox houses in its few narrow winding streets enjoy grand ocean views. Strollers will enjoy crossing the old wooden footbridge to Lobster Cove.

Essex

Just west of Cape Ann, on Route 133, Essex is an antique collector's paradise, with some two dozen specialist shops in the town. Aficionados can find everything from old advertising posters to botanical prints, old maps and ageing wickerwork. There are bargain basements and fancy boutiques, and the dealers all enjoy a bout of bargaining.

It's worth taking a break from the bargain-hunting to visit the **Essex Shipbuilding Museum** (admission fee) at 28 Main Street. The building is crammed with artefacts and pictures illustrating the town's history – a period of 300 years in which more than 4,000 vessels were built, including the unlikely named *Chebacco Dogbody*. This was a two-masted fishing boat built on production line methods so that New England's fishing fleet could be replaced swiftly after being destroyed by the British.

Ipswich

About 5 miles (8km) north of Essex, also on Route 133, is Ipswich, a well-preserved town whose streets are lined with restored houses from the 17th and 18th centuries. More than 40 houses built before 1725 are still in use as homes. The town was founded in 1633, and proclaims itself to be the birthplace of American Independence because it was here that the question of taxation without representation was first raised. Ipswich was the home of the New World's first woman poet, Ann Bradstreet, whose husband Simon was secretary and later governor of the Massachusetts Bay Colony. Some of her poems were written in the house at 33 High Street, privately owned, and published in England in 1650 under the title *The Tenth Muse Lately Sprung Up in America*.

Two of the town's historic houses are open to the public, both administered by the Ipswich Historical Society. The **John Whipple House**, at 53 South Main Street, was built in 1640 and occupied by the Whipple family for more than 200 years. A fine example of an early Puritan home, it is furnished with items owned by the Whipples and has a lovely colonial herb garden. The **John Heard House**, 40 South Main Street, was built by a master mariner in 1795 and displays China trade articles and early American furnishings. There is also a collection of restored carriages on view.

Castle Hill at 200 Argilla Road was the summer home of a more recent New England tycoon, Richard T. Crane, Jr, head of a Chicago plumbing company which was famous in the 1920s for its elegant bathroom fittings. The 59-roomed seaside mansion was built in 1927. A long drive leads through landscaped grounds which include a sunken Italian garden and a rose garden. The Grand Allée is a wide path, lined with spruce trees and statuary, that sweeps grandly from the mansion to the sea. Inside, the rooms have elaborate moulded ceilings 16ft (5m) high, marble fireplaces and chandeliers crafted from crystal and brass. The round surfaces of the entrance rotunda are covered with canvas on which are painted Roman emperors and Corinthian columns and portraits of the Crane children. There is a gallery 63ft (19m) long and a library taken entirely from an estate in Hertfordshire, England. Castle Hill has restricted opening times (Tel: 508 356-7774 for information) and there is an admission charge. There are summer concerts and other performing arts events in the grounds, which are freely accessible to visitors when there are no private functions.

Just below Castle Hill is **Crane Beach**, once part of the Crane estate and now available for public use, though parking fees are hefty, especially at weekends. The beach, though, is magnificent: 4 miles (6.5km) of white sand with dunes and marsh grasses and a lovely view of the Ipswich River. Refreshments are available.

On a more down-to-earth note, Ipswich is famous for its fried clams, available at roadside stalls throughout the area and so much a part of the local psyche that a clam is actually featured as the town's official symbol.

Newburyport

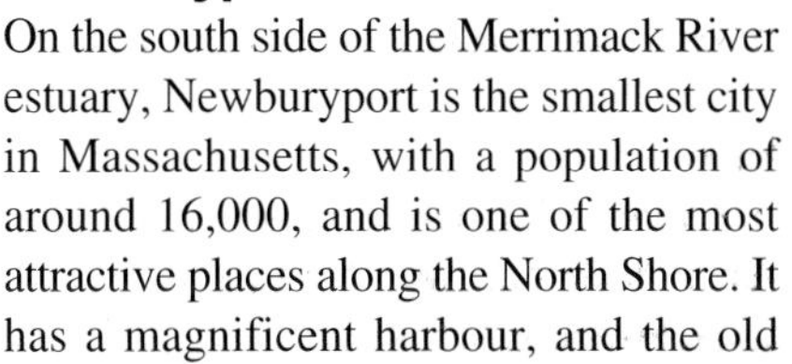

On the south side of the Merrimack River estuary, Newburyport is the smallest city in Massachusetts, with a population of around 16,000, and is one of the most attractive places along the North Shore. It has a magnificent harbour, and the old

LIFE ON THE WILD SIDE

One of the last undeveloped barrier beaches on the Eastern Seaboard is to be found on Plum Island, which juts some 6 miles (10km) into the Atlantic Ocean and is accessible by a causeway from Newburyport. Plum Island is also the site of the **Parker River National Wildlife Refuge** (admission fee), a superb birdwatching area where more than 300 species have been sighted.

The refuge covers 5,000 acres (2,023 hectares) of dunes, wide sandy beaches, bogs, freshwater pools and tidal marshes. There are nature trails, observation towers, boardwalks and camera hides for wildlife photographers.

The beach is closed from April to July or August to protect the endangered Piping plover which nests and raises fledglings at this time of year, but the remainder of the refuge is available to visitors year-round.

Rabbits, deer, woodchucks, turtles and toads roam freely, and there is something to see throughout the year. Birdwatchers can log migrating Canada geese and snow geese in November and December and snowy owls in January. Cranberries and the wild beach plums that give the island its name may be picked by visitors during September and October.

Fishing, cycling and hiking are encouraged, but the number of visitors allowed in the refuge at any one time is limited. Off-season is the best time to visit. Plum Island and the refuge are clearly signposted from Newburyport.

The **Ipswich River Wildlife Sanctuary** at Topsfield also offers a huge treat for nature lovers: 2,000 acres (810 hectares) of remote, wild countryside just off Route 97 east of Ipswich. The sanctuary is the largest property administered by the Massachusetts Audubon Society and there are meadows, swamps, waterfowl ponds, drumlins and kettle holes. There is an observation tower as well as bird-viewing facilities, and at the right times of the year visitors can take guided river trips, watch maple sugaring, rent canoes and cabins, and camp on Perkins Island. There are many nature activities for children. Adults are charged a trail fee.

ambience of a prosperous shipbuilding town has been retrieved through dedicated restoration.

Graceful black iron street lamps, trees and potted plants enhance streets of handsome red brick buildings in the downtown Market Square area of Newburyport, and the city has historic houses in a wide range of styles. The **High Street** contains a row of houses built by sea captains and ranging from Georgian to Federal and Greek Revival to Victorian.

Cushing House (admission fee), at 98 High Street, is a 21-room Federal brick mansion built in 1808 for Captain John Cushing, whose son Caleb became the first US ambassador to China. The beautifully furnished rooms feature a collection of silver, china, glass, clocks, toys and needlework, as well as furniture. There is a carriage house and a French garden which has plants more than a hundred years old. The house, open from April to October, is administered by the Historical Society of Old Newbury.

The **Custom House Maritime Museum**, 25 Water Street, is a Greek Revival structure built in granite in 1835. Its small rooms have brick floors, marble window sills and vaulted ceilings. There are displays of model ships, navigational instruments and other maritime artefacts, as well as antiques and oil paintings. Chests of Ceylon tea and barrels of rum are on show in the office of the Collector of Customs. There is a charge for visiting the museum.

Maudslay State Park on Curzon's Mill Road, on the outskirts of Newburyport, was once the private estate of a wealthy family. The homes of the past are gone, but there are still carriage roads, trails and an avenue of red oaks in its beautifully landscaped grounds. There is a wonderful view of the Merrimack River from a clearing in the woods. The park is in use year-round: performing arts, exhibitions and a children's outdoor theatre in the summer, hay rides in the Fall and cross-country skiing in the winter.

Salisbury

North of the Merrimack Estuary, **Salisbury** was settled in 1638 and is also rich in old world charm, but its major attractions in the summertime are its 5-mile- (8km-) long, white sandy beach and extensive seaside amusement area.

Amesbury, just east of Salisbury, is a sleepy little village missed by many tourists, which is a pity because the place is well worth a visit. One of the most popular American poets of the 19th century, the abolitionist John Greenleaf Whittier, spent 56 of his 85 years at Amesbury, living at 86 Friend Street from 1836 until his death in 1892. Here he wrote his abolitionist articles and poems, including *Snow-Bound* which brought him royalties of $10,000. The Garden Room, in which he wrote, remains as it was during his lifetime. The house is open to the public and there is an admission fee.

Anyone interested in matters maritime – and it's difficult not to be in coastal New England – will want to visit **Lowell's Boat Shop** at 459 Main Street, Amesbury. Telephone first (508 388-0162) because this is very much a working shop, as it has been since as long ago as 1793. Seven generations of Lowells worked here up to 1976. The shop is now a National Historic Landmark.

Until 1793 few boats could cope with the 3 knots (5.5km/h) current at the mouth of the Merrimack River. Simeon Lowell designed a craft that would ride the heavy surf without capsizing. The Amesbury

Coastal Massachusetts has many fine beaches, some within easy reach of Boston.

dory, built of white oak, mahogany and pine, was an instant success. Thousands were carried on board the Grand Banks schooners and 19th-century pleasure yachts. They were used by the US Coast Guard and by the American forces in World War II.

The dories are still in demand today, still made by hand just as they were 200 years ago. The old wooden workshop hasn't changed much either – except that the paint spilt on the floor has become even thicker.

The South Shore

Most people heading south from Boston take I-95 or Route 24, and so miss the considerable attractions of the Massachusetts South Shore. The best highway to take is Route 3A, which hugs the coast until well south of Plymouth, and gives access to some of the state's most historic places. Although it is less prosperous and certainly less popular than the North Shore, it has its fair share of New England charm, with distinctive communities of saltbox and shingled houses set out along a shoreline which is mainly of sandy beaches broken up by salt marshes.

Quincy

Right on the outskirts of Greater Boston and close enough to the metropolis to be ignored by most travellers, Quincy got off to a riotous start when it was first settled in 1624. It was first named Wollaston, after a Captain Thomas Wollaston, but within a year a settler with a more frivolous attitude than the Puritans cared for took over and changed the settlement's name to Merrymount. Merry it certainly was, if the accounts of the Pilgrims are to be believed.

The drop-out settler, Thomas Morton, and his followers made liquor and guns available to the Indians and had a high old time 'dancing and frisking' and taking Indian women as consorts. The Pilgrims had Morton arrested and sent back to England. He was soon back, only to be arrested and sent back again for good.

Today, Quincy makes more of the fact that it was the birthplace of two American presidents, John Adams and John Quincy Adams, and the area has a number of sites connected with both the Adams and Quincy families.

The **Adams National Historic Site**, at 135 Adams Street, was a modest house with only seven rooms when John and Abigail Adams moved in to it in 1787, but as the family fame and fortune increased it expanded to 20. Both presidents used the house while in office, and among the grand guests who visited it were President Monroe in 1817 and Lafayette in 1824. There is a wealth of paintings and furniture – including the wing chair in which John Adams died – and the garden contains the splendid Stone Library, built in 1870.

A combination ticket can be bought giving access to the National Historic Site and the **Adams Birthplaces** in nearby Franklin Street. The John Quincy Adams birthplace (No. 133) was completed in 1663, and the John Adams House (No. 141) in 1681.

Quincy can be reached from Boston on the T's Red Line.

Hingham

Settled in 1635, Hingham has a number of historic buildings, many of them lining Main Street, which Eleanor Roosevelt described as the most beautiful in America. Its best-known structures, both open to the public, are the Old Ship Church, on Lower Main Street, and the Old Ordinary, at 21 Lincoln Street.

The **Old Ship Church** is the oldest church in continuous use in the US. It was built in 1681, with side galleries added in 1730 and 1755, and its name probably comes from the fact that its timber roof structure is similar to a ship's hull. The **Old Ordinary** (admission fee) is a 17th-century tavern which now houses a museum administered by the Hingham Historical Society. The old taproom is exactly as it would have been in the days when the tavern served an 'ordinary meal of the day', with copper tankards, wooden kegs and a simple bar. Thirteen other rooms display an extensive collection of period furniture, paintings, porcelain, glass and locally made artefacts.

A statue of Abraham Lincoln, which is set in a small park opposite the Old Ordinary, is a reminder that ancestors of the 16th president were among Hingham's earliest settlers.

Hull

Set at the end of a spit of land that juts and bends out into Boston Harbor, Hull was a rather upmarket resort at the beginning of this century, with grand hotels and an amusement park to complement the considerable amenity of the white-sand Nantasket Beach, one of the largest on the South Shore. After a period of deterioration, Hull has once more become a lively, respectable place with a resident arts colony. The beach is the main reason for visiting Hull, but the town does have a couple of historic attractions.

The **Lifesaving Museum** (admission fee), set in the nation's first official lifesaving station at 1117 Nantasket Avenue, honours the valiant men who rowed through the surf to rescue shipwrecked mariners. A special tribute is paid to Captain Joshua James, who was the first to command the station when it opened in 1889. Captain James dedicated his life to sea rescues when his mother and baby sister were drowned at sea, and he became the most decorated lifesaver in the US, rescuing some 540 people from 86 wrecks. Among the memorabilia and dramatic photographs are a breeches buoy and a 19th-century surfboat.

Telegraph Hill, behind the museum, is the highest point on the South Shore, with a great view of Boston Harbor, the islands and the ocean beyond. **Fort Revere**, at the top of the hill, has been an outpost of defence for Boston since the 1600s and is rich in history. During the Revolutionary War it was fired on by the British.

Cohasset

One of the best-known coastal drives in New England winds along the rocky coast, passing secluded beaches, from Route 228 in Hull to Cohasset where it becomes Jerusalem Road, noted for its beautiful homes with glorious ocean views. Among the earliest European visitors to Cohasset was Captain John Smith, who landed here in 1614 while surveying the coast. During the 18th and 19th centuries the town prospered from fishing and shipbuilding and is now a charming New England village whose secluded but picturesque harbour is complemented by a town green complete with duck pond and white steepled church. Across the green is the granite church of St Stephen's, famed for its carillon concerts which have been performed since 1924. The carillon has 57 bells cast in England and is the largest in New England.

In the early 19th century the waters off Cohasset were notoriously treacherous and there were many shipwrecks. One of the worst occurred in November 1849 when the *St John*, carrying Irish immigrants to Boston, foundered and sank with massive loss of life on Grampus Ledge, a mile and a half (2.5km) offshore. The tragedy happened while the original Minot's Light was under construction. Two years later – and one year after the light was finished – the iron tower and its two keepers were swept away in a storm. It was replaced by the present lighthouse, a granite tower with a height of 114ft (35m), built two and a half miles (4km) offshore and completed in 1860.

THE ARMY OF TWO

In the village of Scituate, just south of Cohasset on Route 3A, they tell the legend of 'The Army of Two', dating from the War of 1812. According to the story, the teenage daughters of the lighthouse keeper spotted two barges laden with British troops about to land in the harbour. Grabbing a fife and drum, the girls hid behind some trees and played hard and loud. Believing themselves to be outnumbered by an American force, the British turned tail and sailed away.

Scituate today is a busy little port with an active fishing fleet and plenty to interest visitors among the quaint shops, galleries and restaurants along Front Street.

Marshfield

Route 3A continues prettily across tidal marshes and crosses the North River on its way to Marshfield. Now a picture of rural tranquillity, the river once throbbed with activity from shipbuilding yards on both its banks. More than a thousand vessels were constructed along the river, including the Boston Tea Party brig *Beaver*. Those wishing to explore the river can rent a boat or canoe at Marshfield.

Settled in 1632, Marshfield stands on the site of marshes which were drained in the 19th century for the cultivation of cranberries and strawberries. The town's chief attraction is the **Winslow House,** originally built in 1699 for Judge Isaac Winslow, grandson of Edward Winslow, Pilgrim governor of Plymouth Colony. It

Cape Cod attracts all kinds of travellers – a man and his Harley-Davidson contemplate Horseneck Beach.

was rebuilt in 1750 and has now been restored and furnished with Pilgrim and Georgian items. There is a Jacobean staircase, and Georgian panelling in the drawing room conceals a secret chamber in which runaway Tories are supposed to have hidden. The law office of the great orator and statesman Daniel Webster (1782-1852) has been reconstructed in the grounds. Webster spent the last 20 years of his life in Marshfield. The grounds also contain a blacksmith's shop and a one-room schoolhouse. Winslow House is on the corner of Careswell and Webster Streets and there is an admission fee.

Duxbury

Founded around 1627 as an overspill from nearby Plymouth, Duxbury included among its earliest settlers such illustrious names as John Alden, Miles Standish and Elder Brewster.

The **John Alden House**, at 105 Alden Street, was built in 1653 and was the home of John and Priscilla Alden, married after Alden successfully wooed Priscilla away from Miles Standish – the story is told in Longfellow's poem, *The Courtship of Miles Standish*. The modest house (admission fee) is dark and severe, its ceilings plastered with a mixture of crushed oyster and clam shells. In contrast, **King Caesar House** (admission fee), King Caesar Road, is filled with light and luxury. The Federal-style mansion was built in 1809 by the millionaire shipbuilder and merchant, Ezra Weston II, whose power and wealth earned him the nickname 'King Caesar'. There are period furnishings, oriental treasures and local history exhibits.

Duxbury's **Arts Complex Museum** is a contemporary building housing two galleries. The museum features travelling collections of works by well-known artists, and among its permanent collection are Asian art, and Shaker and American works. The grounds contain a Japanese teahouse from Kyoto, and traditional Japanese tea ceremonies are demonstrated on occasion.

Duxbury Beach, clean, well maintained and more than 5 miles (8km) long, is reached by passing over Powder Point Bridge, the longest wooden bridge on the eastern seaboard at 2,200ft (670m). Alcohol is forbidden on the beach, but barbecues are allowed (permits from the bath house). There are lifeguards, showers, restrooms, refreshments, a restaurant and parking for 1,400 cars.

Plymouth

Plymouth calls itself 'America's Home Town', and in many ways it certainly epitomizes Small Town, USA, with a jumble of motels, filling stations, fast food outlets, bumpy road surfaces, and the best and worst of architectural styles. Its waterfront is by no means the most attractive in New England, and on a dull, chilly day it isn't difficult to imagine how the Pilgrims felt when they landed here in the winter of 1620. That, of course, is what Plymouth is really all about, and in spite of the odd outbreak of 20th-century tackiness it does its job extremely well, drawing in more than a million visitors each year.

None of it was here, of course, when the *Mayflower* dropped anchor in the harbour and 102 settlers scrambled ashore on Plymouth Rock on 21 December 1620. They hadn't really meant to land here. Their intention when they left England more than

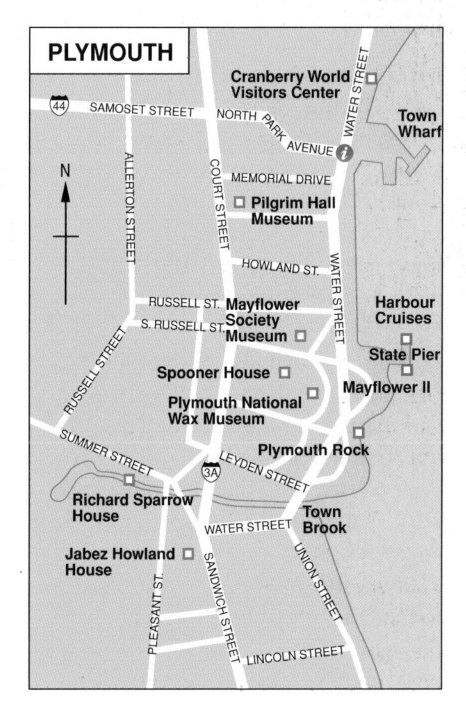

3 months earlier had been to establish a settlement much further south. Blown off course, the *Mayflower* sailed first into Cape Cod Bay, and a small party went ashore at what is now Provincetown.

The Pilgrims decided to seek a more hospitable location, and after explorations along the coast found Plymouth, an ideal spot with a good harbour, strategically high ground, and fresh water. Unfortunately, it was the wrong time of year for pioneer work, and the settlers were ill-prepared. They had poor provisions, no cattle or horses, and no equipment suitable for tilling the rough ground.

Undaunted, they set to work on Christmas Day building a shelter to house the entire group, using the *Mayflower* as a home as construction progressed. Conditions on the ship were cramped, and after weeks at sea many suffered from scurvy and other diseases. Every day someone died. Before their first American winter ended, the Pilgrims' number had been halved through deaths from pneumonia and influenza. Salvation came as a result of help from the friendly Wampanoag Indians, who showed the white people how to live off the land.

Plymouth today is a compact town and many of its attractions can be reached on foot. The **Pilgrim Path**, a leisurely self-guided walking tour, is marked by Pilgrim hats painted on the sidewalks. There are also narrated trolley tours. Maps and brochures may be obtained from the Visitor Information Center in North Park Avenue, and there are other centres near Plymouth Rock and at Exit 5 on Route 3.

Plymouth Rock, on the beach at Water Street, is enshrined beneath an imposing canopy supported by 16 classical columns. For a time, historians doubted that this was the actual place where the Pilgrims first set foot, but current scholarly thinking supports the popular belief. The bodies of those who failed to survive that first winter were buried on Coles Hill, opposite the rock. The burials took place at night and the unmarked graves were planted with corn so that the Indians would not know how many had died. Exhumed remains are now entombed in a sarcophagus on the hill. There are more 17th-century graves, including that of Governor Bradford, at Burial Hill, School Street. This was the site of the Pilgrims' first meeting house and fort. At the top of Coles Hill, at 16 Carver Street, the **Plymouth National Wax Museum** (admission fee) portrays the Pilgrim saga from the early days in England to the landing in the New World.

Moored at State Pier, just along the waterfront from Plymouth Rock, ***Mayflower II*** is a full-size replica of the vessel that brought the Pilgrims to Massachusetts. Accurate in every detail, the 104ft- (32m-) long ship is manned by costumed interpreters who portray some of the people who actually made that first voyage. *Mayflower II* was built in England and set sail for America on 20 April 1957. The voyage lasted 54 days, compared with 66 days for the original crossing between Plymouth, Devon, and the Cape Cod landfall.

Plymouth's oldest surviving house is the **Richard Sparrow House**, built in 1640 and one of three that are open to the public after being restored and furnished in Pilgrim style. The **Sparrow House**, at 42 Summer Street, is occupied by the Plymouth Pottery Guild which features crafts and 17th-century pottery designs, and provides demonstrations of pottery-making. The **Jabez Howland House**, at 33 Sandwich Street, dates from 1667 and is the only surviving property in which a Mayflower Pilgrim actually lived. The **1677 Harlow Old Fort House**, 119 Sandwich Street, is believed to have been built with timbers salvaged from the original Plymouth fort. Costumed guides demonstrate traditional crafts such as weaving, spinning, dyeing and candle-dipping. There is an admission fee charged at both properties.

The **Mayflower Society Museum** (admission fee) is in a 1754 house which also serves as headquarters of the General Society of Mayflower Descendants. Its nine rooms feature furnishings from the 17th to 19th centuries. The museum is at 4 Winslow Street. The **Pilgrim Hall Museum**, 75 Court Street, was opened in 1824 and is the oldest public museum in the US. It also has the distinction of housing the nation's most complete collection of Pilgrim possessions, which includes chairs, chests, clothes and household items. Here, you can take a look at Miles Standish's sword, Governor Bradford's Bible and the cradle in which Peregrine White slept, who was born during the *Mayflower* crossing.

There are other things to see and do in the Plymouth area besides trudging around museums and looking at historic sites and monuments. Just north of Town Wharf, on Water Street, **Cranberry World Visitor Center** tells the story of the fruit that is to turkey what stars are to stripes. There is an outdoor working cranberry bog, demonstrations of harvesting and displays of wetlands flora and fauna. Visitors learn about the many uses the Indians had for cranberries before the settlers arrived, including making dye and treating wounds, and how the Pilgrim women soon caught on to the berry's culinary potential.

A new attraction in Plymouth is the **Children's Museum** on Main Street. It is open daily (admission fee), and holds regular toddler playgroups, as well as offering activities for older children of all ages.

Town Wharf is where the Plymouth fishing fleet lands its catches, but if you want to catch your own there are deep-sea fishing cruises that leave from here and from Manomet, 3 miles (5km) south of the town. Alternatively you could try your luck from the docks, jetties or the beach. If you would prefer to take a look at some of the largest sea creatures, whale-watching cruises leave daily during the summer from Town Wharf and State Pier.

Conservation and recreation come together on **Plymouth Beach**, which serves as a stopover and nesting area for migratory birds, especially terns and sandpipers. The birds are protected in fenced areas, but they may be observed nonetheless. Three miles (5km) south of the town, the beach has restrooms and lifeguards. There is a parking fee during the summer months. Other public beaches are the Nelson Street Beach, near Cranberry World, Stephen's Field, a mile (1.6km) south of town off Route 3A, and White Horse Beach, Manomet.

If you want to get away from it all for a while, try **Miles Standish State Forest**, about 8 miles (13km) south west of Plymouth (Exit 5 on Route 3, then follow Long Pond Road). The park is popular, but you are unlikely to feel overcrowded with some 15,000 acres (6,250 hectares) to roam around in. The park has 15 ponds, two beaches, paths for motorcyclists, cyclists, horseriders and hikers, and there are campsites (467 pitches) with restrooms, hot showers, fireplaces and picnic tables. Camping is on a first-come, first-served basis for a nightly fee.

To Be a Pilgrim...

Before you get 'all pilgrim'd out' in Plymouth, take a trip two-and-a-half miles (4km) out of town – and some 370 years back in time. It would be easy to dismiss **Plimoth Plantation** as just another living history museum, but the 17th-century village is so real, its inhabitants so convincing, that many visitors really feel they have stepped into a time warp.

A non-profit-making organization, Plimoth Plantation is a peculiar experience. At first it seems like any of the historic theme parks now found all over the world: lots of parking for cars and tour buses, a visitor centre, dining facilities and restrooms. Then you pass a sign reading 'You are now entering the 17th century' – and by jingo, you do!

The plantation's centrepiece is the **Pilgrim Village**, which is an authentic re-creation of the Plymouth Colony in 1627, with a palisaded blockhouse, thatched houses lining an unpaved lane, gardens, pigs, poultry, cattle, and above all, people. Real people wearing rough, homespun clothes and going about their ordinary, everyday 17th-century tasks.

In one house, working on a rough table, a middle-aged housewife prepares dough to be baked into bread in the colony's communal oven. Further down the street, Goodman Kempton, stocky and bearded, mends his fence and cheerily asks a Danish tourist if he will be making his home in the colony.

Costumed interpreters play their parts with total dedication at Plimoth Plantation.

Visitors to Plimoth Plantation can see for themselves what life was like in the 17th-century Wampanoag Indian homestead.

Governor William Bradford, in cape and tall hat, strolls between the houses, politely – even deferentially – answering visitors' questions.

The line of illusion is never crossed by the museum staff – the 'Interpreters' – who play these figures from the past with total dedication. They are completely immersed in the 17th century and can discuss anything from how long it takes to correspond with friends and relatives back in England to the problems of bringing up children in an alien land. They work, they play games, they tell stories. And they are probably as familiar with the backgrounds of their assumed personalities as they are with their real 20th-century lives. Between them, the Interpreters speak in 17 dialects from the countryside of Jacobean England.

In addition to the Pilgrim Village, Plimoth Plantation contains a re-created Wampanoag Indian homesite of the same period, a wild riverside nature reserve, and a crafts centre where artisans weave cloth, create pottery and basketware, and demonstrate joinery and the crafting of fine furniture in 17th-century style. Reproduction artefacts are sold in the centre.

The plantation runs a programme of lectures and workshops focusing on 17th-century experiences and presents a series of day-long workshops on 17th-century cooking. The visitor centre houses two orientation theatres and an exhibition gallery.

Plimoth Plantation is well sign-posted and is reached from Exit 4 on Route 3, south of Plymouth – about an hour's drive from Boston. A general admission fee covers entrance to the plantation and to *Mayflower II*, moored on State Wharf in downtown Plymouth, where visitors can experience the same kind of time warp in conversations with Ship's Master Christopher Jones and members of the crew – all a bit fed up with the New World and eagerly looking forward to their return to England.

New Bedford

Herman Melville would not feel out of place today in New Bedford's beautifully restored historic district near the waterfront. The 'patrician-like houses' and 'flowery gardens' he described in *Moby Dick* are still there, and the delightful waterfront still bustles, for the city is the most active fishing port in the US. The whaling ships that Melville knew have long gone, but the industry in which it once led the world is commemorated and brought to life in the **New Bedford Whaling Museum**, founded in 1902 and now America's largest museum devoted to whaling.

The museum has a large collection of figureheads, ships' logbooks, scrimshaw, harpoons and other whaling tools. The story of life aboard whaling vessels is dramatically illustrated in a number of paintings, including a huge panoramic mural created in 1848, and a film of a whaling chase is shown daily. Also displayed is a roster from the vessel *Acushnet*, listing

Melville as a crew member. Pride of place goes to the *Lagoda*, a half-scale model of a fully rigged whaling ship, 89ft (27.1m) in length. The New Bedford Whaling Museum is at 18 Johnny Cake Hill, and there is an admission charge.

Across the street from the museum is the **Seamen's Bethel,** the 1832 chapel in which the Reverend Mapple in *Moby Dick* delivered a blistering sermon from the prow-shaped pulpit. Whaling men, including Melville, would visit the church before setting off on a voyage and many of them did not return, as memorial tablets on the walls testify.

Another maritime attraction is the 1894 schooner *Ernestine*, built in Essex, Connecticut. She spent 25 years fishing the Grand Banks, carried explorers into the Arctic and finally ended her working life after shipping immigrants from the Cape Verde Islands.

New Bedford's grandest thoroughfare – there has been extensive and tasteful restoration throughout the city's historic district – is County Street, on a ridge overlooking the Acushnet River. This is where wealthy 19th-century sea captains built their homes, and some Federal-style and Victorian mansions still remain. At No. 396 the **Rotch-Jones-Duff House and Garden Museum** (admission fee) was originally the home of a whaling merchant, and the Greek Revival house was designed by Richard Upjohn and built in 1834. Rooms display opulent furnishings from the mid-19th to the 20th centuries and the picturesque grounds include a wildflower walk, a dogwood allée and a rose garden. There are summer concerts in the grounds.

Another grand home, the 1821 **Benjamin Rodman Mansion**, stands at 50 North Second Street. Nearby, at 47 North Second Street, is the city **Visitor Center**, where you can obtain brochures of walking tours prepared by the New Bedford Preservation Society.

Just opposite New Bedford, across the mouth of the Acushnet River, is the old

The famous prow-shaped pulpit in the Seamen's Bethel, New Bedford.

The World War II battleship USS Massachusetts *is the centrepiece of Battleship Cove, the floating naval museum at Fall River.*

shipbuilding town of Fairhaven, which flourished during the heyday of the whaling industry. Many old houses and buildings used by 19th-century chandlers, shipwrights and merchants are to be found in the streets on Poverty Point from where the eccentric Captain Joshua Slocum began his historic solo circumnavigation of the world in 1895.

Fall River

Down in the southern corner of coastal Massachusetts, right on the Rhode Island state line, Fall River was a major textile centre from about 1870 to the 1920s, when it fell victim to spirited competition from the South. The town has seen better days – although some of the derelict mills and warehouses are now occupied by high-tech electronics and metals industries, while others have been given over to the factory retail outlets for which the city has become well known. Most of the outlets are on Quequechan and Quarry Streets (follow the signs marked with a heart after leaving Route 24 at Exit 2, Brayton Avenue). The heavily discounted goods – many with internationally known names – include clothing, leather goods, jewellery, craftware, cosmetics and books.

Fall River's other attraction is **Battleship Cove**, on the Taunton River, where a number of wartime naval vessels serve as a floating museum (admission fee). The

battleship *USS Massachusetts* is the official memorial to the state's 13,000 servicemen and women who fell in World War II. The huge vessel – she had a crew of 2,300 – was commissioned in 1939 and served as flagship for the invasion of North Africa in 1942 before moving on to two years of action in the Pacific. Other World War II ships open to the public are the submarine *USS Lionfish*, launched in 1943, and two high-speed PT craft used for launching torpedoes. The destroyer *USS Joseph P. Kennedy, Jr*, was launched

in 1945 and served in Korean waters and in the blockade of Cuba. The Fall River carousel, crafted in the 1920s for a local funfair, was restored to its original glory and moved to a purpose-built site at Battleship Cove in 1992. It makes this a particularly attractive place for children.

Ashore, at 70 Water Street, the **Marine Museum** (admission fee) features the days of sail and steam – especially passenger services between New England ports and New York City – in an exhibition which includes a collection of more than 150 model ships, including a 28ft (8.5m) long model of the *Titanic* used in the 1952 Twentieth Century Fox film.

The **Fall River Heritage State Park**, next to Battleship Cove at 200 Davol Street West, is an attractive waterfront park with a new building modelled on the city's old mills. Displays include historical photographs, and a 20-minute audio-visual presentation tells the story of the textile industry and the conditions under which its workers toiled. There is no charge for admission.

Thar She Blows!

In the early 19th century, New England's whaling ships brought a new light to the world – and a new shape to the female form! Up to that time, homes in America and elsewhere were mainly lit by candles made from tallow, which is a by-product of animal or vegetable fats. The candles provided a dim, smoky light, and the lamps devised to hold them needed constant cleaning to prevent a rapid build-up of soot and wax.

Then someone discovered that the oil extracted from whale fat – blubber – produced a purer, cleaner light. Blubber was first taken from beached whales, then frequently found all along the coast. Whenever a beached whale was sighted, whole communities would turn out to cut off the blubber and render it down on the beach in tryworks – iron cauldrons heated over driftwood fires.

The whaling industry that soon dominated New England ports was born when fishermen realized there were big profits to be made by hunting down the whales at sea. The world's first factory ships were built, primitively equipped with their own on-board tryworks and a nest of dories. Dories were specially designed oar-powered small boats – fast, seaworthy and made to be slotted one into another for easy stacking on deck. Eventually, larger craft were used for the hunt – sleek, strong double-bowed rowboats that also carried a sail. To this day boats of this particular design are known throughout the world as 'whalers'.

A whaling ship would spend months, sometimes years, roaming the seas to fill its hold with casks of oil refined on its own decks. The lookout would perch in the crow's nest high in the mainmast,

Whalers at work: mural in the New Bedford Whaling Museum.

The Lagoda, *a half-scale whaling ship, is a feature of the New Bedford Whaling Museum.*

scanning the horizon for the sudden plume of spray that would announce the presence of a surfacing whale. The whole crew would spring to their stations as he sang out, 'Thar she blows!'

The whaler would be put over the side, the men would bend to their oars, and the harpoonist would be poised in the bow, ready to strike. As the harpoon bit, the whaler, now tethered to the whale, would skim across the waves on a 'Nantucket sleighride', sometimes for miles, the oarsmen praying that the terrified beast would not make a sudden dive into the ocean depths.

Different types of whale provided oil of different qualities. The best came from the sperm whale, which also produced ambergris, a wax-like substance used in the manufacture of perfume. The right whale – now the most endangered of all the world's great whales – was sought because it provided good supplies of quality oil and whalebone.

The figures of Victorian ladies were kept in their wasp-waisted shapes by corsets with stays made from baleen, the light and springy whalebone. Ivory-like whalebone was also used decoratively – as inlays on furniture and objets d'art, for example – and functionally, as knife handles, crochet hooks, knitting needles and the like. It was also used as the medium for a craft invented by whaling seamen. Scrimshaw, the carving or whittling of a design on whalebone, saved the sanity of many a sailor whiling away the hours on a long, long sea voyage. Scrimshaw was carved by all ranks, from ship's master down to cabin boy, and designs ranged from clumsy outlines of the ship, with the carver's name and the date, to the sophisticated embellishment of hairbrushes, combs, jewellery boxes and ornaments that sometimes amounted to works of art in themselves.

Scrimshaw, which may have gained its name from one of its early practitioners, is a fascinating subject, providing a unique aspect on 19th-century life. It is keenly sought by collectors, some of whom concentrate on individual carvers, some on the work produced on particular vessels, and others on certain types of design or artefact. Scrimshaw can be bought in antique shops all along the New England Coast, and there are exhibitions in many maritime museums. There is a particularly fine collection of 800 pieces in the Stillman Building at the Mystic Seaport in Connecticut.

Humpback whales are the species most commonly sighted along the New England coast.

The use of gas and electricity for lighting, the development of petroleum by-products, plastics, and probably changes in the way women shaped themselves, all contributed to the decline of whaling. But the whales themselves play an important role in one of New England's newest industries – tourism. Whale-watching cruises depart from ports all along the coast, even from the heart of Boston itself.

Most of the whale-watching vessels head for Stellwagen Bank, a shallow underwater deposit of sand and gravel in Massachusetts Bay, where huge quantities of plankton – tiny plants, algae, small crustaceans and fish larvae on which several marine animals feed – attract many whales of different species.

Provincetown, on the furthermost tip of Cape Cod, is the closest port to Stellwagen Bank, and whales are frequently encountered within minutes of a cruise vessel's departure. The species most often seen are humpback and fin whales, but the rare right whale is sometimes spotted, too. Scientists from the non-profit-making Center for Coastal Studies at Provincetown, who accompany each Dolphin Fleet departure, have been able to identify individual whales who frequent the area. The scientists provide whale-watchers with an informative and authoritative commentary while gathering new data themselves.

A few whale-watching hints. Take warm clothing, even if you don't need it ashore – better to shed layers than freeze. Wear rubber-soled shoes. Take sunglasses and a sunscreen lotion. Don't forget the camera and binoculars. The best-designed vessels have a long 'pulpit' overhanging the bows which gives the best viewpoint. It is also the place where the vessel's pitching is most evident, especially when conditions are a bit choppy, so you'll need good sea legs.

Cape Cod

Because of the Cape Cod Canal, the cape has actually been an island since 1914, and it would have been one earlier if 17th-century technology had been up to the job. Miles Standish, the Pilgrims' trouble-shooter, came up with the idea of a canal in 1624.

Cape Cod was, of course, the first piece of America on which the Pilgrims set foot in 1620, but it was seven years before the cape's first settlers arrived to set up the Aptucxet Trading Post, at present-day Bourne. The original Cape dwellers, however, were the Wampanoag Indians who had already been fishing and farming on the Cape for about 3,500 years by the time the *Mayflower* landed.

'The bared and bended arm of Massachusetts,' as Henry David Thoreau described it, Cape Cod was named in 1602 by the explorer Bartholomew Gosnold, who had seen vast shoals of cod in the region. In the 17th century dense hardwood forests covered the interior, but these were soon stripped by the Europeans. By the time Thoreau arrived in the mid-19th century, the cape had little more than a thin covering of stunted brushwood. Reafforestation projects since then have enabled scrub pines to flourish.

The Pilgrims were soon trading with the Dutch in New Amsterdam (now New York City) and their trading post was

Boating is a way of life in Cape Cod.

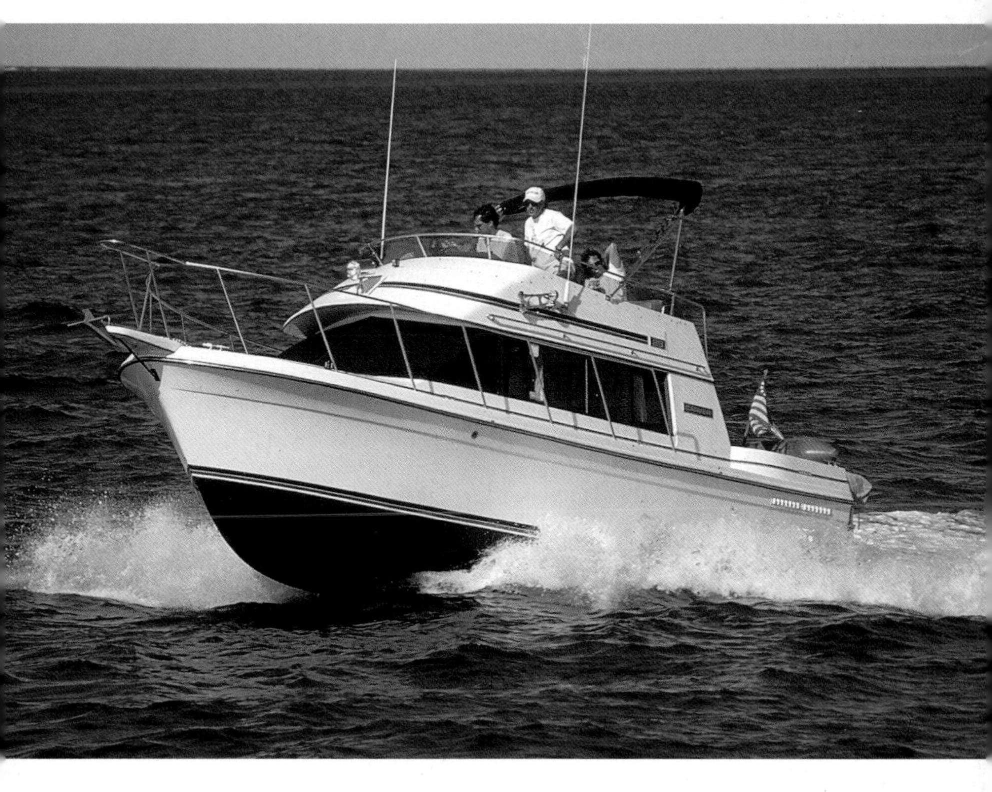

located between the Scusset Creek, which flowed north east into Cape Cod Bay, and the Manomet River, which flowed into Buzzards Bay in the opposite direction. Cargoes were taken by boat, then portaged over the 3 miles (4.8km) of land separating the two streams. Miles Standish's canal, had it been built, would have saved the settlers a lot of hard work – and for those using larger vessels a 100-mile (160km) voyage in hazardous waters around the cape.

The Canal

George Washington took up the idea of a waterway during the Revolution, and actually got as far as having a survey carried out and plans drawn up. But the Cape Cod Canal, 17 miles (27.3km) long and 500ft (152m) wide – the widest sea-level waterway in the world – was not completed until 1914. It is crossed by two graceful bridges, the Sagamore and the Bourne, both completed in 1935, and is used by 20,000 vessels a year. The canal is maintained by the US Army Corps of Engineers, and its story is told in a visitor centre on Academy Drive, Buzzards Bay, on the mainland.

Trips along the canal itself are offered by Cape Cod Canal Cruises (Tel. 508 295-3883). The cruises start from Onset Town Pier, last two to three hours, and take place daily from late spring through to autumn (weekends only during early spring). Onset is just off Route 6 on the mainland, between Buzzards Bay and Wareham.

Cape Cod is 70 miles (112km) from end to end and has 15 towns strung along three major highways. Route 6 traverses the entire cape, taking a middle course from Bourne Bridge to Provincetown, missing all the built-up areas. Route 6A, known as the Old King's Highway, was laid out in 1684, following Indian paths and wagon trails. It winds in leisurely style along the north coast from Sandwich to Orleans. Route 28 is the busiest highway, especially in high summer, looping along the south shore from Bourne to Chatham, then up to Orleans.

Immensely popular with tourists, the cape is at its busiest in June, July and August when the weather is at its best and prices at their highest. At this time no one will be wondering how to spend the day. There are golf courses, tennis courts, plays and concerts; there is swimming, fishing, sunbathing, boating and whale-watching. There are shopping malls, factory outlets and fast food restaurants. Nature-lovers and all who like the quiet life will prefer the spring and autumn, the best seasons for bird-watching, hiking and leisurely country drives. During the winter much of the Cape's tourism industry shuts down, but some inns and B & B places stay open, providing an opportunity for bargain winter breaks.

Sandwich

The first community to be reached along the Old King's Highway after crossing the Sagamore Bridge was originally settled in 1627 by some of the Pilgrims who arrived to establish the Aptucxet Trading Post. During its first 200 years, the village earned a living from farming and inshore whaling. In 1825 the Boston and Sandwich Glass Company opened a factory and began producing wares that were to become collectors' items. Deming Jarves, the company's founder, had chosen Sandwich because of its abundant water, and because its rural situation would present no fleshpot temptations to his employees. The factory closed in 1888 after an acrimonious labour dispute, but many of its wares are on show in the **Sandwich Glass Museum**

Onset Marina on Buzzards Bay. Cruises along the Cape Cod Canal are available from Onset town pier.

(admission fee) at 129 Main Street.

Surrounding the 1834 Greek Revival town hall, the **Town Hall Historic District** includes 47 houses dating from the late 17th to the 19th centuries, among them the **Hoxie House** (admission fee), on Water Street, believed to have been built in 1637 and possibly the oldest house on the cape. The saltbox building, one of a number overlooking the Shawme Pond, has authentic 17th-century furnishings. Nearby is the **Dexter Grist Mill** (admission fee), which was in use for more than two centuries from the 1650s. Visitors can watch demonstrations of old milling techniques.

Also on Water Street is the **Thornton W. Burgess Museum**, the former cottage home of the man who wrote *Old Mother West Wind* and *Peter Cotton Tail*. Overlooking a picturesque duck pond, the museum (admission by donation) could well be in one of the children's book illustrations displayed in its rooms. There is a collection of the author's books and a gift shop, and the museum floor is painted with rabbit footprints.

Burgess's theme is continued at the **Green Briar Jam Kitchen** and **Old Briar Patch Conservation Area**, at 6 Discovery Hill Road, East Sandwich, where the Thornton W. Burgess Society operates an old-fashioned kitchen in woodland beside yet another pond. The society produces and sells jams, jellies, pickles and preserves made to recipes from the days of the author's boyhood. Visitors can work up an appetite on nature trails through the 57-acre (23-hectare) conservation area.

Sandwich Heritage Plantation (admission fee), at Grove and Pine Streets, has collections of antique cars and militaria and an art museum featuring a collection of antique weathervanes and the largest collection of Currier and Ives lithographs open to the public. The plantation is in 76 acres (30.7 hectares) of carefully tended grounds, with trails, picnic areas and a windmill.

Barnstable

The next community on Route 6A was founded in 1639. Its **West Parish Congregational Church**, on Route 149, is believed to be the oldest of its kind in America. Built in 1717, it has a bell cast by Paul Revere. Barnstable profited from whales which became stranded on Sandy Neck, an 8 mile- (13km-) long barrier beach stretching between Barnstaple and Sandwich. Later it prospered from a brisk maritime trade, and many ships' captains' houses survive. The former Custom House, built in 1855, now houses the **Donald G. Trayser Museum** (donations requested) in Main Street. Named after a local historian, the museum has a collection of local artefacts, Indian tools and ships in bottles. Barnstable also has a number of inns, restaurants, stores and antique shops.

Yarmouth Port

The cape's third oldest town, founded in 1639, has two historic homes. The **Winslow-Crocker House**, on Route 6A, was built around 1780 in West Barnstable and moved to its present location in 1935. Maintained by the Society for the Preservation of New England Antiquities, the house has mellow wood panelling and a fine collection of American furniture. The Greek Revival **Captain Bangs Hallett House**, 11 Strawberry Lane, also displays elegant furniture and a collection of antique toys. An admission fee is charged at each house.

CYCLING CAPE

Dennis, just east of Yarmouth on the Old King's Highway, is the start of the **Cape Cod Rail Trail**, a 14-mile (22.5km) tarred cycle path that follows a former railroad right of way to Eastham on the Upper Cape.

A flat easy ride, the trail passes through some attractive and varied terrain: woodland, farms, cranberry bogs, salt marshes and beaches. It starts at Route 134 in Dennis, and there are more than a dozen clearly marked access points along Routes 6 and 6A.

Other cycle trails are to be found in the 1,700-acre (687-hectare) **Nickerson State Park**, east of Brewster, and within the **Cape Cod National Seashore**, which stretches from Chatham to Provincetown.

Bicycle rental shops can be found in almost every town on Cape Cod.

Brewster

Brewster was never more than a packet landing stage with services to New York and Boston, but it had strong maritime connections between 1780 and 1870 when its most prominent residents were well-to-do clipper captains who sailed the Far East routes. Many of them had learned their seamanship on the local packet boats, and when they became successful they built the stately homes and public buildings that can be seen in Brewster today. At one time, it was said, the town had more captains and mates than any other community of its size.

A legend connected with the French Revolution surrounds the names of two of Brewster's most famous sea-going sons. According to the story, Captain David Nickerson, whose name has been given to the Nickerson State Park, just outside the town, was handed a baby boy when he was in Paris at the height of the Revolution. The boy, named René Rousseau, was smuggled to Brewster where local people were – and still are – convinced that he was the Dauphin, the child of Louis XVI and Marie Antoinette. Captain Nickerson and his adopted son, who also became a master mariner, were both lost at sea.

Although none of Brewster's mansions is open to the public, some of them have become inns and B & B establishments. The town has a wide range of accommodation from campgrounds to cottages and condominiums, and there is a variety of cafes and restaurants to suit most palates. The town has eight public beaches, all accessible from streets leading off Main Street. Fresh water beaches for swimming and boating are to be found in **Nickerson State Park**. **Punkhorn Parklands** has 45 miles (72km) of scenic trails through oak and pine forests, meadows, marshes and ridges overlooking kettle hole ponds.

On Main Street, **Stony Brook Mill**, built in 1873, was originally part of a small industrial complex. Grist milling demonstrations take place, and there is a small museum upstairs. The **New England Fire and History Museum** (admission fee), 1439 Main Street, has one of the country's largest collections of early American fire engines and lots of whistles and bells – literally. Rather quieter is the **Cape Cod Museum of Natural History** (admission fee), also on Main Street, where visitors can relax on nature trails, browse among exhibits, watch films, and keep an eye on bees in a working hive.

Bourne

Back at the western end of Cape Cod, Route 28 starts at Bourne, where the Plymouth Pilgrims set up their trading post in 1627. Re-created in the 1930s, the **Aptucxet Trading Post and Museum** (admission fee) calls itself 'the Birthplace of American Free Enterprise' and features a saltworks, grist mill and a railroad station built for holiday use by President Grover Cleveland.

Falmouth

Falmouth was founded in 1660 by a breakaway group who had become Quakers. The **Friends Meeting House** in the town was built in 1842 on the site of one built in 1755. Falmouth's village green, used as a military training ground in the 18th century, is elegantly surrounded by homes and inns from the 18th and 19th centuries. The **Congregational Church** here has a bell cast by Paul Revere and installed in 1797.

The Falmouth Historical Society maintains two museums facing the green (combined admission fee). The **Julia Wood House**, built in 1790, has wide-board floors, leaded-light windows and a colonial kitchen, and displays furniture, toys, baby clothing and embroidery. The 1794 **Conant House** features whaling artefacts, scrimshaw, silver, glass and chinaware.

About 1,000 holly trees, including varieties from America, the Far East and Europe, are to be found in the Massachusetts Audubon Society's **Ashumet Holly and Wildlife Sanctuary**, 45 acres (18.2 hectares) of woodland, ponds and meadows on Ashumet Road, off Route 151, 6 miles (9.6km) north of Falmouth. There are hiking trails in the sanctuary which is open daily (admission fee) from dawn to dusk.

Wood's Hole

This small town at the south west corner of the Cape is known as the departure point for ferries to Martha's Vineyard and is a world-famous centre for marine research. The Wood's Hole Oceanographic

Institution has an **exhibit center** (a donation is requested) showcasing the institution's many expeditions, including the successful discovery of the *Titanic* in 1985. The National Marine Fisheries Service maintains a small **aquarium** (no charge) exhibiting regional sea life, a rehabilitation centre for rescued seals, and hands-on displays for children.

Hyannis

This busy and commercial resort town is not quite as classy as its Kennedy connections might suggest. The Kennedy family actually lives in a strictly private compound at Hyannis Port, and curious visitors rarely catch a glimpse of them, in spite of the many sightseeing buses that hang around the area like bees round a honey pot. Those of you desperate for a Kennedy fix may gain satisfaction from the new **John F. Kennedy Hyannis Museum** at 397 Main Street (admission charged). The John F. Kennedy Memorial plaque and fountain is on Ocean Street, overlooking Lewis Bay.

Cranberry bogs are a distinctive feature for travellers in the Cape Cod area.

East of Hyannis, Route 28 degenerates into a rash of gas stations, motels and fast food joints, but sanity is restored at Harwich Port, where Main Street and its surrounding thoroughfares have been designated an historic district. The **Brooks Academy Museum**, on Sisson Road, is maintained by the Harwich Historical Society and located in a former school building dating from 1804. The museum features nautical displays and equipment used in the production of cranberries, a major local industry.

Chatham

Chatham is a stylish town, right on the elbow of Cape Cod's bent arm – a good base from which to explore the upper and lower regions. There's a wide choice of accommodation and eating places in the town itself, and enough recreational facilities – including excellent beaches and a superb playground for the children – for those who would like to stay put for a little while. Its Main Street was made for strolling, with boutiques, craft and antique shops and restaurants. There is an information booth at 533 Main Street.

Chatham Light, built in 1877, stands on a bluff where Main Street meets Shore Road and overlooks a spectacular view, with Nauset Beach and Pleasant Bay to the north, Monomoy Island to the south, and Nantucket Sound to the west. At low water, it also presents a good view of the 'Chatham Break', a channel sliced through an offshore barrier beach during a violent storm in 1987.

Not far from the lighthouse, at 347 Stage Harbor Road, is the **Old Atwood House**, which is maintained as a museum by the local historical society (admission fee). The house was built in 1752 by a sea captain and was occupied by the same family for five generations. There is a collection of antiques dating from 1635, and other displays feature sea shells, Sandwich glass, equipment from the Chatham Light and memorabilia relating to Joseph Lincoln, a popular Victorian writer of sea stories. A barn in the grounds houses a

Everyone finds it easy to relax in downtown Hyannis.

collection of murals by Alice Stalknecht Wight, who depicted local people of the 1930s in biblical settings.

Just offshore from Chatham, the **Monomoy National Wildlife Refuge** is located on a sandy barrier island which was split in two during a blizzard in 1958. The refuge is a great place for hiking and birdwatching, though parts of it are closed to the public. Thousands of birds use it as a staging post during their spring and autumn migrations: some 300 species have been recorded here. Guided day trips to Monomoy are organized by the Cape Cod Museum of Natural History, Box 1710, Route 6A, Brewster, MA 02631 (Tel. 508 896-3867), and the Wellfleet Bay Audubon Society, PO Box 236, South Wellfleet, MA 02664 (Tel. 508 349-2615). The museum also organizes weekend tours for visitors, which offer accommodation in the island's restored 19th-century lighthouse and keeper's cottage as part of the deal.

North of Orleans

Here the landscape changes into what might be termed 'Thoreau's Cape Cod' – the big skies, windswept moors, waving marsh grass and awesome dunes described by the spartan naturalist in the 1850s. Route 6 is the only real highway in this part of the cape, linking a sparse handful of communities until it turns back on itself in a loop at Provincetown.

Much of the area has been designated since 1961 as the **Cape Cod National Seashore**, encompassing expanses of wide ocean beach, towering dunes, swampland, marshes, wetlands and scrub. The seashore is administered by the US National Park Service, and there are trails for walking, cycling and horseback riding. Seasonal

WATCH THE BIRDIE

Bird lovers will find a rare shop catering exclusively for their needs at Orleans, where Routes 28A and the Old King's Highway converge. The **Bird Watcher's General Store** is on Route 6A, just outside the town, and is stocked with everything from field guides to binoculars, telescopes, bird tables and feeders. A host of birding bric-a-brac includes carvings, jewellery, T-shirts, puzzles, notecards, place mats and bookmarks.

lifeguard services and other facilities are available at half a dozen beaches within the protected zone. Surf-fishing is permitted from beaches, but a state licence is required for freshwater angling. There are no camping facilities in the seashore area. National Park Service rangers lead daily nature walks and give lectures. Salt Pond Visitor Center, on Route 6 at Eastham, and Province Lands Visitor Center, on Race Point Road, Provincetown, each contain exhibits, audio-visual programmes, publications and information services.

Provincetown

Almost encircled by Sahara-like dunes, Provincetown is a hotchpotch of good and bad taste: elegant homes, hamburger joints, gourmet restaurants, souvenir shops and art galleries. The people it attracts are just as varied – from local fishermen to artists and writers from Boston, New York and beyond. The town became a popular art colony about the turn of the century when it attracted celebrities of the calibre of Sinclair Lewis and Eugene O'Neill.

You can't help feeling that P-town, as the locals call it, has come a long way since the *Mayflower* landed here in 1620, an event which is immortalized by the **Pilgrim Monument**, a granite tower more than 250ft (77m) high. An observation deck near the top of the tower provides a stunning view of Cape Cod Bay. A small museum (admission fee) at the foot of the monument documents the town's history and includes a diorama of the *Mayflower*, together with displays of model ships, whaling equipment, scrimshaw and maritime artefacts. Further seafaring items are to be found at the **Heritage Museum**, at 356 Commercial Street in the centre of town. A huge model of a fishing schooner takes up the whole of one floor, and other displays feature hand-painted furniture, photographs and paintings.

A frequent ferry service for foot passengers links Provincetown with Boston.

An active port, Provincetown draws fishermen, writers and artists.

Martha's Vineyard

No one knows for certain who Martha was, but the island is supposed to have

ROLL OUT THE BARREL

The first cooper to practise his craft in Massachusetts was John Alden, who came over with the *Mayflower*. The state's last practising cooper is another Englishman, Anthony Bridgewater, who runs the **Cape Cod Cooperage** on Queen Anne Road, Chatham.

Housed in an old shingle-hung barn set on a rural crossroads, the cooperage was founded by yet another Englishman, a Captain Small, nearly a century ago. Anthony and his wife Barbara took over the business in May 1991.

In its early days the cooperage supplied boxes and barrels for local fishermen and cranberry growers. Now it sells a wide range of furniture and decorative goods for the home and garden. Many of the items are made on the premises, and some are hand-painted by a resident artist. There is also a blacksmith who produces wrought ironwork in a forge behind the old barn.

been named by the English explorer Bartholomew Gosnold, who discovered it in 1602 and was impressed by the many wild grapes he found growing there. Some people say Martha was his daughter, others his mother.

Whatever the origins of its name, there's no denying the popularity of an island whose population swells from 14,000 to 80,000 at the height of summer. Martha's Vineyard is reached by ferry services from Cape Cod (Wood's Hole, Falmouth and Hyannis), New Bedford and Nantucket, with trips taking between 40 minutes and two and a quarter hours. The island can also be reached by air from Boston or New York. Whichever route you choose, book early in summertime.

More or less triangular, the Vineyard – as locals prefer to call it – extends some 10 miles (16km) north to south and 20 miles (32km) east to west. Three major car rental companies have bases on the island, and visitors can also rent beach buggies and mopeds. Residents are generally hostile to mopeds which can be dangerous on the narrow lanes and are certainly irritatingly noisy. Shuttle buses operate regularly between the island's major centres, and taxis are available.

There are three main towns: Vineyard Haven and Oak Bluffs in the north, and Edgartown, about halfway down the east coast, where there is a crossing to Chappaquiddick Island. Each has a reasonable selection of shops, lodgings and places to eat, but liquor can be purchased in restaurants only in Edgartown and Oak Bluffs. Elsewhere, you can take your own. There are five public beaches, four wildlife and nature areas and a state forest. Cycle paths in the north and eastern parts of the island connect with trails through Martha's Vineyard State Forest in the centre. Fishing, golf, horse-riding, sailing and other water sports are available.

Vineyard Haven

Most visitors arrive first at Vineyard Haven, officially named Tisbury, a lively and charming little town which has attracted writers since that prince of the pulp writers Dashiell Hammett spent his summers here in the 1930s. Much of the old town was destroyed by fire in 1883, but many of the white clapboard sea captains' homes survived on William Street. Opposite the ferry terminal on Union Street is the **Seamen's Bethel**, which was opened in 1892 as a chapel and refuge for mariners. Now restored, it houses a museum with displays of photographs, scrimshaw and nautical memorabilia. Nearby, on Beach Road, the 1804 Federal-style **Jirah Luce House** (admission fee) has displays in eight rooms depicting local life in the 19th century. A

Vineyard Haven, officially named Tisbury, is a lively and charming little town.

third museum is the **Old Schoolhouse**, at 110 Main Street, which features whaling and Revolutionary memorabilia. Operated by the Daughters of the American Revolution, the museum stands on the site where three girls blew up the town's flagpole rather than let it fall into the hands of British sailors who wanted it to replace a broken spar on their warship.

Oak Bluffs

Another cheerful community, this is best known for its 'Cottage City', about a thousand Victorian cottages ornately decorated with Gothic windows and gingerbread railings. The eccentric development, entered from Circuit Avenue, the town's main street, was built by followers of a charismatic Methodist preacher who held summer camps here from 1835. On Illumination Night, a festival held in mid-August each year since 1869, hundreds of oriental lanterns are strung from the cottages.

Edgartown

About 5 miles (8km) south of Oak Bluffs, Edgartown was founded in 1642 and has been a prosperous port for much of its history. The magnificent homes of 19th-century sea captains remain along North

Oak Bluffs is known for its 'Cottage City', an eccentric development of Victorian homes.

and South Water Streets, overlooking the harbour. The **Vineyard Museum** in the Thomas Cooke House, at Cooke and School Streets, contains a research library and maritime museum (admission fee), which exhibits whaling gear, period costumes, scrimshaw, and the lens used in the Gay Head Lighthouse from 1856 to 1952.

Up Island

The western half of Martha's Vineyard is known as Up Island, a rather more rural area than the east with rich farmland and the major part of the 4,000-acre (1,620-hectare) state forest. In the far south west are the towering Gay Head Cliffs, spectacularly striped in half a dozen hues as a result of glacial action thousands of years ago. The approach to the cliffs is lined with food and gift shops operated by the Wampanoag Indians whose reservation is nearby.

Nantucket

Tiny Nantucket – it covers only 36 square miles (92km^2) – was a giant in the days of whaling. Nantucketers led the world in the hunt for the sperm whale for 150 years, and the busy little island, 30 miles (48km) out in the open Atlantic, earned great wealth. Its isolation also brought times of great distress. The Revolution, the War of 1812 and the use of kerosene as fuel all resulted in depression for the sturdy, seafaring islanders. Then a new prosperity came with the introduction of tourism at the beginning of this century.

The town of Nantucket, preserved by strict regulation, is a National Historic District.

Often shrouded in fog, Nantucket mirrors the extremes of American culture. On one side, a windswept landscape of wild moorlands and weatherbeaten saltbox cottages; on the other, chic restaurants and boutiques to rival those in Mayfair or Manhattan. The town of Nantucket, preserved by very strict regulation and the only one

on the island, is an official National Historic District with streets just made for a Gilbert and Sullivan chorus. The island can be circuited by car in 30 minutes and by bicycle in about two hours, but only the most neurotic would be in such a rush.

There is much to see in Nantucket town whose streets contain dozens of homes from the 18th and 19th centuries. Its cobblestoned lanes, narrow and winding, are a joy to walk, and there are many places where you can flop on to a bench and watch the world go by.

The best place to begin a stroll around town is the wharf at the foot of Main Street. The **Thomas Macy Warehouse**

A renowned whaling centre in the past, Nantucket maintains its links with the sea.

was built in 1846 by the man who founded the famous New York store (the Macys were an old Nantucket whaling family). The two-storey brick building houses a small museum with historical, geological and art displays and a large diorama showing what the waterfront was like before it was ravaged by a great fire in 1846.

Broad Street contains two museums side by side. The **Whaling Museum** is housed in a candle factory of 1846 and includes a superb collection of scrimshaw, a whaleboat and the skeleton of a whale 43 ft (13.2m) long. The **Peter Foulger Museum** portrays Nantucket home life through photographs, drawings and treasures brought to the town from the Far East and elsewhere by traders and whaling men.

The town's grandest homes are to be found on Main Street, beyond Fair Street where the business district ends. Most of the homes are privately occupied, but the Greek Revival **Hadwen House**, at 96 Main Street, is a museum of Regency, Empire and Victorian furnishings. The house, built in 1844, has an imposing portico, a grand

circular staircase, fine plasterwork and carved Italian marble fireplaces.

The **Maria Mitchell Science Center**, on Vestal and Milk Streets, farther along Main Street, commemorates the Nantucket astronomer who discovered a comet in 1849 and became the first woman member of the American Academy of Arts and Sciences. The centre has a natural science museum, a library, aquarium, observatory and the astronomer's birthplace.

The **Jethro Coffin House** on Sunset Hill is the oldest dwelling on the island, built in 1686 and extensively renovated after being struck by lightning in 1987.

A single ticket provides admission to most of the town's historical attractions.

Siasconset – everyone says 'Sconset' – is a bijou village of rose-covered cottages and picture postcard streets alongside a beach 7½ miles (12km) from Nantucket town on Milestone Road. Continuing north along Polpis Road you cross open moorland, pass the Sankaty Light, one of three lighthouses on the island, and come to the 205-acre (83-hectare) **Windswept Cranberry Bog**, where visitors can watch cranberries being harvested in the autumn.

Nantucket has ferry links with Hyannis on Cape Cod and Oak Bluffs on Martha's Vineyard. Reservations should be made as early as possible during the high season and are a must for cars. There are air services from Boston. Cars and jeeps may be rented on the island, and shuttle buses run between Nantucket town and the Jetties, Siasconset and Surfside beaches. Bicycle rentals are available in profusion.

Safely boxed and all ready to go – just a part of Nantucket's autumn harvest.

RHODE ISLAND

Small, but Packed with Interest

Rhode Island has a universe of experience contained within a minuscule area. The state is the smallest in the Union – no more than 48 miles (77km) from north to south and 37 miles (60km) from east to west. Yet packed within its total of 1,214 square miles (3,144km^2) are some 400 miles (640km) of coastline, 100 public beaches, 18,000 acres (7,300 hectares) of parkland and more than 20 percent of the nation's Registered Historic Landmarks.

As if the contrasts of size and content were not enough, Rhode Island also spans the social and historical spectrums. It was founded on principles of religious freedom by refugees who had fled from the harsh intolerances of Massachusetts in the 1630s. It was the first colony to ban slavery and the first to declare independence from Britain.

Here, America's Industrial Revolu tion began in 1793 when the first water-powered textile mill went into production at Pawtucket. As poor immigrant labourers flocked to the factory towns of the north, America's wealthiest families – the unimaginably rich Astors, Belmonts, Vanderbilts and their ilk – spent dreamy summers in Newport, vying with each other in the size of their yachts and the splendour of their marble 'cottages'.

The Breakers, one of the 'summer cottages' built at Newport, Rhode Island, by the rich and famous in the 19th century.

Bordered by Massachusetts to the north and east and Connecticut to the west, the Ocean State – as its inhabitants like to call it – is crossed from north east to south west by Interstate 95, from which a good network of roads spreads in all directions. Providence, the capital, is served by both I-95 and US Highway 1, which creeps in from Connecticut in Rhode Island's extreme south-west corner and roams along the shores of the Atlantic Ocean and Narragansett Bay. Newport lies aloof at the southern end of Aquidneck Island,

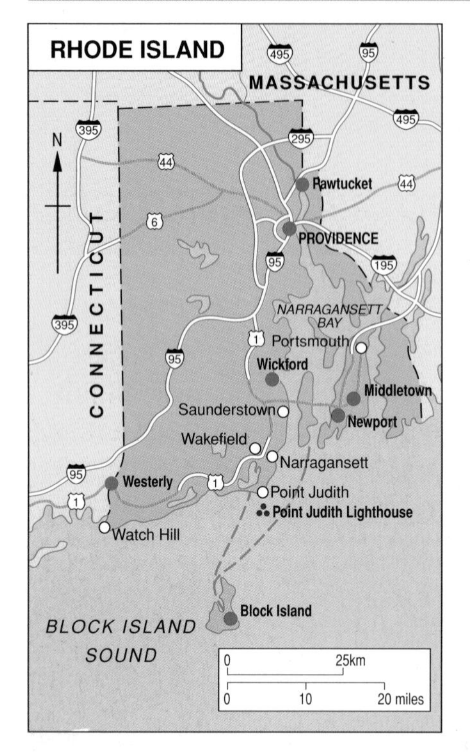

connected to the mainland by bridges in the north and south. The coastal strip straddling US 1 between Narragansett and the aptly-named Westerly is known as South County, though it is actually a part of Washington County. Thirteen miles (21km) offshore is Block Island.

Providence

Rhode Island's capital city has two things in common with Rome: it is built over seven hills, and its skyline is dominated by a huge marble dome. Providence was founded in 1636 by Roger Williams, a religious exile with a good eye for a town site. There was a fine, sheltered harbour with good access to the open sea, and rivers to serve both as highways and power sources. The city began as an agricultural plantation, but by the 18th century was deeply involved in the molasses, rum and slaves trade triangle.

After the Revolution, Providence prospered in the China trade, in which the four Brown brothers were leading figures; each left a lasting mark on the city. The mansion built for John Brown, slave trader and shipping magnate, is a major attraction to this day. The architecture of Joseph Brown brought a new look to Providence.

The liveliest spots in Providence are to be found in the neighbourhoods. Of these, College Hill, home of Brown University, probably has the greatest vitality, thanks to its student population, its boutiques, restaurants and book shops.

Students apart, the real spirit of Providence springs from its ethnic make-up. **Federal Hill**, west of downtown, lies at the heart of the city's Italian community. It's all so ethnic, in fact, that even the line down the middle of Atwells Avenue – the main street – is painted red, white and green. Italy's national colours also adorn street benches. Nearby **Broadway Boulevard**, also Italian, was first populated by Irish immigrants during the 1830s. The elaborate, rambling gingerbread houses were built during the time of the Irish, but properties ranging from Greek Revival to Gothic Revival by way of Italianate and Queen Anne were developed as the area became more Italian. At the mouth of the Providence River, **Fox Point** has long been the focus of the city's Portuguese community, although this is beginning to change as the gentrification process progresses.

Overlooking the city, Rhode Island's **State House**, on Smith Street, is impossible to miss. Completed in 1904, it is built of marble from Georgia, and after St Peter's in Rome its huge dome is the

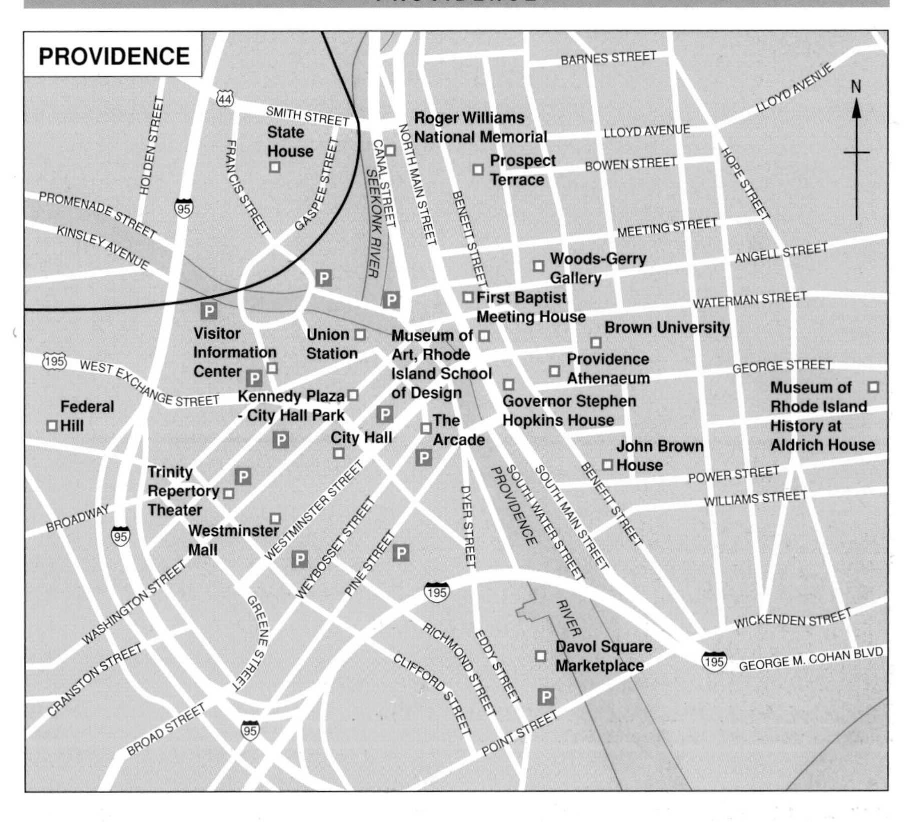

second largest unsupported dome in the world. It is topped by George T. Brewster's gilded statue of Independent Man. Visitors to State House can see the parchment charter granted to the colony of Rhode Island by King Charles II in 1663. Also on permanent display is a full-length portrait of George Washington by Gilbert Stuart, who also created the first president's likeness on the $1 bill. Changing exhibits feature different parts of the state's collections.

Across the river from State House, at 65 Weybosset Street, along Westminster Mall, is **The Arcade**, America's first indoor shopping mall. It was built in 1828 and is now a National Historic Landmark. Occupying three floors of an elaborate Greek Revival structure with six Ionic columns and cast iron balcony rails, The Arcade has many speciality shops, including clothing, toys, jewellery and stationery. Other major shopping areas are Westminster Mall, on Westminster Street, Wickenden Street, Fox Point and two waterfront locations, Davol Square Marketplace and South Main Street.

Back on the eastern side of the river, on Market Square, is **Market House**, designed by Joseph Brown and built in 1775 as a maritime trading centre. Soon after its opening it became a focus of political activity. Meetings were held there, tea was burned in protest, and during the Revolution it was used as a barracks. In the mid-1800s it served as the city's seat of government. It is now owned by the Rhode Island School of Design (RISD).

OLD STONE BANK

Providence, Rhode Island's capital city, has a rich and varied architecture.

Just around the corner, at 224 Benefit Street, is the **RISD's Museum of Art** (admission fee), a small institution housing a comprehensive range of collections, including French Impressionist works, Paul Revere silver, porcelain and antiquities from Egypt and the Far East. There is a regular programme of changing exhibitions.

The **First Baptist Church** – the first in America – is at 75 North Main Street, a block north of the Museum of Art. The congregation was established in 1638 by Roger Williams, but the present church was built in 1775 to the design of Joseph Brown. Its steeple is 185ft (57m) high, and its elegant interior is enhanced by a chandelier of Waterford crystal. Citizens of Providence will tell you that the predominantly timber-built church survived disastrous storms in 1875 and 1938 because it was built by ships' carpenters.

Benefit Street, running parallel with North and South Main Streets, is a 'Mile of History', believed to contain America's highest concentration of historic buildings. The street was first developed in the 1750s, and its architectural styles range from colonial and early Federal to Victorian. The **Providence Athenaeum**, at No. 251, was one of the first lending libraries in the US, founded in 1773, although the present Greek Revival building dates from 1838. It houses a collection of Rhode Island art. The **First Unitarian Church**, on the corner of

The First Unitarian Church in Providence was built in 1816, and its tower contains the largest bell that was cast in Paul Revere's foundry.

George Washington really did sleep in the John Brown House in Benefit Street, Providence.

Benefit and Benevolent Streets, was built in 1816. Its bell tower contains a bell weighing 2,500lbs (1,136kg), the largest ever cast in Paul Revere's foundry.

The most striking building in Benefit Street is the **John Brown House** (admission fee), on the corner of Power Street. This is the mansion Joseph Brown built for his brother, the slave trader John, in 1786. George Washington really did sleep here. The three-storey house has 14 elegant rooms displaying Rhode Island furnishings, silver and china, as well as pewter, glass and Chinese porcelain from the days of the China trade.

Brown University, on College Hill was founded in 1764 as Rhode Island College and is the seventh oldest in the US. Its main entrance is through the Van Wickle Gates, but these are opened only twice a year – at convocation when they are opened inward and at commencement when they are opened outward. **University Hall**, built in 1770, is the oldest building on the campus. It was used as a barracks by American and French troops during the Revolution.

Pawtucket

This city, 3 miles (5km) north east of Providence, gets its name from an Indian word meaning 'the place where water falls'. With abundant supplies of wood and waterpower, it became an important industrial settlement when iron ore was discovered in 1650. This is where America's industrial revolution began in 1793 when Samuel Slater, utilizing the skills he had learned while working with Richard Arkwright in England, harnessed the waters of the Blackstone River to create a factory capable of mass-producing cotton yarn.

Today the restored mill is part of the **Slater Mill Historic Site** (admission fee) at 727 Roosevelt Avenue, Pawtucket. There are classrooms – instruction is offered in weaving, basketry and other crafts – an audio-visual theatre, gift shop and ancient machinery which includes a 16,000-lb (7,258kg) waterwheel. The site is a National Historic Landmark.

Younger travellers are certain to enjoy the **Children's Museum of Rhode Island** (admission fee, but no charge on the first Sunday each month), at 58 Wolcott Street, Pawtucket. The kids can handle anything they like and can put their ingenuity to the test in the Puzzle Room. Great-grandma's Kitchen will give them a taste of yesteryear, and they can explore the geography of Rhode Island on a room-sized map.

Near Providence

Another family entertainment centre is the **Rocky Point Amusement Park** at Warwick Neck, about 10 miles (16km) south of Providence on Route 117A. Spreading over 76 acres (31 hectares), it is the largest park of its kind in New England, with more than 100 rides, including the white-knuckle Corkscrew Rollercoaster and the eight-storey-high Free Fall.

On the outskirts of Providence, the **Roger Williams Park Zoo** (admission fee) covers 430 acres (175 hectares) and features sea-lions, penguins, polar bears, gibbons, wolves, endangered species, and animals of the African plains. A wetlands area is maintained in its natural state and features native birds and plants. Indoor exhibits include a nature centre and a tropical America display, both with computers to enable visitors to learn more about rain forests. The park has picnic areas, paddleboats, pony rides, a miniature train, a carousel, Japanese gardens and a playground. The zoo is on Elmwood Avenue, reached from I-95 south Exit 17 or I-95 north Exit 16.

Newport

Newport city was founded in 1639 by religious dissidents from Boston, and soon became a haven for Quakers and Jews. The settlement grew rapidly, with most of its inhabitants engaged in shipbuilding and trade by the 1650s. Within a hundred years it was a major New World port, and went on to greater prosperity through the triangle trade, privateering and downright piracy. Captain Kidd was among those who used Newport as a base.

The British decided to crack down on Newporters for piracy, smuggling and tax evasion, and blockaded the harbour. It was the beginning of a hard time for the Aquidneck islanders. Filled with revolutionary determination, Rhode Island declared independence two months before the other colonies, on 4 May 1776. Seven months later, 6,000 British troops landed in Newport and stayed for three years. By the end of the occupation, the city had lost most of its population, many of its buildings, and all of its trade. Its problems were compounded by the combined effects of the War of 1812 and development of the railways, which killed any hope of regaining its position as a leading seaport.

Only when the Civil War ended did Newport begin to climb out of its

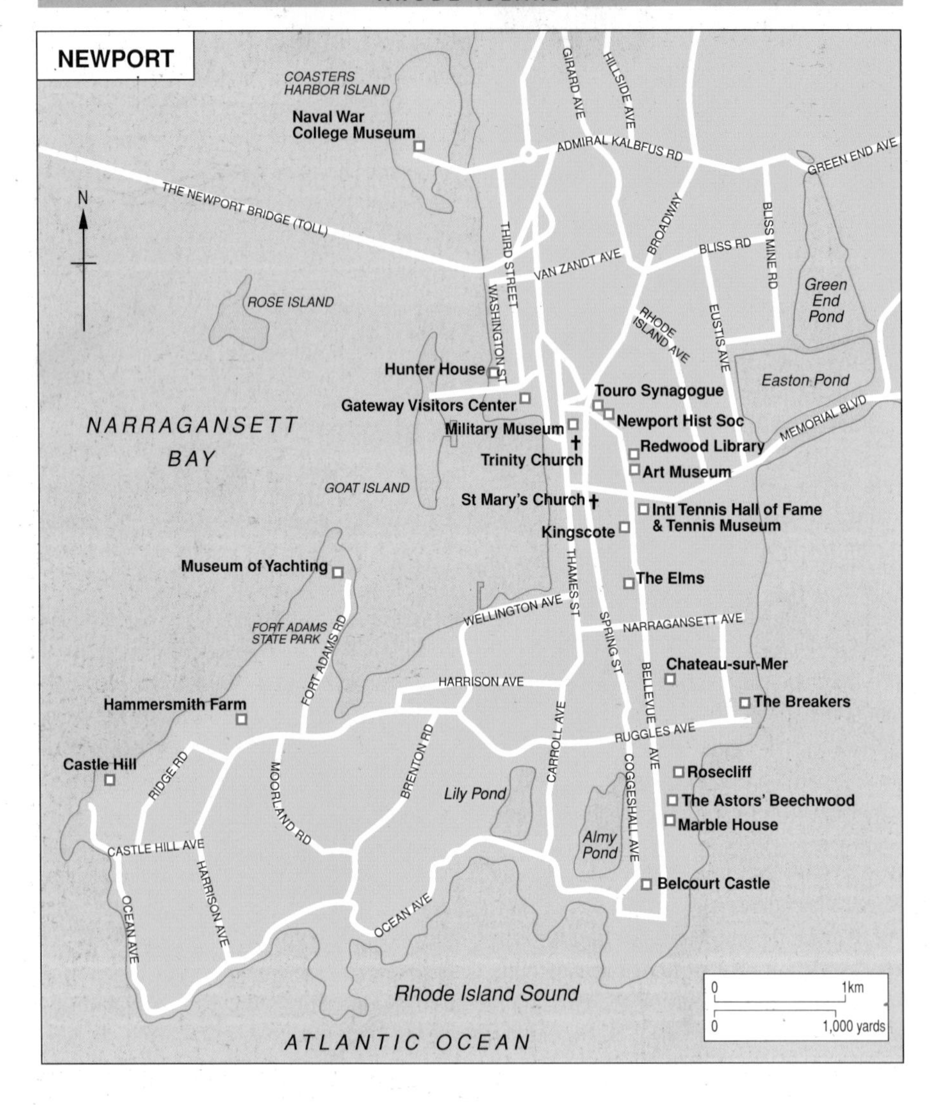

depression. Then it did it in style. New York City's wealthy socialites swooped in and began building their summer 'cottages', and the old port began a new incarnation – this time as a leisure haven for immensely rich yachtsmen.

Newport today is an attractive amalgam of old and new; the old manifested in its cobblestoned streets and charming buildings; the new in its progressive attitude towards the arts and tourism, with its renowned jazz and other festivals and a programme of year-round events.

One of the world's most famous yachting centres, Newport, is the home base for many traditional sailing craft.

The major activity associated with the city is sailing, and although the America's Cup is no longer the major annual event, scarcely a summer week goes by without a grand regatta of some kind being staged. One of the most spectacular is the Classic Yacht Regatta, held each September over the Labor Day weekend, when some of the most beautiful traditional sailing vessels in America are raced and reviewed. A number of important marine shows also take place, including the Small Boat Show in spring and the Newport International Sailboat Show and the International Powerboat Show, both held in September.

There are plenty of sailing opportunities for those who would rather take part than watch. The **Sail Newport Sailing Center**, at Fort Adams State Park (Tel. 401 846-1983), on Ocean Drive, for example, is a non-profit-making organization that offers recreational sailing, three-hour charters and rentals, and instruction. For a real treat you can rent a J-Class yacht. Sir Thomas Lipton's 120-ft (37m) *Shamrock V*, built as an America's Cup contender in 1930, costs around $6,000 a day plus expenses, but it can take up to 30 people (sleeps 8) so you can share the cost. (Contact J-Class Management, Tel. 401 849-3060.)

Newport's **Museum of Yachting** (admission fee), housed in a 19th-century building on the waterfront at Fort Adams State Park, features the great J-Class boats in its America's Cup Gallery. Another section honours single-handed round-the-world sailors, and there are many exhibits of small craft, yachting artefacts, models, photographs and memorabilia.

The city has established itself as a major centre in the field of music. Newport Music Festival, when classical concerts are staged at the mansions and in other locations, takes place in the second half of July, and the internationally renowned jazz and folk festivals are staged in August.

Tennis and golf are very popular and played to a high international standard. Professional tournaments are staged each summer at the recently expanded **International Tennis Hall of Fame**, at the Newport Casino, at 194 Bellevue Avenue, Newport. Major events are the Miller Lite Hall of Fame Tennis Championships and the Hall of Fame Invitational.

A National Historic Landmark, the Casino also houses a museum (admission fee) with the world's largest collection of tennis memorabilia. American tournament tennis began at the Casino in 1881 with the first US National Lawn Tennis Championship, forerunner of the US Open.

The Newport Casino opened in 1880 as one of the first country clubs in the US. For a time it was the country's most complete resort facility, with a theatre (in which Oscar Wilde once appeared), a restaurant and bachelor apartments. The Casino was founded by James Gordon Bennett Jr, publisher and yachtsman, in retaliation for being expelled from the Newport Reading Room, then the city's snootiest social club. Bennett had dared his friend, the British polo player Captain Henry Candy, to ride a horse onto the club's porch. Bennett's Casino soon became the gathering ring for Newport society.

The Hall of Fame's 13 grass courts are the world's oldest continuously used competition grass courts and the only ones in the US open to the public for play (fee). The City of Newport has free courts at five locations.

Newport Country Club, on Harrison Avenue, is in most years the venue for the PGA Seniors golf tournament in July. Opened in 1893, the private club was the location of the first American amateur golf championship. There are four courses open to the public within easy reach of Newport.

Newport and neighbouring Middletown are fringed by five excellent beaches. Easton's Beach, also known as First Beach, is the area's largest – three-quarters of a mile (1km) long, with parking (fee) for some 700 cars. **Sachuest** or Second Beach, in

The Newport area is noted for its excellent beaches.

Middletown, is the most popular, with dunes and parking (fee) for up to 1,000 cars. **Third Beach**, on the Sakkonet River, also in Middletown, is smaller, less crowded and a favourite with windsurfers. Again, there is parking for a fee. **Fort Adams State Park** has a small beach on the south side of Brenton Cove. Picnic tables and barbecue grills are available and there is a small entrance fee for out-of-state cars. **King Park Beach**, on Wellington Avenue, Newport, is handy for town and has free parking. There are picnic tables and barbecue grills, as well as free bath houses, swings, slides and a marked shallow area for children.

On summer weekends and holidays, Newport can get snarled up with traffic. On-street parking is free, but a two-hour limit is strictly enforced, and parking in some streets is for residents only. There are also a few municipal and privately operated parking lots. A regular commuter bus service throughout Newport and Middletown is operated by the Rhode Island Public Transit Authority. Buses stop at major shopping centres and the beaches. Viking Tours operates trolleys which serve downtown Newport and the mansions on Bellevue Avenue. Bicycles can be rented on an hourly, daily or weekly basis from Ten Speed Spokes at 18 Elm Street (Tel. 401 847-5609).

Alternatively you can walk. Newport's charming historical district, with some 200 colonial homes and other buildings, is best seen on foot. Anita Rafael, director of Newport On Foot (Tel. 401 846-5391), has become as familiar as many of the landmarks she points out as she guides groups along routes chosen from ancient maps of the city. Striding along in pristine tennis shoes, Anita leads visitors past the old meeting house, the first State House, and into the old burying grounds, teaching them how to 'read' a house – working out from its appearance how it was built and how old it might be – as they go.

During the summer months, walking tours are also offered by Newport Historical Society (Tel. 401 846-0813).

Tourist information, brochures and maps can be obtained at the Newport Gateway Visitors' Center, 23 America's Cup Avenue (Tel. 401 849-8098). The centre is open seven days a week, has a 16-screen audio-visual presentation, sells tickets for local attractions, events and tours and is within walking distance of hotels, shops and restaurants. There are public restrooms, telephones and vending machines, and visitors can park under cover free for half an hour.

Colonial Newport

With more colonial houses than any other US city, many of them still in use as homes, Newport is a living museum in the truest sense, and its most significant historical buildings are within easy walking distance of each other. The best of the colonial homes – indeed, it is said to be one of the most beautiful 18th-century mansions in the country – is the **Hunter House** at 54 Washington Street (admission fee). Built in 1748, the house is a National Historic Landmark. It has been lovingly restored by the Preservation Society of Newport County and furnished with pieces made by Townsend and Goddard and other Newport craftsmen of the colonial era.

The Hunter House is noted for its fine woodwork and staircase, and there are displays of silver, porcelain and paintings in its elegant rooms. The carved pineapple in the pediment over the front door is a traditional symbol of hospitality found throughout New England. In the days when much of the region's livelihood came from the sea, a woman would place a pineapple at the front door to announce that her seaman husband had returned home safely.

Washington Square was the centre of everything that mattered in colonial times. Here goods and gossip were exchanged, offenders punished, proclamations read and troops drilled. Here, too, early anti-British demonstrations were staged. The square is dominated by the dignified **Colony House**, built in 1739 of bricks imported from England. The seat of colonial and until 1900 state government, the building has been the setting for a number of historical events, including Rhode Island's declaration of independence on 4 May 1776, and the meeting at which George Washington and the French General Rochambeau planned the defeat of the British at Yorktown. There are free tours of Colony House daily from July to early September.

THE CLIFF WALK

Independent walkers with good footwear might like to tackle the Cliff Walk, which follows the coast for 3 miles (5 km) between Easton's Beach and Bailey's Beach near the southern end of Bellevue Avenue.

A public footpath, the walk provides spectacular sea views across Rhode Island Sound and gives hikers close-up backyard peeks at some of Newport's opulent mansions. At one point it passes within yards of the Chinese teahouse in the grounds of Marble House, the extravagant summer 'cottage' built for William K. Vanderbilt.

Efforts by mansion owners to close the walk at various times have been vigorously opposed – when one owner built walls across it, Newporters tore them down and threw the wreckage into the sea. Today, erosion and weather are the greatest threats to the path's existence, but maintenance is in the hands of the US Army Corps of Engineers. Care is needed when following the walk.

Brick Market, opposite Colony House, was designed by Peter Harrison and completed in 1762 as part of the Long Wharf development. During colonial times, Long Wharf was the busiest wharf on Newport's waterfront. The Brick Market followed the British style with storage rooms above a central market area. In its time, the market has served as town hall, theatre and art gallery and now houses shops. Since the end of 1993 it has also been the location of the new **Museum of Newport History**.

Just north east of Washington Square, at 17 Broadway, is the **Wanton-Lyman-Hazard House** (admission fee), believed to be the oldest in Newport. It was built in the 1690s and has the steeply pitched roof and central chimney typical of early settler homes. Some of its interior walls are covered with the original plaster made from ground shells. Among its early residents was the Tory, Martin Howard Jr, who had to flee from an enraged mob during the Stamp Act Riot in 1765. He managed to board a British ship and never set foot in Newport again. Demonstrations of 18th-century cooking are given in the house, and there is a restored colonial garden at the back.

North of the square, at 26 Marlborough Street, is the **White Horse Tavern**, which was built around 1673 and is America's oldest tavern. Its first liquor licence was issued to the pirate William Mayes in 1687. Carefully restored by the Preservation Society, the White Horse Tavern is still in business.

Nearby, on the corner of Marlborough and Farewell Streets, is the **Friends' Meeting House** (admission fee), the oldest Quaker meeting house in the US. It was built in 1699, enlarged in 1729 and 1807 and has recently undergone extensive renovations. Maintained by Newport Historical Society, the two-storey meeting house has wide-plank floors, a lofty ceiling, and houses models, architectural displays and exhibits of Quaker life and dress. The Quakers were persecuted in Massachusetts but welcomed in free-thinking Newport, although their pacifist stance incurred the wrath of patriots during the Revolution.

Newport's White Horse Tavern, America's oldest, has held a liquor licence since 1687.

Another monument to Newport's religious tolerance at a time when blind prejudice assumed the mantle of faith is the **Touro Synagogue**, south east of Washington Square, at 72 Touro Street. Designed by Peter Harrison, the building was completed in 1763 and is the oldest synagogue in the US. The Jewish community had been established in Newport for about a century, worshipping in private homes, when Harrison was commissioned to build the synagogue.

A sombre exterior gives no hint of the elaborate elegance within, where a gallery for women worshippers is supported by 12 Ionic columns representing the Tribes of Israel. George Washington addressed the Touro congregation during a visit to Newport in 1790 when he promised religious freedom without restraint. Until the Revolution Jews were not allowed to vote, although they were free to practise their religion. Washington's declaration containing the promise that America would give 'to bigotry no sanction, to persecution no assistance' is read at the synagogue each year.

The headquarters of Newport Historical Society are at **82 Touro Street**, where work by Newport craftsmen, including fine examples of furniture made by local cabinetmakers, is displayed. There is a recreation of a merchant's parlour, and a marine museum displays models, maritime art and navigational equipment.

South of Washington Square, at 23 Clark Street, is the **Armory of the Newport Artillery Company**, yet another first for the city. The Greek Revival-style Armory (admission fee) was built in 1836 and houses military uniforms and weapons going back to colonial times, but the company was founded in 1639 and chartered by King George II in 1741 and is thus the country's oldest militia in continuous service.

Standing delightfully at the corner of Spring and Church Streets, **Trinity Church** displays all the elegance of a Christopher Wren design, on which it was modelled, except that it is structured in timber, rather than the off-white masonry of a London church. Trinity was built in 1726 by Richard Munday. Among the church's notable features are its graceful white spire and its Tiffany stained-glass windows. Its triple-decked wineglass-shaped pulpit is the only one in America. The organ, installed in 1733, is the second oldest in the country. It was made by Richard Bridge of London and there is a belief that Handel once played it.

On the corner of Spring Street and Memorial Boulevard is the **Church of St Mary**, seat of the oldest Catholic parish in Rhode Island. Designed in English Gothic style by Patrick Keeley of New York, it was completed in 1852. It was here that Senator John F. Kennedy and Jacqueline Lee Bouvier were married on 12 September 1953. As President and First Lady, they frequently returned to Newport. St Mary's was designated a National Shrine in 1968.

The **Redwood Library**, at 50 Bellevue Avenue, is the nation's oldest library in continuous use and still occupying its original building. Built of wood treated to look like stone and designed in the form of a Roman temple by Peter Harrison, the building was completed in 1748. The library was named after Abraham Redwood, merchant and owner of a West Indian plantation, who donated £500 for books. Apart from a collection of rare books, the library also displays Early American paintings, furniture and historical items. Although membership is private, visitors are freely admitted.

TOWER OF MYSTERY

Some people believe that the round stone tower in Touro Park, off Bellevue Avenue, was built by Viking explorers in the 11th century, either as a church or a lookout tower. They bolster their argument with Norse sagas and archaeological evidence of Viking settlements in Newfoundland.

The fact that there are no records of the tower's construction and that several excavations have failed to prove its origin serves only to thicken the web of attractive mystery cast over it. Historians say the tower is most probably the base of a mill built during colonial times.

Newport's **Art Museum** (admission fee) is housed in a curious but picturesque building at 76 Bellevue Avenue. Designed by Richard Morris Hunt and built in 1863 as the Griswold Mansion, a private home, it is a gabled 'stick style' structure and is listed on the National Register of Historic Places. Regular exhibitions of work by internationally known artists are staged in the **Griswold House** and in the adjacent **Cushing Memorial Gallery**, which was built in 1921. There is also a permanent collection of work by 19th- and 20th-century American artists.

Newport's Summer 'Cottages'

Whatever else Newport has to offer, its most popular attractions, drawing more than a million visitors a year, are the mansions located mainly along Bellevue Avenue. During the late 19th and early 20th centuries the cream of New York society and the most flamboyantly successful of America's nouveaux riches flocked to Newport to spend their summers and their money in an awesome display of wealth.

The railroad barons, bankers and industrial tycoons of the Gilded Age strove to outdo each other, spending millions on their homes, and thousands on a single party. They employed Old World craftsmen to build the stately homes they modestly described as 'cottages', and imported shiploads of marble, antique furniture, tapestries, paintings and sculpture. Some 60 mansions were built in the area, eight of which are now open to the public, serving as monuments to the grotesquely overblown lifestyle of an age in which there was no income tax and the rich could indulge themselves.

Six of the mansions are maintained by the Preservation Society of Newport County, and combination tickets can be purchased giving admission to any two or more of the buildings. Guided tours last about an hour. Free parking is available at each of the properties. Bus tours including admission to one or two of the mansions are run on a shuttle basis from the Gateway Visitor Center on America's Cup Avenue by Viking Tours (Tel. 401 847-6921).

One of the oldest and least flamboyant of the mansions is **Kingscote**, on the corner of Bowery Street and Bellevue Avenue. Designed in Gothic Revival style by Richard Upjohn and completed in 1839, Kingscote was built for a plantation owner from Georgia who proved to be a trendsetter in deciding to have his summer residence erected outside the city area. It contains furnishings installed by the China trade merchant William Henry King, who bought the property in 1864.

A block south of Kingscote, on Bellevue Avenue, is **The Elms**, modelled on a French chateau and built in 1899 for a coal tycoon from Pennsylvania. The mansion is lavishly furnished with 18th-century pieces, and is surrounded by 14 acres (5.8 hectares) of grounds with sunken gardens, terraces, statuary and fountains.

Chateau-sur-Mer was built in 1852 as a relatively modest villa for William Shepard Wetmore, a China trader. Twenty years later Richard Morris Hunt renovated and enlarged the house, setting a standard for the grandeur that was to follow. There is an elaborately panelled library and a hall with a ceiling 45ft (14m) high. Many original furnishings are on show, and there is a charming collection of Victorian toys. The gardens contain many exotic plants.

The Breakers is away from Bellevue Avenue, on Ochre Point Avenue at the end of Victoria Avenue, but it's a diversion not to be missed. The four-storey 'cottage', completed in 1895 for Cornelius Vanderbilt, contains 70 rooms and covers one whole acre (0.4 hectare) of an 11-acre (4.5-hectare) site grandly overlooking the Atlantic Ocean. It took some 2,500 workmen two years to build the mansion, which Richard Morris Hunt designed in the style of a 17th-century Genoese palace. The Breakers has a two-storey ballroom, a music room with a gold ceiling and a dining room with rose alabaster pillars. The grounds, featuring many unusual trees and shrubs, were landscaped by Frederick Law Olmsted.

The entire exterior of **Rosecliff**, back on Bellevue Avenue, is covered in glazed white terracotta. The 40-room mansion was designed by Stanford White inspired by the Grand Trianon at Versailles and completed in 1902. It has a heart-shaped grand staircase, a Court of Love, and a ballroom 72ft (22m) long, the largest of any Newport mansion. Rosecliff has

Beechwood, a Newport mansion, was the summer home of members of the Astor family.

featured in a number of films, notably in the 1974 version of *The Great Gatsby*, starring Robert Redford.

The Astors' **Beechwood**, at 580 Bellevue Avenue, is Newport's only living history tour, with actors in period costume playing the parts of members of the Astor family, including Caroline Astor, the 'queen' of New York society. Beechwood was designed by Calvert Vaux and Andrew Jackson Downing, and was completed in 1852.

Marble House, so called because of the many types of marble used in its construction and decoration, was built in 1892 by William K. Vanderbilt as a gift for his wife, Alva. Three years later she divorced him – and kept the house as part of her settlement. Sumptuously furnished, the house was designed by Richard Morris Hunt, inspired by the Petit Trianon at Versailles. Its Gold Ballroom is decorated with real gold. The Chinese tea house in the grounds was built by Mrs Vanderbilt in 1913.

Belcourt Castle, at the southern end of Bellevue Avenue, was built for Oliver Hazard Perry Belmont, who married Alva Vanderbilt after her divorce. Designed by Richard Morris Hunt and modelled on a Louis XIII hunting lodge, the castle was built in 1892. It has a wealth of stained glass and carved wood, and a $3 million collection of antiques and art from 32 countries.

Belmont and Alva were an odd couple, to say the least. He kept a stable of horses in the lap of luxury: they slept on white linen sheets and were provided with morning, afternoon and evening clothes. At Marble House, Alva had a miniature railway built so that footmen could serve tea in her Chinese tea house, and on one occasion served a ten-course dinner in the Gold Ballroom – for 100 dogs.

As a contrast to the eccentric opulence of the 'cottages', take a trip along Ocean Drive to **Hammersmith Farm** (admission fee), overlooking Castle Hill Cove and Narragansett Bay. This was where Jacqueline Bouvier spent her childhood summers and where the reception was held after her marriage to Senator John F. Kennedy. It served as the summer White House during the Kennedy Administration. The only working farm in Newport, Hammersmith is informal and welcoming, and filled with Kennedy memorabilia.

Beyond Newport

Newport's neighbours on Aquidneck Island are Middletown and Portsmouth. Each has attractions that make an excursion worthwhile.

Middletown

Whitehall, at 311 Berkeley Avenue, Middletown, was the home of the philosopher Dean George Berkeley, later Bishop of Cloyne, Ireland, from 1729 to 1731. During his stay, Berkeley enlarged the original farmhouse, installing a cruciform hall and introducing several unusual architectural features. British troops were billeted in the house during the Revolutionary War. Restored and furnished with period pieces, Whitehall (admission fee) is on the National Register of Historic Sites and is maintained by the Rhode Island chapter of the National Society of Colonial Dames.

Prescott Farm (admission fee), at 2009 West Main Road, Middletown, consists of a group of 18th-century buildings rebuilt on the site by the Newport Restoration Foundation. The complex includes a windmill originally built in 1811 and still used to grind corn. Corn meal, honey and herbs grown on the property are sold in the farm store. The original farm earned a place in the history books on 9 July 1777, when a band of colonists rowed ashore at midnight and kidnapped the British commander, General William Prescott, in his night clothes.

For wildlife lovers, the **Norman Bird Sanctuary** (admission fee) on Third Beach Road, Middletown, has 450 acres (182 hectares) with well-marked trails, a variety of trees, shrubs and vegetation, streams and rock ledges. A natural history museum is located at the entrance. More than 200 species of bird have been recorded in the area, and the sanctuary provides nesting grounds for 60 species. Guided birdwalks are held on Sunday mornings. A major attraction is **Hanging Rock**, 50ft (15m) high and overlooking the Atlantic Ocean.

Another natural phenomenon at Middletown is **Purgatory Chasm**, a deep, narrow cleft in the rocky cliff overlooking Second Beach. An observation bridge

The fishing is great in the waters of Narragansett Bay.

THE NAVY IN NEWPORT

Newport can justifiably claim to be the birthplace of the US Navy because the first seaborne engagement of the Revolutionary War took place in Narragansett Bay in June 1775, when the sloop *Katy* defeated a sloop of the Royal Navy. Six months later *Katy* was re-named *Providence* and became part of the new American fleet.

The Navy's first shore-based recruit-training station was established at Newport in 1883, followed a year later by the Naval War College, the oldest institution of its kind in the world. There are now so many educational and training centres on Coasters Harbor Island, just north of Newport Bridge, that the area is known as 'the Campus of the Navy'.

The history of the US Navy in Narragansett Bay is told at the **Naval War College Museum**, which also explores the history of the 'art and science' of naval warfare. Admission to the museum is free (access through Gate 1 of the Naval Education and Training Center on Coasters Harbor Island). All graduations, pass-out parades and award ceremonies are open to the public (Tel. 401 841-4052).

enables visitors to watch as surf gushes into the chasm. Local legend tells that the chasm was formed when the devil took an angry swipe at an unwilling Indian maiden.

Portsmouth

Ten miles (16km) north of Newport, Portsmouth was Rhode Island's second settlement after Providence. It was settled in April 1638. The Battle of Rhode Island, the only major engagement in the state during the Revolution, took place at Portsmouth in August 1778. A flagpole and stone monument stand at the junction of Routes 114 and 24 as a memorial to the 1st Rhode Island Regiment which inflicted heavy casualties on Hessian troops fighting on the British side. The monument is known as the Black Regiment Memorial. The members of the 1st Rhode Islanders were all slaves earning their freedom through military service.

Portsmouth's major attraction is **Green Animals** (admission fee), a 7-acre (3-hectare) estate featuring a profusion of animal shapes among 80 pieces of topiary. Located on Cory's Lane, Portsmouth, these fascinating gardens were developed over a period of some 60 years from 1905 and are now maintained by the Preservation Society of Newport County. The main house features its original furnishings and also has on display a Victorian toy collection.

Green Animals is included in the combination tickets that cover the society's Newport Mansions (see p. 185). If you want a change from the car, the estate can be reached on the Old Colony and Newport Railway, which follows an 8-mile (13km) route along Narragansett Bay. The trip from Newport to Green Animals takes about an hour and a half. Tickets can be purchased at the Gateway Information Center or at the railway station at 19 America's Cup Avenue, just north of the information centre.

South County

Officially, there's no such place as South County. The southern part of mainland Rhode Island, between Wickford on Narragansett Bay and Westerly on the Connecticut state line, is actually part of Washington County, but everybody calls it South County, and nobody knows why. The area is undeniably attractive – peaceful, bucolic, picturesque and quaint

– with areas of farmland, swathes of sandy beach, wilderness, historic sites and charming small communities.

Wickford

This colonial town thrived as a shipbuilding centre and fishing port during the 18th and 19th centuries, and many houses from that period are to be seen in the village. On Church Lane, off Main Street, is **Old Narragansett Church,** one of the nation's oldest Episcopal churches. It was built a few miles south of the village in 1707 and moved to its present location in 1800. Just outside Wickford, on Route 1, is **Smith's Castle** (admission fee), built in 1678. Rhode Island's founder, Roger Williams, preached here on many occasions. About 5 miles (8km) south of Wickford, signposted to the west of Route 1A, is the **Gilbert Stuart Birthplace** (admission fee), the gambrel-roofed house in which the portraitist who painted George Washington was born in 1755.

Saunderstown

The **Silas Casey Farm** (admission fee) on Boston Neck Road, Route 1A, Saunderstown, has been cultivated for nearly 300 years. It was founded as a plantation in the early 1700s and was the home of Thomas Lincoln Casey, engineer of the Washington Monument. The 360-acre (150-hectare) farm is still worked. Period furniture, paintings and documents are on display in the 19th-century farmhouse.

Narragansett

Continuing south, Route 1A crosses a stretch of water to reach Narragansett, an important resort and steamer stop on the Newport-New York line at the turn of the century. It's not so busy now, but is still a good centre for touring South County. Many Rhode Islanders believe **Narragansett Town Beach** to be the best in the state. At the height of the town's Victorian popularity crowds would flock to the **Narragansett Pier Casino** to dine and be entertained, but the massive building, designed by the fashionable architects McKim, Mead and White in 1885, was ravaged by fire in 1900. Now only the turreted structure known as The Towers remains. It serves as headquarters for the local chamber of commerce.

At the north end of Narragansett, in the grounds of Canonchet Farm, is the **South County Museum** (admission fee), where traditional crafts are demonstrated in a number of reconstructed buildings. Ocean Road runs south of the town to reach **Point Judith**, where there are fine beaches and a striking ocean view. Just north west of Point Judith is the busy little harbour village of **Galilee**, which has some excellent seafood restaurants. From Galilee you can take the ferry to Block Island, or take a boat trip around the point and across to the village of Jerusalem. Whale-watching trips also start from here.

Wakefield

Route 108 from Point Judith takes you back to Route 1 and the village of Wakefield, where you can see what life has been like in the area during the past three centuries and catch a glimpse of what it was like to be a prisoner in New England's early days. Pettaquamscutt Historical Society maintains a museum in the old **Washington County Jail**, built in 1792.

Further West

West of Wakefield, Route 1 skirts a coastline of beautiful sandy beaches and clear water. One or two of them are crowded at times, but you won't have far to travel to find peace and quiet. **Ninigret Park National Wildlife Refuge**, just south of Charlestown, off Route 1, is a sanctuary for many waterfowl and other bird species and its 400 acres (162 hectares) includes such amenities as picnic areas, cycle paths and a nature centre. The refuge is maintained by the US Fish and Wildlife Service.

Watch Hill, prettily located at the extreme south-west corner of Rhode Island, has been an active resort since Victorian times. It's a good place for shopping, dining, walking and just soaking up a tan on excellent beaches. Children will love the town's **Flying Horse Carousel**, located at the foot of Bay Street. It is believed to be the oldest merry-go-round in the US, dating from around 1867. There are more rides, roller-skating, miniature golf and a giant waterslide at Atlantic Beach Park at **Misquamicut**, just outside Watch Hill.

Block Island

Less well-known than Martha's Vineyard and Nantucket, Block Island has nevertheless enjoyed the following of keen holiday aficionados since the 19th century. The attractions of this dewdrop of an island, 13 miles (21km) offshore, are its unspoilt beauty and the quiet lifestyle of its inhabitants.

Don't get the impression, though, that Block Island, covering a mere 11 square miles ($28km^2$) is dead. There are shops selling T-shirts and salt water *taffy*, jewellery and books, as well as restaurants and inns, and a couple of bars that feature live music. But camping is illegal, motorcycles are not be ridden between midnight and 6am, and mopeds, while available to rent, are frowned upon by locals.

There are good beaches, 365 freshwater ponds, enough gradients to make cycling a pleasure, grassy moors for walking and first-rate birdwatching opportunities in five wildlife refuges. There is only one village, Old Harbor, which has a number of Victorian hotels, as well as the shops and restaurants mentioned above.

Block Island's first residents were Narragansett Indians who used to discourage visitors by tossing them from **Mohegan Bluffs**, the 200ft (61m) cliffs on the southern shore. The island is named after the Dutch navigator Adriaen Block, who claimed it in 1614. The first white settlers, refugees from religious persecution, arrived in 1661. Their names are listed on **Settlers' Rock**, a monument erected on the shores of Chaqum Pond in 1911.

There are ferry services from Galilee State Pier, Point Judith, and from Providence via Newport (summer only). Other summer boat services operate from New London, Connecticut, and Montauk, Long Island. Air services operate from Westerly State Airport and Groton, Connecticut.

Cars and cycles can be rented on the island, and there is a handful of taxi companies. Sailboats, rowing boats, sailboards and surfboards can also be rented.

THE GREAT OUTDOORS

Arcadia Management Area, located in the triangle bordered by Route 165, I-95 and the Connecticut state line, is Rhode Island's largest recreation area, with thousands of acres of wilderness. Crossed by the Appalachian Trail, the park is great hiking country, and there are excellent facilities for boating, freshwater swimming, fishing and picnicking. Year-round camping is available on a private site. The park's entrance is off Route 165 at Arcadia.

Land of the Long River

Because its south-western border is so close to New York City, Connecticut is often claimed to be the gateway to New England. It's certainly an easy state to reach and cross. Interstate 95 runs right along the coast from New York to Rhode Island, paralleled much of the way by Route 1, the old Boston Post Road. I-91 heads north from New Haven through Hartford and on through Massachusetts and Vermont to Canada. I-84 crosses the state from south west to north east.

Measuring only 90 miles (144km) from west to east and 55 miles (88km) from north to south, Connecticut is the third smallest state in the Union, covering an area of less than 5,000 square miles (12,950km^2). Situated more or less centrally, Hartford, the capital, is barely 100 miles (160km) from either Manhattan or Boston.

Bradley International Airport, at Windsor Locks, about 12 miles (20km) north of Hartford, is served by major airlines with connections all over the US. Three smaller airports – Groton-New London, Tweed-New Haven and the Igor Sikorsky Memorial Airport at Bridgeport – are spaced along the coast. For rail travellers, Amtrak's main line runs between New York City's Penn Station and Boston, with stops along the coast and a link from New Haven to Hartford. Metro North carries passengers between New York's Grand Central Terminal and New Haven, with connections from Stamford to New Canaan, South Norwalk to Danbury, and Bridgeport to Waterbury. Scheduled interstate bus services for most points in Connecticut are provided by Greyhound/Trailways and Bonanza lines.

Lighthouse Point Park on Long Island Sound has a public beach, nature trails, a picnic grove and a bird sanctuary.

The Indians called the state Quinnehtukut – 'the place beside the long tidal river'. The Connecticut River, the longest in New England, is certainly a dominant

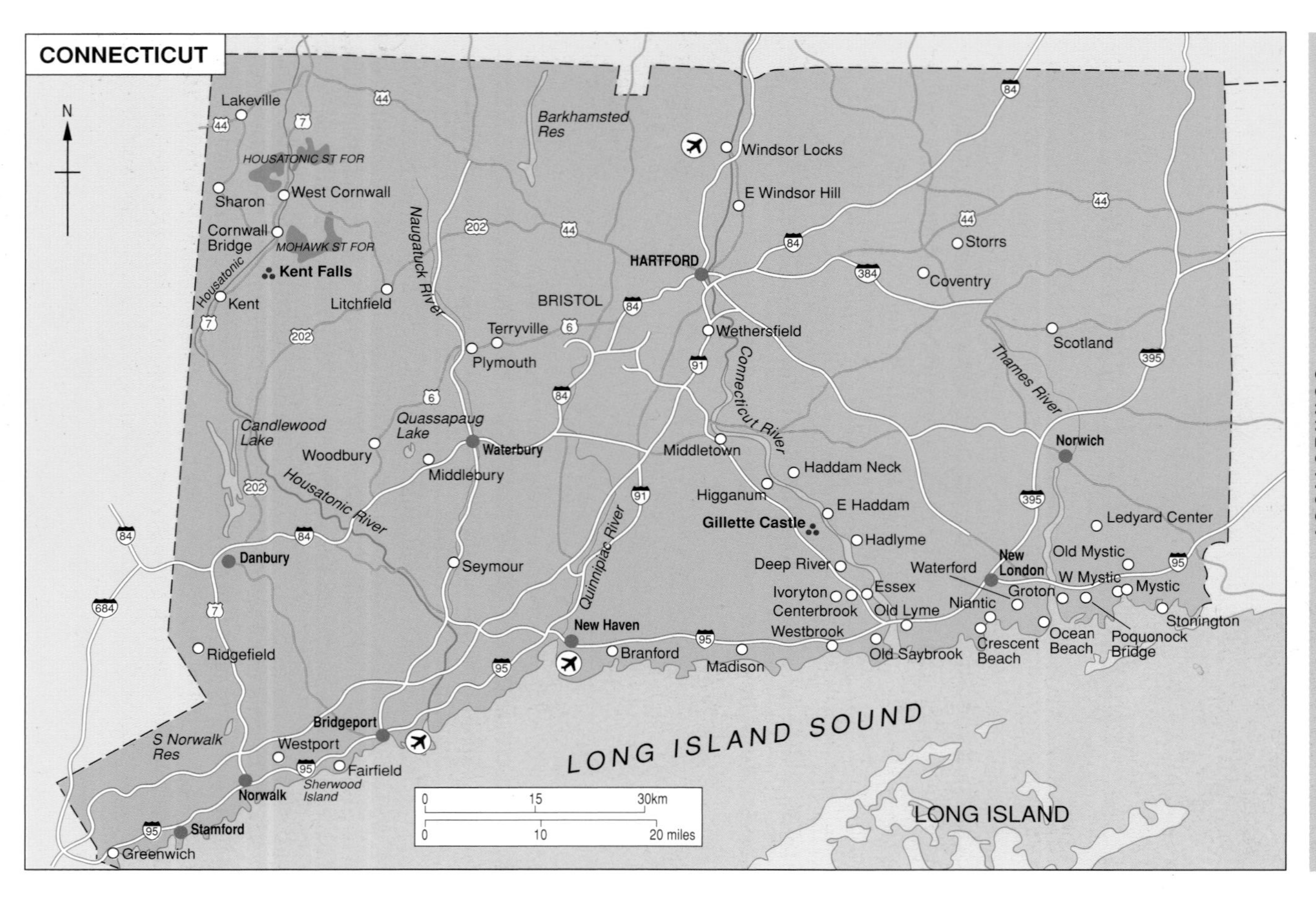
CONNECTICUT
N
Lakeville
HOUSATONIC ST FOR
Sharon
West Cornwall
Cornwall Bridge
MOHAWK ST FOR
Kent Falls
Housatonic
Kent
Litchfield
Naugatuck River
Barkhamsted Res
Windsor Locks
E Windsor Hill
HARTFORD
BRISTOL
Terryville
Plymouth
Wethersfield
Storrs
Coventry
Scotland
Thames River
Connecticut River
Candlewood Lake
Quassapaug Lake
Woodbury
Waterbury
Middlebury
Middletown
Haddam Neck
Higganum
E Haddam
Gillette Castle
Hadlyme
Norwich
Ledyard Center
Housatonic River
Danbury
Seymour
Quinnipiac River
Deep River
Ivoryton
Centerbrook
Essex
Old Lyme
Westbrook
Old Saybrook
Waterford
New London
Niantic
Groton
Crescent Beach
Ocean Beach
Old Mystic
W Mystic
Mystic
Poquonock Bridge
Stonington
New Haven
Branford
Madison
Ridgefield
Bridgeport
Westport
Fairfield
Sherwood Island
S Norwalk Res
Norwalk
Stamford
Greenwich
LONG ISLAND SOUND
LONG ISLAND
0 15 30km
0 10 20 miles
84
44
7
202
6
384
91
395
95
684

The Connecticut River, the longest in New England, splits the state in half and is a great leisure amenity.

feature, splitting the state from north to south into two neat halves. The jagged coastline, sheltered for much of its length by Long Island, covers a total of 253 miles (405km). The great river valley and the natural harbours of the coast attracted settlement first by Native Americans and later by Europeans.

Connecticut is known as 'the Constitution State' and 'the Nutmeg State'. The first appellation stems from the Fundamental Orders of 1639, a written constitution claimed as the world's first and accepted as a basis for governing the Hartford Colony, founded in 1633 by settlers from Massachusetts. The nutmeg reference originated in the days when itinerant and persuasive Yankee peddlars, mainly from Connecticut, could sell anything on the doorsteps of America – even wooden nutmegs.

The state has thrived not only on salesmanship but also on inventiveness and industry in such fields as textiles, engineering, firearms, shipping and insurance.

Although manufacturing industries have played an important role in Connecticut's economy since the Industrial Revolution, much of the state is actually rural, with vast areas of forest, state parks and nature reserves, and hundreds of miles of well-marked hiking trails. In addition to the beaches, the coast offers a wealth of picturesque villages and harbours where a visitor can spend hours painting, sketching, taking photographs, hunting antiques, experiencing the past, or just plain relaxing.

The South-West Shore

Although it forms part of the Manhattan commuter belt, Connecticut's south-west shore has an appealing ambience and a range of scenery and attractions packed into a stretch of coast less than 45 miles (72km) long, from Greenwich near the New York State line to New Haven at the mouth of the Quinnipiac River. Lightly wooded, the area climbs inland to about 800ft (245m). The coastline is broken up by small bays and inlets, and the countryside is dotted with lakes and ponds. The climate is tempered by Long Island Sound, providing pleasant summers and mild winters with more rain than snow.

Many of the area's communities were established in the early 18th century and were soon linked by the Boston Post Road, along which trade and travellers moved in a parade of horse riders, stage-coaches and wagons. This was the start of tourism, and a network of inns and eating places sprang up to meet the needs of those on the move. The network is still there, and so is the old road, now better known as US Route 1, running along the coast in tandem with I-95.

Greenwich

This picturesque commuting suburb was settled in 1640 by two big-spending Englishmen from Massachusetts who paid the Indians a mere 25 cents for the land. The town had a hectic time during the Revolution when British troops destroyed a saltworks and burned down several houses.

Putnam Cottage (admission fee) on Route 1, was built around 1690 and was originally known as Knapp's Tavern. Legend has it that General Israel Putnam, a commander at the battle of Bunker Hill, was attending a meeting at the tavern when British dragoons appeared. He fled and is said to have escaped by spurring his horse over a cliff. Putnam's Cottage is hung with unusual scalloped shingles and has a huge fieldstone fireplace and colonial furniture. It is set in an attractive old herb garden.

The **Bush-Holley House** (admission fee), 39 Strickland Road, is a classic, central-chimney saltbox home built in 1685, and now a National Historic Landmark in which works by Childe Hassam, John Twachtman, Elmer Livingstone MacRae, John Rogers and Leon Volkmar are exhibited. From 1890 to 1925 the house was run as an inn where writers and artists gathered, including those whose work is now displayed there. The house is furnished with pieces from the 18th and 19th centuries.

Stamford

First settled in the 1640s, Stamford is a centre of commerce and industry where the friction clutch, the spring scale and a steam-driven wagon were invented in the 1850s by Simon Ingersoll and where the Yale lock was first manufactured. Local history exhibits, including furniture, quilts, tools and dolls are displayed at the **Stamford Historical Society Museum** (donation) at 1508 High Ridge Road. The society also maintains the 1699 **Hoyt-Barnum House** at 713 Bedford Street (admission by appointment).

New York's prestigious **Whitney Museum of American Art** has its Fairfield County branch at Champion Plaza in downtown Stamford. There is a regular programme of changing exhibitions and special events, and there are permanent displays of sculpture and folk art. There is no charge for admission.

Just north of the town, at 39 Scofieldtown Road (reached from Exit 35, Route 15), the **Stamford Museum and Nature Center** (admission fee) includes a working farm, country store, an observatory and a planetarium on its 118-acre (48-hectare) site. Demonstrations of 19th-century agricultural methods, as well as bee-keeping, cookery and blacksmithing, are given on the farm, and there are permanent exhibits of tools and Native American cultures. In the grounds there are wildlife trails and picnic areas.

Compulsive bargain-hunters will not be able to resist a trip to **United House Wrecking**, at 535 Hope Street, off Route 106. Here the spoils of estate sales and demolitions are up for sale in acres of warehouses and open space – everything you can imagine from antiques to navigational instruments.

Norwalk

South Norwalk, affectionately shortened to SoNo by its citizens, is a lively, revitalized seaside village with lots of galleries, boutiques and restaurants. SoNo's major attraction, however, is the new **Maritime Center** (admission fee), built on 5 acres (2 hectares) around a restored 19th-century factory on the waterfront at 10 North Water Street. There is a huge aquarium and visitors can board a 56ft (17m) oyster sloop, a 30ft (9.2m) steam tender and other vessels. There are demonstrations, exhibitions and an IMAX theatre with a six-storey high screen – all devoted to the ecology and history of Long Island Sound.

To the north, at 295 West Avenue in Norwalk proper, is the **Lockwood-Matthews Mansion Museum** (admission fee), known as 'America's first chateau'. The magnificent mansion has 50 lavishly decorated and furnished rooms and was built in 1864 by Le Grand Lockwood, who was treasurer of the New York Stock Exchange. It cost him $1.2 million.

Westport

This picturesque town attracted a colony of artists at the turn of the century. Today it offers amenities for a restful stop for those bustling along the coast. Just north of the town, at 10 Woodside Avenue (Exit 41, Route 15), the **Nature Center for Environmental Activities** (admission fee) is a 62-acre (25-hectare) wildlife sanctuary with trails and a museum featuring natural science exhibits. The sanctuary also has an aquarium, a live animal hall and a discovery room. Westport's principal summer attraction is **Sherwood Island State Park** (parking fee), which has one and a half miles (2.4km) of sandy beach, two large picnic groves, and provides facilities for fishing, scuba diving, field sports and food.

Fairfield

Fairfield was settled in 1639 and was almost entirely destroyed during a raid in July 1779. The four houses which survived stand to this day on **Beach Road**. More than 100 Revolutionary soldiers are buried in Fairfield's **Old Burying Ground**, also on Beach Road.

A collection of art, furniture, silver, china, glassware, textiles and artefacts from the 18th to 20th centuries is displayed in the **Fairfield Historical Society Museum** (admission fee) at 636 Old Post Road. The society also maintains the **Ogden House** (admission fee), an 18th-century saltbox farmhouse which has been furnished to portray life during the Revolutionary era. The Ogden House is at 1520 Bronson Road.

Fairfield Nature Center (admission fee), maintained by the Connecticut Audubon Society, is a 160-acre (65-hectare) wildlife sanctuary, with 6 miles (9.6km) of trails, and walks for the blind, disabled and elderly. There are natural history exhibits, a compound for injured birds, a reference library and a shop. The nature centre is at 2325 Burr Street, Fairfield (Exit 21, I-95). The society also maintains the **Birdcraft Museum and Sanctuary** (admission fee) at 314 Unquowa Road (Exit 21, I-95). The museum highlights local natural history with dioramas, wildlife exhibits and a children's activity corner. The sanctuary has 6 acres (2.5 hectares) of trails and ponds.

Bridgeport

Connecticut's largest city has a unique claim to fame: it was the first city in the world to produce rust-proof corsets! A rather more enduring achievement was the production of the world's first gramophone, invented by Alexander Graham Bell. The city was founded on the site of a Pequonnock Indian village in 1639 and became an important industrial centre during the 19th century, manufacturing metal fittings, heavy machinery, carriages and ammunition. More recently its industries have suffered a recession.

Its most popular attraction today, however, is undoubtedly the **Barnum Museum** (admission fee) at 961 Main Street, dedicated to the 'Greatest Show on Earth' and the Great Showman himself, Phineas T. Barnum, circus king and one-time mayor of Bridgeport. The museum features permanent exhibits associated with Barnum, General Tom Thumb, and 'the Swedish nightingale' Jenny Lind. There are lots of circus items, and a model of the showman's famous three-ring circus. Tom Thumb, born Charles S. Stratton in Bridgeport in 1838, stopped growing at the age of 7 months, and at a height of just over 2ft (0.61m) became a famous figure on Barnum's world tours. The two men are buried in the city's Mountain Grove Cemetery, on the corner of North Avenue and Dewey Street.

Captain's Cove, at the end of Bostwick Avenue, is an historic waterfront area with craft shops, restaurants and a fish market. Band concerts and special events take place on Sunday afternoons. A big attraction here is a replica of *HMS Rose*, a 24-gun frigate at the time of the Revolutionary War. There is an admission fee for boarding the vessel, which is not always in port.

Beardsley Zoological Gardens (admission fee) houses some 200 animals, ranging from North American mammals to exotic rain forest species, on a site of 36 acres (15 hectares) at Beardsley Park (Exit 27A, I-95). There is also a children's zoo standing in a New England farm setting, as well as pony rides, a picnic area and snack bar.

Bridgeport's **Discovery Museum** (admission fee) is an interactive art and science museum with about 100 hands-on exhibits, a planetarium, and the Challenger Learning Center where visitors can take part in computer-simulated space missions. There is also a children's museum. The art galleries have a wide range of exhibits, from the Renaissance to contemporary works. The Discovery Museum is at 4450 Park Avenue (Exit 27, I-95 or Exit 47, Route 15).

New Haven – Downtown

Right from the start New Haven was dedicated to the good life. Led by wealthy Theophilus Eaton, the 500 settlers who arrived from England in 1638 were pledged to found a colony based on sound finances and a minimum of the discomfort encountered by previous New World pioneers. Attracted to the area by its excellent harbour, the settlers soon had their new town laid out on a gridiron pattern. By the 1800s New Haven was an established shipping and industrial centre, so successful that from 1784 to 1875 it shared the status of state capital with Hartford. Although it still earns much of its revenue from manufacturing industries, the city today is best known as the seat of **Yale University.**

The gridiron on which those first settlers laid out their town was based on nine squares with a large green at the centre.

Covering 17 acres (7 hectares), the old green still forms the heart of the city with its three fine churches – the Georgian-style **Center Church,** Federalist **United Church** and the Gothic Revival **Trinity Church** – all built between 1812 and 1815. Most of the city's sightseeing attractions are within walking distance of the green.

New Haven's cultural and social character is largely influenced by the presence of Yale University. There are three theatres, important art galleries and libraries, and a thriving music scene. Shops range from campus bookstores to upmarket boutiques. Chapel Square Mall, opposite the green, contains more than 60 shops. For diners the choice ranges from lowly student cafes and fast food joints to haute cuisine establishments.

New Haven was founded in 1638 as a colony based on sound finances and a minimum of discomfort.

The **Beinecke Rare Book Library,** 121 Wall Street, provides a double treat. Its collection includes a *Gutenberg Bible*, illuminated manuscripts and original Audubon bird prints, and the building itself, erected in 1963, features windows of translucent marble and a sunken sculpture garden with works by Isamu Noguchi.

Yale University's **Peabody Museum of Natural History** (admission fee), at 170 Whitney Avenue, is one of the oldest university museums of its kind in the US and the largest in New England. There are dinosaur fossils and exhibits of Neolithic, Pacific, Mesoamerican and ancient Egyptian cultures. Connecticut's wildlife and Native American culture is also featured. Nearby, at 114 Whitney Street, the **New Haven Colony Historical Society** maintains a museum which features historical and industrial exhibits and houses a permanent display of decorative tableware.

YALE UNIVERSITY

Yale University campus is entered at Phelps Gate, 344 College Street, facing New Haven Green. The university's oldest building is **Connecticut Hall**, a Georgian brick structure dating from 1717. **Harkness Tower**, also on the Old Campus, is a bell tower 221ft (67m) high, bearing the university's motto, 'For God, for country, and for Yale.'

There are 12 self-contained colleges on the campus. Most of the dignified buildings, their walls covered in ivy, were built between 1919 and 1941. Visitors may wander the campus on their own – maps are available from the information office near Phelps Gate. Guided tours leave the information office twice daily.

Also in the area, at 15 Hillhouse Avenue, is the **Yale Collection of Musical Instruments** (donation suggested), a museum displaying 850 instruments from the 16th to the 20th centuries.

Two other Yale institutions open to the public, both free, are the **Center for British Art** at 1080 Chapel Street and the **University Art Gallery** at 1111 Chapel Street. The first is a museum and research institute with a collection of British paintings, drawings, prints, rare books and sculpture from Elizabethan times to the present day. The art gallery, the oldest college art museum in the country, has a collection of some 75,000 works, ranging from ancient Egypt to the 20th century. A major attraction is its reconstructed Mithraic shrine.

The **Connecticut Children's Museum**, at 22 Wall Street, is designed to encourage discovery and the use of imagination in children aged seven and under, who must be accompanied by an adult. A play village has shops, a hospital and a restaurant.

New Haven Environs

Half a dozen of New Haven's attractions are away from the downtown area, and all but one provide an opportunity for some fresh-air sightseeing.

North of the city, at East Rock Road (I-91, Willow Street exit), **East Rock Park** is New Haven's largest park, with a bird sanctuary, nature trails, playgrounds, recreation facilities and picnic sites. Further west, on Wintergreen Avenue (Exit 59, Route 15), is the **West Rock Nature Center**, a year-round zoo covering 40 acres (16 hectares) and featuring native birds, reptiles and mammals. There are picnic facilities and hiking trails, including the Regicide Trail which leads to a cave in which two of the men who had signed the warrant for the execution of

Black Rock Fort, one of two reconstructed forts guarding New Haven harbour.

England's King Charles I hid after the restoration of the monarchy.

South of the downtown area, on Woodward Avenue, are **Black Rock** and **Nathan Hale Forts**, reconstructed defences from the Revolutionary and Civil Wars. Both provide spectacular views of New Haven harbour.

Lighthouse Point Park is an 82-acre (33-hectare) park on Long Island Sound with a public beach, nature trails, a picnic grove and a bird sanctuary. There is a fee for parking. Nearby, at 325 Lighthouse Road, is the **Pardee-Morris House** (admission fee), a restored colonial home built in 1780 and featuring furnishings from the 17th to 19th centuries. The house stands on the site of a home built 30 years earlier and burned down by British troops in 1779.

Four miles (6.4km) out of town, across New Haven Harbor, is the **Shore Line Trolley Museum** (admission fee) at 17 River Street, East Haven. A registered National Historic Site, the museum has a collection of nearly 100 classic trolleys, including the first electric freight locomotive, the oldest rapid transit car and a vintage parlour car. Visitors can take trolley rides.

The South-East Shore

Tourism has taken over from whaling and fishing in many of the towns and villages along the coast from New Haven to Stonington. There are a number of historic homes, art galleries and museums to visit.

Westbrook

On the coast near the mouth of the Connecticut River, is the **Military Historians Headquarters**, a museum with the largest collection of American military uniforms in the country. Restored and working vehicles range from a World War II Weasel to a Desert Storm truck. The museum is located on North Main Street and is open Tuesday to Friday from 8am to 3.30pm.

About 7 miles (11km) west of Westbrook, at Madison, is **Hammonesset Beach State Park** (parking fee), the biggest shoreline park in Connecticut, with camping, picnicking, boating, sea water fishing, swimming, hiking and scuba diving.

Old Lyme

Old Lyme was known as an artists' colony in the early 1900s when patron of the arts Florence Griswold opened her home at 96 Lyme Street to painters to study and work in the area. Noted American Impressionists and others who stayed there are represented at what is now the **Florence Griswold Museum** (admission fee).

New London

Once a busy port, New London draws visitors today with its historic, literary and marine connections. It is the home of the **US Coast Guard Academy** – one of the nation's four military academies. When she is in port, the tall ship *Eagle* can be viewed (Friday to Sunday afternoons). The Visitors' Pavilion features a multimedia show on cadet life. Cadet dress parades often take place on Fridays at 4pm in spring and fall. The 200-acre (81-hectare) campus can be toured, and visits may coincide with a concert by the US Coast Guard Band.

New London's oldest surviving house, the 1678 **Joshua Hempsted House**, at 11 Hempsted Street, and the mid-18th-century **Nathaniel Hempsted House** in

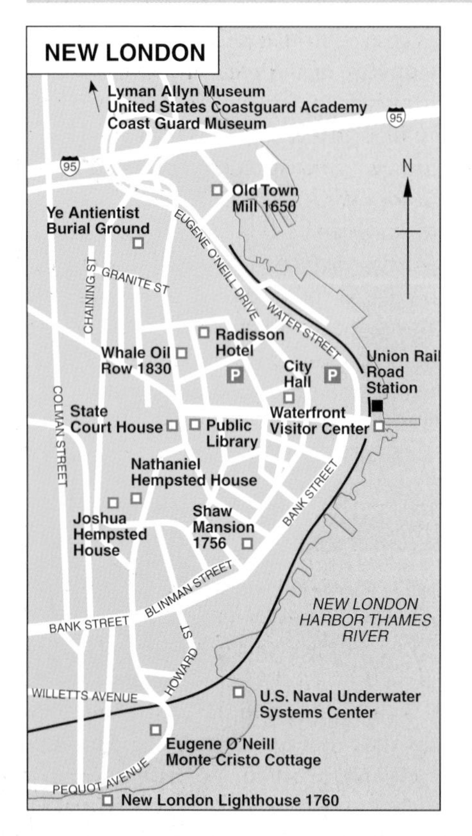

the grounds (one admission charge covers both properties) are open Thursday to Sunday from noon to 5pm from mid-May to mid-October. Early American furnishings are shown at Joshua's house. Nathaniel's is noted for its rare cut-stone architecture, its projecting stone beehive oven and its period furnishings.

The boyhood home of Eugene O'Neill, considered by many to be America's greatest playwright, is **Monte Cristo Cottage** (admission fee), on Pequot Avenue, New London. The cottage contains memorabilia and gives an insight into the sometimes difficult family relationships of the writer. A visit starts with a short multimedia presentation. Visiting writers

Visitors may tour the campus of the US Coast Guard Academy at New London. It is one of four military academies throughout the country.

can sometimes be seen working in an upstairs room.

As well as permanent and changing exhibits of fine and decorative arts, Old Master drawings, Impressionist paintings and colonial and federal furniture, the **Lyman Allyn Art Museum** (donation suggested) at 625 Williams Street, displays antique dolls, dolls houses and toys.

Ocean Beach Park, on Long Island Sound, has a beachfront boardwalk, rides and waterslides, playground and pool for small children, mini-golf and a variety of watersports.

Niantic

Just south of New London, Niantic grew along with the arrival of the railroad during the mid-1800s, which brought summer visitors from New York. Today, the scenic Niantic River, Nehantic State Forest and **Rocky Neck State Park**, with its extensive, crescent-shaped sandy beach, attract people from more distant places. Rocky Neck has a picnic pavilion, hiking trails, a woodland campground and excellent fishing – mackerel, flounder and striped bass make up the main catches.

The **Millstone Information and Science Center** on Main Street, Niantic, shows that science can be fun. Visitors can play energy and computer games and are challenged to light up an entire house with a bicycle generator.

The **Thomas Lee House** (admission fee) on West Main Street is the oldest wooden

Monte Cristo Cottage in New London was the boyhood home of Eugene O'Neill, and gives an insight into the playwright's family relationships.

UP AND DOWN

If you want a bird's eye view of things, why not try a balloon trip over the Litchfield Hills? These are offered all year round by Watershed Balloons, Watertown (Tel. 203 274-2010).

frame house in Connecticut still standing on its original site. It dates from 1660. Also can be seen the 1734 **Little Boston School**, the first district school between New York and Boston. The house and school are open Tuesday to Sunday afternoons between late June and early September.

Waterford

Here the Historical Society operates a replica of a **Colonial Village** at Jordans Green. Buildings include a 1740 schoolhouse, an 1840 farmhouse and a blacksmith's shop. A museum and education centre are on-site. For shopping, Waterford has the two-storey Crystal Mall, with a food court and 150 stores, including Filene's and Sears.

Groton

I-95 takes you across the estuary of the Thames River to Groton, where you can tour the world's first nuclear-powered

The history of the US Navy submarine force can be traced at the Nautilus Memorial Museum, Groton.

submarine. The **Nautilus Memorial/ Submarine Force Library and Museum** has working periscopes and midget submarines, and depicts the history of the US Navy submarine force.

Fort Griswold Battlefield State Park at Groton is the site of the 1781 killing of American defenders by British troops in a battle that lasted only 40 minutes. The park is open all year. The museum and 134ft (41m) high granite monument are open during the summer when historic displays take place.

Mystic

As well as the seaport, Mystic has a **Marinelife Aquarium**. This is open all year round except during the last week in January and the major holidays (admission fee) and presents beluga whales and bottlenose dolphins who demonstrate their physique and intelligence in their pool in a 1,400-seat theatre. There are 6,000 living specimens of underwater life grouped in 50 major exhibits. Penguins and seals can be observed out of doors in their natural habitats.

It's pleasant on a sunny day to watch the **Bascule Bridge** (a drawbridge) operating as world class yachts move along the Mystic River. Another ideal place for strolling is **Olde Mistick Village**, at Coogan Boulevard, a colonial-like centre of 60 shops, restaurants and a theatre, which was built in 1720s style. The shops sell unusual goods imported from around the world and individual items handcrafted around Mystic.

The Village has a pond with turtles and ducks, a stream, and lanes with such

A WHALE OF AN ATTRACTION

Mystic Seaport is the state's major attraction, a restored 19th-century village with tall ships, working craftspeople and a whaling history.

You can board the last wooden whaling ship, the *Charles W. Morgan,* to see the crew's cramped quarters in the fo'c's'le and the captain's stateroom with en suite facilities.

It's worth devoting several hours, or even a couple of days to **Mystic Seaport** (admission fee). The 17 acres (7 hectares) of living museum fronting the Mystic River include a planetarium explaining navigation by the stars, rigging and sail lofts, and demonstrations of wooden boat-building, wood carving, and ironworking. There's a smokehouse for preserving fish, as well as a cooperage, a children's toy and play museum, a sailors' tavern, a non-denominational chapel, and many other active exhibits reflecting life in Mystic's shipbuilding and whaling heyday.

Galleries exhibit nautical items from ships in bottles to ships' figureheads. Five shops under one roof sell books, contemporary marine art, nautical prints, confectionery and a wide range of quality gifts. There are catering outlets and waterside clambakes over open wood fires.

As well as the 1882 training ship *Joseph Conrad* and the 1921 fishing schooner *L.A. Dunton* bobbing at anchor, America's last coal-fired steamboat can be often be seen at its mooring. Short cruises past historic homes and fishing communities leave half-hourly in summer.

Mystic Seaport can be toured by horse-drawn wagon (at an extra charge). Special events take place throughout the year, including lantern-light tours in December.

The museum was founded in 1929. It is a privately-operated, non-profit-making educational institution which pursues the collection, preservation and exhibition of artefacts and skills related to maritime history and its influence on American life.

Cramped quarters for the captain of the Charles W. Morgan, *last of the wooden whaling ships, now moored at Mystic Seaport.*

names as Button Ball Lane, Dingley Dell and Featherbed Lane. Musicians, dancers and storytellers provide free entertainment in the Victorian gazebo and the colonial meeting house.

Sea creatures entertain in natural surroundings at Mystic Marinelife Aquarium.

Stonington

Just east of Mystic is Stonington, the last Connecticut coastal community before the Rhode Island state line. The best way to see Stonington on a fine day is by hay wagon. David Farm Horse-drawn Hayrides operate one-hour trips by wagon pulled by Belgian/Amish horses, all year, by reservation (Tel. 203 599-5841). For a view of the area from above, you can take a champagne flight in a hot-air balloon with Mystic River Balloon Adventures (Tel. 203 535-0283). The company operates year-round, weather permitting.

Stonington is the home port of Connecticut's only fishing fleet. Fishing and whaling gear, toys and Stonington-made firearms and stoneware are among the exhibits in the **Old Lighthouse Museum** (admission fee) at 7 Water Street.

THE TRIBE THAT HIT THE JACKPOT

Casino gambling is illegal in many states, including Connecticut, but Indian reservations are exempt, and a number of tribes have set up casinos since obtaining federal recognition.

Foxwoods High Stakes Bingo and Casino, on Route 2 at Ledyard, north of Mystic, is vast, and still growing. Free parking places are numbered in thousands with at least 1,200 slots for the employees alone.

This is the story of the tribe that hit the jackpot. The Mashantucket Pequot Indians were in decline earlier this century because of a down-turn in their major cottage industry, basket-making.

In the mid-1970s a welder and pipe fitter, Richard 'Skip' Hayward, chairman of the Mashantucket Pequot Tribal Council, wanted to get the tribe back together. It owned 214 acres (87 hectares), but tales told by tribal elders led Skip Hayward and others to believe land had been stolen from the tribe in the past.

Research into the history of land transference to non-Indians enabled them in 1976 to bring a suit with the aid of the Native American Rights Fund. The US Congress enacted the Mashantucket Pequot Indian Land Claims Settlement Act, settling the claim and providing federal recognition. Few Indian tribes in the US have had land returned on such a scale as the Pequots. By 1991 their holding had increased to 1,795 acres (726 hectares).

Following the lead taken by other federally-recognized tribes, the Pequots opened a high stakes bingo operation on their reservation, in an 1,800-seat hall opened in July 1986. In February 1992 the casino, which offers at least a dozen games, from blackjack to roulette and as many types of poker, and has hundreds of slot machines, was open for business 24 hours a day. 'We haven't closed since we opened,' said Pequot tribe member and its former marketing executive, John Holder. 'I don't even know where the key is.'

Two and a half million people live within a two-hour drive of Foxwoods, which attracts about 14,000 people every day.

Indian tribes are exempt from state tax, but the Pequot tribe voluntarily contributes millions of dollars a year to Connecticut. Tribe members employed at the casino complex get an annual share-out of profits on top of their pay. Money is invested in a continual learning programme for the tribe, and the children are encouraged to go for further education.

Since the casino opened, work has continued on extending it, and adding a Native American museum, a 280-room inn, a 312-room luxury hotel, golf courses, monorail, shops, extra restaurants and a Cinetropolis – a state-of-the-art theatre and nightclub.

'We haven't had to borrow a dime, yet,' said John Holder.

Conducted winery tours, with tastings, are offered by **Stonington Vineyards** on Taugwonk Road, 2 1/2 miles (4km) north of Exit 91 off I-95.

The North East

Connecticut's north-east region is known as the Quiet Corner. Some of its dense forests, lakes and rolling hills are state parkland, and much of it remains undeveloped. Here also is the state's main agricultural area.

The University of Connecticut is situated at Storrs. Nearby is Coventry, where most of the attractions are pastoral, such as the **Caprilands Herb Farm**, which grows more than 300 different herb varieties and serves its visitors herbal teas, and the **Nutmeg Vineyards Farm Winery,** where vineyard walks and wine tasting can be enjoyed. Caprilands, at 534 Silver Street, Coventry, offers garden tours at noon on weekdays, from April to December. The Vineyards, at 800 Bunker Hill, Coventry, are open at weekends all year round.

Visitors interested in horse riding through the region can call the Diamond A Ranch (Tel. 203 779-3000). If you prefer paddling about in a canoe, you can rent boats at the River Bend Campground in Sterling (Tel. 203 546-3440).

River Country

The great Connecticut River is the longest in New England, flowing across the region for 350 miles (560km). It reaches Long Island Sound between Old Saybrook and Old Lyme (see p. 201). There is no port at its mouth because of a sand bar which prevents deep-water navigation.

An excellent way to see the area is by train and boat. Both modes of transport are provided by the Valley Railroad Company, with whom you can ride the **Connecticut Valley Line** by steam or diesel-hauled train. You can return by rail or transfer at Deep River to the company's multi-deck riverboat, the *Becky Thatcher*, for an hour's cruise back to Essex. Not all departures connect with the boat, so check at Essex Station when you buy your ticket. A commentary goes with the train ride, which is in restored vintage rail cars. Reservations are required for a two-hour excursion in the beautifully restored 1920s dinner train, the North Cove Express (Tel. 203 621-9311). This runs on Friday and Saturday evenings. Valley Railroad Company trips operate from May to December, with 'specials' like a Halloween Ghost Train ride and Santa's North Pole Express. Other trip boats ply on the river, and fishing boats and pleasure cruisers can be rented.

Old Saybrook

On the western side of the estuary, Old Saybrook is a pleasant place for a stroll and the birthplace of David Bushnell, a farmworker from boyhood who saved hard for years until at the age of 31 he could study at Yale. In 1775 he invented the first submarine, *The Turtle*, a replica of which can be seen in the **Connecticut River Museum** just up-river at Main Street, Essex (Route 9, Exit 3). The museum (admission fee) has many exhibits, models of ships and a waterfront park.

Essex

Essex has an attractive main street of 18th- and 19th-century buildings. It has been placed second in Norman Crampton's book, *Best Small Towns in America*. It was an important shipbuilding centre from the mid-1800s to the mid-1900s, but today the river serves the needs of recreational boating.

Next door to Essex is Ivoryton, where martial music is played on July and August evenings at the **Museum of Fife and Drum** on North Main Street. The museum (admission fee) presents America on Parade, from Revolutionary War days right up to the present.

Chester

The **National Theater of the Deaf** is based at West Main Street, Chester, though performances in sign language and the spoken word take place in several locations (Tel. 203 526-4971).

Travelling Upstream

Gillette Castle stands imposingly on a rocky bluff above the Connecticut River at River Road, Hadlyme, providing a wonderful view. The 24-room property opens for tours, the grounds surrounding it are a state park enjoyed by hikers and picnickers (admission fee). The mansion was completed in 1919 as a private home for the actor William Gillette, who was known for his portrayal of Sherlock Holmes. Hand-carved fixtures inside are the work of Gillette, who died in 1937.

At East Haddam (Route 82) is the **Goodspeed Opera House**, built in 1876, on the eastern bank of the river. It incorporates a library of the American Musical Theater, with sheet music dating back nearly 150 years, video cassettes and old theatre programmes.

A ferryboat crosses the Connecticut River between Mystic and Hadlyme.

Farther upstream is Haddam Neck (Route 9, Exit 7), with the **Connecticut Yankee Information and Science Center** in the grounds of a nuclear power plant in Injun Hollow Road. This has exhibits on energy and nuclear power, environmental monitoring and emergency preparedness.

Formal gardens in 17th- and 18th-century style, with herb shop and tea room, can be seen at the **Sundial Herb Garden** at Brault Hill Road, Hagganum, off Route 81.

Middletown

The town mid-way between Old Saybrook and the state capital, Hartford, is called Middletown. It became prosperous in the late 18th century when shipbuilding and trading with the West Indies were flourishing. The Wesleyan University was founded at Middletown in 1831. In spite of its name, however, the university has always been non-sectarian.

Memorabilia of the two world wars is exhibited at the **Submarine Library Museum** at 440 Washington Street. Displays include a complete set of model World War II submarines. The museum (no charge) is open weekends only, all year.

Middletown has an impressive craft gallery at 350 South Main Street. **Wesleyan Potters** has changing craft exhibits, with hand-made items for sale. There are pottery and weaving studios.

Hartford

Standing in an area known for tourism purposes as the 'Crossroads of Connecticut', Hartford, together with West Hartford, offers a range of cultural, historical, literary and recreational attractions.

The **Old State House**, at 80 Main Street, now a museum and home of the city's visitor centre, is the oldest in the nation. It is on the site of the signing of what is believed to be the world's first written constitution. It was built in Federal style between 1792 and 1796, and became the city hall for a number of years.

Hartford is known as 'Insurance City', and some of its grand buildings are insurance company headquarters. The first such business was founded in the city in 1810. Its history is chronicled at **The Hartford Exhibit** at ITT Insurance Group, Asylum Avenue, with multimedia presentations and displays on weekdays. **Travelers Companies Tower**, the office of another pioneer company, at Tower Square, Main Street, provides views of the surrounding area from its observation deck.

Hartford's prosperity during the 18th century was based on shipping and manufacturing. Samuel Colt invented the revolver here. The city's old and new buildings sit comfortably together, and **Bushnell Park** provides a pleasant green centre in the downtown area. Here, for a very small outlay, you can ride a famous 1914 carousel with 48 prancing horses carved by Stein and Goldstein. Music is provided by a 1925 Wurlitzer organ.

Free one-hour tours of the gold-domed **State Capitol and Legislative Office** building on Capitol Avenue are given on weekdays, and on Saturdays, too, during the summer. The building opened in 1879. Flags riddled with bullet holes and Lafayette's camp bed are on display.

Connecticut's state capital, prosperous Hartford, is known as Insurance City.

DELTA
AIR LINES

A number of homes from the 18th and 19th centuries are open to the public in Hartford and its environs. Among them are those of two literary figures – Harriet Beecher Stowe, whose works included *Uncle Tom's Cabin,* and Mark Twain, author of *Huckleberry Finn, A Connecticut Yankee in King Arthur's Court* and other works. Both homes (admission fee) are on Farmington Avenue, at Woodland Street, Hartford. The **Mark Twain Memorial Home** of 1874, all turrets and balconies, has interiors by Louis Comfort Tiffany and is a National Historic Landmark. Mrs Stowe's 1871 cottage is in a more restrained style. Guided tours and a gift shop are available year-round.

Wadsworth Atheneum (admission fee, but free on Thursdays and 11am-noon, Saturdays), at 600 Main Street, is the nation's oldest continuously operating public art museum. It opened in 1842 and houses more than 45,000 works covering a large range of 19th- and 20th-century paintings and decorative arts. There are changing exhibitions of contemporary art. The museum is closed on Mondays and major holidays.

The worlds of science, nature and technology are explored at the **Science Museum of Connecticut** (admission fee) at Trout Brook Drive, West Hartford. A planetarium, mini-zoo, touch tank of marine life, computer laboratory and discovery room appeal to children.

Nearly 6,000 people, including 17th-century settlers and victims of the Revolutionary War, have their final resting

The eccentrically styled Mark Twain Memorial Home, built in 1874.

The outsize foot of Tyrranosaurus Rex *is one of the exhibits at Rocky Hill Dinosaur State Park, near Hartford.*

place in the **Ancient Burying Ground** at the corner of Gold Street and Main Street.

Dinosaur tracks from the Jurassic Period – which makes them 185 million years old – can be seen beneath the impressive dome at the **Rocky Hill Dinosaur State Park,** about 10 miles (16km) south of Hartford (off I-91). Visitors can make plaster casts of dinosaur footprints. The park has nature trails and a picnic area. There is an admission charge to the Exhibit Center.

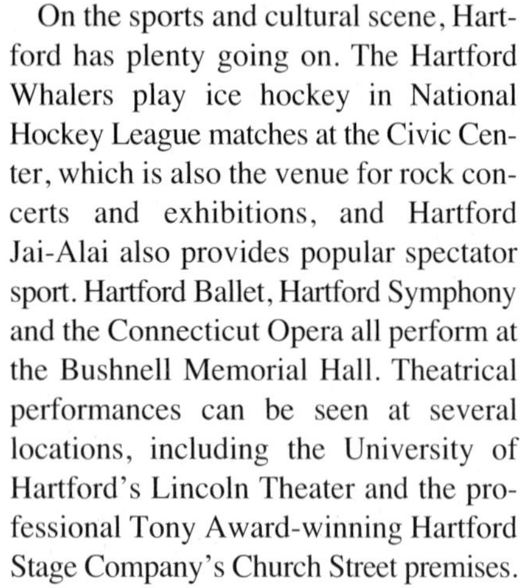

On the sports and cultural scene, Hartford has plenty going on. The Hartford Whalers play ice hockey in National Hockey League matches at the Civic Center, which is also the venue for rock concerts and exhibitions, and Hartford Jai-Alai also provides popular spectator sport. Hartford Ballet, Hartford Symphony and the Connecticut Opera all perform at the Bushnell Memorial Hall. Theatrical performances can be seen at several locations, including the University of Hartford's Lincoln Theater and the professional Tony Award-winning Hartford Stage Company's Church Street premises.

Old colonial homes are a feature of **Wethersfield**, a town on the southern outskirts of Hartford, which claims to be the first permanent settlement in Connecticut (Windsor makes a similar claim).

Restored homes of the 18th and 19th centuries, with the appropriate furnishings, are open to the public in the **Old Town**, with a museum, church and 17th-century burial ground.

North of Hartford

Follow US Route 5 north out of Hartford towards Windsor, turning on to Route 140 for East Windsor and the **Connecticut Trolley Museum** in North Road (admission fee). More than 50 trolley cars dating from 1894 to 1949 are displayed, and visitors can take a three-mile antique trolley ride (Tel. 860 627-6540).

At the western end of nearby Windsor Locks, at Bradley International Airport (Route 75) is the **New England Air Museum** (admission fee), which has the largest indoor display of aircraft in the north-eastern US. Here you can get a good look at bombers, fighters, helicopters, gliders, and classic private and commercial planes from 1909 through both world wars to the present. You can also 'fly' a jet plane with the aid of a flight simulator. Aviation films are shown throughout the day and there's a gift shop.

A brief drive north takes you to East Granby and a chance to tour the underground caverns of the earliest copper mine in the US, which dates from 1707.

The New England Air Museum, near Windsor Locks, has the largest indoor display of aircraft in the north-eastern US. This is the Gee Bee Racer.

Together with the ruins of the **Old New-Gate Prison,** where debtors, adulterers, thieves and others were flung, to live in appalling conditions, it is a National Historic Landmark (admission fee).

Litchfield Hills and The Valleys

Connecticut's western region includes the Litchfield Hills, and in the central and southern parts, The Valleys – an area with a network of rivers, including the Nangatuck and the long Housatonic River.

The Hills

Route 7 keeps the Housatonic company through the Northwest Hills and the Housatonic State Forest. It is a wonderfully scenic drive, passing near the town of Kent where the covered Bulls Bridge crosses the river into New York State. A little farther north, on Route 128, the West Cornwall covered bridge has been in continuous use since 1837.

Litchfield, set amid the hills, has conscientiously preserved its character over the years. Today, people visit the town to enjoy its common, dating back to the 1770s, and to see its 18th- and 19th-century architecture. The town and its surrounding area have become home to a number of celebrities in search of rural peace.

Excitement rather than peace is what you will get if you visit **Lime Rock Park** in Lakeville, in the state's north-west corner. Actor Paul Newman has been known to take to the motor-racing track there from time to time.

Driving south from Lakeville you will find Sharon, on Route 4. The **National Audubon Society's Northeast Center**, a 680-acre (275-hectare) sanctuary (admission fee) is here, with self-guiding trails, wildflower and herb gardens, an interpretive centre, book and gift shops and a discovery room for children. The sanctuary opens daily, 9am-5pm, Sun 1-5pm, but is closed on major holidays. Trails are open from dawn to dusk.

Nature lovers will also enjoy two free attractions in the Litchfield area. One is **White Flower Farm** on Route 63. The gardens here are open from spring to fall, but the peak time for colourful blooms is between June and September. The other attraction is the **White Memorial Foundation** on Route 202. This is Connecticut's largest nature centre and wildlife sanctuary, with 4,000 acres (1,620 hectares) and 35 miles (56km) of trails. Hiking, horseriding, fishing and cross-country skiing are among the activities.

The **Lourdes in Litchfield Shrine** has a pilgrimage season from May to mid-October (for schedule Tel. 203 567-1041). A replica of the grotto at Lourdes in France is in a 35-acre (14-hectare) shrine, maintained by Montfort Missionaries.

To the east, on Maple Street, Bristol, off Route 6, is the **American Clock and Watch Museum.** The 1801 house (admission fee) contains more than 3,000 timepieces, from novelty watches to grandfather clocks. A tour traces Bristol's clock-making history. There is also a sundial garden.

More illustrations of craftwork of the past can be seen at nearby Terryville, where the **Lock Museum of America,** on Main Street, houses 22,000 locks and allied artefacts, and the **Kerosene Lamp Museum** at Winchester Center (100 Old Waterbury Turnpike) in the far north of the state. A private collection of more than 500 lamps in use between 1852 and 1880 can be seen. An admission fee is charged at the Lock Museum.

Driving south, those interested in antiques should visit the pretty town of **Woodbury**, where Main Street is dubbed 'Antiques Avenue'.

The Valleys

This region in the south west, once a centre of mill towns and manufacturing industries, today has a mixture of industry and commerce. There are large lakes and reservoirs used for swimming and boating in the Housatonic Valley area. One, Lake Quassapaug, is at Middlebury, where the **Quassy Amusement Park** offers more than 30 rides and games.

If some of the scenery in this region seems familiar, perhaps you saw the Danny De Vito film *'Other People's Money'* or *'Stanley and Iris'*, starring Robert de Niro and Jane Fonda. Scenes for the first film were shot in Seymour and for the second in Waterbury.

The hat-making industry put Danbury on the North American map. In Main Street the **Scott-Fanton Museum** has the John Dodd Hat Shop (1790), with exhibits from 'Hat City's' millinery heyday. There are Revolutionary War exhibits and memorabilia relating to the musician Charles Ives, who was born in Danbury. Blues, jazz and other concerts are held during the summer at the outdoor Charles Ives Center in Danbury.

At Ridgefield the **Keeler Tavern Museum,** at 132 Main Street, is a tavern with a British cannonball embedded in its wall. The missile has remained there ever since a conflict in the Revolutionary War of Independence.

The oldest copper mines in the United States, which date from 1707, can be found at East Granby.

Mountains, Maple Syrup and Snow Galore

The Green Mountains which give Vermont its name form a slightly off-centre spine down much of the state. Lake Champlain borders most of the west, with New York State on the other side of the water and the northernmost part of the lake spilling into Canadian territory. Ninety miles (144km) of Vermont adjoins the Canadian province of Quebec.

Hundreds of miles of hiking trails criss-cross the Green Mountains, which are gentle, richly forested and mostly under 4,000ft (1,220m). Many people enjoy inn-to-inn hikes or bike rides in summer. In winter, an average of 200 inches (500cm) or more of snow falls, and it is constantly topped up with the artificial sort on the ski slopes. Alpine and cross-country skiing have a long season. One resort, Killington, provides the longest ski season in the United States. The sport can run until as late as June with the aid of state-of-the-art snow-making technology. More than half of the season's snow in Vermont falls after mid-February.

Leaf-peeping is an autumn pursuit of thousands of visitors to Vermont.

Lake Champlain, 120 miles (192km) long, provides heart-lifting views from Vermont across to the Adirondack Mountains. The boundary with New York State runs down the middle of the lake. Ferries cross regularly, one of them operating year-round. Islands in the lake can be reached by causeway on Route 2 north of Burlington, Vermont's biggest city. This has a population of around 40,000. Motorists can also cross close to the border with Canada. Camping, boat rentals and nature trails are available in a public recreation area on Grand Isle on the lake.

Vermont is dotted with dozens of covered bridges, the oldest, the Pulp Mill Bridge, built in 1820, is at Middlebury. The newest, at Woodstock, is as recent as 1969.

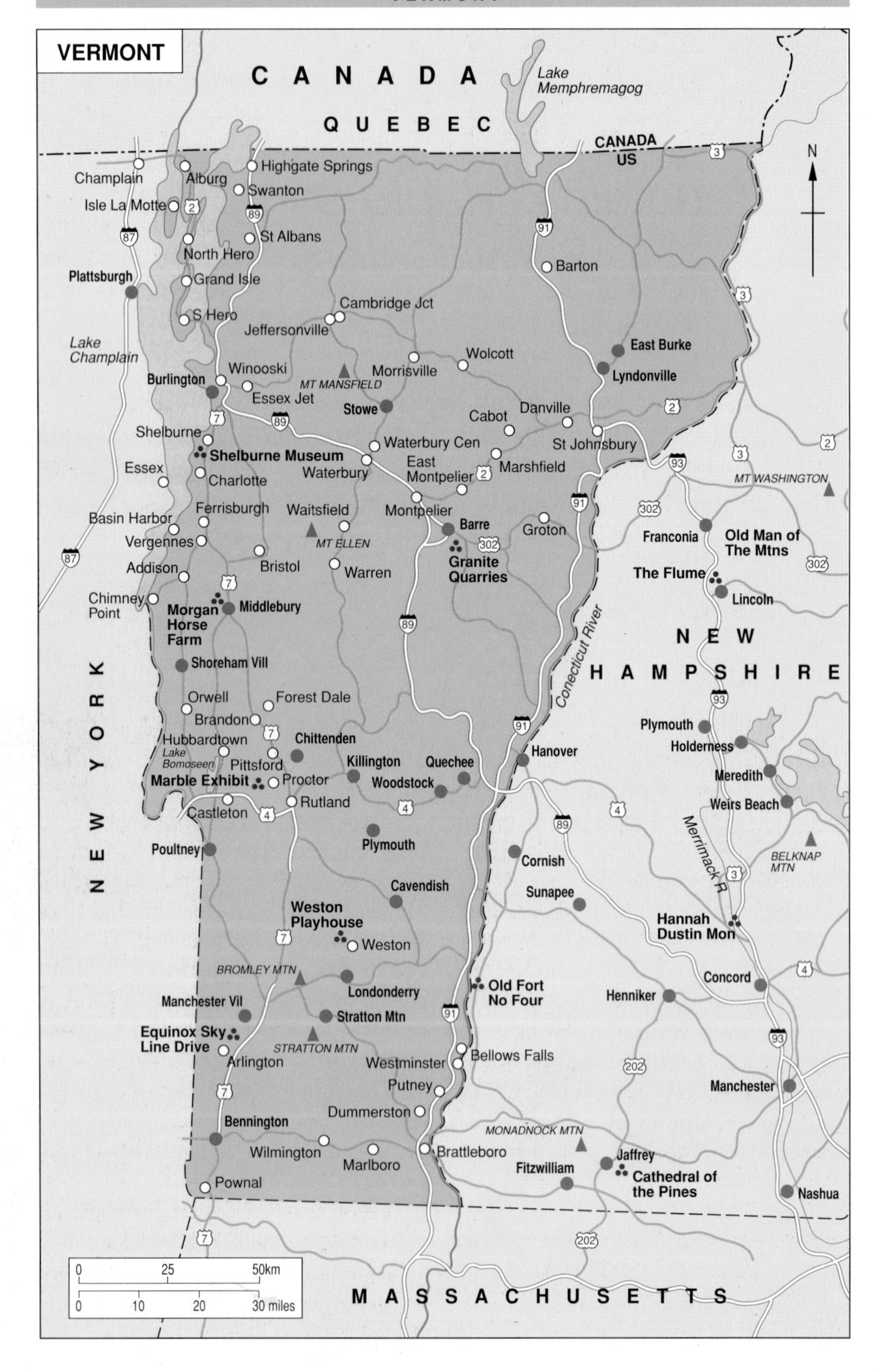
VERMONT
CANADA
QUEBEC
Lake Memphremagog
CANADA
US
N
Champlain
Alburg
Highgate Springs
Swanton
Isle La Motte
St Albans
North Hero
Plattsburgh
Grand Isle
Barton
Cambridge Jct
S Hero
Jeffersonville
Lake Champlain
East Burke
Wolcott
Winooski
Morrisville
Lyndonville
Burlington
MT MANSFIELD
Essex Jct
Stowe
Danville
Cabot
Shelburne
Waterbury Cen
St Johnsbury
Shelburne Museum
Essex
East Montpelier
Marshfield
Waterbury
Charlotte
MT WASHINGTON
Ferrisburgh
Waitsfield
Montpelier
Basin Harbor
Barre
Groton
Franconia
Old Man of The Mtns
Vergennes
MT ELLEN
Addison
Bristol
Granite Quarries
Warren
The Flume
Chimney Point
Lincoln
Morgan Horse Farm
Middlebury
Conecticut River
NEW HAMPSHIRE
NEW YORK
Shoreham Vill
Orwell
Forest Dale
Brandon
Plymouth
Hubbardtown
Chittenden
Holderness
Lake Bomoseen
Pittsford
Killington
Quechee
Hanover
Meredith
Marble Exhibit
Proctor
Woodstock
Rutland
Weirs Beach
Castleton
Merrimack R
Poultney
Plymouth
Cornish
BELKNAP MTN
Cavendish
Sunapee
Weston Playhouse
Hannah Dustin Mon
Weston
BROMLEY MTN
Concord
Old Fort No Four
Londonderry
Henniker
Manchester Vil
Stratton Mtn
Equinox Sky Line Drive
STRATTON MTN
Bellows Falls
Arlington
Westminster
Putney
Manchester
Dummerston
Bennington
MONADNOCK MTN
Wilmington
Brattleboro
Jaffrey
Marlboro
Fitzwilliam
Cathedral of the Pines
Pownal
Nashua
0
25
50km
0
10
20
30 miles
MASSACHUSETTS

Basically a farming state, with dairying and stock raising, Vermont is a year-round tourism state. Swedish immigrants at Stowe introduced the sport of skiing to Americans early this century, and the first recorded descent of Mount Mansfield – Vermont's highest peak at 4,393ft (1,339m) – was made in 1914. Natural attractions range from a wildflower farm to a mile- (1.6km-) long chasm called the Queechee Gorge.

Visitors can tour a remarkable number of places producing food and drink – a cider mill, a brewery, a winery, a dairy, a smokery, sugar-houses and the famous Ben and Jerry's ice cream factory. Locally produced goods include handwoven baskets, pottery, wooden bowls, marble products and teddy bears.

The world's largest granite quarries can be visited in Vermont. Museums, art centres, historic preservation sites, vintage train rides, gondola or chairlift rides up a mountain, alpine slides down again, lake trips aboard the replica of a vintage sternwheeler – there's plenty to see and do. It should be borne in mind, however, that many of the summer attractions have a short season, and may not open regularly until May or even June. Others, such as the State Craft Center at Frog Hollow, Middlebury, the Kennedy Brothers' Factory Marketplace at Vergennes and the Vermont Teddy Bear Company at Shelburne, are open throughout the year.

Montpelier is the smallest state capital in the US, with a population of around 8,400. It has an arrestingly beautiful State House set well back from the street, and a number of other architectural and cultural attractions.

AMERICA'S MOST RURAL STATE

Vermont is the nation's most rural state. It is 150 miles (240km) long and 90 miles (144km) across at its widest point. The population is about 567,000, the most populous regions being Burlington and Rutland, where the electronics industry has burgeoned since the 1970s. Vermont was declared an independent republic in 1777, and became the first state to join the original 13 in 1791. The state tree is the sugar maple: Vermont is the largest producer of maple syrup in the US. Vermont has a number of firsts to its credit: its constitution of 1777 was the first to abolish slavery; the first US canal was built at Bellows Falls in 1802; and the nation's first ski tow opened at Woodstock in 1934.

The Old Courthouse at Montpelier, the smallest state capital in the US.

Southern Vermont

Make **Bennington Museum** (admission fee) your first stop in Southern Vermont and you can acquire some background knowledge of the area's history. The history is brought to life with artefacts and documents relating to the American Revolution and the turbulent Civil War. There are also toys, tools, hand-blown glass, pottery and other decorative arts.

The museum, founded in 1928 and located on West Main Street, incorporates the Grandma Moses Gallery in a separate wing. This is the largest public display of her works in North America. The accent is on the many paintings of rural life in New England by Grandma Moses, whose talent manifested itself when she was in her mid-70s. Her works are exhibited in the timber-framed schoolhouse reconstructed at the museum after being transported from Eagle Bridge, about 20 miles (32km) away in New York State.

Bennington

Bennington is one of Vermont's four biggest cities, with a population of about 16,500. The Chamber of Commerce has a walking tour map which guides visitors among the lovingly-preserved 18th- and 19th-century buildings of old Bennington. The **Old First Church**, an attractive white building with wooden columns on the green in Monument Avenue, dates from 1806. The adjacent burial ground is pleasant to browse in. The poet Robert Frost (1874-1963) rests there.

Fall foliage provides a blaze of roadside colour in the Green Mountain National Forest.

Standing like a tall sentinel over the town is the 306ft (94m) **Bennington Battle Monument** (admission fee). The limestone monolith was built in 1891 to commemorate a Revolutionary War battle on 16 August 1777, when America's General John Stark's men attacked General Burgoyne's troops.

Gracious colonial buildings set in 550 acres (229 hectares) surrounded by lovely views can be seen at **Bennington College**, north of the city. The Suzanne Remberg Usdan Gallery within the campus, has changing art exhibitions and is open on weekday afternoons during term time.

The **Park-McCullough House** (admission fee), at Park and West Streets, North Bennington, is on the National Register of Historic Places. The 35-room 1865 Victorian mansion in the classic style of the French Second Empire displays furnishings and personal belongings of Trenor and Laura Hall Park, for whom the mansion was built as a summer home. The Park-McCullough family produced two governors of Vermont. Vintage carriages can be seen in a barn, and there is a children's playhouse in the grounds.

Bennington has more than purely aesthetic attractions. Many visitors make a beeline for the direct sell shoe factory outlets on Northside Drive. Men's and women's styles in leather can be found at up to 50 percent off the normal price.

Pownal

South of Bennington, down Route 7 – the Ethan Allen Highway – is Pownal, where you can take in spectacular views on horseback, on a covered waggon ride, or, in winter, a horse-drawn sleigh. Phone Valley View Horses and Tack Shop (Tel. 802 823-4649). If you want your own horse they'll sell you one.

Arlington

The works of Norman Rockwell, the noted illustrator and painter, are celebrated at his home town, Arlington, where the permanent **Norman Rockwell Exhibition** (admission fee) is housed in a church dating from the 1800s. Patrons may be tempted to peer at some of the staff as well as the pictures, as Rockwell's friends and neighbours, some of whom now work at the gallery, posed for him. On display are hundreds of Rockwell's *Saturday Evening Post* covers and numerous sketches, illustrations and large prints. A 15-minute film show provides information on the man and his output.

The exhibition also features photographs of Rockwell's former home and studio in the 1940s and early '50s beside a public covered bridge in River Road, West Arlington. The 1792 farmstead home, with fishing, swimming, canoeing and skiing nearby, is now the Inn on Covered Bridge Green. It is elegantly furnished with antiques, and has tennis courts and a library among its facilities for guests. The inn is a no-smoking property.

In East Arlington's Old Mill Road are a couple of unusual shops which many visitors find interesting. One is the **Candle Mill and Music Box Shop**. The ground floor of the old grist mill offers thousands of candles, and you can dip some for yourself. The music boxes are upstairs, a collection from many parts of the world. The other store is a place to entice anyone who enjoys cooking, amateur or professional. For a start, there are a thousand cookbooks – addicts should allow themselves plenty of browsing time. There is a wide choice of crockery, from pottery to fine chinaware and cookware, and cutlery of chef quality as well as crystal glassware table linen and accessories.

Manchester

Continue north on Route 7 through mountain and wooded scenery for Manchester Village and Manchester Center, allowing time to deviate left for a stretch of toll road, the Mount Equinox Skyline Drive. **Manchester Village** is pleasant to stroll in and the Center has good shopping, with some of the country's most prestigious designer stores. The area has many beautiful inns, some with Jacuzzis and fireplaces in romantic guestrooms featuring canopy beds and lacy coverlets and cushions.

One of the region's most visited properties, **Hildene**, is at Manchester Village. Descendants of Abraham Lincoln lived here until 1975. The restored mansion (admission fee) which Robert Todd Lincoln, President Lincoln's son, built in Georgian Revival style in the early 1900s, has 24 rooms with original furnishings and a number of family effects, including an Aeolian organ. The gardens are vivid with colour in June, when more than a thousand peonies other flowers bloom.

Southern Vermont Art Center (admission fee), off West Road, Manchester, has 11 galleries of paintings, prints and photographs by contemporary artists, and special loan exhibitions. The 400-acre (160-hectare) estate has a sculpture garden, a botany trail, a cafe, library and gift shop. Music and dance performances take place in the Arkell Pavilion, a theatre seating 360. Special events, workshops and classes are held.

Vermont State Craft Center has three locations, including a gallery across the road from the Equinox Hotel in Manchester Village. (The others are at Burlington and Middlebury.) Open daily, all year round, with free admission, it displays contemporary and traditional crafts from more than 200 Vermont craftspeople.

TAKE A RIDE ON THE SLIDE

Alpine slides provide exciting rides at your own pace: you can control the speed, but fast is best. Several Vermont ski resorts have them. About 6 miles (10km) east of Manchester is the **Bromley Alpine Slide**, on Bromley Mountain. This is a summer and Fall activity, weather permitting. You go up in the chairlift and whizz down the narrow, specially constructed slide seated on a little plastic 'sledge'. You can also descend in slow and stately style, taking in the multi-state scenery as you go. The Bromley Alpine Slide has three tracks, each two-thirds of a mile (1.05km) long. A shop selling gifts, ski wear and sports clothes is open year-round.

The **American Museum of Fly Fishing** (admission fee), at Route 7A and Seminary Avenue is devoted entirely to the sport of fly fishing. It has a gift shop and gallery, and opens daily from April to October (closed weekends from November to March).

A place to delight the young and revive childhood memories for others is the **Enchanted Doll House**, in the Manchester Center. In a 12-room farmhouse there are dolls, dolls' clothes, dolls' carriages and cradles, and dolls' houses with tiny furniture. There are also babies' toys, stuffed animal toys, mechanical toys, musical toys, games and classical children's books.

Weston

Just a little farther north, on Route 100, is Weston, not a place to hurry through. For a start, there's a bowl mill, which has more than 400 Vermont-made wooden household and gift items, including hundreds of bowls on offer in the mill and its annexe. There are 'seconds' available, too. **Weston Bowl Mill**, founded more than 90 years ago, opens every day, all year.

Weston Village Store, a traditional country store, has been attracting shoppers for more than 100 years.

Weston Village Store is more than a century old, with its original 1891 tin ceiling and offers a host of unusual gift ideas. It houses the Vermont Cheese Emporium and a needlework shop called the Mountain Stitchery. Across the street is the **Vermont Country Store**, famous for its mail-order catalogue offering nostalgic items such as tooth powder, maple syrup, bottled pickles and wooden sleds. **Weston House Inc** is the home of a large collection of hand-made Amish, antique and modern quilts and wall hangings. Goose-down comforters, pillows and duvet covers manufactured in the state are on sale.

Vermont's oldest professional theatre is the Weston Playhouse on the Village Green. It is noted for its revivals of Broadway musicals and plays. There is a theatre restaurant, and a cabaret show follows the evening performance.

The southernmost region of Vermont is narrow – only about 40 miles (64km) as the crow flies from the state line of New York to the New Hampshire border. You could zig-zag about the area mopping up all the attractions it offers.

Due south of Weston are Londonderry, South Londonderry and the Magic Mountain Ski Area. There's the **Ball Mountain Dam** picnic recreation area, which has picnic facilities, tent and trailer sites, foot trails and swimming.

Stratton Mountain

Nearby is **Stratton Mountain**, Southern Vermont's highest peak with an altitude of 3,936ft (1,200m). The Stratton Resort – among the state's foremost – has the Starship XII gondola, which provides a lift to the summit in eight minutes with a 360-degree view of four states. Gondola rides are available daily except Wednesdays from late June to mid-October. Mountain bikers can take their bikes up in the gondola and then pick their way down through forest paths and mountain trails.

A 27-hole golf course at Stratton Mountain Country Club is recognized by Ladies' Professional Golf Association players as a real challenge. Tennis, hiking, and horseriding – the resort has its own stables – are among other summer sporting pursuits. For skiers there are 92 trails, a Frequent Skier card and special offers for multi-day tickets. The resort offers daycare for children over 6 weeks old.

The mountain also hosts a juried annual arts festival from September until mid-October, with some 200 Vermont artists and craftspeople displaying their work.

Brattleboro

Brattleboro is the cultural centre of this corner of the state. Built where two rivers converge (the Connecticut and the Whetstone), it has a museum, art centre, school of dance, opera theatre, music centre and a brass band – all in a town of 12,250 people. There are plenty of good restaurants. Its shops range from a Main Street department store selling designer clothes at discounted prices to Tom and Sally's Handmade Chocolates in Eliot Street. Here you can watch the luxury chocolates and specialist lines – cowpie candy bars, cowlick lollipops – being made.

Scenic, historic and Sunday brunch cruises on the Connecticut River, aboard the *Belle of Brattleboro*, are available through Connecticut River Tours Inc (Tel. 802 254-1263).

South west of Brattleboro, in off-the-beaten-track country, is Jacksonville, where the **North River Winery** gives free tours and tastings daily from late May to the end of December. Between January and late May the winery is open on Friday, Saturday and Sunday. Also free is the scenic 1850s farmstead setting of this award-winning winery.

Six miles (9.6km) north of Jacksonville is Wilmington. Between here and West Dover to the north, lumbering thrived for many years. The industry abandoned this highland region long ago, but relics of it remain and are worth exploring. Fashionable resort communities have developed, offering skiing and golf.

From Wilmington take Route 9 east for Marlborough and the 2,410ft (734m) Hogback Mountain. From up here you can see 100 miles (160km) on a clear day. Onward to Dummerston, where the British writer Rudyard Kipling and his American wife, Carrie, lived for four years around a century ago. The house, in private ownership, is in Kipling Road, but is not open to the public.

Putney

Just north of Dummerston, on Route 5, is Putney and **Santa's Land,** the place for people who wish it was forever Christmas. This is a Christmas theme village, where everyone can buy presents in the shops and children can do a host of other things. They can chat with Santa Claus, visit the Elves' Home, the Little Red Schoolhouse and animals in the petting area, have a train ride, a carousel ride, and enjoy themselves in the playground. There's a picnic park and the Igloo Pancake House which serves, among other delights, a dozen different sorts of pancake.

Established in 1956, Santa's Land (admission fee, but free for all children under three) is closed on Christmas Day itself, but it opens every day from May 1 to Christmas Eve.

BASKETS AND BUCKETS

Basketville, Putney, imports baskets from around the world, and has been handweaving and selling them for more than 150 years. Cassius Wilson, who had 11 children, started the business in 1842, and as the children grew up they set to work weaving and selling.

The company, still run by the Wilson family, is the country's major producer of genuine American splint baskets. They are hand-crafted on site. Splints of ash are produced in the Basketville sawmill. Local craftspeople working in an adjacent building carry out the 46 individual hand operations entailed in making each basket. The basketmakers follow the same techniques as those used by the Native Americans and early settlers.

Wooden buckets are also hand-made at Basketville – produced in the same way as those in which the early settlers stored maple sugar.

Silk flowers, home accessories and wickerware, including furniture, are on sale. Basketville is open daily year-round. There is no admission charge.

Grafton

A white painted church with a steeple; probably a green; a cluster of timber-framed clapboard houses, no two alike, painted in various colours; plenty of trees and shrubs – Vermont has a wealth of such picturebook New England villages. They are alike, and yet different. Grafton, about 20 miles (32 km) north west of Putney, is a prime example.

Officially called Historic Grafton Village, it is freely on view all year, seven days a week from 10am to 4pm. The 19th-century buildings have been restored by the Windham Foundation, and the community is recognized as one of the finest examples of rural New England architecture and village life. One of the oldest buildings is the **Old Tavern** (1801). Customers of the past are said to include Oliver Wendell Holmes, Ulysses S. Grant and Rudyard Kipling. Accommodation is still available there. There are museums, an award-winning cheddar cheese factory open to visitors, and self-guided walking tours. A cross-country skiing centre is another popular attraction. Details are available from the Information Center on Townshend Road.

Grafton has a couple of gift shops in Main Street. One, Eaglebrook, is on the National Register of Historic Places. It sells handicrafts, folk art, paper goods and jewellery. It also has a 'summertime' shop, The Croft, selling plant pots, baskets and garden-related items. The other shop is called Tickle Your Fancy Gift Shop, and no doubt some of the goods will.

Bellows Falls

About 12 miles (19km) eastwards is Bellows Falls on the Connecticut River, which marks the boundary with New Hampshire. The first US canal was dug at Bellows Falls in 1802. Here, the Green Mountain Flyer operates from mid-June to mid-October, with two daily departures in restored coaches pulled by vintage diesel locomotives through beautiful country to Chester Depot. In the Fall you might take the Ludlow Special or the Sunset Special. On the basic narrated ride you'll travel beside the Connecticut and Williams rivers. You will see the Brockways Mills Gorge, two covered bridges, farmland and pastoral scenery. The service is closed on Mondays, except on public holidays. The historic coaches used on the railroad date from the 1890s to 1931.

From Bellows Falls it is only 15 minutes to Westminster and the **MG Car**

Museum, the world's largest private collection of one make of car. Currently there are 29 MGs on display, and others are at various stages of restoration waiting to go on show. The museum (admission fee) has a collection of MG and other motoring artefacts, a gift shop and library.

Windsor

Tourists taking Route 103 direct from just north of Bellows Falls to Rutland are going to miss out on a lot of attractions. It is better to continue north along the Upper Connecticut River Valley on I-95. The **Vermont State Craft Center**, at 54 Main Street, Windsor, displays the work of Vermont artisans and furniture makers, and at 106 Main Street the **American Precision Museum** shows Industrial Revolution and machine tool exhibits.

Go west along Route 106 to the junction with Knapp Brook to see 'Indian Stones' at Reading. Slate markers were set up in 1799 to commemorate the birth of Elizabeth Johnson, born while her parents were held captive by Abnaki Indians.

Central Vermont

Take I-91 north some 15 miles (24km) to White River Junction, where the **Catamount Brewing Company**, based at 58 South Main Street, is open for free tours and tastings daily from 1 July to the end of October and on Saturdays throughout the year. A former granary built in 1884, it opened as a brewery in 1986 – the first brewery to open in Vermont for more than a century. Visitors can watch the various stages of producing English-style ale, using traditional ingredients, and 'drink in' the distinctive aroma of hops and freshly milled barley.

Vermont's largest gift and wool clothing store is at White River Junction. Its name, 25,000 Gifts and Woolens, alerts you to the idea of being spoilt for choice.

Rural Vermont offers a wealth of picturebook New England scenes.

Woollen shirts, jackets, sweaters and a wide selection of gifts, including Vermont products such as maple syrup, are offered under one roof. The store, which has been in business for more than 55 years, opens daily from 15 May to 31 December.

Quechee

A short drive westward on Route 4 brings you to Quechee, and a look at a magnificent geological manifestation of the last Ice Age. This is where the Ottauqueechee River forms a gorge 165ft (50m) deep and a mile (1.6km) long. The gorge was the only outlet for a large glacial lake. A bridge spanning the gorge to carry the Woodstock Railroad was built in the 1870s. A steel-arched bridge replaced it in 1911. In 1933 the railroad tracks were removed and the present Route 4 was laid on the same roadbed.

A gorge-side walk extends for nearly a mile (1.6km) in one direction, and a short walk the other way leads to an impressive waterfall. There are also fine views from the road bridge. A gift shop and restaurant beside the gorge opens from 1 May to 31 October. It overlooks the Quechee Gorge State Park which has picnic facilities.

Close by Quechee Gorge, still on Route 4, is **Quechee Gorge Village**, and anyone who likes nosing around for antiques and collectibles, arts and crafts is advised to allow plenty of time here. The village has some 450 antiques and bric-a-brac shops, and the work of 200 craftspeople is sold by 165 dealers. There's also an antique carousel, a Christmas Loft, an original 1946 diner, a basket mart and a Vermont Country Store. You can ride on a miniature railroad and take a horse-drawn hay ride or sleigh ride, according to season. Timber Village, which opened in 1985, can be visited any day of the year between 9am and 5pm. It has a restaurant and snack bar.

On the way to Woodstock you may care to take a detour along back roads from the Taftsville Covered Bridge on Route 4 up Hillside Road for 3 miles (4.8km) to **Sugarbush Farm**. Seven varieties of cheese can be sampled here, and the sugar-house can be visited. There is a 'maple walk' through the woods, where signs and photos explain the maple sugaring process.

Quechee Gorge, 165ft (50m) deep and a mile (1.6km) long, is a spectacular legacy of the last Ice Age.

Maple syrup produced at the farm and Vermont mustards and jams are on sale. Visiting is 7am to 4pm weekdays, and 9.30am to 4pm weekends. From December to May ring first to check road and weather conditions (Tel. 802 457-1757).

Woodstock

Woodstock is a gracious place with well-cared-for old houses, shops and galleries and electricity cables hidden away to protect the ambience. It has the state's newest covered bridge, which was built in 1969.

In Church Hill Road, Woodstock, is the **Vermont Raptor Center**, in the Vermont Institute of Natural Science. The outdoor Raptor Center (admission fee) houses nearly 30 species of hawks, owls and eagles, all native New England birds. They are all birds suffering permanent injuries which prevent their release into the wild. Their home is in an 80-acre (32-hectare) nature preserve with self-guided nature trails and a beaver pond.

Nearly 30 species of New England hawks, owls and eagles may be seen at the Vermont Raptor Center at Woodstock.

At **Dana House Museum**, 26 Elm Street, the Woodstock Historical Society presents furnishings from the 18th and 19th centuries, silver, portraits, costumes, dolls and toys. The museum (admission fee) also displays the town charter, while the barn holds a lovely old sleigh.

Just north of Woodstock on Route 12 is **Billings Farm and Museum** (admission fee), one of the leading agricultural museums in the US. It shows a working farm of more than a century ago. Visitors can sniff what's cooking on the woodstove in the 1890s farmhouse kitchen. In the basement creamery visitors can see how butter was churned and prepared for market.

Life on a 19th-century Vermont family farm is depicted in barns and outbuildings – dairying, planting, harvesting, maple sugaring, the life of the farming community, and the heavy horses. Vegetables, flowers and herbs can be seen in the gardens outside the farmhouse.

At the Billings Dairy Farm, where the Jersey herd established in 1871 has won many prizes, visitors can watch the afternoon milking and admire the calves. Chickens and Southdown sheep have been added to the livestock, and draught horses can be seen at work in the fields.

There are audio-visual programmes, a museum shop and a dairy bar. The complex is open daily for six months from 1 May then at weekends only in November and December.

PUTTING THE PAST TO GOOD USE

You don't see overhead power lines in Woodstock. Close your eyes and ears to the traffic that crawls along Prospect and Elm Streets – the police frown on drivers exceeding 25mph (40kph) – and you could imagine yourself back in the 18th century.

The power lines are hidden. The white clapboard houses, substantial buildings with important front doors, reflect the gracious living of prosperous professional people of 200 years ago. Today these homes are still beautifully maintained.

Every inch a New England community, Woodstock has three covered bridges crossing the Ottauqueechee River – Taftsville (1836), Lincoln (1877) and Middle, built beside the village green as recently as 1969 – and a board on which the local news is chalked. The board is known as the Woodstock Town Crier.

There's an annual croquet tournament in August. A hand-milking contest is held each June at Billings Farm, a living, working museum whose Jersey cow, Rosanne, was the breed's North American champion in 1989. Polo matches are held at nearby Quechee.

Hunting, trout fishing, hiking, climbing, trail riding (on horseback and bicycle), canoeing, golf, tennis and squash are among Woodstock's summer recreations. Movies are shown in the 400-seat Town Hall Theater at weekends. In the winter there's ice hockey, skating and skiing. December sees the annual Wassail Celebration, with wassail dancing and a parade of riders and carriages.

Woodstock is now a town of 3,500 residents, a number magnified by the visitors who flock in at all seasons. Having experienced Woodstock once, many of them return again and again. They browse among the sort of shops they don't see at home. Elisha Morgan, on the green, is an association of graduate gemologists delighted to share their knowledge while presenting their jewellery. In the art gallery in Central Street, Robert O. Caulfield offers his distinctive oils and watercolours of New England landscapes and street scenes that are attracting attention through the US. 18 Carrots in Pleasant Street is a source of organically grown produce, natural remedies, herbs and spices, and also has a vegetarian restaurant and take-out delicatessen. There's the Gifted Llama gift shop whose stock includes slightly eccentric items – the fluffiest ear-muffs, the droopiest earrings.

The Village Butcher on Elm Street also sells wines, cheeses, breads, pies and deli foods, and opens seven days a week. Church Street Antiques Gallery features porcelain, crystal, silver, lamps, mirrors, prints, original paintings and country furniture.

Woodstock was chartered by George III in 1761. The railroad came in 1875 – and went 58 years later, its demise bringing a decline in industry and population. Then in 1934 America's first rope tow was installed at Woodstock, and winter sports entered a new era. Woodstock Inn and Resort opened for business in 1969, replacing the old Woodstock Inn which opened in 1892 on the site of the Eagle Hotel, which had opened as Richardson's Tavern in 1793.

In spite of the gentle image of a bygone age which it unashamedly promotes, Woodstock has avoided becoming a town locked in a timewarp. Poised on the brink of the 21st century along with the rest of the world, it continues to put its 18th-century heritage to good use while keeping an alert business eye on the growth of the winter sports industry, tourism and golf mania.

The resort's Woodstock Country Club has the oldest golf course in Vermont. It is open to the public and recently reached its century. The inn has an impressive reception lobby with an enormous fireplace and plenty of comfortable sofas. There are conference facilities.

PUTTING THE PAST TO GOOD USE continued

As well as the golf course, there are indoor and outdoor tennis courts and swimming pools, croquet, squash and racquetball courts, putting green and a well-equipped sports centre.

The resort is deeply 'green', ensuring maximum recycling. The policy also ranges from energy-efficient lighting to donating waste paper to local farmers as bedding for stock.

The historic Suicide Six Ski Resort, with challenging terrain for all grades of skier, is run by the Woodstock Inn. Guests ski free from Sunday to Thursday, provided no public holiday intervenes. There are 37 miles (60km) of free skiing for them at the Woodstock Ski Touring Center.

Woodstock acknowledges three ecologically-minded citizens who have helped make the town what it is. The first was George Perkins Marsh, born in 1801 in a cottage on the slopes of Mount Tom, Woodstock. He was destined to be lauded as a forerunner of the conservation movement in North America. A diplomat and the man largely responsible for the Smithsonian Institute, he wrote *Man and Nature*, which became the ecologist's bible.

Next was local-boy-made-good Frederick Billings (born 1823) who returned to Woodstock in 1869, having made a fortune as a San Francisco lawyer and as president of the Northern Pacific Railroad. He bought the Marsh estate on Mount Tom, applying many of Marsh's principles on conservation and land use as he developed Billings Farm.

Then Laurance S. Rockefeller, grandson of philanthropist John D. Rockefeller, entered the scene, marrying Frederick Billings's granddaughter Mary in 1934. It was he who donated money to keep Woodstock's power lines out of sight. In 1961 Laurance Rockefeller bought the Suicide Six Ski Area and the Woodstock Country Club, enlisting Robert Trent Jones to re-design the golf course, and in 1968 acquired the Woodstock Inn. The Inn and Resort is one of the Small Luxury Hotels of the World – and the only New England property in the organization.

In 1992 President George Bush signed legislation creating the Marsh-Billings National Historic Park – the first in Vermont. Early in 1993 Mr and Mrs Rockefeller donated their restored mansion and its surrounding woodland to the park, retaining a lifetime right to the estate, after which it will be open to the public.

Plymouth

Turn left off Route 4 west of Woodstock to State Highway 100A and the Coolidge State Forest, beyond which is Plymouth Notch and the **President Coolidge Homestead** (admission fee). Calvin Coolidge, who was born here, became the 30th President of the United States. Seven restored buildings include the homestead, the birthplace, a store and church. Coolidge was sworn in as President at the homestead at 2.47am on 3 August 1923, following the sudden death of President Warren G. Harding. A museum and visitor centre are also on the site

Ludlow

To the south on Route 100 is Ludlow, the only village at the base of the Okemo Mountain ski area. A year-round tourism region, it offers both downhill and cross-country skiing, golf, tennis, cycling and hiking. There are antique and art and craft shops, a winery and a wide choice of country inn accommodation.

Shrewsbury

Take Route 103 north west and after 15 miles (24km) turn right to Shrewsbury – this is back-of-beyond country and well worth seeing. The church is also the town

America's most rural state, Vermont is especially noted for the quality of its home-grown produce.

hall. In Lincoln Hill Road is W.E. Pierce Groceries, a country store run by the same family for nearly 160 years. Shrewsbury also has a herb farm, where you can relish a heady cocktail of scents.

Outdoor Attractions

East of Rutland is the extensive Killington ski area, Vermont's largest resort, with a famous ski school and 77 miles (123km) of trails ranging from the steepest to the most gentle in New England. Dozens of inns in the area also cater to summer and Fall tourism. **Killington Peak**, at 4,241ft (1,293m), is the highest in the region. Adjacent Little Killington is 3,939ft (1,200m) high. At Pico Ski and Summer Resort you can take in the wonderful mountain views from an alpine slide and chairlift, looking across to New Hampshire and New York State. The slide has fast and slow tracks open daily from the end of May to early October when the weather is suitable. At Pico's Summit people go hiking, mountain biking and picnicking. The resort, at Sherburn Pass, has 17 miles (27km) of ski trails across four peaks. It also has a sports centre and mini-golf.

North of Rutland is the central part of the vast **Green Mountain National Forest.** It has a variety of hiking trails, some nature trails, wild, tumbling rivers and more gentle streams for experienced or novice canoeists, picnic areas – some with rest rooms – and occasional Forest Service Stations. The forest is home to a number of animal species, including black bears, white tail deer and moose. Among the birdlife are wild turkey and birds of prey, including peregrine falcons.

Aficionados of the watercolour artist Al Friedman may like to visit his studio at Chittenden, a village in the National Forest near Rutland. Workshops and classes are held there. The **Trailside Art Studio and Gallery**, close to the Mountain Top Inn and Resort, is usually open between 10am and 3pm from Thursday to Monday, and sometimes also at unspecified times. Telephone 802 483-6058 to check. Original watercolours and limited edition prints are shown.

Rutland

Rutland is a good base for exploring the central western area of Vermont. It is the state's second largest city in terms of population, although with 18,250 inhabitants it is less than half the size of Burlington.

A commercial and shopping centre, it has some interesting and unusual shops. The Lamb's Yarn Shop, on Kendall Avenue, sells everything for knitters and for needlepoint, embroidery and rug-making addicts. Vermont Canvas Products, on Woodstock Avenue, makes its cotton canvas and cordura bags in more than 60 styles on the premises, and sells at discount prices. Also on Woodstock Avenue is the Wagon Wheel, a card and gift shop specializing in Vermont maple products. Vermont cheddar cheese, deerskin gloves and moccasins and a loft full of baskets are on sale. Boutique International, on North Main Street, has a variety of imported goods from around the world – jewellery, crystal, cut glass, ceramics, art works, linens, collectors' dolls and gourmet delicacies. The city also boasts some art deco architecture – of which the nine-storey **Service Building** and the newly restored **Paramount Theater** are outstanding examples; the **Midway Diner** also merits attention.

Changing monthly exhibits are on display at the **Chaffee Center for the Visual Arts** at 16 South Main Street. More than 200 artists are featured in eight galleries. Many of the works on show are for sale, and there is also a craft shop.

Castleton

West of the city, off Route 4A, is Castleton, and the **Christine Price Gallery** at Castleton State College. The emphasis here is on the work of contemporary artists. The gallery opens from 8.30am to 4.30pm, Monday to Friday, during academic terms. Poultney, 20 miles (32km) south of Castleton, has changing art exhibits at **The Gallery**, Green Mountain College, open from 10am to 5pm, Monday to Friday, in term time.

Proctor

Just outside Rutland, to the north, is Proctor, off Route 4 on the West Proctor Road.

WALKING ON MARBLE

Proctor's sidewalks are made of marble. The town is the centre of Vermont's historic marble industry. At 61 Main Street you will find the **Vermont Marble Exhibit**, the world's largest marble museum. It has historical displays and a Hall of Presidents, all carved from the purest white marble. Forty-one, including George Bush, are on parade, and the sculptor, who is employed full time, was working on President Clinton in 1993 at the Marble Company's establishment which opened more than 60 years ago.

The technique and talent of a professional artist can be observed as the marble is carved and polished. A colour film illustrates the formation of marble deposits more than 400 million years ago, its quarrying and use. Marble and stone products are on sale in the gift shop.

Detail of a stained glass window at Wilson Castle, Proctor, which houses a rare mix of antiques and museum pieces.

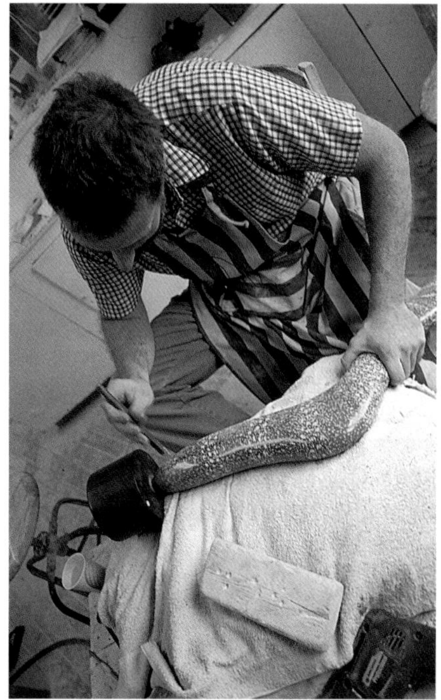

A resident sculptor works full-time at the Vermont Marble Company's museum at Proctor.

A rare mix of antiques and museum pieces is on show at **Wilson Castle** (admission fee), a restored mid-19th-century edifice regarded as an architectural masterpiece set in a 115-acre (48-hectare) estate with neat lawns and pathways in which to stroll. Guided tours of the castle reveal the historic value of European and Far Eastern antique furniture, ornaments and decorative arts.

Pittsford

About 8 miles (13km) north of Proctor, on Route 7, is Pittsford, and another popular attraction, the **New England Maple Museum and Maple Market** (admission fee). The full story of maple sugaring from sap to syrup is told here.

The development of the maple sugaring process from the times of the early settlers to today's techniques is illustrated. Demonstrations and a slide show are given, and visitors can sample maple syrup and other products.

Newly incorporated into the museum's display of photographs is a large collection of black and white pictures of sugaring during the early 1900s. The rare collection of 'live' sugaring scenes of bygone days was donated by Vermont Maple Orchards of Essex Junction, near Burlington.

The museum, which opens from mid-March to December, has the largest and most complete collection of maple sugaring equipment in existence. From July to mid-October visitors can see how maple sugar candy is made, and sample it. Vermont crafts and foods, as well as maple syrup and allied products can be bought in the gift shop.

Hubbardton

Military history buffs may like to visit the **Hubbardton Battlefield and Museum** at East Hubbardton, 7 miles (11km) off Route 4. Located on the site of the Revolutionary battle of 7 July 1777, the museum can be visited from late May to mid-October, from Wednesday to Sunday, between 9.30am and 5.30pm.

Hubbardton is on the northern shores of the huge Lake Bomoseen. There are obsolete slate quarries within **Bomoseen State Park**, which has tent and trailer sites, showers, rest rooms and picnic facilities. Walking and nature trails, swimming, boat rentals and fishing are among the amenities.

To the north west of Hubbardton, 6 miles (9.6km) west of Orwell, off Route 73A, is another Revolutionary War site. Here Mount Independence was named after the Declaration of Independence. There are the remains of the stockade, the foundations of the fort, block houses, gun batteries and hospital, and more than 3 miles (5km) of trails. This is fine weather territory, and is open from late May to mid-October except on rainy days, from Wednesday to Sunday.

In Orwell there is a place called **Stratford House** (Route 22A), where 'new' antiques are sold. Hand-crafted reproductions of primitive pine furniture are made to resemble 18th-century pieces with hand-wrought iron and traditional hinges. Shaker-style chests and tables are on sale. The store is open all year, seven days a week.

Brandon

On the way north on Route 7 between Rutland and Middlebury, turn off at Brandon to join Route 73 for a splendidly scenic drive through the **Brandon Gap**. Wherever you go in Vermont you encounter wonderful scenery, but here it almost surpasses itself, with steep mountains, fast-flowing rivers and heavily wooded slopes.

Brandon Town is the birthplace of Stephen A. Douglas, born in 1813. He contested the 1860 presidential election but was defeated by Abraham Lincoln. The town has another claim to fame: Thomas Davenport invented the electric motor here in 1837.

Middlebury

Middlebury (population 8,000) is a college town with a bandstand on its green. East of the town, on Route 125 South, **Middlebury College Snow Ball** offers terrain for all skiing abilities. Middlebury has the oldest covered bridge in Vermont, the **Pulp Mill Bridge** built in 1820. The Robert Frost Wayside Area and Trail near Ripton, south east of Middlebury, is named after the local poet whose name is nationally and internationally revered. From here, you may fancy a drive south east towards Route 100 to enjoy the beauty of the **Middlebury Gap** and **Texas Falls.**

Back in Middlebury, on Main Street, is the **Vermont Book Shop**, specializing in

Frost – he shopped there himself – and books on Vermont. It stocks thousands of books on many subjects, and also sells cassettes and CDs. Another interesting shop, on Route 7 South, is Wood Ware. Crafted goods in dozens of native woods are on sale. Other crafts and Vermont foods are also available.

Vermont Folklife Center, at 2 Court Street, Middlebury, is an exhibition of folk art and videos introducing the people, places and traditions that make the state distinctive. There are regularly changing exhibits. **Vermont State Craft Center** at Frog Hollow – one of the state's three centres – is at 1 Mill Street, Middlebury. Contemporary and traditional work by more than 200 Vermont craftspeople is featured.

Texas Falls: a beauty spot in the heart of the Green Mountain National Forest.

The **Sheldon Museum**, on Park Street, depicts local history, with a marble merchant's house of 1829, a research centre and gallery. Vermont paintings, furniture, toys and decorative arts are displayed. Tours of special appeal to children are arranged. There is a museum shop.

Weybridge

Less than 3 miles (5km) north of Middlebury is the University of Vermont **Morgan Horse Farm**, at Weybridge, home to some of the best bloodlines there are in the history of breeding Morgan horses. Set in rolling pasture and woodland, the farm (admission fee) is a National Historic Site and a working farm with more than 60 horses. Visitors can take a guided tour of the stalls, watching the staff at work and learning, and perhaps seeing, how the horses are trained. A short walk from the 1878 barn, mares can be seen with their foals. Audio-visual shows are given. The farm is open daily from 1 May to 31 October.

Addison

From Weybridge it is a short distance north west to Addison, where guided tours of the **John Strong Mansion** are available from Friday to Monday (9am to 5pm) between mid-May and mid-October. The mansion has antique furniture and effects of the Federal and Victorian periods. **Chimney Point**, south west of Addison, is the site of a 1690 stockade. The name comes from the chimney ruins of a French fort of 1795. A museum depicts the part played by Native Americans and French settlers in Vermont. Chimney Point opens Wednesday to Sunday (9.30am to 5pm) from late May to mid-October.

South of Chimney Point, on Route 74, is **Larrabee's Point**, Shoreham, where the new 60ft (18.2m) M/V *Carillon* embarks four times a day from Teachout's Wharf for a 90-minute narrated tour of southern Lake Champlain. The luxury cruise boat also docks at Fort Ticonderoga, in New York State. Shoreham has a 108ft (33m) long covered railroad bridge built in 1897.

Northern Vermont

Vergennes is proud to be the smallest city in the US – all 1.8 square miles (4.6 km^2) of it. It can also boast that it was chartered before Boston, in 1788.

A big attraction in Vergennes is the **Factory Marketplace** at Kennedy Brothers, a huge brick building that was originally a creamery. In 1987 it opened as a centre for more than 200 local craftspeople and antique dealers and dozens of artists from the region, all offering their wares in an open marketplace atmosphere. Kennedy Brothers have been manufacturers of oak and pine goods since 1937 and their products are on sale. A delicatessen, ice-cream shop, country store, children's play area, sculpture garden and picnic facilities are other attractions available at the site.

Basin Harbor

West of Vergennes, at Basin Harbor, is the **Lake Champlain Maritime Museum** (admission fee). It illustrates the cultural, military, commercial and technological history of Lake Champlain, demonstrating how the lake is arguably the most historic body of water in North America.

There are six exhibition buildings grouped in a lakeside setting, including an 1818 reconstructed stone schoolhouse, where the history of the Champlain Valley is outlined, a working 18th-century-style blacksmith's forge, and a fully operational boat shop in which boat-building demonstrations, classes and workshops are presented.

Other buildings house a collection of regionally-built small craft and an exhibit illustrating the Revolutionary War in the Champlain Valley. The latest building, added in 1993, contains a variety of large and small craft, and other artefacts, including the pilot house from the steamship *Reindeer*.

The engine room of the sidewheeler vessel SS Ticonderoga, *a National Historic Landmark, on show at the Shelburne Museum.*

At a public recreation area at nearby Button Bay you can rent a boat on the lake. Swimming, camping, nature trails and foot trails are available. Facilities include restrooms and hot showers.

Ferrisburgh

Just north of Vergennes, on Route 7, is **Dakin Farm**, Ferrisburgh, where a variety of Vermont's foods are prepared in the traditional way. Cheeses, preserves, maple and honey products and a range of smoked meats are produced, using well-tried family recipes. Visitors can sample more than 30 varieties of food. Maple-cured ham, bacon and poultry are seen (and savoured) smoking slowly over fires of smouldering corn cobs in the smoke house. In the sugar-house and cannery top quality maple syrup is produced and packed for despatch. The selection, maturing and waxing process of Vermont cheddar cheese can also be seen.

Dakin Farm has been in operation since 1792 and is open daily all year from 7am to 5pm. From June to mid-October a slide show presented at 30 minutes past each hour outlines how the traditional Vermont methods of food production originated. Admission is free.

Charlotte

A short drive north west of Ferrisburgh on Route 7 is Charlotte, and an attraction that draws nearly 40,000 visitors during its six-month-long season. Growing wildflowers used to be a hobby for Chy and Ray Allen. Now the **Vermont Wildflower Farm**, which they started in 1981, is a flourishing business – the biggest wildflower seed supplier in the eastern United States, and serving one of the fastest-growing aspects of gardening in the whole of the country.

Six acres (2.5 hectares) of colourful labelled wildflowers provide seeds which are despatched nationwide. The farm (admission fee) has an information centre and seed shop. There is also a mini-theatre which constantly shows a 30-minute video on creating a wildflower meadow.

Shelburne

With its magnificent museum, Shelburne is just north of Charlotte. The entrance fee to the museum is fairly high, so don't drop in just for an hour or two: allow a full day, if you can. Even then you won't be able to take in the 80,000 exhibits.

The **museum**, on a 45-acre (18.26-hectare) site offers good value, with some 40 buildings covering a variety of themes. A circus museum has an old carousel and a long procession of circus characters, human and animal, in miniature. A steam locomotive with a private rail car, and the 220ft- (67m-) long sidewheel steamship *Ticonderoga* – a National Historic Landmark – attract much attention.

There are architectural exhibits: a typical one-room New England schoolhouse from 1830, the Colchester Reef lighthouse, a round barn, and the only covered bridge with two lanes and a footpath left in the US. The 168ft- (52m-) long bridge was moved to the museum site from Cambridge, in north-west Vermont. Working demonstrations are given in printing, weaving and blacksmith's shops.

Another building displays hundreds of wildfowl decoys. Several buildings are devoted to the museum's American folk art collection, the largest in Vermont, with quilts, scrimshaw, weather vanes, hooked rugs and other items. There are hats, costumes, lace and perfumes dating back nearly 200 years. Toys, dolls and dolls houses intrigue the children.

The museum's latest addition, opened in 1993, is Owl Cottage, a family centre where visitors can 'become' people from a century and a half ago. Children – and the rest of the family – can dress up in mid-19th-century rural clothes, such as sun bonnets, pinafores, waistcoats and mob caps. In these costumes they can call at the 1840 general store, and decide what they would have bought if they had been customers doing their shopping in the mid-19th century.

The Shelburne Museum opens all year, but has a limited schedule in winter. The museum store opens daily throughout the year from 10am to 6.30pm.

THE BEAR FACTS

To find out 'How a Bear is Born' take one of the free tours at the Vermont Teddy Bear Company's factory at Shelburne and see the processes which create hand-made, jointed teddy bears.

The stuffing of each bear is crucial to produce just the right degree of huggability. There's a good selection of teddy bear clothes, too. Children are not the only recipients of Vermont teddy bears. There's a great Mother's Day market, and more and more bears are turning up as executive teddies in city offices.

The factory is at 2031 Shelburne Road. There is a gift shop, and tours take place between 10am and 4pm Monday to Saturday, and 1-4pm on Sunday throughout the year.

This round barn is one of many architectural exhibits at the huge Shelburne Museum near Burlington.

Crafts in Common, a showcase for 75 regional craftspeople, and is located on the Common in Shelburne. Another local attraction is **Shelburne Farms**, off Route 7 at Bay and Harbor Roads. Tours can be made of this 1,400-acre (405-hectare) property on Lake Champlain's shores, which is open daily from mid-May to mid-October. The 19th-century former estate of railroad magnate William Seward Webb includes formal landscaped gardens – the original landscaping was by Frederick Law Olmsted – with statuary, historic buildings and a children's farmyard. Visitors can watch cheese being made – and sample it. There are 24 authentically restored rooms in the property. These are used as an inn, which comes complete with a full-service restaurant (closed in winter).

Burlington

Burlington's urban sprawl – it's far and away the biggest city in Vermont (population 39,150) – begins 7 miles (11km) north of Shelburne. There are lovely views across Lake Champlain to New York's Adirondack Mountains.

Burlington has great downtown shopping at **Church Street Marketplace**, where there is parking for 3,000 cars. As well as more than 100 shops and some 20 eating places to choose from, you'll find street sellers, with an array of colourful wares, and live entertainment throughout the year, including festivals when the shop windows have animated displays. Marketfest is a lively street festival which takes place in October. Another of Vermont's three state craft centres is located at the Marketplace.

Winooski, just north of Burlington, has shops and restaurants on three floors of a converted woollen mill on Main Street. At the **Outlet Center** in Shelburne Road, South Burlington (Exit 13, I-89, then north on Route 7) two dozen stores offer goods at direct-sell prices.

The Winooski River runs through northern Burlington, skirting the 284-acre (115-hectare) park off Route 127 where the **Ethan Allen Homestead** can be visited (admission fee). There are short walks laid out in the grounds and picnic facilities available. Guided tours of the restored, authentically furnished 1787 farmhouse illustrate the challenges of frontier life two centuries ago.

Ethan Allen himself is famous for forming a military force, the Green Mountain Boys, which sent packing usurpers from New York and New Hampshire. His men also provided the American Revolution with its first key victory when the force took Fort Ticonderoga from the British garrison.

An orientation centre in a re-created tavern features a multimedia presentation outlining life in the surrounding area over a 5,000-year period. There are also exhibits and a gift shop. The Homestead is open from the second week in May until mid-October, Tuesday to Sunday. The **Ethan Allen Burial Place** is at the Colchester Avenue Cemetery in Burlington, where a marble statue of the local hero has been erected.

Decorated sidewalks in downtown Burlington, Vermont's largest city.

Burlington is a major cultural centre, with music, theatre and a number of art galleries. Professional comedy, mystery and musical shows are on the programme during the summer months (June to August) at St Michael's Playhouse at the McCarthy Arts Center in Winooski Park (Tel. 802 654-2535).

TICONDEROGA

Reindeer

Lake Champlain is appropriately depicted in this mural on the waterfront at Burlington (previous page).

Changing exhibitions of paintings, graphics and sculpture are periodically on display at the **McCarthy Gallery**, St Michael's College, Winooski. The gallery is open on weekday afternoons and evenings, and from 1-5pm on Saturday and Sunday.

Changing exhibits are also shown at the **Church Street Center**, open weekdays, 8.30am to 5pm. Permanent and changing exhibits are on display at the **Fletcher Free Library,** 235 College Street, open daily from September to May and on Sunday afternoons.

At the University of Vermont's Williams Hall, the **Francis Colburn Gallery** has changing contemporary art exhibits, open on weekdays during academic terms. Contemporary art representing the visual media can be seen at another University of Vermont establishment, the **Living Learning Center**, open Monday to Saturday from noon to 8pm during term time.

The work of Vermont artists is exhibited month by month by Burlington City Arts at the Metropolitan Art Gallery, City Hall. Opening times are 9am-9pm, Monday to Friday.

The University of Vermont at Burlington stages many changing exhibitions of contemporary art during academic terms.

Lake Champlain Region

Although Vermont is the only New England state with no sea coast, it does have Lake Champlain, which has about 250 miles (400km) of shoreline. Public beaches in the Lake Champlain region include two in Burlington. North Beach is at Leddy Park, North Avenue, and at South Burlington there is a beach at Red Rocks Park, off Route 7.

Cruising the Lake

The cheapest way to cruise the lake is to take a ferry. Lake Champlain Ferries, King Street Dock, Burlington, has been running since 1826 (Tel. 802 864-9804). Their one-hour car ferry service between Burlington and Port Kent, in New York State, operates between late May and mid-October, from 7.15am to 7.45pm in the summer and between 8am and 5.30pm in the spring and autumn. **Grand Isle**, Vermont, in Lake Champlain, is easily accessible by road from the mainland (Route 2). The ferry company has a 12-minute crossing between Grand Isle and Plattsburgh, New York, operating between 5am and 1am year-round. Their third crossing is from Charlotte, Vermont, to Essex, New York. The company can also provide private charters, and offers a two-hour narrated tour of the lake on the M/V *Essex* during the summer.

Lake Champlain Ferries' fleet includes the *Vermont*, launched in 1993. M/V *Vermont*, 196ft (60m) long, is on the Grand Isle–Plattsburgh run. It can carry 300 passengers and up to 50 cars. The company's vessel *Adirondack*, on the Burlington–Port Kent route, was built in 1913, and is the oldest in-service double-ended ferryboat listed in the US Registry of Shipping.

For a narrated cruise aboard a triple-deck cruise ship amid spectacular scenery, take a trip on the *Spirit of Ethan Allen II*, which docks at the Burlington boathouse in Burlington's waterfront park. The *Sprit* has two fully enclosed and heated decks, and operates in all weathers. There is a full restaurant and a bar on board. The 500-passenger ship offers 90-minute daytime shoreline cruises between late May and mid-October. From mid-June to early September there are also brunch cruises, mystery cruises, sunset cruises, moonlight cruises and dinner cruises. For reservations (these are required for the dinner cruises), contact Lake Champlain Shoreline Cruises (Tel. 802 862-8300). Passengers are told to keep a lookout for Champ, Lake Champlain's answer to Scotland's Loch Ness monster. Champ is said to have manifested himself to 70 passengers on the *Spirit of Ethan Allen* in July 1984, during the vessel's first season.

Grand Isle

To explore the Lake Champlain Island region take I-89 north out of Burlington, turning left at Chimney Corner across the causeway to Grand Isle. This area is the most north-westerly part of Vermont, and joins the Canadian province of Quebec.

Route 2 leads to Grand Isle, first through South Hero, where there is a public beach. **Camp Skyland**, half a mile (0.8km) south of Route 2, is a private campground open from mid-June to early September, offering swimming, fishing and boating. **Grand Isle State Park** has tent and trailer sites, fishing, boating, walking and nature trails, with restrooms and showers.

The **Hyde Log Cabin**, near the northern point of Grand Isle, is the oldest log cabin in the US. It was built in 1783 by Jedediah Hyde, who had served in the

Revolutionary War. Some of the original furniture and implements are still there.

From early July to Labor Day (the first Monday in September) the North Hero stables of the **Hermann's Royal Lipizzaner Stallions** are open daily to the public (no charge). Entertainment is provided by these superb performing horses four times a week (Tel. 802 372-5683).

Knight Point State Park is at North Hero, with swimming, boat rentals, fishing and trails. Swimming is for campers only at North Hero's other state park, called... North Hero! Boating and trails are available.

Isle La Motte

The westernmost island is Isle La Motte (Route 129). Many tourists call here to see **St Anne's Shrine** at West Shore Road. The Roman Catholic shrine, tucked away among pine trees, is on the site of Fort St Anne, which is Vermont's oldest white settlement, built in 1666 by Captain Pierre La Motte. Within the grounds are a grotto, a sandy beach, an open-air pavilion, a picnic area and a statue of Our Lady of Lourdes. There is also a statue of Samuel de Champlain which was sculpted at Expo '67 in Montreal.

A French explorer, de Champlain was in Canada when he heard about the great fresh water lake from Algonquin Indians. He travelled up the St Lawrence River from Quebec, a journey which brought him to the lake. He commandeered it and the surrounding land as French territory. The lake he named after himself, and although during the next two centuries the British and Dutch tried to claim it, it retains the French adventurer's name.

The shrine and its surroundings are a pleasant place to relax in the sun. Facilities include a souvenir shop and a cafe, and a jetty where those visiting by boat can moor. Eucharists are held at St Anne's Shrine daily, including weekends, from mid-May to early October.

Other Attractions Near Lake Champlain

Travel northward amid the Alburgs – South, Center, East and Alburg Springs – and you'll soon find yourself at the international frontier. There's still a lot more of Vermont to see, so take Route 78 eastward. The road accompanies the track of the Champlain Valley Railroad through lovely countryside which includes the **Mississquoi National Wildlife Refuge**.

At Swanton join Route 7 south to St Albans, where the **St Albans Historical Museum** has a railroad display, children's room and historical exhibits relating to Albans Raid. The museum is open in the afternoons from Tuesday to Saturday during June to October, and by appointment at other times (Tel. 802 527-7933).

About 5 miles (8km) or so along Route 36 fork left, then right for the **President Chester A. Arthur Historic Site** at Fairfield. The birth and career of Arthur, the 21st US president, are charted through an interpretive exhibit in the 35-acre (14.5-hectare) park, open Wednesday to Sunday between late May and early October.

Essex Junction, near Burlington's eastern boundary is a busy commercial centre midway between the Green Mountains and Lake Champlain.

The **Discovery Museum** (admission fee) at 51 Park Street, Essex Junction, is a hands-on museum for children, with nature, history, science and art exhibits. Live animals native to New England can be seen in the Native Wildlife Learning Center. There are a nature trail, public park and picnic facilities.

A Banquet of Chefs

Nobody is likely to complain that the 97-room Inn at Essex, near Burlington, is understaffed. The restaurant and catering are the responsibility of 18 world class chefs and 100 assistants.

The inn, at Essex Junction, has two restaurants, Butler's and the Birch Tree Cafe, as well as the more informal Chimney Point Lounge, where light fare is served. Even with the special functions, banquets and receptions at the inn, and the outside catering it undertakes, it may seem excessive to have 18 chefs and all those helpers.

The inn, which opened in 1989, is a campus of the New England Culinary Institute. Another 100 students learn their art at nearby Montpelier, at a restaurant, two cafes and a bakeshop.

A busy chef and trainees preparing dinner in the spacious kitchens of the Inn at Essex, part of the prestigious New England Culinary Institute.

The students come from many parts of the world, including Britain, Mexico, Peru, France, Belgium and North America. Small groups work with each chef for a couple of weeks, learning and practising a succession of specialist skills. The expert eye of a chef watches each plate as it is about to leave the million dollar kitchens for the restaurants.

While one group is catering for the restaurants another is producing several courses for a wedding reception or banquet in one of the function rooms.

Displays of finger buffet food – symphonies in pink, green and white flanked by an intricate ice sculpture – contribute to the guests' pleasurable anticipation. For set banquets each plate is an art form. A partially hollowed jacket potato may be fashioned to form a basket with a handle, filled with peas, slender green beans or sliced carrots. Presentation of the food is as important as its preparation.

Students' training includes spells of duty in all aspects of providing impeccable meals. Everyone takes a turn at

A proud chef and a covey of the students with their latest creation at the Inn at Essex.

waiting on table. Each waiter knows what each item on the menu is and how it is made, and can describe it clearly to a diner.

The food is as good as any you will find in the top restaurants of the world, but at a fraction of the price. Tipping is forbidden. Chef instructors instil into their trainees the fact that they are catering for paying guests who expect perfection: a pork chop with pecan stuffing and onion cider sauce, maybe, or pan-roasted partridge with couscous, currants and greens.

The students range in age from late teens to retired people who have decided on a new career. Their average age is around 27. They are in a learning, creative and extremely busy environment, working against the clock. There is neither room nor time for prima donnas.

The Inn at Essex is a low white building; its guests have access to nearby health and fitness facilities, hiking trails and a view of the distant Adirondacks. Every room is furnished and decorated differently, and about a third have open fireplaces. There is a library with board games for guests. Joining the public part of the inn with the conference and function rooms in a separate building is an underground art gallery. Works by New England and other American artists are exhibited.

The Inn at Essex is the only hotel in Vermont on which the American Automobile Association has bestowed its Four Diamonds Award.

Cocktail parties, business lunches and dinners, special group functions and wedding receptions are all catered for. With its renowned catering and attractive interior and exterior backgrounds for photographs, it is in great demand for weddings. One member of the staff is a professional 'bride's mother', responsible for organizing the complete reception, from the first phone call making a reservation to the moment before guests go into dinner. 'Then the banqueting manager takes over,' she says. 'Me, I do my job. I calm people's nerves, I wear beige and I keep my mouth shut!'

North Central Vermont

Vermont's north central area has many mountain peaks, great skiing and snowmobiling trails and mountain resorts.

Montpelier

The smallest state capital in the US, Montpelier's State House, one of the nation's oldest and best-preserved, has a magnificent gold leaf dome. A statue of Ethan Allen stands at the door, and topping the gleaming dome, which is made of wood and sheathed in copper beneath the gold leaf, is a 14ft (4.3m) statue of Ceres, the Roman goddess of agriculture.

The **State House** has been in use since 1859. Its exterior walls are made from granite quarried at nearby Barre. The Grecian-style portico and pillars were originally on a previous building, modelled after the temple of Theseus in Greece and destroyed by fire in 1857.

The Vermont Senate sits in the east wing and the House of Representatives occupies the centre. Sixty-five flags used by Vermont units in the Civil War, and another 14 used in other wars, can be seen in the building. A 20ft by 10ft (6m by 3m) painting of the Civil War battle of Cedar Creek is displayed in the Governor's Reception Room.

The State House opens from 8am to 4pm Monday to Saturday year-round and admission is free. There are free guided tours from July to mid-October.

Vermont Historical Society Museum (admission fee), on State Street, has exhibits revealing many aspects of the state's rich history. The past comes to life through costumes, furnishings, implements, posters, games, novelties and paintings, and through those soldiers, industrialists and craftspeople who left their mark.

The development of Vermont and the inhabitants who influenced it, from the Abenakis to the Yankees, Europeans, African-Americans and people from many parts of the world, is outlined in an easily-absorbed style. Family roots can be traced and the lives of past Vermonters researched in the library, which has collections of

The gleaming dome of Vermont's State House at Montpelier is sheathed in copper covered with gold leaf. The building has been in use since 1859.

maps, photographs and manuscripts, as well as books.

Montpelier's **T.W. Wood Art Gallery** is in College Hall, a fine building on the Vermont College campus of Norwich University on College Street. The gallery (admission fee) was founded in 1895 by Thomas Waterman Wood (1823-1903), one of America's leading portrait painters of his time, and a native of Montpelier. Many of his portraits and landscapes are displayed among selections from the permanent collection. The main gallery is devoted to temporary exhibits of works by contemporary painters and sculptors, the accent being on Vermont artists.

While in Montpelier, you may care to take the opportunity to sample the breads, pastries, desserts and chocolates freshly made at **La Brioche Bakery and Cafe**, 89 Main Street. They are the creations of chefs and students of the New England Culinary Institute, owners and operators of the enterprise. The same organization owns and runs **Chef's Table** at 118 Main Street, a full-service haute cuisine restaurant.

Maple Sugar

The maple sugaring process, from trees to finished product, can be seen at **Morse Farm and Sugarhouse**, 2 1/2 miles (4km) from downtown Montpelier. Travel north on Main Street until it becomes County Road, where there are signs to Morse Farm. A short slide show narrated by one of the Morse family explains the tradition and detail of the maple sugaring business. Visitors can walk the maple trail, tour the sugar-house, taste the syrup and call at the maple products, crafts and mail order shop. Morse Farm is open throughout the year, from 8am to 8pm in summer and 9am to 5pm in winter.

Harvest time for the maple crop is from around late February to mid-April. Conditions have to be exactly right – freezing nights and warmer days – for the sap to flow. Once this happens, the maple farmers and helpers go into action, with long hours and hard work.

At **Bragg Farm Sugarhouse**, 6 miles (9.6km) east of Montpelier (Route 14 North) holes are drilled in 2,000 trees, spouts fixed and buckets hung below them to gather the sap. It takes 40 gallons (182 litres) of sap boiled in large vats over a wood fire or oil-fired furnace, to make one gallon (4.55 litres) of syrup. The average maple tree yields about 10 gallons (45 litres) a season.

Traditionally, horse-drawn sledges were used to collect the buckets of sap, and this still happens on some farms. A more modern method is to fix up enormous lengths of plastic piping through the woodland to allow the sap to flow from the tree to the sugar-house. Visitors to Bragg Farm, which like Morse Farm opens all year, are offered free samples, and the complete range of maple products is on sale.

Another East Montpelier sugar-house which welcomes daily visitors is **Dan-**

GRANITE CITY

About 10 miles (16km) south east of Montpelier is the more workaday town of Barre (pronounced 'Barry'). This is Granite City, home of the world's biggest monumental granite quarry. The quarry, called **Rock of Ages** (admission fee), is reached from Exit 6, I-89. An elevated platform at the visitor centre gives an overview of the 30-acre (12.5-hectare) site, and there are shuttlebus tours on weekdays between 9.30am and 3.30pm. There is a craft centre where visitors can watch tombstones being prepared.

forth's (Route 2 East). It has a gift shop and tastings, as well as a display of equipment and a video showing the history of maple sugaring.

Waterbury

North west of Montpelier, take Route 100 off I-89 to reach Waterbury, which might just as well be called Feastville. For a start, there's the **Cold Hollow Cider Mill**, at Waterbury Center. The cider press operates throughout the year. From a viewing area visitors can watch cider being produced at the rate of 600 gallons (2,730 litres) an hour, and have a free taste. Apple products, cheeses and other Vermont foods are on sale at the mill, and there is also a snack bar. Breads, scones, cookies and muffins are made at the mill's natural foods bakery. Cold Hollow, which was founded in 1974, is open daily and admission is free.

Waterbury's biggest attraction – and the top attraction in the whole of Vermont – is **Ben and Jerry's Ice Cream Factory** (admission fee). It gets nearly a quarter of a million visitors a year, and every one of them comes out with at least one of the multitudinous and unusual ice cream flavours. Choose a big cone and you get something that looks like the Olympic torch. One of the biggest selling flavours of the 1990s has been Chocolate Chip Cookie Dough ice cream, while Blueberry Cheesecake and Rainforest Crunch have been runners-up.

Visitors can watch the ice cream making process from a viewing platform, while enjoying frozen yoghurt samples and a whacky narration at the same time. There's a video presentation and a gift

Anyone can get in the picture at Ben and Jerry's Ice Cream Factory at Waterbury – Vermont's top attraction.

THE RELUCTANT TYCOONS

Ben Cohen and Jerry Greenfield met as schoolboys. A few years later, they sent away for a $5 correspondence course in ice cream making. They experimented with their own recipes, and everything happened from there.

They started the business in 1978 in a converted filling station in Burlington, with high ideals about improving the quality of life locally, nationally and internationally. Their policy of 'caring capitalism and linked prosperity' has survived in spite of the enormous growth in sales, from $9.8 million in 1985 to $132 million in 1992. From the start, people went for their offbeat flavours and great chunky ingredients.

But Ben and Jerry hadn't reckoned on being big businessmen. All they had wanted to be was ice cream men, keeping their small, grassroots image. Presiding over a young and growing goldmine was not what they'd planned. The financial side left them bemused. One day they shut up shop and put a notice on the door: 'We're closed because we're trying to figure out what's going on.'

An executive with a sound business head was appointed and sales went even higher. Ben and Jerry remained socially conscious, donating through a foundation 7.5 percent of their pre-tax profits to charitable and social causes. Most American companies contribute less than one percent.

The company has a rule that no one shall be paid more than seven times the earnings of the lowest-paid fulltime employee, despite the fact that this does not ease executive recruitment. Ben and Jerry campaign for environmental concerns through their products. The nuts in Rainforest Crunch ice cream are from rainforest trees, discouraging destruction. The berries in Wild Maine Blueberry flavour are bought from Passamaquoddy Indians in Maine, supporting traditional elements of their economy. The admission charge for touring the Waterbury plant provides money for other worthy causes.

Federal support programmes for dairy farmers were cut in 1991, resulting in a 25 percent decline in milk prices. Ben and Jerry's continues to pay its Vermont dairy farmer suppliers a premium price equal to the pre-reduction rate.

Over the years Ben and Jerry have had occasional marketing blitzes across the country in a 'cowmobile'. These days it's a high-tech 'New Vaudeville Circus Bus', with free ice cream and entertainment.

The annual shareholders' meeting is followed by Ben and Jerry's One World, One Heart Festival, a two-day jamboree of free music, activities and crafts open to the public. The company, which incorporates an independently reviewed social performance assessment in its annual report to shareholders, has nearly 100 franchise scoop shops in the US.

If any of this has a familiar ring, you've probably seen the hit movie *City Slickers*. Two of the characters in it were parodies of Ben and Jerry.

shop that is good fun, with Ben and Jerry hats and T-shirts, novelties and stylized cow-related items.

Ben and Jerry's is high-priced ice cream, and very rich, with a butterfat content of up to 17 percent. The low-fat frozen yoghurt was introduced in 1992 for those who wanted a less rich treat. Its sales soon exceeded expectations, without affecting the ice cream sales.

Stowe

There's an assortment of eating places and places to stay along Route 100 towards Stowe, north of Waterbury, and even more up the Mountain Road (Route 108) to the

Animals sculpted in wood can be seen on show at the Spinning Wheel craft centre near Waterbury.

ski areas – country inns, international class hotels, motels, bed and breakfast accommodation, chalets and cabin sites. Stowe, two centuries old, has a typical New England main street with steepled church, shops, cafes, boutiques and white clapboard houses.

A 5-mile (8km) paved recreation path, through mainly privately owned land and accessible to the handicapped, was completed in 1989. It starts in the village and ends at the Brook Road covered bridge, off Route 108. It is for human-powered recreation only – walking, running, biking, in-line skating and cross-country skiing.

Stowe people were introduced to skiing as a sport by Swedish immigrants early this century, and in 1914 a librarian, Nathaniel Goodrich, made the first recorded descent of the state's highest peak, 4,393ft (1,338m) Mount Mansfield. The first official ski trail was cut early in the 1930s, and in 1938 Stowe, which had come to be known as the Ski Capital of the East, hosted the first US National Ski Championships.

Stowe Mountain Resort

Six miles (9.6 km) from the village is **Stowe Mountain Resort**, one of Vermont's great holiday areas, in winter and summer. The world's fastest eight-passenger state-of-the-art gondola gets you to the top of Mount Mansfield in under six and a half minutes. There are ten other lifts – five of them more than a mile (1.6 km) long. The 3,270ft (997m) Spruce Point is also at Stowe.

Winter activities at Stowe Mountain Resort include moonlit sleigh rides, ice skating, snowshoeing, tobogganing, snowmobiling and illuminated night

skiing. Mount Mansfield and Spruce Peak offer skiers 2,360 vertical feet (720m) of skiing on 45 trails. To ensure good sport throughout the season, snow-making machines supplement nature's already generous contribution.

In summer there are hiking trails, golf, tennis, gondola rides, and the only alpine slide in north Vermont. The 2,300ft (700m) Stowe Alpine Slide, operating daily from late May to early October, provides an exhilarating way of descending Spruce Peak, winding your way through woods and meadows. The cost per ride is reduced if you buy five or ten rides at a time. Children aged five and under ride free when accompanied by an adult.

Mountain rides in the world's fastest gondola are available only at weekends from the last week in May to mid-June, but from around 20 June to mid-October they operate daily. From the top there's a short hiking trail to Mount Mansfield's peak for superb views to New Hampshire, Lake Champlain, the Adirondack Mountains in New York State and Quebec province in Canada.

Mount Mansfield Auto Road, constructed in 1922, provides a winding, scenic route to a point 3,850ft (1,173m) above sea level, with panoramic views. The 4½-mile (7.2km) road follows the course of a carriage road built in the mid-1800s to serve two guest houses. The present road replaced it to accommodate motor traffic. It is open daily from the last week in May to mid-October (tolls charged).

Village churches like this one at West Topsham are a pristine complement to the Vermont countryside.

Stowe Mountain Resort owns and operates skiing facilities on Mount Mansfield and Spruce Peak, Stowe Country Club, Tennis Center, the Inn at the Mountain, adjacent condominiums and nine restaurants. Learn-to-ski programmes and day care for children are provided. The resort's ski school offers instruction from novice to advanced levels.

The Stowe Winter Carnival has been held annually since 1921. The ten-day spree includes an ice sculpture contest, fireworks, a fancy costume parade, international dog-sled races and many other fun events.

Umiak Outfitters, at 849 South Main Street, Stowe (Tel. 802 253-2317) rent equipment for summer and winter activities and provide instruction. Pursuits include canoeing, snowshoeing and inn-to-inn hiking.

Smugglers' Notch

Smugglers' Notch is another top-notch Stowe skiing area. The mountain is 2,162ft (660m) high. The notch itself is an awe-inspiring narrow pass between stark, steep mountains in **Smugglers' Notch State Park**. It was used as a secret route linking Canada and the US during the 1812 war between the British and the Americans, and today it provides a memorable drive.

Weird rock formations in the park resemble birds and animals, and dark, chilly caves can be explored. It is a popular area for climbers. The small, 25-acre (10.2-hectare) state park has hiking trails, rest rooms, hot showers, picnic tables, public telephones and a camp site open from late May to mid-October.

Smugglers' Notch mountain vacation resort is renowned for its children's programmes and childcare facilities, and has been named America's Number One Family Ski Resort – a *Family Circle* magazine award – at least twice in the current decade. A Discovery Ski Camp for three- to six-year-olds includes games on skis and many other activities, and tots from the age of two can take part in a 'Mom and Me...Dad and Me' programme. This helps a parent to teach the youngest in the family to ski. In summer a similar programme is applied to swimming. For those aged 7 to 12 there's an Adventure Ski Camp, and young teenagers have an Explorer Ski Programme. Summer equivalents are run for the three age groups.

Average annual snowfall at the resort is 276 inches (700cm), and this is augmented by extensive artificial snow. Smugglers' Notch has 58 trails and slopes, most of which are in the 'most difficult' and 'more difficult' categories, with a few easier ones. The longest slope is 3 miles (4.8km) and the longest continuous run is 4½ miles (7.2km).

Three inter-connected mountains comprise the biggest vertical drop in northern Vermont – 2,610 ft (795m). Morse Mountain, favoured by novices, is close to the resort village. Sterling Mountain appeals to intermediates, and Madonna Mountain provides world class sport.

The resort village itself has restaurants, lounges, cafes, ski rental and sports shops, Scandinavian spa, swimming pool, sauna, indoor tennis courts and après ski activities. There is an illuminated outdoor ice-skating rink. Accommodation, all slopeside and close to facilities, ranges from one-room motel units to five-bedroom condominiums.

Several golf courses in the area include Stowe Country Club's par 72 championship course. There are also local stables where horses can be hired and instruction given.

The Lamoille Valley

At Jeffersonville on Route 108 **Vermont Horse Park** offers trail-riding, hay rides and carriage rides in the summer and sleigh rides in the winter. Antiques and New England crafts in pottery, glass, wood and metal can be found at **Smugglers' Forge**. Another place to find gifts and souvenirs in Jeffersonville is the **Vermont Maple Outlet**, where locally made maple syrup and other maple products are sold, along with Vermont cheddar cheeses, smoked meats, clothing and handicrafts. The village also has art exhibitions at the **Mary Bryan Memorial Gallery** and **Art Center**, open daily from June to October.

Route 15 links Jeffersonville and Morrisville, following the course of the Lamoille River. In between is Johnson, a small place set in lovely countryside with three covered bridges. Two retail outlets in Johnson make for great browsing and buying. **Johnson Woolen Mills Factory Store**, on Route 15, has been trading for more than 150 years and sells masses of items in wool and natural fibre at direct-sell prices. Seconds are also available. You can wander around the factory choosing sweaters, ties, hats, scarves and mittens. There are blankets, blazers, dress coats and rugged outerware. The other store, on Route 100C, in premises 150 years old, is the **Vermont Rug Makers' Gallery**. Rugs and hangings, from small to room size, are displayed at this internationally-renowned designer and handweavers' gallery.

At Morrisville, scenic train rides can be enjoyed on the historic **Lamoille Valley Railroad**, operating from July to October. The only covered railroad bridge still in use in the US – the Fisher Covered Bridge – is about 2 miles (3.2km) east of Wolcott village on Route 15.

The Mad River Valley

To explore the Mad River Valley and the ski areas around Waitsfield and Warren – beauty spot areas with covered bridges – take I-89 north out of Montpelier, turning on to state Route 100B which accompanies the Mad River to Waitsfield.

Horse lovers will want to see the pure-bred mounts at the **Vermont Icelandic Horse Farm** in Waitsfield (Tel. 802 496-7141). Inn-to-inn treks, weekend tours and day rides on woodland trails, through fields and along dirt roads are available. For cyclists, the **Mad River Bike Shop** at Waitsfield, just south of the junction of Routes 100 and 17, has mountain bikes and racing and touring models for rental. It can also provide information on any organized rides being offered by bike clubs in the area.

Quilts in traditional and contemporary designs, including babies' quilts and Mennonites' hand-made quilts, can be seen at **Cabin Fever Quilts** in Waitsfield Village. Call, too, at the nearby showroom of the **Luminosity Stained Glass Studios** to see the windows and lighting in which the company specializes.There are Tiffany-style lamps, paperweights, vases, bronzes and various arts and crafts items.

All sorts of things that appeal to the dedicated cook and gourmet can be found at **The Store** in Waitsfield. Cooking utensils, gadgets, cookery books, and table linen are offered for sale in the setting of a former Methodist meeting house dating from 1834.

Sugarbush Ski Area

South of Waitsfield, **Sugarbush Ski Area** is amidst the highest peaks in the Green Mountain National Forest, just over 4,000ft (1,220m). A good choice of accommodation is handy for the three ski areas – Sugarbush North, Mad River Glen and Sugarbush Valley.

Sugarbush ski resort, with 111 trails for all abilities and what is claimed to be the world's fastest chair lift, has been operating since 1958 and has developed into a popular year-round centre. It has two dozen tennis courts and a tennis school – said to be the only one in the country to guarantee that students will be better players when they leave. Its classic 18-hole mountain golf course is open to the public (proper attire required). The resort offers daycare for children over six weeks.

The resort's activities are located in Sugarbush Village, Sugarbush South. They include squash, racquetball, indoor and outdoor swimming, aerobic and step classes. There's also a well-equipped exercise room.

Another exercise room and indoor pool are at the Sugarbush Inn's pavilion, where there is also a games room with pool table and video games. Summer activities include fly fishing, mountain biking, volleyball, chairlift rides and hay rides. Children from 6 to 14 years have a camp programme, and there's a day school for fives and under. Four and five-year-olds can take swimming lessons.

East of Montpelier

Take Route 2 east from Montpelier towards St Johnsbury, then head south on state Route 232 to enjoy lake, mountain river and woodland scenery in five state forests and parks in a compact area between Marshfield and Groton. These are called New Discovery, Big Deer, Boulder Beach, Ricker and Stillwater. Some have campgrounds, and facilities at Ricker and Stillwater include boat rentals.

The next diversion off Route 2 is to Cabot, a small and pretty town famous for

its **Cabot Cooperative Creamery** (admission fee). A video shown in the visitor centre briefs you on farm history and the cheesemaking process. During the tour you find out how naturally matured mild, sharp and extra sharp cheddar cheeses are made. You also see low fat cheeses and other dairy goods in production. There's a chance to taste award-winning cheeses, jams, jellies, sauces and dips and to buy gourmet products and locally-made craft items in the retail store.

St Johnsbury

Rejoin Route 2 at Danville – there are picnic tables near the water at Joe's Pond here – and head for St Johnsbury, the largest town in the Northeast Kingdom. The whimsical name, which reflects the remote region's rugged independence, was coined in 1949. The **Fairbanks Museum and Planetarium** (admission fee) on Main and Prospect Streets is a major attraction. Housed in a century-old historic Victorian building, the museum exhibits cover natural science, rural history, astronomy and the arts. An Arctic World section was added in 1993.

Groups of stuffed bears and big cats occupy the museum. They are part of a collection of 2,500 mounted mammals and birds. There is also a collection of 2,500 antique dolls. Historic scales form another collection – the museum was founded by the Fairbanks family, inventors of the platform scale. In the museum shop the accent is on environmental gifts, including bird feeders and nest boxes. A planetarium, Hall of Science, and the Northern New England Weather Center are also based in the building.

Maple Grove Farms of Vermont, claimed to be the world's largest and oldest maple candy factory, can be toured in Portland Street, St Johnsbury. Visitors walk through the working factory (admission fee), with a guide explaining the production processes. As well as maple syrup and Vermont candy, the factory, established in 1915, produces salad dressings, savoury sauces and raspberry syrup. The sugar-house can be visited.

The factory's gift shop contains a sampling table with maple syrup and gourmet dressings. Factory seconds are available with savings of up to 50 percent of the usual retail price. The factory is open year-round. Guided tours are held from mid-May to late October.

St Johnsbury has a big gift shop on Route 2, the **Farmer's Daughter Gift Barn**, where the selection is bigger and prices are lower than in most similar stores. Sheepskin products, moccasins, hand bags, foods and a range of attractive goods are offered. The barn opened some 35 years ago. A new development is the Sugar Shack, which tempts visitors with delicious butter fudge, waffle cones, ice creams and candies.

Lyndonville

Route 5 takes you to Lyndonville, just north of St Johnsbury. Lyndonville has two covered bridges. A large collection of paintings and prints depicting Vermont's North Country is displayed in a barn in the grounds of the **Wildflower Inn** at Darling Hill Road.

Harness racing, cattle exhibits, and assorted events relating to agricultural and

A huddle of farm buildings near St Johnsbury, in the heart of the Northeast Kingdom region (previous page).

rural life provide four days of entertainment at **Mountain View Park**, Lyndonville, in mid-August, at the Caledonia County Fair, which has taken place annually for nearly 150 years. Telephone 802 626-5538 for dates and information.

North of Lyndonville

Just north of Lyndonville is East Burke, where Burke Mountain has had the reputation of being a real skier's mountain for half a century. This is the home of Burke Mountain Academy, the nation's premier race training school, and there is always the chance of seeing Olympic hopefuls skiing the upper trails. The lower slopes are ideal for beginners. Ski Burke offers trailside lodging, a ski school, a rental shop and other facilities.

From Lyndonville you have a choice of road – I-91 or Route 122 – north to Barton. If you take the state highway you can call at the **Bread and Puppet Museum**, near Glover, just short of Barton at the junction with Route 16. There is some lovely lake country to explore on minor roads west of Glover.

Sugarmill Farm and Museum, 200 yards (185m) off I-91 (Exit 25) is a relaxing place to visit. Admission to the sugar-house and syrup samples are free, but the charge for a hay wagon ride through the maple orchard is well worth the money. The Auger family is into its third generation of sugar producers at Sugarmill Farm, having started farming in 1923. Now 4,800 rock maple trees are tapped each year. Some of the syrup flavours Ben and Jerry's maple walnut ice cream. As well as a museum, gift shop and ice cream parlour, there are two trout ponds, and visitors can borrow fishing equipment. The farms opens from 8am to 8pm daily all year.

North-East Vermont

The extreme north east of Vermont is a sparsely populated but beautiful region of mountains and rivers.

The **Jay Peak** region, in north central Vermont, is close to the border with Canada. The Jay Peak ski resort has 63 diverse trails and offers slopeside accommodation. Childcare for children aged 2-9 years is provided free between 9am and 9pm for guests at the resort (others are charged a fee). As well as lifts, Jay Peak has the only aerial tramway in the state. It carries 60 passengers and offers views of four US states and the Canadian province of Quebec.

The tramway operates between 10.30am and 4.30pm from late June to early September and again for foliage time, from mid-September to mid-October. Telephone 802 988-2611 for times and rates.

Lots of Tax-Free Fun

Natural beauty with heart-lifting views, a wealth of outdoor activities in an uncommercial setting, and historic inns make New Hampshire an ideal holiday destination for those who love rural life and rural touring. And the state's trump card is the fact that it has no sales tax. Factory outlet complexes and more than 50 state liquor stores offer shoppers tremendous value.

Mountains with gently-rounded summits, forests of mixed woods which bring visitors by the thousands in the Fall, lakes, waterfalls and rivers entice New Hampshire people from their small towns and villages to enjoy whatever season it happens to be. Pre-school-age children learn to ski, snowmobilers have an extensive network of trails, and the intrepid take up ice climbing. Dog-sledding is fun, as are white water rafting, canoeing and tubing, mountain climbing and mountain biking.

America's Stonehenge at North Salem is said to form an accurately aligned astronomical calendar.

New Hampshire has only 18 miles (29km) of sea coast, but makes the most of its resorts and beaches. It has a short northern border with Canada, and the lion's share of the White Mountain National Forest, which covers 773,000 acres (312,833 hectares), a fraction of which intrudes into Maine. In the north of the State, at Clarksville, the 45th parallel is midway between the Equator and the North Pole.

Although mainly rural in character, New Hampshire was the first state to develop industry after the Revolutionary War, setting up textile mills and shoe factories. The Amoskeag Mill in the state's biggest city, Manchester, was once the largest textile mill in the world.

'Live Free or Die' is New Hampshire's motto. The Granite State, as it is also

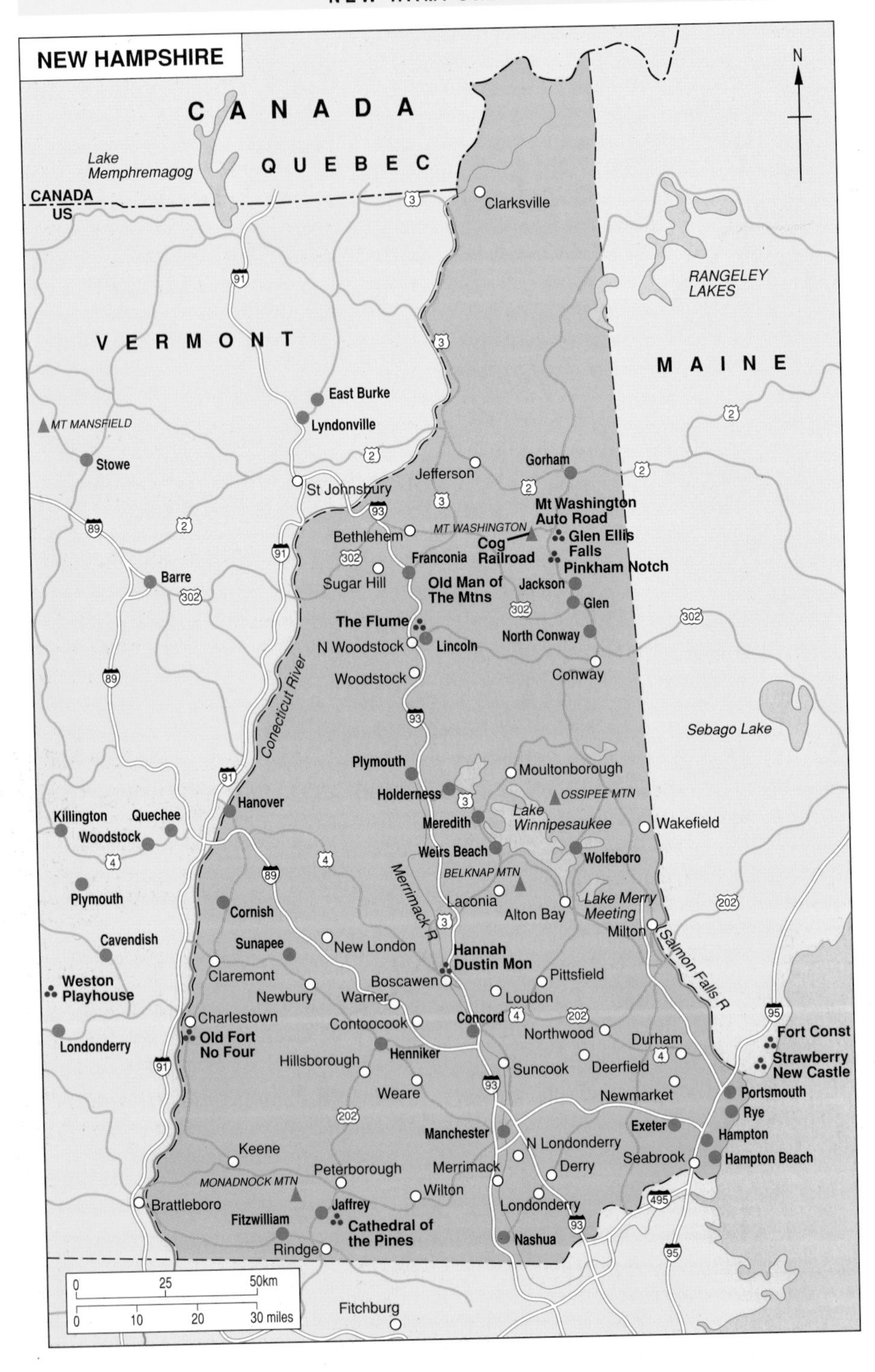
NEW HAMPSHIRE
CANADA
QUEBEC
Lake Memphremagog
CANADA
US
VERMONT
MAINE
RANGELEY LAKES
Clarksville
East Burke
Lyndonville
MT MANSFIELD
Stowe
Jefferson
Gorham
St Johnsbury
Mt Washington Auto Road
MT WASHINGTON
Glen Ellis Falls
Cog Railroad
Pinkham Notch
Bethlehem
Franconia
Sugar Hill
Old Man of The Mtns
Jackson
Glen
Barre
The Flume
N Woodstock
Lincoln
North Conway
Conway
Woodstock
Conecticut River
Sebago Lake
Plymouth
Moultonborough
Holderness
OSSIPEE MTN
Hanover
Lake Winnipesaukee
Meredith
Wakefield
Killington
Quechee
Woodstock
Weirs Beach
Wolfeboro
Merrimack R
BELKNAP MTN
Plymouth
Cornish
Laconia
Alton Bay
Lake Merry Meeting
Milton
Salmon Falls R
Cavendish
Sunapee
New London
Hannah Dustin Mon
Claremont
Weston Playhouse
Boscawen
Pittsfield
Newbury
Warner
Loudon
Charlestown
Contoocook
Concord
Northwood
Old Fort No Four
Londonderry
Durham
Fort Const
Strawberry
New Castle
Hillsborough
Henniker
Suncook
Deerfield
Weare
Newmarket
Portsmouth
Rye
Exeter
Manchester
Hampton
N Londonderry
Keene
Seabrook
Hampton Beach
Merrimack
Derry
Peterborough
MONADNOCK MTN
Wilton
Brattleboro
Londonderry
Jaffrey
Cathedral of the Pines
Fitzwilliam
Nashua
Rindge
Fitchburg
0 25 50km
0 10 20 30 miles
N

known, has a population of nearly 1,114,000, and a land area of nearly 9,000 square miles (23,300km^2) divided into six regions in which its people live very freely indeed. It is 200 miles (320km) long and at its widest, at the state line with Massachusetts to the south, about 100 miles (160km). The capital is Concord (population 36,000) in the Merrimack Valley Region. There are nearly 70 state parks, forests, historic sites and roadside picnic areas. A dozen state parks have camping facilities. One-sixteenth of the surface of New Hampshire is covered by water – more than 2,000 lakes and 40,000 miles (64,370km) of streams.

New Hampshire has plenty of wide, open spaces, much to the delight of cross-country skiers.

The state's Office of Travel and Tourism Development provides toll free, up-to-the-minute reports on snow and Fall foliage conditions. For foliage reports in September and October telephone 1-800-258-3608. From November to March skiers may phone 1-800-262-6660 (cross-country), or 1-800-258-3608 (alpine). For snowmobile trail inquiries (the state has 6,000 miles (9,650km) of trails) the number is 1-800-258-3609 (November to April).

The Sea Coast Region

The Sea Coast Region is the smallest in the state. More than half of the 18-mile (29km) Atlantic coastline is public land, with sandy beaches. Route 1A follows the coast from Portsmouth, where the Piscataqua River forms the border with Maine, to Hampton Beach, close to the Massachusetts state line.

Portsmouth

Portsmouth is the Sea Coast Region's largest town (population 26,000). It has performing arts, galleries, historic homes, antique shops, seafood eateries, gourmet restaurants and museums, the largest of which is **Strawbery Banke** (admission fee). The story goes that a group of English settlers sailed up the Piscataqua River in 1630, keeping an eye open for land with a source of fresh water. They found a bank of strawberries and the area became Portsmouth's original neighbourhood. Through workshops, artisans' galleries, more than 40 furnished historic homes and costumed guides, the open-air museum on a 10-acre (4-hectare) waterfront site at Marcy Street gives an insight into local life from the 17th to the mid-20th centuries. Strawbery Banke is open daily, 10am to 5pm, from May to the end of October.

Also in Marcy Street is the **Children's Museum of Portsmouth** (admission fee), open year-round from Tuesday to Saturday, 10am to 5pm, Sunday 1-5pm, and on Monday, too, in summer and during school vacations. The place is great fun, and some children hold their birthday parties there.

Six historic houses with different architectural styles and furnishings come under the auspices of Portsmouth Historic Associates (Tel. 603 436-1118). These are the **Warner House** (1716) with early murals, the **John Paul Jones House Museum** (1758), the **Wentworth-Gardner House** – considered to be one of the finest Georgian houses in America – the **Moffatt-Ladd House** (1763), the **Governor Langdon House** (1784) and the **Rundlet-May House** (1807). As well as these, all open to the public from mid-June to mid-October, Portsmouth has one of the oldest surviving houses in New Hampshire, the 1664 **Jackson House** on Northwest Street. Its opening times are limited to the first Saturday afternoon of the month from June to October.

On Little Harbor Road, 2 miles (3.2km) south of downtown Portsmouth, is the **Wentworth-Coolidge Mansion**, the 42-room home of Benning Wentworth, New Hampshire's Royal Governor from 1741 to 1767 (telephone 203 436-6607 for opening times).

At Albacore Park, 600 Market Street, the experimental 205ft (63m) submarine *USS Albacore* which was in service from 1953 to 1972 can be toured. The crew of 55 lived for months at a time in the floating laboratory. The *Albacore* is part of the **Port of Portsmouth Maritime Museum** (admission fee). A short film is shown in the visitor centre, and there is a Memorial Garden. The museum is open from late May to early October. Telephone 603 436-3680 for winter hours.

On the cultural side, Portsmouth has a number of theatres, one of which presents original plays in a former warehouse, a 900-seat music hall, a repertory company and a ballet company. The work of more than 300 craftspeople is represented at the **N.W. Barret Gallery** at 53 Market Street. Limited edition gold and silver jewellery, home furnishings and marine-related fine art and model ships are on sale. Shopping in the city ranges from modern malls to quaint shops in the Olde Port area, along the restored waterfront. There are enough restaurants to earn Portsmouth the tag, 'the San Francisco of the east'.

Tours

Horse and carriage tours go from Market Square daily from May through October and at weekends the rest of the year (Tel.

GO GUNKHOLING

Sea kayaking is a growing sport at Little Harbor, Portsmouth. Sea kayaks are wider, larger and more stable than river kayaks and the basic techniques are different. Sea kayaks can get to places no other boats can reach and are great for wildlife watching and 'gunkholing' – poking into inlets and caves. Gunkholing trips in the Portsmouth area are organized by John and Nancy Halloran, of the Adventure Learning Centre, Merrimack, Massachusetts (Tel. 508 346-9728).

603 427-0044). For walking and motoring tours of Portsmouth and the region call Insight Tours on 603 436-4223. The Isles of Shoals ferry operates from Barker Wharf. Harbour and river trips, and cruises to the Isles of Shoals are operated by Portsmouth Harbor Cruises, Tel. 603 436-8084. Captain Whittaker's Oceanic Whale Watch Expeditions, with a naturalist guide on board and a chance to see sharks and various seabirds, are run from Barker Wharf (Tel. 800 441-4620).

Water Country, on Route 1 at Portsmouth, is the place for families to splash out. You can go tubing along a river, through waterfalls, caves and a 'rain forest', or belt through raging rapids. There are giant water slides, including the Double Geronimo – 'the fastest in New England' – a huge whirlpool, bumper boats, and more gentle activities in shallow pools with mini-slides for tots.

New Castle, Portsmouth's next-door neighbour to the east, has two of the forts – now forming a National Historic Landmark – built along the coast. One is **Fort Constitution**, formerly called Fort William and Mary, a British stronghold, originating from the 17th century. Little remains of this, but the fort, captured by colonists in 1774, was rebuilt in 1808. It is on Route 1B at the US Coast Guard Station. The second fort is **Fort Stark**, at Wild Rose Lane, overlooking Little Harbor. It has been used as an active fortification in every conflict from the Revolutionary War to World War II.

Rye

Odiorne State Park, on Route 1A midway between Portsmouth and Rye Beach, is a great place to learn about the area's environment and ecology. The park has a visitor centre, an aquarium, a museum and a sea-coast science centre. There are nature trails and bird walks among its 230 acres (93 hectares). The park is the site of New Hampshire's first European settlement.

Wallis Sands State Beach at Rye is long and wide with a bath house and good parking. At low tide gnarled old stumps of a sunken forest – a legacy of the Ice Age – can be seen off Rye. Snaking around the tree stumps is the original Atlantic cable, laid in 1874. The receiving station for the cable is in Old Beach Road, Rye. Whale-watching trips and cruises to the Isles of Shoals are available from Rye Harbor. Of the nine islands, four belong to New Hampshire and five to Maine.

ANOTHER RIDE FOR REVERE

13 December 1774 was a hectic day for the Sons of Liberty, and one which helped to spark off the Revolution. Paul Revere galloped from Boston to Portsmouth to warn that the British planned to remove gunpowder from their garrison at Fort William and Mary. Hundreds of men overpowered the fort and grabbed several tons of gunpowder, which were subsequently used by the New Hampshire Militia at the Battle of Bunker Hill.

Hampton

Formal gardens, including a Japanese garden, a conservatory and an all-American rose display garden, can be visited daily from May to October (donation suggested) at **Fuller Gardens**, 10 Willow Avenue, North Hampton (off Route 1A). North Hampton's factory outlet centre, which has more than 30 stores, is on Lafayette Road.

North Beach, Hampton, offers good swimming, with lifeguards on duty. At Hampton Beach, a town of 900 people, events take place all summer, mostly on the extensive beach, which is a state park. They include a regatta, a seafood festival, weight-lifting contests, fireworks and free concerts at the Seashell Complex. For an events list telephone Hampton Beach Chamber of Commerce (603 926-8717).

Hampton Beach, known for its three-mile (4.8km) boardwalk, attracts swimmers, parasailers, surfers and kite fliers. In summer, flea markets and backyard sales are held all along the coast from Portsmouth to Seabrook.

Durham

One of the sea coast region's inland towns is Durham, west of Portsmouth and adjacent to the campus of the University of New Hampshire, at the north-eastern corner of Great Bay. Durham's **museum** on Maine Street (Route 108) is run by the local Historic Association (Tel. 603 868-5436). It opens on weekday afternoons from June to August and on Tuesday and Thursday afternoons the rest of the year, or by appointment.

Little Bay Buffalo Company, on Langley Road, Durham, is where the American bison roam. It is open daily from 9am to sunset, and bison meat and bison burgers are available.

From Adams Point, Durham (or by boat via Little Bay and the Piscataqua River) the **Great Bay National Estuarine Research Reserve** can be reached. The 'inland' Atlantic Bay has nearly 4,500 acres (1,820 hectares) of tidal waters and mud flats and nearly 50 miles (80km) of shoreline. Habitats and environments in the estuary include saltmarsh, tidal creeks, woodland and fields, with interesting flora and fauna.

South of Durham, on Route 108, is **Newmarket**, a town of fewer than 500 inhabitants, noted for its dance floor and dancing to big band sounds. Call the Rockingham Ballroom for details (Tel. 603 772-2622).

Exeter

The new **American Independence Museum**, on Governor Street, Exeter, west of North Hampton, has rare documents and military items relating to the Revolution. The museum (admission fee) is open Wednesday to Sunday, noon to 5pm, from May through October (Tel. 603 772-2622). Also in Exeter, at 12 Water Street, is the **Gilman Garrison House**, built in 1690 to protect John Gilman's sawmills, and re-modelled in the 18th century.

Seabrook

Formerly a whaling community, Seabrook now has a nuclear power industry, and is the southernmost town on New Hampshire's coastline, close to the border with Massachusetts. The **Yankee Science and Nature Center**, the state's only hands-on energy, science and wildlife study centre, is here. Allow time for a bus tour, a nature walk and a visit to the energy theatre.

Another popular venue west of the town is **Seabrook Greyhound Park** on Route 107. A bet on the races can be combined with a meal in the restaurant. The park is open year-round, and there are matinee and evening races.

A **railroad museum** in a restored 1873 railroad depot at Sandown, in the west of the sea coast region, has plenty of memorabilia and a telegraph system, and opens at weekends (1-5pm) from June to October or by appointment (Tel. 603 887-4621).

The Merrimack Valley

Three of New Hampshire's major cities are in the Merrimack Valley region, which is nevertheless mainly rural. Manchester, the textile town on the Merrimack River, with a population of nearly 100,000, is the biggest city in the state. Concord, with well under 40,000, is the state capital. Nashua (80,000), a mill town with a history of fur trading, is now a centre for high-tech industry and commerce.

Four times a Pulitzer Prize winner, America's revered poet, Robert Frost, who died in 1962 at the age of 88, spent ten years in the early 1900s living in a white clapboard farmhouse at Londonderry, just south of Derry on Route 28. Now a National Historic Landmark, the property is open to the public daily from 10am to 6pm in summer and at weekends in spring and autumn (Tel. 603 432-3091).

Gray Goose Village Shoppes at nearby Londonderry provide an unusual shopping experience. Thirty speciality shops selling crafts and gifts are within two restored New England homes (closed Sunday).The **Children's Metamorphosis**, at Rockingham Road, Londonderry, is

A rock chamber on North Salem's Mystery Hill – just one of the puzzles posed at America's Stonehenge.

AMERICA'S STONEHENGE

Choose a fine day to visit a wondrous woodland site of more than 30 acres (12.1 hectares), at North Salem, east of Nashua. This is **America's Stonehenge**, formerly known as Mystery Hill (admission fee). To find it, take Route 111 east for about 5 miles (8km) to Island Pond and Haverhill Roads. Follow Haverhill Road south to the entrance.

America's Stonehenge does not look like England's Stonehenge, but like its counterpart it is believed it was built by an ancient people who knew about astronomy and stone construction. Situated among woodland at the top of a granite hill, America's Stonehenge is a series of chambers forming a megalithic astronomical complex. It is believed to be around 4,000 years old, the oldest site of its kind in North America.

Standing monoliths line up with the Equinox sunset on 21 March and 21 September and others line up with the summer solstice sunrise on 21 June. A 4½ ton (4.6 tonne) stone slab on stone 'legs' forms what is called the Sacrificial Table. It is thought ancient sacrifices were made here.The largest chamber on the site has two passageways in the shape of a T. There are capstones on the site weighing up to 11 tons (11.2 tonnes), posing similar puzzles to those of England's Stonehenge: who transported the huge stones to the site, how did they do it – and why?

It is only since 1958, when America's Stonehenge was first opened to the public, that it has been proven that the stones form an accurately aligned astronomical calendar. Research continues into artefacts – stone tools and pottery shards – found on the site.

The site (Tel. 603 893-8300) is open daily from June to early September, from 9am to 5pm, and from 10am to 4pm in May and October. In April and November it opens at weekends only from 10am to 3.30pm.

as much an activity area as a museum. It has a construction site, nature centre, waterplay area and hands-on exhibits, and is open Tuesday to Saturday, 9.30am to 5pm (to 8pm on Friday) and Sunday afternoon.

The region's main cities are strung along the Merrimack River – Nashua, Merrimack, Manchester and Concord, going from south to north. They are linked by the F.E. Everett Turnpike, Interstates 93 and 293 and Route 3. Nashua's evolution as a mill town in the 1800s, later diversifying into other industries, unfolds at **Nashua Historical Society**'s premises at 5 Abbot Street. Merrimack also developed as a mill town, though today visitors are more likely to be aware of the brewing industry. Free guided tours of the **Anheuser-Busch Brewery** are held all year at the Daniel Webster Highway premises (Tel. 603 595-1202). Visitors are shown the brewery's Clydesdale draught horses. Tours take place daily, 9.30am to 5pm, May to October, and Wednesday to Sunday, 10am to 4pm, November to April.

Manchester

Manchester is an industrial and cultural centre, home of the New Hampshire Symphony Orchestra, several art galleries and the Palace Theater in Bridge Street, where Broadway-style shows can be seen in summer. Built in 1915, the Palace had a basic but effective conditioning system – a massive block of ice and an outsize fan.

The city's most prestigious gallery, regarded as one of the finest small art museums in the US, is the **Currier Gallery of Art**, in Orange Street. Paintings and sculptures by European and American artists represent the work of seven centuries (admission fee). Transport is provided from

Friday to Monday to the **Zimmerman House** – reservations are required for this (Tel. 603 669-6144) – a 1950 home designed by Frank Lloyd Wright, architect of New York's spiralling Guggenheim Museum. The Currier Gallery opens Friday 11am-9pm, Sunday 11am-5pm, and other days 10am-5pm (closed Tuesday).

Manchester's economy was founded on textiles, its **Amoskeag Mill** housed 700,000 spindles and 23,000 looms, turning out 1,500,000ft (457,200m) of cloth each week. Today, the historic mill, on Commercial Street, houses the **Science Enrichment Encounter**, a fascinating learning centre open in summer and school vacations on weekdays 10am to 3pm, and at weekends all year from noon to 5pm.

Artefacts of the Amoskeag Manufacturing Company, the Revolutionary War and Indian exhibits can be seen at **Manchester Historic Association's library/ museum** on Amherst Street (open Tuesday to Friday, 9am to 4pm, Saturday 10am to 4pm).

The reproduction of a French medieval castle contains a world of collectible dolls, dolls houses, doll paraphernalia, musical boxes, miniature building materials and an old world Christmas shop. All can be seen at **The Little Red Doll House**, open daily on Union Street.

The **Mall of New Hampshire**, at South Willow Street, Manchester, has some 100 stores and handcart stalls bright with clothes and gifts, jewellery and housewares. One of the stores is Filene's. Bargains, remember, are even better in New Hampshire where there is no sales tax.

State Parks

To the south of Suncook, between Manchester and Concord, is **Bear Brook State Park**, off Route 28 at Allenstown. Nearly 10,000 acres (4,050 hectares) of thickly wooded country contain two archery ranges, a snowmobile museum, a fitness course, nature centre, nature trails, an interpretive centre, a new (1993) **Museum of Family Camping**, and facilities for mounting biking, hiking, fishing, ski towing and camping (Tel. 603 485-9874).

Other state parks in the Merrimack Valley region are **Pawtuckaway**, east of Bear Brook – a popular campground with a lakeside beach – and smaller **Clough**, at Weare, south west of Concord, where an extensive river pool provides swimming and a beach.

At Deerfield, west of Bear Brook Park, Gay Nineties buggy rides and romantic sleigh or hay rides are offered at **Point of View Farm** (Tel. 603 463-7974).

Concord

Concord's **State House**, completed in 1819, is the seat of the New Hampshire State Legislation, the oldest legislature building in the US in which both houses continue to sit in their original chambers. It is built of locally quarried granite. The State House, at 107 North Main Street (Tel. 603 271-2154), opens at the weekend during August to October, from 11am to 4pm, for self-guided tours. Reservations are required for conducted tours.

Furniture, folk and decorative art, tools and toys, and the ornate Concord ceremonial coach, all produced in the state, are among exhibits at the **Museum of New Hampshire History,** at 30 Park Street (Tel. 603 225-3381). Revolutionary War battle flags and White Mountains paintings are displayed. The museum (donation requested), run by the New Hampshire Historical Society, opens Tuesday to Saturday 9am to 5pm (to 8.30pm Thursday), and weekends noon to 5pm.

The State House and the museum are in the downtown area, where you can wander around and see more than a dozen other places of historic interest, all of which are listed in the Coach and Eagle Trail walking tour map and brochure, available from the Greater Concord Chamber of Commerce, at 244 North Main Street.

The **Kimball-Jenkins Estate**, on Main Street, is one of these sites. Tours of the 1882 mansion and formal gardens are available during the summer, and the carriage house is open all year round.

Traditional and contemporary crafts are displayed at the League of New Hampshire Craftsmen's **Gallery**, less than two blocks south of the State House, on North Main Street. The gallery is open year-round on weekdays, 9am to 5pm.

The **Christa McAuliffe Planetarium**, on Institute Drive, is a new and technologically advanced museum (admission fee charged) named after the New Hampshire social studies teacher who lost her life in the Challenger space shuttle explosion. Visitors can navigate the solar system without leaving the safety of the 40ft (12.3m) dome, all with the aid of computer graphics. A certain amount of space exploration can be accomplished by pressing a button at your seat. Reserva-

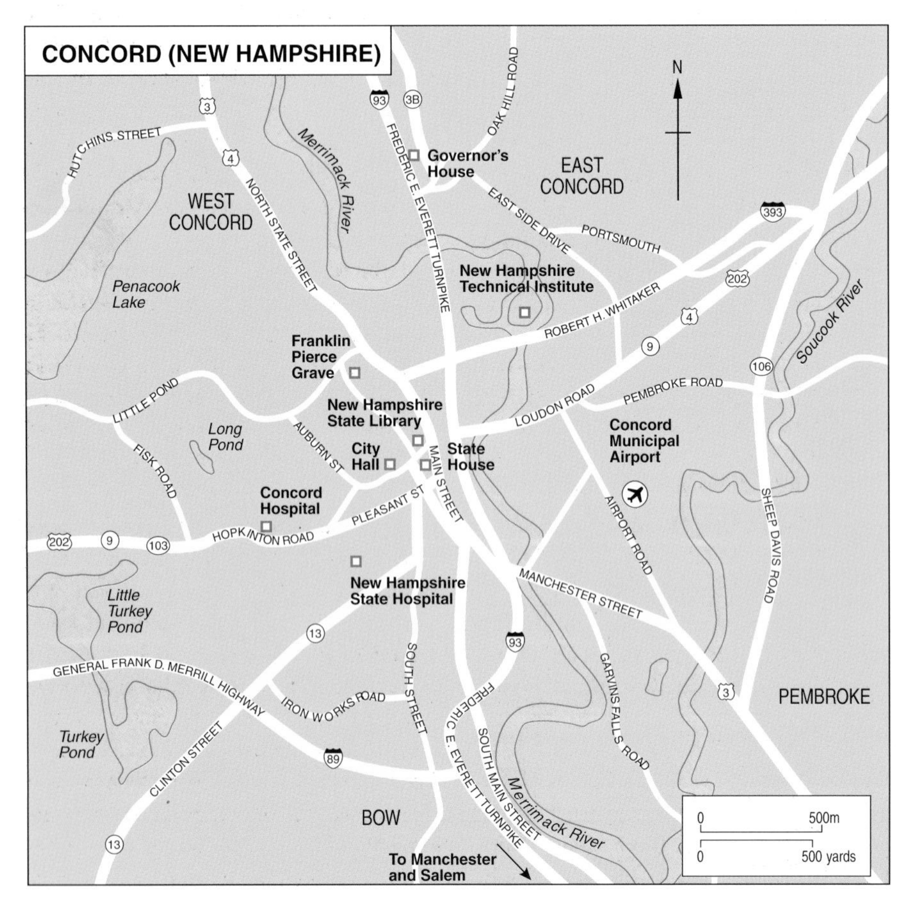

tions for the dome show should be made in advance, by telephoning 603 271-STAR or by calling in at the box office in person during opening hours – Tuesday to Sunday from 9am to 4pm.

Concord is not memorable for its nightlife, but on Tuesday evenings in June, July and August the Nevers 2nd Regiment Band plays some stirring military music at outdoor concerts in Bicentennial Square.

CANTERBURY SHAKER VILLAGE

Canterbury Shaker Village is less than a half-hour's drive north of Concord. To get there, leave I-93 at Exit 18 and follow signs to the Shaker village (admission fee) for about $6^1/_2$ miles (10.5km).

The village's 24 buildings, where Shakers followed their way of life for more than two centuries, can be witnessed. The Canterbury Shaker Village was founded in the 1780s, and at its peak in the mid-1800s there were 300 people and 100 buildings on a 4,000-acre (1,620-hectare) site. They observed equality of race and sex.

In their workshops the Shakers made beautiful furniture with simple lines. Today, skilled craftsmen in the village continue to practise traditional Shaker crafts, including broom-making, oval box-making, spinning, basket-weaving and herbal crafts.

Light lunches or sandwiches are served daily from May to October, with brunch available on Sundays in April, November and December. Dinner by candlelight, followed by entertainment, is available on Friday and Saturday year-round by reservation (Tel. 603 783-9511). Original Shaker recipes are used.

From May to the end of October the village is open 10am to 5pm daily. In April, November and December it is open only on Friday, Saturday and Sunday.

North of Concord

At Boscawen, on Route 3 north of Concord, members of the New Hampshire Art Association exhibit their paintings, sculpture, prints and photography at their **gallery** at 150 King Street. The gallery is open all year, Wednesday to Sunday, 11am to 5pm.

North east of Concord, on Route 106, is the **New Hampshire International Speedway** at Loudon, where 55,000 seated spectators can watch Indy cars, stock cars, formula cars, motor cycle and kart racing from April to the end of October. Telephone 603 783-4931 for schedules and ticket information.

A fascinating place to visit at Contoocook, west of Concord (I-89, Exit 6) is **Cole's Bird Carving**, where exquisite shorebirds, songbirds, ducks and other waterfowl are hand-carved and painted, and can be made to order. Telephone 603 746-4056 for an appointment and directions.

If there's a horse lover in the family it may be worth driving north east out of Concord to Pittsfield, where the equine occupants of **White's Miniature Horse Petting Farm**, and other friendly farm animals are happy to be hugged by small visitors. Visitors with disabilities are especially welcome (Tel. 603 435-8258 for further details or to arrange a visit). Open May to September, 10am to 5pm; there is an admission charge.

Northwood

From Pittsfield, Route 107 leads to Northwood, which is 18 miles (29km) east of Concord on Route 4. Northwood is well known for its dozens of antique shops and its wide variety of craft and speciality establishments. With a flea market, a designer and manufacturer of bird feeders, a company which buys, sells and restores golf carts, another dealing in old toy railroads, doll houses and models, a military surplus store and lots of other odd specialists, there is plenty to keep browsers happy for hours.

Northwood has winter appeal, too, as a ski centre. In January the local Lions Club sponsors snowmobile races on Northwood Lake. A local company, ABC Quilts, donates quilts to babies born with AIDS and other disorders. Late July is the time for the annual Bean Hole Bash, when beans are baked underground as they were in colonial times.

The Monadnock Region

The Monadnock Region, in the south-west part of New Hampshire, takes its name from Mount Monadnock, the 3,165ft (965m) peak that is claimed to be the most-climbed mountain in North America. It dominates the region's landscape of farmland, woodland, lakes and villages. The only town of any size is Keene (with a population of 22,500), which is said to have the world's widest paved main street. There are nearly 40 other towns and villages.

State Parks

One of the region's parks, **Rhododendron State Park**, at Fitzwilliam, is a National Natural Landmark. It has 16 acres (6.5 hectares) of the colourful shrubs. A trail provides a good view of Mount Monadnock in **Monadnock State Park**, situated to the north east. This park, 4 miles (6.4km) north of Jaffrey, has 40 miles (64km) of trails to Monadnock summit. There are picnic grounds, tent sites with year-round camping, and ski touring. Note that this is one state park in which pets are not allowed.

Mount Monadnock is visible from many parts of the region. The **Cathedral of the Pines**, off Route 119 at Rindge, provides a good view of it. The 'Cathedral', open between 9am and dusk from May until the end of October, is an outdoor shrine in memory of the service men and women from the area who have lost their lives during times of conflict. The congregation sits on makeshift pews during services which are presented for worshippers of all faiths from May to the end of September.

Jaffrey, just to the north west, offers a choice of ancient and modern ways of viewing the scenery. Silver Ranch Stables arranges hay rides or sleigh rides, while a horse-drawn carriage goes through field and forest (Tel. 603 532-7363). And from Silver Ranch Airport you can take a flight over the region (Tel. 603 532-8870) for a unique bird's-eye view.

The Monadnock Region has a variety of state parks. A drive to the top of 2,300ft (701m) Pack Monadnock goes through glorious scenery in **Miller State Park**, and there are walking trails. The park, 3 miles (4.8km) east of Peterborough, off Route 101, was established in 1891, honouring a hero of the 1812 war, General James Miller.

North east of Miller State Park is **Wapack National Wildlife Refuge**, nearly 17,000 acres (6,880 hectares) on North Pack Monadnock Mountain. It provides mixed habitats of forest, swamp, bare rock ledge and cliffs. It is a hawk migration area. People go there to observe wildlife and take photographs. Hiking, ski towing and snowshoeing are other popular activities.

Wildlife

Soils in New England generally are not good, but are frequently gravelly and stony. There are large areas of rock, sand or gravel with little topsoil, and wetlands are to be found throughout the region. These were among the factors which helped bring on agricultural decline when development of America's fertile Midwest began to accelerate in the 19th century. But decline on the one hand means preservation on the other, and New Englanders today benefit from an wide range of native vegetation and wildlife.

Wilderness areas, such as Acadia National Park, provide opportunities for appreciating nature.

There are extensive forests of birch, beech, maple and hemlock, especially in the north. Spruce fir covers large parts of Maine and the higher mountain areas, and Cape Cod has oak-pine forests. The tall and stately white pine, believed to live as long as four centuries, is the most commonly found conifer in southern New England. The paint factory explosion of autumn, when colours that ought to clash combine in a riotous and triumphant harmony, is provided mainly by the beech and oak, the birch, maple and hickory, with contributions from the delicate sumac and pin cherry.

Spring and summertime sees a profusion of colour as wildflowers burst into bloom throughout New England. Lupin, goldenrod, purple aster and black-eyed Susan gladden the hearts of anyone travelling the highways, or

The grey squirrel is one of New England's most common mammals.

visiting parks, forests and recreation areas. Dogwood, mountain laurel and rhododendron also put on magnificent displays, while the beach rose, fuchsia, huckleberry and blueberry flourish along the shore. Swathes of crimson in bogland areas serve as a reminder that the small but flamboyant cranberry was decreed by nature to be the perfect complement to another New England native, the turkey.

Birdlife is abundant throughout the region, where more than 400 species have been sighted. The best time for birdwatching is during the spring migration. With so much water about, both salt and fresh, wildfowl and sea birds will provide the readiest material for a birdspotter's notebook. Among endangered species enjoying sanctuary in New England are the bald eagle, peregrine falcon, piping plover, roseate tern, short-eared owl and the upland sandpiper. At the other end of the scale, visitors to the **Dead Creek Wildlife Refuge** at Addison, Vermont, can enjoy the spectacle of 10,000 snow geese lifting off at once from a migration stopover.

The most common mammals in the region are the grey squirrel and the eastern chipmunk, both seen everywhere – in parks, backyards, even in city streets. The moose, whose presence is advertised on frequent roadsigns throughout northern New England, and the black bear are the largest land mammals, followed by the white-tailed deer. Beaver, porcupine, possum, raccoon and the red fox abound. Only two poisonous snakes are found in the region. The northern copperhead and the timber rattlesnake are both said to be shy and retiring – good news for all the frogs to be found there.

Peterborough

Peterborough Historical Society has a **museum** of local history on Grove Street, and a mill house, colonial kitchen, Victorian parlour, country store and a display of antique toys. You can see it all on weekdays, 10am to 4pm (museum 1-4pm).

In the best Hollywood tradition, Peterborough Players have run a professional summer theatre on a farm since 1933 (Tel. 603 924-7585).

Sharon

About 5 miles (8km) south of Peterborough, on Route 123, is Sharon, where the **Sharon Arts Center** and its prestigious Killian Gallery hosts changing exhibitions, and there is a well-stocked craft shop.

Wilton

To the east, off Route 101, is Wilton, where **Frye's Measure Mill** presents a water-powered mill, and Shaker and colonial reproductions, country crafts and a blacksmith's shop. Tours take place on Saturdays at 2pm from June to October (fee charged). The property is open from Tuesday to Saturday, 10am to 5pm, from May to mid-December.

Harrisville

Nearby Harrisville is a carefully preserved mill village which demonstrates the textile history of the US, with its mill ponds, mill races, mills and the homes of mill owners and workers. On Main Street is the **Weaving Center of Harrisville Designs**, with floor looms, beginners' looms and weaving accessories to be seen, and some woven items in Harrisville colours for sale.

Keene

A college town west of Harrisville, Keene has several museums, which include the **Monadnock Children's Museum** (admission fee) at 147 Washington Street. The **Wyman Tavern Museum,** at 339 Main Street, is the site where trustees met in 1770 to found Dartmouth College.

The town's pièce de resistance is its **Colony Mill Marketplace**, West Street, where Country Artisans Fine Handcrafts presents the work of some 400 American craftspeople in a former woollen mill. More than 40 stores are grouped under one roof. Crafts available include musical instruments, pottery, jewellery, quilts, woven goods, clothing, ironwork, baskets, toys, stained glass and items for the home.

Dartmouth-Lake Sunapee Region

Occupying the west central area of New Hampshire, the Dartmouth-Lake Sunapee Region is named after Dartmouth College at Hanover and Lake Sunapee, and its neighbouring mountain in Mount Sunapee State Park. Predominantly rural, with few cities, this is a picturesque region of rolling hills, old villages and small towns with classic New England architecture, and a rich culture centred on Dartmouth College.

Dartmouth

The Ivy League college, founded in 1669, is home to the **Hood Museum of Art**, where ten galleries feature permanent and changing exhibitions. Permanent exhibits range from ancient art to Picasso, and collections encompass European Old Masters and Native American and African art. The museum is open daily, except Mondays, and there is no charge for admission. The college's **Hopkins Center**, on which New York City's Metropolitan Opera House is

based, presents performances of dance, music, theatre and film, as well as exhibitions of fine art.

Grafton

South east of Hanover, just off Route 4, is **Ruggles Mine**, at Grafton, the oldest mica, feldspar and beryl mine in the US – mica was produced here in 1803. The admission ticket permits visitors to collect their own minerals. The open-pit mine is interesting not only for its mineral deposits, but also for its many rooms and tunnels, used to illustrate how mountains were formed over a period of 300 million years. The mine is open daily from 9am to 5pm mid-June to mid-October and weekends only mid-May to mid-June.

Cornish

Off Route 12A, just a few miles north of Claremont, the region's largest town, is Cornish, where the world's longest two-span covered bridge crosses the Connecticut River to provide a link with Vermont. The Cornish-Windsor Bridge is 449ft (138m) long. It cost $9,000 to build in 1866, and $4.2 million to repair in 1989.

Two miles (3.2km) north of the bridge, also off Route 12A near the Connecticut River, the gardens, studios and

home of the American sculptor Augustus Saint-Gaudens, who died in 1907, may be visited between June and the end of October (admission fee). Many of his works, including larger ones and some replicas, are displayed.

Saint-Gaudens, whose works included the statue of Admiral David Farragut in Madison Square, New York City, and the Abraham Lincoln statue in Chicago's Lincoln Park, lived and worked at Cornish for the last 20 years of his life. He called the house Aspel after his father's birthplace in France. He himself was born in Ireland to an Irish mother, and he moved to the US in infancy. The property (Tel. 603 675-2175) is a National Historic Site managed by the National Park Service, and is open daily from 8.30am to 4.30pm. Chamber music is performed at 2pm in the studio on Sundays in July and August.

The Saint-Gaudens National Historic Site stands as a monument to the period between the late 1800s and the early 1900s when Cornish became a well-known cultural centre which attracted a colony of noted artists, writers, poets and musicians, including the landscape painter Willard Metcalfe and the actress Ethel Barrymore.

Claremont

Some 10 miles (16km) south of Cornish, Claremont offers good shopping and a walking tour of its **Historic Mill District** – a map is available from the Claremont Chamber of Commerce on Tremont Square, Main Street (Tel. 603 543-1296).

Lake Sunapee

Lake Sunapee in the centre of the region is a popular holiday location. The lake, which has three lighthouses, is 10 miles (16km) long and 3 miles (4.8km) wide, with crystal clear water. Among boat trip operators is Mount Sunapee II Tours (Tel. 603 763-4030) at Sunapee Harbor, whose clients get a narrated tour. Steamboat trips on the lake began in 1875, becoming so popular with holidaymakers that hotels were built around the shores to accommodate them.

Artefacts of old-time Sunapee and the lake's steamboat era are displayed in the **Historical Society Museum**, located at the harbour.

Mount Sunapee, rising 2,743ft (836m) from the lake's south shore, provides wonderful views, and **Mount Sunapee State Park** has good skiing and snowboarding, hiking trails, picnic sites and playgrounds, and fishing for trout and salmon. There are facilities for year-round camping in the area.

Newbury, on Route 103A on the lake's southern shore, was the summer home of John M. Hay, writer, statesman and private secretary to President Abraham Lincoln. Now known as the Fells Historic Site at the **John Hay National Wildlife Center**, the property is open at weekends and public holidays from late June to the end of October (Tel. 603 763-5041). There are nature trails and a formal garden.

New London

At the northern end of the lake is New London (I-89, Exit 11), where nostalgia rules at **Baynham's Country Store and Cafe** on Main Street. There's a 1950s soda fountain and an array of handcrafted goods and unusual items from around the world. Local craftspeople offer a large selection of pottery, woodware, jewellery, blown glass, stained glass, paintings, garments and toys at **Artisans' Workshop**, Main Street.

Bog plants unique to the area can be viewed from wooden walkways at **Cricenti's Bog**, a nature reserve just outside the centre of New London. A resident naturalist is on duty.

Andover

A classic 1874 railroad station, authentically furnished and complete with Station Master's office, is open at weekends from June to mid-October at **Andover Historical Society Museum** at Potter Place, Andover, where Routes 4 and 11 intersect east of New London. The museum (donation requested) is open Saturday 10am to 3pm and Sunday 1-3pm.

Warner

Guided tours of a major museum (admission fee) on North American Indians – their artefacts, medicinal woods and other extensive exhibits – are available at **Mount Kearsarge Indian Museum** at Warner (I-95, Exit 8 north, Exit 9 south). The museum is open daily May through October and at weekends in November and December (1-5pm).

Charlestown

In the south west of the region, off Route 12 south of Claremont, is Charlestown, where settlers built a stockade around a watchtower and domestic buildings and successfully held out against a French attack in 1747. Today, a faithful reproduction of **Fort No. 4** with 13 buildings, costumed personnel talking about their 18th-century lives, and varied exhibits can be visited (admission fee). There are demonstrations of traditional crafts, and military scenes from the days of the French and Indian wars are frequently reenacted. Times are variable from June to mid-October (Tel. 203 826-3327).

Charlestown has an extensive historic district, with 45 noteworthy buildings, for which a self-guided tour booklet is available (Tel. 203 826-5821).

Hillsborough

Hillsborough, in the region's south-east corner (Route 9) has the **Parkside Gallery** on West Main Street, where a cooperative of 30 craftspeople offers home accessories, pewterware, quilts, woven goods and a whole range of arts and crafts. Close by, near the junction of Routes 9 and 31, is a National Historic Landmark: the **Franklin Pierce Homestead Historic Site**. This is the recently restored opulent mansion built in 1804 for Pierce, 14th President of the United States. It is open daily mid-June to early September and some weekends (Tel. 603 464-5858).

The Lakes Region

The Lakes Region, the mid-eastern section of New Hampshire, did not get its name for nothing. Every one of its 40 communities borders at least one of the region's lakes and ponds, almost all of which have sandy beaches. The film *On Golden Pond* was made on Squam Lake.

In summer a variety of watersports attracts people to the region, and there are all sorts of land-based attractions to visit. Winter brings dog-sled racing and ice fishing, there's good downhill and cross-country skiing, and some towns have their own winter carnivals. All parts of the Lakes Region are easily accessible by car.

Around Lake Winnepesaukee

The largest lake, Winnipesaukee, occupies 78 square miles (202km^2), has 283 miles (453km) of shoreline, and is dotted with 365 islands, 274 of which are habitable.

Weirs Beach

On the western shore of Lake Winnipesaukee, this is the place for fun and thrills, with three major activity attractions. M/S Mount Washington Cruises operates four cruising vessels and a sailing sloop from the port. From south to north, the attractions are Surf Coaster, Weirs Beach Water Slide and Funspot.

Squam Lake was the setting for the award-winning film On Golden Pond.

A covered bridge in New Hampshire's Lakes Region – the state has more than 50 in total.

Surf Coaster (Route 11B) water park has a giant wave pool, many huge slides for all ages and levels of daring, a children's play park and a fast-food outdoor dining area. **Weirs Beach Water Slide** (Route 3) is smaller, but has a variety of exciting slides, among them a twister and an express. Both attractions open at weekends from late May to mid-June, and daily to early September. **Funspot** (Route 3), open all year, offers ten-pin bowling, a golf driving range, children's bumper cars, mini-golf, an outdoor play area and hundreds of video games. There are spectacular firework displays at the weekend, and seasonal attractions including craft fairs and elephant rides.

Weirs Beach has a sandy public beach with illuminated night swimming, go-karts, and boat rentals. Concerts and barbershop singing are presented at the bandstand. The town caters for family dining and lodging, and the area is very busy at weekends and during the summer. The *Mount Washington* cruise vessel and its sister ships sail from Weirs Beach.

Meredith

Meredith, north of Weirs Beach, is the home of **Annalee's Gift Shop Museum**, off Route 3 or 104, where exhibits include distinctive collectible dolls (admission fee). There is also a **Children's Museum** with hands-on exhibits. The **Old Print Barn**, on Winona Road, Meredith, has hundreds of prints from Old Masters to contemporary works. It opens daily, year-round, and there is no admission charge.

Meredith's showplace shopping centre is at **Mill Falls Inn and Market Place**, a former linen mill open daily all year. Some two dozen specialist stores, eateries and a 54-room inn stand over a dramatic millrace that rushes beneath the building.

If you want to retrace your steps and let someone else do the driving, why not take the train? The Winnipesaukee Railroad follows the western lake shore between Meredith and Lakeshore, Laconia, stopping at Weirs Beach.

Moultonborough

Castle in the Clouds at Moultonborough is a mansion set within some 6,000 acres (2,430 hectares) of the Ossipee Mountain range, with a vista of Lake Winnipesaukee and panoramic views. You may need some imagination to see it as a castle, but it is certainly impressive, having been built at summit level in the early 1900s by a boot and shoe millionaire who paid $7 million for the property. There are wagon rides, horseriding, hiking trails, picnic grounds, tours of the mansion and of the source and bottling plant of Castle Springs natural spring water. Castle in the Clouds is open (admission fee) at weekends May to mid-June then daily until mid-October.

Wolfeboro

On Route 109 at the south-eastern end of Lake Winnipesaukee, Wolfeboro has been tagged the oldest summer resort in America. This is because Governor John Wentworth built the first known summer house in the country here in 1763 beside a lake now called Lake Wentworth. It is a pretty place with a colonial atmosphere, and it fronts on to two other lakes besides Wentworth and Winnipesaukee.

Colonial techniques are used by craftsmen creating ornaments, candlesticks and other items at the **Hampshire Pewter Company**, 9 Mill Street, Wolfeboro. The workshop is open year-round, with tours held from Monday to Friday in summer and Fall.

Three buildings on South Main Street – a one-room schoolhouse, a firehouse museum and an 18th-century home, the Clark House – constitute the **Wolfeboro Historical Society Museum**, which is open in July and August from 10am to 4pm Monday to Saturday (donation requested). More than 500 artisans have work for sale displayed daily throughout the year at **New England Craftsmen** on Main Street.

Alton Bay

Route 28 leads from Wolfeboro round the southern tip of Winnipesaukee to Alton Bay, which boasts a dance pavilion and a Victorian-style bandstand for outdoor concerts. Watersports, and hiking on Mount Major, which is part of the Belknap Range, are recreational options. An ice fishing derby is held on the lake in February, and a springtime contest involves guessing the exact time that the ice will melt.

Laconia

Follow Route 11 for a splendid view of the lake as you skirt the Gunstock Ski Area and drive to Laconia, where the **Belknap Mill** at the Mill Plaza is the oldest unaltered brick-built textile mill in the US. The Belknap Mill Society runs it as a year-round arts centre, with concerts, exhibits and a museum of the knitting industry. The mill is open weekdays 9am to 5pm, Saturday 9am to 1pm.

Between Laconia and Weirs Beach, off Route 3, is **Endicott Rock**, an historic site in the form of a large boulder bearing some of New England's earliest graffiti. Here are initials which were inscribed in 1652 by the surveyors commissioned by Royal Governor John Endicott of the Massachusetts Bay Colony.

Plymouth

At the north-west corner of the Lakes Region is Plymouth, and just to the west, off Route 25, are the **Polar Caves** (admission fee). Set in a woodland park are the awe-inspiring glacial caverns with imaginative names. Wear outdoor clothing – there is sometimes ice in August in the Cave of Eternal Chill. The park opens daily, 9am to 5pm, from early May to mid-October, weather permitting.

Holderness

On Squam Lake's south-western point is Holderness (Route 113), where the **Science Center of New Hampshire** has activity buildings and a trail featuring the state's native animals in natural enclosures. These include bears, bobcats, owls, eagles, deer, otters, foxes and hawks. The centre is open daily, though the trail is open only from 1 April to 1 November.

FEEDING THE MIND

Route 113 takes you round the west and north of Squam Lake to the large township of Sandwich, flanked by the Squam and Sandwich mountain ranges. On Thursday evenings from November to the end of May, dinner at the Corner House Inn, Center Sandwich, is accompanied by story telling (Tel. 603 284-6219).

GETTING AFLOAT

In a region called The Lakes, it would be a pity not to get afloat. People trailing their own boats should purchase the relevant navigational charts. These are available for several waters, including Ossipee Lake, Newfound Lake, Lake Winnisquam and Lake Winnipesaukee. The charts are sold at many marinas and gift shops.

Boat or canoe rentals are available at many campgrounds, and boats with inboard or outboard motors are available for rent at marinas around the major lakes.

Public boat trips and cruises are offered on some lakes. Two-hour guided cruises aboard all-weather vessels are operated on Squam Lake by two companies based at Holderness. They are Squam Lake Tours (Tel. 603 968-7577) and The Original Golden Pond Tour (Tel. 603 968-3348). Loons are frequently sighted on Squam Lake.

Queen of Winnipesaukee, a 48ft (15m) sailing yacht, has 90-minute and two-hour trips from Weirs Beach. The sloop is a sister craft of three other vessels operated by Mount Washington Cruises at Weirs Beach (Tel. 603 366-BOAT). These are the 68ft (21m) *Doris E*, which plies between Weirs Beach and Meredith and cruises the lake's northern waters, the 76ft (23m) *Sophie C*, which carries on the US Mail delivery tradition begun in 1872, and the *M/S Mount Washington*. All can be chartered for special occasions.

The biggest sister is the elegant *Mount Washington*, 230ft (70m) long. In July and August there are moonlight dinner-dance cruises, with special theme nights from June to October. Fabulous Fifties, Caribbean Carnival, Lobsterfest, Country 'n' Western and Forties Swing are some of the themes.

The whole ship or one of its lounges may be chartered for wedding receptions – or wedding ceremonies. The captain is a Justice of the Peace and can perform the wedding ceremony in a romantic setting on board.

Daytime cruises are informal, but there are one or two guidelines for passengers on evening cruises. The minimum age is 21, except for minors accompanied by adults or with spouses over 21. Smart casual evening wear is required, and men's shirts must have collars.

Wakefield

Close to the region's north-eastern border with Maine is Wakefield (Route 109), with ten lakes and a major ski area providing plenty of sport. The **Museum of Childhood** at Wakefield Corner has 3,000 dolls among its attractions in ten rooms. It is open daily except Tuesday from late May to early October, 11am to 4pm, Sunday 1-4pm.

Milton

Take Exit 18 off the Spaulding Turnpike for the **New Hampshire Farm Museum** (admission fee) at Milton, south of Wakefield. It has workshops and demonstrations of such early skills as natural dyeing, stone wall repairing and rock splitting with hand tools. The museum is open Tuesday to Saturday, 10am to 4pm, Sunday noon to 4pm, from mid-June to early September, then weekends only until mid-October.

Franklin

One mile (1.6km) south of Franklin, off Route 127 in the south west of the region, is the **Daniel Webster Birthplace Historic Site.** The two-room farmhouse, restored in 1913, was where the distinguished statesman and orator was born in 1780. The building contains antique furniture and effects. Telephone 603 934-5057 for opening times.

The White Mountains

Well endowed by nature with gently rounded mountains, notches (narrow passes), gorges, forests, waterfalls and

A walk on the wild side amid the stunning beauty of New Hampshire's White Mountains.

The Mount Washington Cog Railway operates on the world's steepest tracks. It was completed in 1869.

wilderness, the White Mountains Region has added some superb resort accommodation, friendly country inns, scenic railroad rides – including the breathtaking Mount Washington Cog Railway – theme parks, more than 50 covered bridges, and great skiing. This is New

THE PEAK OF TOURISM

Mount Washington, at Pinkham Notch, Gorham, is the highest mountain in north-eastern North America. It can be climbed on foot, and in summer and autumn by the Auto Road, opened in 1861 and considered to be the nation's first man-made tourist attraction. It can also be scaled on the exciting Cog Railway, on the world's steepest tracks. This, the first rack and pinion railway in the world, was completed in 1869. It's wise to make reservations well in advance for the three-hour round trip.

The Mount Washington Auto Road, an 8-mile (13km) toll road – drivers are given an audio-tour cassette – can be a hairy low-gear trip, not one for a novice or nervous driver. An alternative is to take a 90-minute guided tour in a chauffeur-driven vehicle, with a half-hour visit to the Tip Top House and Observatory Museum at the summit.

The view from the top is stupendous: 130 miles (208km) on a clear day, taking in the neighbouring states, Canada and the Atlantic Ocean. On scorching days people go up there to cool off – snow has been recorded at the summit in every month of the year.

The Auto Road is open from mid-May to late October, weather permitting – 7.30am to 6pm in high summer, shorter hours either side of the main season.

The opulent Mount Washington Hotel and Resort opened in 1902. It employs a staff of 350 to service its 180 rooms.

Hampshire's most-visited region, and late May to mid-October is the most popular period for tourism, the last three weeks being the peak Fall foliage time.

Almost every town and village is within or bordering the 773,000-acre (312,830-hectare) **White Mountains National Forest**. The Saco, Connecticut, Merrimack and Androscoggin Rivers have their headwaters in the region, which also has **Mount Washington**, at 6,288ft (1,917m) the highest peak in north-eastern North America. The seven well-known notches (narrow gaps or passes between mountain peaks) are: Kinsman, Franconia, Crawford, Bear, Pinkham, Dixville and Evans.

Seventeen major attractions are promoted through the White Mountains Attractions Association. Many are grouped in the Lincoln-Woodstock area (Route 3) and the Jackson-North Conway area (Route 16), both connected by the Kancamagus Highway, a National Scenic Byway climbing to nearly 3,000ft (914m) and running alongside the Pemigewasset and Swift rivers for much of its 35 miles (56km). Both areas make good bases in which to stay for a few days.

The Lincoln-Woodstock Area

From the south, I-93 and Route 3 lead to the Lincoln-Woodstock area – take Exit 32 off the Interstate. If, after the drive, you'd like to kid yourself you arrived by rail, the place to eat is the former Lincoln railroad station, attached since 1984 to the **Woodstock Inn** at North Woodstock. You can hardly see the join. Old sewing machine tables and antique theatre seats enhance the Victorian atmosphere. The 16-page menu offers Main Line Fare, Cattle Car (beef) Specials and Coastal Express (seafood), with Long Hauls and Loose Caboose among the drinks.

North Woodstock

In spring the Pemigewasset River gallops at full belt beside Route 3, carrying the melted snow off the mountains. At the northern end of North Woodstock (Exit 33 off I-93) is **The Basin**, a 20ft (6m) wide pothole in the rock in which the Pemigewasset's water swirls powerfully. A 15-mile (24km) trip around the river valley by train with restored vintage coaches is operated by the Hobo Railroad, Lincoln (Tel. 603 745-2135). Dinner aboard a restored Pullman car of 1924 is one of the options.

There's a strong railroad atmosphere at the Woodstock Inn, North Woodstock, where meals are served in a former train station.

Water entertainment is provided by nature at **Lost River Reservation** (admission fee), North Woodstock (from Route 3 take Route 112 west). From boardwalks at the gorge you can see the river disappearing and reappearing under boulders, and you can also view Paradise Falls. Rocks and caves add to the fun. A gift shop, picnic area, snack bar, nature garden and geological displays are open from mid-May to late October. Wear footwear with good-gripping soles.

Clark's Trading Post, North Woodstock, provides varied entertainment – a bit of mystery, a steam train ride, bumper boats, museums, antique music machines, Americana – and from July, performing bears. The post (admission fee) is open

Accommodation is provided in timber-built cabins at this North Woodstock motor inn.

daily from late June to early September and weekends only before and after the main season.

Lincoln

Nearby, in Lincoln (Route 3) is a water park, the **Whale's Tale**, with gentle pools for tots, a wave pool and fast slides. Admission is charged by height! Children under 36 inches (91cm) and those over 65 years (however tall) get in free. Variable opening hours from late May to early September (Tel. 603 745-8810).

Loon Mountain Park (admission fee), off the Kancamagus Highway (Route 112) at Lincoln, offers self-guided nature trails, a glacial caves walk, hiking and mountain bike trails, horseriding, rollerskating, archery, laser trap shooting, and a ride up the mountain by enclosed aerial lift.

In winter, Loon Mountain is one of the area's most popular ski resorts, with a vertical of 2100 feet (640m). There are two base lodges connected by a miniature railway, family and expert terrain, and childcare facilities are available.

The Old Man of the Mountains measures 40ft (12.3m) from forehead to chin, and is formed by five granite ledges.

Franconia Notch State Park

Just north of Lincoln and North Woodstock, I-93 becomes the Franconia Notch State Parkway, and in the state park is the **Flume Visitor Center**, (admission fee) where a 15-minute film tells what there is to see in the 6,440-acre (2,506-hectare) park. There are also historical displays, a gift shop and cafe at the centre, where between late June and mid-October a shuttle bus service operates to the base of the 800ft- (243m-) long gorge. You can see the gorge and its sheer 70ft (21.5m) walls from a wooden walkway. The centre is open daily (weather permitting) from mid-May to the end of October.

It costs nothing to admire another piece of nature's work, the **Old Man of the Mountain**, whose granite features measure 40ft (12.3m) from forehead to chin. Formed by five ledges 1,200ft (366m) above Profile Lake, he is best viewed from the lake shore.

The Franconia Notch State Park is a vast wilderness area just north of Lincoln. Activities available in the park are outlined at a visitor centre.

A covered bridge crosses Flume Brook in Franconia Notch State Park.

An 80-passenger aerial tramway takes only five minutes to glide above the tree line to the 4,200ft (1,280m) summit of Cannon Mountain, where there are easy walking trails and 26 miles (42km) of ski trails and slopes. Vermont and Canada can be seen from the observation deck. Admission is free to the **New England Ski Museum** at the top, where a vintage ski film is shown. Money-saving combination passes are available for those visiting The Flume and taking the aerial tramway ride. The tramway operates daily from mid-May through October and on most pre- and post-season weekends.

Cannon Mountain is one of the oldest US ski resorts, and is owned and operated by the state of New Hampshire. The cold, north-facing mountain is popular with advanced skiers for its narrow, steep trails and challenging upper slopes. It also has a slope for children and offers childcare provision. Being further from Boston than resorts such as Loon, it is rarely crowded.

A number of well-marked hiking trails, including the **Appalachian Trail**, go through the state park.

Franconia

Leaving the park, drive north to Franconia town and turn on to Route 116 for the **Frost Place** (admission fee), a cultural centre with a poet-in-residence. This is the 1859 farmhouse where the poet Robert Frost lived for five years from 1915, winning a Pulitzer Prize during that time. His writing desk and signed first editions of his works can be seen here. The centre is open on spring weekends and daily (except Tuesday) from 1-5pm in summer and autumn.

Mount Washington Cog Railway is accessible from Route 302 at Bretton Woods. Just north east of Franconia, on Route 302, is Bethlehem, at 1,500ft (460m) above sea level probably the highest occupied village east of the Rockies, and provides a welcome retreat for hayfever sufferers because of its virtually pollen-free air.

Jefferson

From Bethlehem turn north to join Route 116, then take Route 2 for **Santa's Village** at Jefferson. This is his summer home. Children can meet Santa and his elves, ride the monorail Skyway Sleigh and the Santa Express Train, watch the trained macaws and splash down the Yule Log Flume. The village is open daily from late June to early September, and then on weekends only to mid-October. The admission fee is valid for unlimited rides and shows.

Nearby, in Jefferson (Route 2 east), is **Six Gun City** (admission fee), with great Wild West cowboy entertainment, rides, waterslicks, a display of miniature horses, and a collection of more than 100 horse-drawn vehicles. It is open daily mid-June to early September, then weekends only to early October.

The Jackson-North Conway Area

About 15 miles (24km) east of Jefferson is Gorham, where Route 2 intersects with Route 16. North of Gorham is the North Country Wilderness, an unspoilt region of forests, lakes and rivers, where the activities are hunting, fishing, snowmobiling, canoeing and white water rafting. Moose Brook State Park, just outside Gorham, has a campground and picnic facilities. **Gorham Historical Society Museum** (donation suggested) presents a 1907 railroad depot, a 1911 steam locomotive and other treasures from the past. The museum is open summer and autumn on Monday, Wednesday and Friday afternoons.

Mount Washington Auto Road is south of Gorham, off Route 16. A little farther south is **Wildcat Mountain** at Pinkham Notch. For views of Mount Washington and the Presidential Range, soar to 4,000ft (1,220m) by gondola to brookside nature trails, a restaurant and gift shop. The gondola service operates at weekends from late May to late June, then daily until early October. The 65ft (20m) Glen Ellis Falls are at Pinkham Notch.

Jackson

The pretty town of Jackson offers a wide choice of accommodation for winter and summer visitors. On Dinsmore Road is **Nestlenook Farm**, on the Ellis River, where visitors can feed deer, meet farm animals and ride on a horse-drawn trolley or sleigh. The 65-acre (27-hectare) Victorian estate has riverside walking and riding trails through woodland, and ice skating and skiing lessons are available.

Glen

Heritage New Hampshire, at Glen, some 2 miles (3km) south of Jackson, provides

a simulated journey through 350 years of the state's history, starting with settlers setting out from English villages in 1634 and ending with a simulated Fall foliage train ride through Crawford Notch. The centre (admission fee) is open daily from late May to mid-October.

At **Story Land**, also in Glen, the world is child-sized, and little ones can meet fairy-tale characters, sail on a pirate ship and try a dozen other rides and adventures daily from mid-June to early September, and at weekends only until early October. Children under four get in free.

Those wanting a different kind of thrill should travel west out of Glen to Bartlett, on Route 302, for **Attitash** – an Indian word for blueberry – where they can enjoy a chairlift ride to the **White Mountain Observation Tower** and descend by the Alpine Slide. Guided horseback rides, hay rides, waterslides, a golf

Visitors take a swan boat trip at Story Land in the White Mountains town of Glen.

driving range and a nature trail are available. Opening times are variable (Tel. 603 374-2368). In the winter Attitash is a popular ski resort.

North Conway

Three miles (4.8km) south on Route 16 is North Conway, where the dedicated shopper will be thrilled at the prospect of countless bargains and will doubtless need to be prised away from the factory outlet stores. As you drive south, pause to take in the **Intervale Scenic Vista**, a panoramic view of the Presidential range, in which all the peaks are named after US Presidents. Because of a low-lying flood plain in the foreground, no development has taken place and the view has been more or less the same for centuries.

Now to the shops. North Conway and Conway Village have dozens of stores where goods are sold direct from the manufacturers at up to 75 percent off normal retail prices. Many are clothing stores – sportswear, casuals, outerwear, formal and classic clothes, and footwear. The goods on offer include top name designer labels. There are also hand-crafted goods, luggage, kitchen fittings, beds, bedding, baths and books – one warehouse has thousands of books with up to 90 percent off the publishers' prices. And no sales tax to pay either.

At Main Street, North Conway, the **League of New Hampshire Craftsmen** has a gallery (Tel. 603 356-2441). Here glassware, woodware, textiles, ornamental ironwork, pottery and jewellery are among the crafts offered.

A memorable way to see the Mount Washington Valley is by the **Conway Scenic Railroad**: 11 miles (18km) aboard old-time cars or enclosed coaches. Alternatively you can go first class in a restored 1898 Pullman observation car. The **North Conway Depot** has a museum and a yard with a locomotive turntable. It is open early May to pre-Christmas, daily in high season, otherwise weekends only (Tel. 603 356-5251).

The Conway Scenic Railroad provides a memorable way to see the Mount Washington Valley during an 11-mile (18km) trip aboard vintage coaches.

The Big Country

Maine, the big one into which the other five New England states could all comfortably fit, has 17 million acres (6.8 million hectares) of forest, 6,000 lakes and ponds and 32,000 miles (51,200km) of rivers and streams. In the Western Lakes and Mountains region it has the tail end of the White Mountains National Forest spilling over from neighbouring New Hampshire, though its highest peak, the 5,268ft (1,605m) Mount Katahdin is in Baxter State Park in the north.

For all the state's rural beauty, it is the rugged Maine coast and the lighthouses – more than 60 of them – the inlets and bays, the old shipbuilding towns, cliff walks and oceanside resorts and villages that attract thousands of visitors every summer. Maine is about 320 miles (510km) long and 210 miles (340km) wide. Its has 3,478 miles (5,565km) of deeply indented coastline. US Route 1 provides access to most of the coastal sights and attractions as it winds from Kittery, in the south west, to the state's north-east corner on the border with New Brunswick.

Fine churches are found throughout New England. This one is at Bath.

To the north the Maine coastline is rocky, rugged and remote. Beach areas total less than 100 miles (160km), of which more than 30 are in the South Coast region, the south-westernmost part of the state. Notably, there is a 7-mile (11km) stretch of dazzling white sand at the resort of Old Orchard.

Maine's capital is Augusta (population 21,500), in the Kennebec/Moose River Valley region, where the high dome of its Capitol is visible above the trees as you approach the city. The state's biggest city is Portland (population 64,500).

The evergreens of Maine, known as the 'Pine Tree State', mixed with the brilliant oranges, yellows and reds of the hardwood

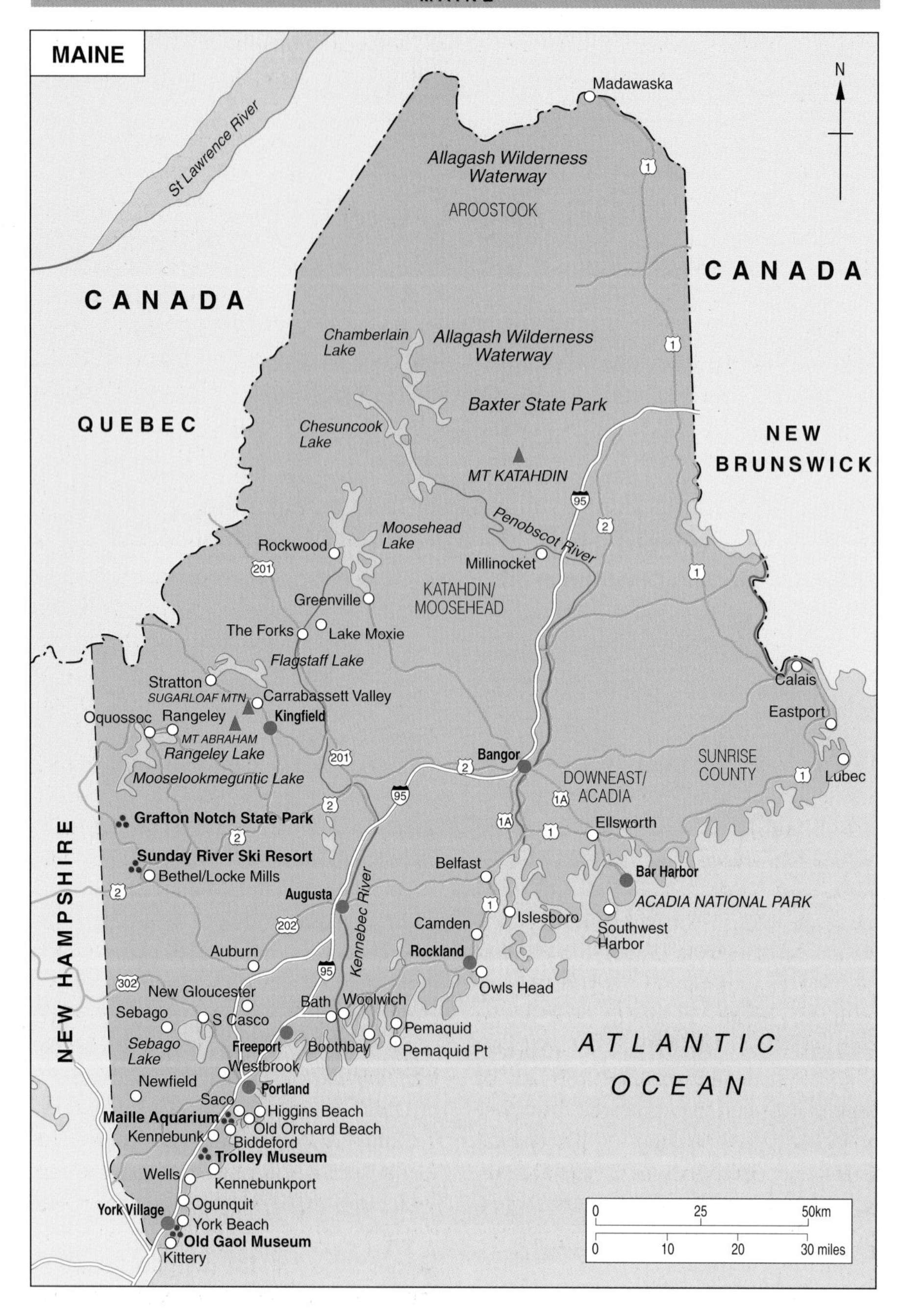

trees, provide a Fall foliage unique in New England. As the largest blueberry producer in the US, Maine also has the deep purples and reds of these plants.

The state announces itself to incoming visitors as 'Maine – the way life should be', and presents itself as a four-season holiday destination, with summer and then Fall attracting the most visitors. Spring brings tree blossom, flowers and bargain off-season rates. The weather is usually good for motor touring and it isn't necessary to reserve accommodation far in advance. In winter there is good alpine and cross-country skiing. Ice hockey, skating, snowmobiling, tobogganing and dog-sledding are other winter sports.

Acadia National Park – 40,000 acres (16,200 hectares) on rocky Mount Desert Island – is the second most popular national park in the US (only Great Smokeys, North Carolina, gets more visitors). Among the island's peaks, the highest is Cadillac Mountain (1,530ft – 466m) – the highest point on the Atlantic Seaboard north of Brazil.

Maine has an International Park, too, at Lubec in Sunrise County. This is the Roosevelt-Campobello Park, Franklin D. Roosevelt's home, where his family's cottage can be seen.

Puffin watching and moose watching are pursuits mainly for summer. Puffin colonies in Maine were very nearly wiped out by the beginning of this century as a result of excessive hunting. They were hunted for their meat and eggs, then in the 1880s their feathers became a fashion accessory in the millinery trade. The National Audubon Society stepped in and now there are at least three puffin-breeding islands in the Gulf of Maine, each protected by resident wardens throughout the summer breeding season.

Puffins are best viewed from the water, or from a bird hide on one of the island sanctuaries. A number of companies operate puffin trips, among them Hardy III Tours New Harbor (Tel. 207 677-2026) and Albert Bunker, Matinicus Island (Tel. 207 366-3737).

There are noted moose-watching locations in Maine, which claims to have a bigger moose population than any other part of North America. Moose are more likely to be seen early in the morning or early evening, between mid-May and late July. For likely moose-watching sites contact the Maine Publicity Bureau Inc, PO Box 2300, Hallowell, Maine 04347-2300 (Tel. 207 623-0363).

Whale watching – humpbacks, minkes, white-sided, finbacks and dolphins among them – is another option. One company that is often successful in introducing its passengers to some of the species is Friendship Whale Watching, with sailings from Harbor Place, 1 West Street, Bar Harbor (Tel. 207 288-3322). Its 90ft (27m) fast boat seats 149, and has a naturalist on board.

A local sea creature which has achieved international renown is the lobster. In 1990 a record lobster harvest of more than 28 million pounds (12.7 million kilograms) was achieved.

Bargain shopping at outlet stores is made easy along a stretch of Route 1 between Kittery and Freeport, where many outlets are grouped together in malls. Other outlet stores can be found throughout Maine.

Every US state has its adopted state animal. Maine's is, of course, the moose, but it also has a state cat – the Maine Coon cat. The state tree is the white pine, which can grow to a height of more than 200ft (62m). In the 18th and 19th centuries countless sailing ships had masts of Maine white pine.

Maine, the 23rd state, joined the Union in 1820. It was formerly part of

Acadia National Park, the second most popular national park in the US, is located on Mount Desert Island.

Massachusetts. York, in the South Coast region, is claimed to be America's first chartered city, having received its charter in 1641.

The population of this large state is only 1,233,500. It has vast areas of dense forests and lakes, and it is one of the few remaining wildernesses east of the Mississippi. The temperature averages 70°F (20°C) in summer and 20°F (–6.7°C) in winter.

Maine has northern boundaries with the Canadian provinces of New Brunswick and Quebec, and is bordered to the west by New Hampshire.

White water rafting, kayaking and canoeing, cycling, fishing and hiking are among the varied pastimes enjoyed in many parts of Maine's sparsely-populated interior. The Appalachian Trail, starting in Georgia, ends in Baxter State Park, in northern Maine.

The South Coast

Kittery

Route 1 runs a gauntlet of more than 100 factory stores and outlets at Kittery, soon after crossing the Piscataqua River from New Hampshire. Huge shopping malls offer a variety of goods, from shoes to glass ware, kitchen and cookware, children's clothes, menswear, fine china, books and music, sportswear, jewellery, cosmetics, crafts, toys, fashion clothes, underwear, outerwear – almost anything you can think of is there.

The **Whaleback Lighthouse** stands where the Piscataqua River meets the Atlantic Ocean. **Kittery Historical and Naval Museum** is in Rogers Road, off Route 1. Kittery Naval Yard, which was established in 1806, can be seen from the street, but it is not open to the general public. The hexagonal **Fort McClary blockhouse**, originally a private fort, is open daily from late May through to the end of September.

York

At York are the first of the sandy beaches along this stretch of coast. There are two lighthouses in the area: **Nubble**, off Route 1; and **Boon Island**, 6 miles (10km) east of York Beach. Several companies operate fishing charters from York Harbor. Within the National Historic District at York Village (Routes 103 and 1A) are the **Old Gaol**, built in 1720, a one-room **schoolhouse** dating from 1745, the **John Hancock Wharf** (1800), **Jefferd's Tavern** (1750), **Elizabeth Perkins House** (1730) and **Emerson Wilcox House** (1742). For information and opening times telephone Old York Historical Society (Tel. 207 363-4974).

Most of the towns along the coast were settled in the 17th century, and local historical societies have taken great care to preserve some of the early buildings and to provide artefacts and furnishings of the period.

Cape Neddick Light is near York, which marks the start of a stretch of sandy beaches.

The sandy beach at York Harbour, where several companies operate fishing charters.

Ogunquit

Beyond York Beach, Route 1A runs beside the aptly-named **Long Sands Beach**, which runs for 2 miles (3.2km) to the pleasant little resort and artists' colony of Ogunquit. Here, another beach, 3 miles (4.8km) of silver sand, is considered one of the best in the US. New England's only foot drawbridge can be crossed at Perkins Cove to the **Marginal Way Walk**, a cliff footpath looking out over the Atlantic Ocean. Ogunquit's permanent population is around 1,500, but its hotels, motels, inns and cottages welcome thousands more throughout the season.

Visitors soon recognize the seascapes and local scenes displayed on canvas at the **Museum of Art of Ogunquit** on Shore Road. **Ogunquit Art Center** is on Hoyt's Lane. A summer theatre has been presenting performances for more than 60 years.

There's lots of room along Ogunquit's three miles (4.8 km) of beaches for those seeking a quiet place on the sand.

Wells

Just along the coast, Wells is considerably larger than Ogunquit, with more than 8,000 people and numerous accommodations, including more than a dozen campgrounds. The beachfront resort has outlet stores, markets and an assortment of antique shops. **Wells Auto Museum**, on Route 1, has some 70 fine old classic cars of long ago. Rides in a Model T Ford are available for enthusiasts.

There are trails through the extensive **Rachel Carson National Wildlife Refuge**, with its saltmarsh ecology. Nearby is the **Laudholm Farm National Estuary Reserve**, where a 19th-century saltwater farm, and wetlands and wildlife habitats are conserved.

Kennebunkport

Two miles (3km) along the coast and firmly etched on the world map by President George Bush, is Kennebunkport. Walker's Point, Bush's summer White House, is not open to the public. It was built at the beginning of this century by his grandfather, George Herbert Walker.

Dock Square is a good place to start a tour of Kennebunkport's charms. A 200-year-old rum warehouse now houses the **Book Port**, which opens daily all year. It has a section on books about Maine and its coast. It also has a loft and lookout tower from which customers can try to spot ships on the horizon. Once devoted to warehouses, chandleries and sailing lofts, the Dock Square district, beside the Kennebunk River, is now an area of antique shops, galleries, stores and boutiques.

Splendid old houses built by shipbuilding tycoons and merchants of the early 19th century can be seen in the historic areas. One of these Federal-era homes is the **Captain Lord Mansion**, which faces the **Town Green** where George Bush made a speech acknowledging his victory in the presidential election of 1988. The Captain Lord Mansion, listed on the National Register of Historic

Waterfront restaurants overlook the river at Kennebunkport.

Places, has been an inn since the late 1970s. It has 16 guest rooms – 11 with wood-burning fireplaces – with four-poster beds, antique furniture and private bathrooms. This and five other prestigious, privately-owned and operated inns in lovely settings, each about an hour's drive apart, are marketed as the Inns of the Crescent Coast.

Tourism is not Kennebunkport's only industry. It is also very much a working fishing port with a lobster and fish market. Restaurants serve a variety of delectable seafood. Lobsters can be sampled baked, boiled or steamed, or shelled and sautéed. Lobster shacks sell them straight from the sea. People buy lobster sandwiches and rolls to eat by the river or on the beach. **Cape Porpoise** is the picturesque lobstering harbour where you can buy a boiled lobster and eat it on the pier.

The work of some five dozen local artists, all members of the Art Guild of Kennebunk, can be seen in galleries and studios. Amicus, a craftpeople's co-operative, sells scrimshaw, toys, woven goods, jewellery and other crafts. Porcelain and stoneware can be seen at Goose Rocks Pottery.

Up-river from Kennebunkport is the larger community of Kennebunk (population 7,000), where the **Brick Store Museum** (admission fee) has exhibits depicting the area's maritime history. It opens all year, Tuesday to Saturday in summer and Tuesday to Friday in winter.

Follow North Road for about 3 miles (5km) from Kennebunkport to Cape Arundel to visit the **Seashore Trolley Museum**, open from late April to late October (Tel. 207 967-2712). More than 200 old trolleys and their repair shops can be visited. Up to half a dozen of the veterans are 'exercised' daily, offering trips along 3½ miles (5.6km) of track. Once you've bought your ticket you can switch from one trolley to another all day (Tel. 207 967-2800 for recorded information).

Two whale-watching boats go out daily in summer at 10am from Kennebunkport.

Legend has it that the Wedding Cake House at Kennebunk was built by a sea captain for his bride. The house, on Summer Street, is not open to the public.

The trips last five or six hours. Cruises under sail along the coast in a replica 1880s-style craft offer a chance to see shore birds and basking seals on Bumpkin Island, one of several small islands along this stretch of coast. Deep-sea fishing trips are offered by several companies.

Bike rental is popular, and avoids the problem of finding car parking space when visiting beaches. Cape-Able Bike rents out conventional and mountain bikes and all the accoutrements including child seats and helmets.

Two 18-hole golf courses are open to the public at Kennebunkport, though hours are restricted. Non-members are excluded between 11.30am and 1pm from the Webhannet Golf Club, and between 11am and 2.30pm from the Cape Arundel Golf Club – the course where George Bush has played many a round.

Biddeford

Route 9 follows the coast to the substantial city of Biddeford (population 20,000). The beach, village community and the fishermen's base is at nearby Biddeford Pool. Biddeford itself is an industrial city by the Saco River and is light on tourism infrastructure apart from a campground, cottage rental and a few motels. It has an airport, with an aviation company offering scenic flights. Bicycle and moped hire and fishing charters are available.

Saco

Twinned with Biddeford, on the other side of the river, is Saco, an industrial and commercial centre with a population of 15,000. Attractions here include the **Cascade Water and Amusement Park**, the **Aquaboggan Water Slide** and a museum. **Maine Aquarium**, on Route 1 at Saco, has sharks, seals and penguins, and opens daily in May from 9am to 5pm and from June to mid-September between 9am and 9pm.

On Saco's doorstep is an extensive recreation area at **Old Orchard Beach** which includes 7 miles (11km) of sand and Maine's premier beachfront amusement park, **Palace Playland**. The Giant Skywheel is worth a ride for its breath-taking panoramic coastal views. There is plenty of varied accommodation here, which includes a dozen campgrounds. Beachlovers have been visiting Orchard Beach now for more than 100 years, and in the early days harness racing took place on the firm sand.

North of Biddeford

Four state parks line the coast between Biddeford and Portland: **Ferry Beach**, **Scarborough Beach**, **Crescent Beach** and **Two Lights**.

Canoe trips and nature tours are available at the **Scarborough Marsh Sanctuary and Nature Center**, a wildlife and study centre. Scarborough (with a population of 11,400) is a farming community which also caters for holidaymakers. Its biggest attraction is the **Beech Ridge Motor Speedway**, where you can enjoy some professional Saturday night motor racing.

A local registered guide at Scarborough, Stephen Randall (Tel. 207 883-2148) operates two-hour saltmarsh tours by canoe, as well as full-day adventure trips, hiking tours, or fishing and extended wilderness expeditions (accommodation is either camping or sleeping in cabins).

For an evening's horse-racing, Scarborough Downs is the place. Harness racing takes place on Wednesday, Friday and Saturday evenings and on Sunday afternoons from March to October (Tel. 207 883-4331).

Portland

People who live in Portland and people who visit it enthuse about the city, its culture, its curious blend of history and 1990s lifestyle, and its regenerated waterfront, which is still in operation and popular with strolling visitors. Certainly there is no shortage of things to do and see. The well-preserved Victorian residential district is considered one of the best in the US.

Maine's largest city, with a population of around 64,500, Portland has many cultural attractions, with a variety of museums, galleries and festivals, and music ranging from classical concerts to lively evening entertainment in bars. The poet Henry Wadsworth Longfellow, of *Hiawatha* fame, was born in Portland in 1807 and grew up here.

Over the centuries, Portland has overcome some tough situations, suffering Indian raids before the Revolutionary War, and being bombarded and burned by the British in 1775. The Great Fire of 1866 razed much of the city to the ground. Many of the buildings which grew out of

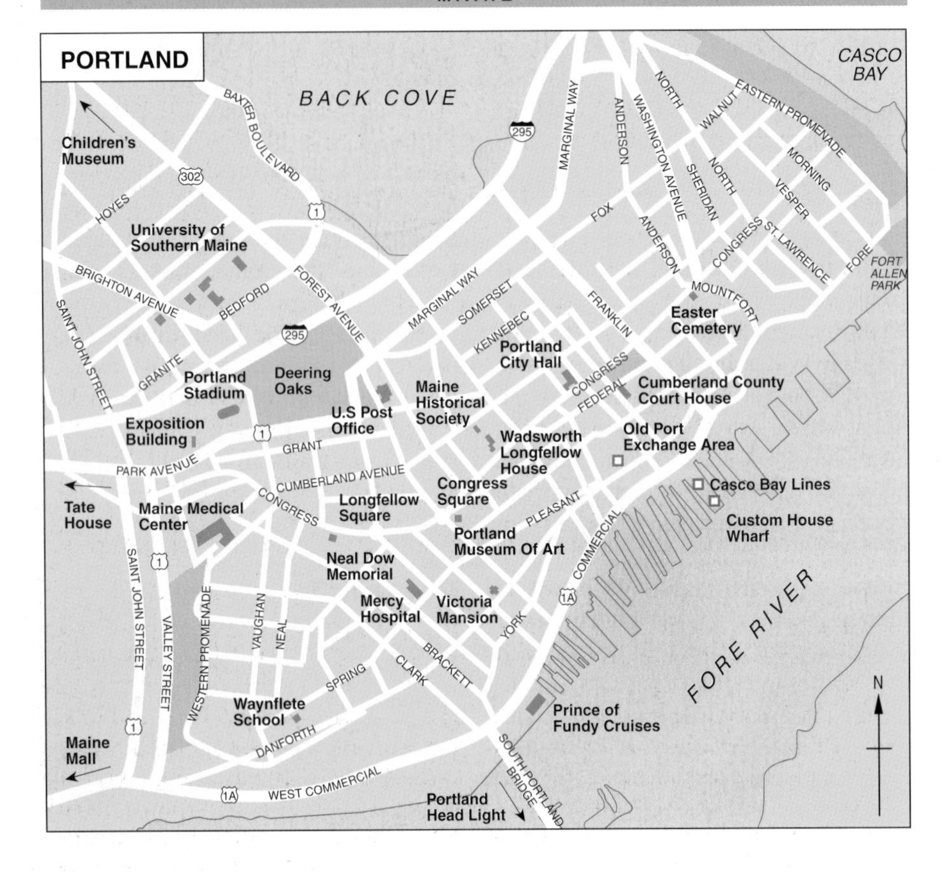

the ashes in the Victorian era survive to this day.

Portland Concert Association (Tel. 207 772-8630, toll-free within the US), one of New England's leading arts movements, presents programmes of dance, opera, musical theatre, jazz, folk and classical music to suit most tastes.

There are more than 300 restaurants in Portland, ranging from the casual to the formal. Specialities here are Maine lobster dinners and other fresh local seafood. The choice of ethnic eating goes from Afghan to Vietnamese. For an unusual evening out try the floating restaurant, Dimillo's, moored at Long Wharf. Sample menus of some of the restaurants can be seen at the visitor Information Center at 305 Commercial Street.

Maritime History

The Greater Portland Association of Maritime Museums has five properties open to the public. The oldest lighthouse in Maine,

The Portland Head Light is the oldest lighthouse in Maine. First illuminated in January 1791, it still guides vessels through the entrance to Portland Harbour.

IDEAL FOR CHILDREN

Compared with the rest of northern New England, the South Coast in general, and Greater Portland in particular, has plenty of recreational activity and organized fun for children during the summer season.

Most of the beaches are sandy and safe, shelving gently, so that the water at the edge is shallow. It is also cold, especially early in the summer, and the farther from the edge you venture the colder it is. The fact that few of the beaches are commercialized adds to their appeal. What you get is what nature provides – sand and sea, and with luck, sun. No fizzy drinks and fast foods, no ice cream stalls and no amenities such as toilets. Car parking near the beaches is restricted, so unless you go early you have to walk a little distance, using a buggy or stroller for the very young.

A fireworks display starts at 9.30pm every Thursday in the summer at **Palace Playland** at Old Orchard Beach, which also has plenty of exciting entertainments, including Maine's largest water slide, a giant arcade and rides.

Route 1 in the Saco area provides a rash of children's attractions. The **Aquaboggan Park** has three water slides and other thrilling chutes, swimming and wave pools, a splash 'n' play area for toddlers, several shuffleboard courts, mini-golf, skid cars, bumper boats, paddleboats and more.

Funtown USA, a theme park on Route 1 at Saco, has 11 major rides and nine kiddies' rides. Baseball and other games can be played. For the child who never tires of rides, an unlimited pass can be bought. American and Mexican food and seafood is available, there's a gift shop and a picnic area, and parking is free.

The **Children's Museum of Maine**, at 746 Stevens Avenue, Portland (Tel. 207 797-5483) has interactive, hands-on art and science exhibits with an in-built element of play. Children can get an insight into the life of a lobster fisherman, play the computers and work gadgets. Admission is half price on Wednesdays. The museum is open Monday to Saturday, 10am to 5pm.

Children's shows are a feature at **Southworth Planetarium** at 96 Falmouth Road, Portland (Tel. 207 780-4249). The planetarium is at the University of Maine's Science Building.

the **Portland Head Light**, first illuminated in January 1791, still guides sea traffic through the entrance to Portland Harbour. Its **museum** (admission fee), at 1000 Shore Road, Cape Elizabeth, South Portland, presents its history and that of neighbouring Fort Williams. Portland Head Light is on the National Register of Historic Places. The museum is open daily between 10am and 4pm from 1 June to 31 October and at weekends in November, December, April and May.

The home of George Tate, a colonial merchant who represented a British firm that supplied masts to the Royal Navy, contributes to Portland's maritime history. The **Tate House**, built in 1755, is now a museum and classed as a National Historic Landmark, and is well worth a visit for the insight it gives into the merchant's lifestyle. Tate House (admission fee charged) is at 1270 Westbrook Street (corner of Congress Street) and opens from early June to early September, from 11am to 4pm from Tuesday to Saturday and 1-4pm on Sunday.

The **Portland Observatory**, at 138 Congress Street, was built in 1807 and is on the National Register of Historic Places. It enabled local shipowners to tell when their ships were returning by a system of signal flags. Visitors who are prepared to climb the 108 steps are rewarded by a good view of the city, the White Mountains and Casco Bay. In July and August the observatory (admission fee charged) opens from 10am to 5pm on Friday and Saturday and 1-5pm on Wednesday, Thursday and Sunday. In June, September and October it opens Friday to Sunday 1-5pm.

Spring Point Museum (admission fee charged), based at Southern Maine Technical College, Fort Road, South Portland (Tel. 207 799-6337) has an exhibit on the development of Portland Harbour between 1865 and 1900. The history of the local neighbourhood is also outlined. The museum opens from late May to the end of October, Wednesday to Sunday, 1-4pm; at other times by appointment only. Telephone on the above number for further details.

Cruises from Portland

Those wanting to get afloat with someone else taking the wheel have a good choice of cruises and tours from Portland. Bay View Cruises (Tel. 207 761-0496) operates several sightseeing trips a day in scenic Casco Bay, with the option of an on-board lobster bake. The cruise is on the 61ft (19m) *Bay View Lady*. Casco Bay Lines (Tel. 207 774-7871) offers narrated two-and-three-quarter-hour mailboat runs at 10am and 2pm, moonlight and sunset runs, a Sunday evening music cruise (lasting three hours) and a Bailey Island cruise (nearly six hours). Boats leave from the Casco Bay Ferry Terminal at Commercial and Franklin Streets.

Harbour cruises, seal-watching cruises, whale-watching and deep sea fishing trips, with catering if required, are offered by Old Port Mariner Fleet (Tel. 207 775-0727). The trips depart from Long Wharf, Commercial Street. Passengers sail by vintage ocean racer with Palawan Sailing on two- or three-hour trips leaving from the historic **Custom House Wharf** (Tel. 207 773-2163).

Prince of Fundy Cruises goes farther afield, operating trips all the way to Yarmouth, in Nova Scotia, from May to October. Packages range from a 23-hour round trip to Yarmouth, to eight-day trips. The company's vessels have 315 cabins and can offer their guests fine dining, live entertainment and a casino. Telephone toll-free within the US: 1-800 341-7540 (nationwide), 1-800 482-0955 (Maine only).

Dozens of tiny islands are dotted about Casco Bay. Passenger and car ferries depart from Customs House Wharf on trips to Peaks Island and the islands of Great and Little Diamond, Long Island, Cliff Island and Great Chebeague. Canoes and kayaks can be rented and guided tours and instruction are available from Norumbega Outfitters, Portland (Tel. 207 773-0910). At Peaks Island, just a short ferry ride from Portland, Maine Island Kayak Company specializes in running one- to ten-day ocean kayak tours along the coast (Tel. 207 766-2373).

Downtown Sights

The sea comes up to Portland's doorstep on three sides. The city's history and the sea go hand in hand, and its restored waterfront remains an active, working area. And it is no surprise to find that the exhibits in Portland's art galleries are strongly influenced by the sea, ships, lighthouses and local matters maritime. Some powerful works by Winslow Homer, who was greatly inspired by the Portland scene and the Maine coast, are on display in the **Portland Museum of Art** at Congress Square. Edward Hopper and Andrew Wyeth are also well represented. Sculptures, furniture and art works of the 18th and 19th centuries are displayed, and part of the museum building itself is a work of art in the ultra-modern style.

Paintings of Portland and Maine, and some limited edition prints are displayed at the **R.N. Cohen Gallery** at 547 Congress Street.

Longfellow's boyhood home, built by his grandfather in 1785, can be visited (admission fee charged) from June to mid-October at **485 Congress Street**. It also happens to be the first brick-built house in the city. Some of the furniture that decorated the house when the poet lived there is still in place. Opening times are Tuesday to Saturday, 10am to 4pm; it is closed on public holidays.

The **City Hall**, built in Second Renaissance Revival style between 1909 and 1912, houses in its auditorium the 6,500-pipe Kotzschmar Memorial Organ which was presented to the city in 1912 by the publisher, Cyrus Curtis. Concerts are performed on Tuesday evenings from mid-June to the end of August, and in winter, by national and international musicians. For schedules telephone 207 774-3427.

Also in Congress Street, at No. 714, is the **1829 Neil Dow Memorial House**, an example of Federal-style architecture, and at Longfellow Square a bronze statue of the celebrated poet can be seen at the corner of State and Congress Streets. Portland's oldest burying ground is the **Eastern Cemetery** (1688) at Congress and Mountfort Streets.

The history of fire-fighting in Portland – the city has had considerable practice at it – is explored through the artefacts displayed at the **Fire Museum** at 157 Spring Street. The building housing the museum was built in 1836 in the Greek Revival style. Portland was redesigned after the 1866 fire which demolished the waterfront area and as a result is a convenient city for walking in. At 312 Fore Street the **US Custom House**, built between 1867 and 1871, is an example of the French Revival style of architecture.

For a significant architectural example of a Victorian house, considered to be one of the best in the nation, the **Victorian**

Mansion, built in 1858, can be viewed at 109 Danforth Street. Original interior rooms have the furnishings, carpets, ceramics, wall decorations and fixtures of the period. The mansion is open (admission fee) from Memorial Day (last Monday in May) to Columbus Day (second Monday in October).

Portland's shopping is a delight, with specialist shops, boutiques, galleries and, in South Portland, **Maine Mall**, with 140 stores open from 9.30am to 9.30pm (noon to 5pm on Sundays), selling fashions, books, gifts, crafts and household goods. The mall has seven major department stores and a food court. Antique hunters can have a field day in the city in shops with such enticing names as Steamer Trunk, Auntie's Things and Nelson Rarities.

The city's pièce de resistance is the regenerated port area, **Old Port Exchange**, with cobblestoned streets, quaint boutiques, cafes and restaurants and speciality shops. This covers five blocks and is good for a couple of hours of strolling, browsing and choosing. **Maine Potters Market** is found here, at 376 Fore Street. It is a cooperative of 14 artists producing hand-made pottery, and it opens daily from 9am to 6pm, until 9pm in summer.

In Temple Street, Green Mountain coffee roasters offers more than 35 varieties of fresh-roasted coffee – straight, decaffeinated or flavoured, and eight varieties of brewed coffee. It also sells mugs and chocolates. Once a Tree, in Exchange Street, sells all sorts of wooden items 'from the functional to the whimsical'.

On Commercial Street, on the waterfront, is the Whip and Spoon, the place for kitchen gadgets and accessories, cookware, Maine-made foods and products and gift baskets. Cross Jewelers, at 590 Congress Street, presents an annual summer collection of Maine tourmaline jewellery. Some 700 pieces – rings, earrings, necklaces, brooches and pendants – are set with many-coloured gems mined in the mountains of western Maine.

'Green' gifts and goods can be found under one environmentally-friendly roof at **Ecology House**, 49 Exchange Street. Environmentally-themed items – clothes, books, games, recycled cards, art prints, music and housewares – can be bought. A portion of the revenue from every purchase goes to human and animal rights and 'green' causes. Just ME (ME is the abbreviation for Maine) displays the area's largest selection of toys, gifts, accessories, foods and other items – all products from throughout the state. Just ME is at 510 Congress Street.

Anyone self-catering for a while in Portland may care to join BJ's Wholesale Club, where name-brand goods spread out in a vast area can be bought at wholesale prices. There are fresh meats, bakery items and confectionery, books, clothing, electronic goods, cosmetics, health goods, wines and beers, toys and other merchandise. Customers pay $25 a year for club membership. Alternatively you ask for a Free Club Card and pay a 5 percent surcharge on the wholesale price of your purchases. Take Exit 8 off I-95, turn on to Riverside Street North, then take the first right into Warren Avenue. BJ's is at 513/515 Warren Avenue.

Westbrook

Route 22 takes you west out of Portland to the inland industrial and commercial town of Westbrook. The attraction here, at 781 Country Road, is **Smiling Hill Farm Barnyard**, a working dairy farm where children can enjoy pony rides, petting various creatures and seeing native

PORTLAND'S FAIRS AND FESTIVALS

Portland is famous for its summer fairs and festivals. The first major one of the season is the **Old Port Festival**, held early in June, which includes craft displays, food booths, children's activities, music and live entertainment. Also taking place in June is the **Holy Trinity Greek Festival** in Pleasant Street, which celebrates with Greek food, arts and crafts, and dancing.

In mid-July the **Rotary Club Crafts Festival** attracts nearly 200 craft booths displaying work from all over the country. Late July is the time for the six-day **Deering Oaks Family Festival**. In the setting of this lovely Portland park visitors can enjoy concerts, arts and crafts, antiques sales, paddleboat rides and puppet shows, and sample the wares of the many food booths.

If you're in town in mid-August you can't avoid a festival. During the **6-Alive's Sidewalk Arts Festival**, in Congress Street, the work of artists from throughout the US is displayed in some 350 booths. Meanwhile, Southern Maine Technical College in South Portland holds the **Spring Point Festival**. This family fun day includes a parade, road race, games and the re-enactment of a Civil War encampment. An **Italian Street Festival** is held at about the same time in Federal Street. This is a lively ethnic celebration featuring band music, children's games, Italian food and novelty entertainment. **Art in the Park**, a few days later, is held at South Portland's Mill Creek Park, where paintings and prints by artists from the entire eastern seaboard are on display.

On 31 December the New Year is ushered in with music, dance and family entertainment – and not a drop of alcohol anywhere in sight.

There are many smaller, and more specialized, events held too. For details and dates of the festivals telephone the Visitor Center on 207 772-5800.

wildlife exhibits. Ice cream is made at the farm, and there is a gift shop.

Westbrook has two golf courses and **Westerly Winds Golf and Driving Range**, which also has miniature golf and baseball/softball pitching machines. It is open from 9am to 9pm, and is five minutes from Exit 8 off the Maine Turnpike.

Falmouth

A short drive on Route 1 brings you to Falmouth, where the headquarters of the Maine Audubon Society are in a solar-heated building at **Gilsland Farm**, on the northern edge of the town. There are bird and other natural history displays and nature walks and picnic areas in the grounds (Tel. 207 781-2330).

Freeport

Many visitors leaving Portland make a 20-minute detour along the coast to Freeport, famous for its bargain outlets, where you can buy anything from a pair of socks and a scented candle to a second-hand yacht, and from a bedspread to a Benetton jacket. There are more than 100 retail outlets with prices up to 70 percent cheaper than normal. The greatest of these is **L.L. Bean**, the outdoor specialist and clothing store, open 24 hours a day, 365 days a year, at 95 Main Street. There is also the L.L. Bean Factory Store on Depot Street (open long hours), with up to 60 percent off discontinued items and slightly imperfect products. Leon Bean set up his massive store in the 1920s.

If anyone in your party can't stand shopping, send them on a seal and osprey watch with Atlantic Seal Cruises (Tel. 207 865-6112). If they've already done that, suggest that they browse in the **North American Wildlife Expo** on Route 1, 2 miles (3.2km) south of L.L. Bean. More than 100 North American animals are on display in the museum, there is a wildlife theme gallery, and there are thousands of gifts and collectibles in the retail outlet store.

Desert safaris are probably the last thing you would expect to find anywhere in New England, let alone coastal Maine, but they take place daily from 8.30am to dusk from early May to early October (admission fee). The **Desert of Maine** is at Desert Road, Freeport, off Route 1 and I-95 (Tel. 207 865-6962). The narrated safari tours are by coach, rather than camel, through the 40-acre (16.2-hectare) natural phenomenon of giant inland sand dunes. There are nature trails and sand design demonstrations, museum exhibits and masses of fine sand, mostly white but some multicoloured. A 1783 barn remains from an old farmstead on which the sand encroached. A gift shop and store are on the site, which has a campground with hot showers and laundry.

Near Freeport, jutting out into the ocean, is **Wolfe Neck Woods State Park**, and the Audubon Society's **Mast Landing Sanctuary**, with hiking trails and nature study opportunities.

The Mid-Coast Area

Keeping to the coast on Route 1, you can soon reach Brunswick, in the Mid-Coast area, home of Bowdoin College with its **Museum of Art**, **Arctic Museum** and the **Maine State Music Theater** on its campus. Broadway musicals are presented here at the state's only professional musical theatre. Bowdoin College has a Winslow Homer collection in its **Walker Art Building**. Brunswick has some lovely old homes and tree-lined streets, and there are several museums, including the **Joshua L. Chamberlain Civil War Museum** at 226 Maine Street.

Civil engineers, industrial archaeologists and anyone interested in unusual structures should take Route 24 south from Cooks Corner, at the eastern end of Brunswick, and drive about 16 miles (25km) through Orrs Island to Bailey Island. This takes them over the 1,200ft-(370m-) long Bailey Island Bridge of cribstone construction – granite slabs set up honeycomb-style without the use of mortar. It is believed to be the only bridge in the world built this way. Don't worry – it has been bearing traffic for more than 65 years.

Bath

The town of Bath, located on Route 1, is near two state beaches, Popham and Reid, and is home to the **Maine Maritime Museum and Shipyard** (admission fee), depicting four centuries of the state's seafaring heritage. More than 4,000 vessels, including almost half the wooden sailing ships built in the US in the last 40 years of the 19th century, were launched

Visitors from all over the world come to New England to appreciate the beauty of the Fall colours. This is a park at Bath.

Bath has been involved in shipbuilding for four centuries and is home to the Maine Maritime Museum.

at Bath. The museum, on Washington Street (Tel. 207 443-1316), has a new Maritime History Building and is open daily from 9.30am to 5pm. There are shipyard tours, a boatbuilding school and waterfront activities, as well as museum exhibits, models and paintings. During the summer trips can be taken on the Kennebec River. Across the river is Woolwich, a farming community on Route 1 with a **farmhouse museum** (admission fee) run by Woolwich Historical Society.

Wiscasset

Ten miles (16km) east of Bath is Wiscasset, considered one of Maine's prettiest villages. It has a 19th-century ambience, a number of antique shops, several museums, and attracts a lot of holidaymakers. Most of the accommodation is bed and breakfast, but there are two campgrounds, cottage rentals, an inn and a motor lodge.

Formerly an important shipbuilding centre and lumber port, Wiscasset has some unusual places open to the public. The **Old Jail**, built in 1811, has walls of solid granite 41 inches (more than a metre) thick. Music boxes, player pianos and other mechanical music players are on view at the **Musical Wonder House**. Among the old mansions which can be visited is **Castle Tucker**, Lee Street at

During summer months boat trips can be taken on the Kennebec River at Bath.

High Street. Built in 1807, it has an elliptical staircase.

Boothbay

Route 27, off Route 1, leads to Boothbay and Boothbay Harbor. Boothbay has museums, galleries and the **Boothbay Railway Village,** a re-created turn-of-the-century New England village with a museum in two restored railroad stations. Steam train rides are available. The railway village (admission fee) opens daily from mid-June to mid-October.

Boothbay Harbor is one of Maine's finest natural harbours, with a fishing industry, some boatbuilding and a sea aquarium. It is very much a busy summer resort, with boat trips, galleries and museums and sport fishing charters.

Local roads lead to interesting shore areas on two tidal rivers, the Damariscotta and the Sheepscot. Phone Tidal Transit Kayaks and Bike Rentals (207 633-7140) if you would like to explore the area with paddle or pedal power.

Damariscotta

Follow the local road northwards along the western shore of the Damariscotta River to Damariscotta, on the east bank. Nearby is a massive **shell mound** – a 3-acre (1.25-hectare) expanse of oystershell heaps 30ft (9m) deep in places, left beside the river by Indian tribes. It is believed the shells were deposited over a period of 2,000 years. In mid-July Damariscotta has an annual Oyster Festival. The 7-mile (11km) **Lake Pemaquid**, to the south, has a family camping ground with pine cabins and sites for trailers, tents and camper vehicles. There are multi-recreational facilities available.

Pemaquid and New Harbor

Just south of Damariscotta lies Pemaquid, which is part of Bristol, and just off Route 30 is **colonial Pemaquid**, where old buildings have been restored. **Fort William Henry**, built in 1690, is off Route 130 at New Harbor. A short drive south takes you as far as you can go to Pemaquid Point, where the **lighthouse**, dating from 1827, has been captured by countless painters and photographers, professional and amateur alike.

At Pemaquid Point, housed in what used to be the lighthouse keeper's home, is the **Fishermen's Museum**, displaying old lobstering and fishing equipment and illustrating the techniques used to harvest the ocean's products.

In summer you can visit **Monhegan Island** from New Harbor, a voyage of about 15 miles (24 km). There are a few cottage rentals and guesthouses, but new building is limited to preserve the island's character. The local population, many of them lobstermen and fishermen, is little more than 100, but in summer artists and other visitors move in to enjoy the incredible scenery – cliff, woodland and several hundred wild flower species. Year-round ferries serve Monhegan Island from Boothbay Harbor and Port Clyde. Cars from the mainland are not allowed on the island. The *Hardy III* sailings may include a puffin trip, a seal watch and, on Wednesdays and Saturdays, a lobster bake. For further information telephone 207 677-2026.

Rockland

Back on the mainland, Rockland was a commercial shipping centre for more than a century. Now it is known for its fishing and lobstering, and in early August it is the site of the four-day annual Maine Lobster Festival.

Rockland's natural harbour is marked by a long breakwater, culminating in the **Rockland Breakwater Lighthouse**, built in 1888, which provides a panoramic view of the harbour and city. Walking tours of the waterfront and historic districts are offered (Tel. 207 596-0376). There are a number of privately operated boat trips, and the state ferry service goes to the islands of North Haven, Vinal Haven and tiny Matinicus (population 66).

Civil War memorabilia and US Coast Guard light and sound signals augment the displays of lighthouse equipment, navigational buoys and nautical life-saving aids at the **Shore Village Museum** on Limerick Street. The **Farnsworth Library and Art Museum** on Elm Street contains a substantial collection of the works of Andrew Wyeth, including 'Her Room' and 'Christine's World', and paintings by other members of the celebrated Maine family of artists, N.C. Wyeth and Jamie Wyeth.

Owls Head

South of Rockland, on Route 73, is Owls Head, which has an 1826 **lighthouse** and the **Owls Head Transportation Museum** (admission fee). The museum, open daily, has a rare collection of pioneer aircraft and fine old cars and other vehicles. Aircraft demonstrations take place on most summer weekends (Tel. 207 594-4418 for events schedule).

Rockport and Camden

North of Rockland are Rockport and Camden, neighbouring village resorts which please vacationers with their lobster boats, summer homes, arts and crafts, shops, windjammer cruises and coastal scenery. Strong on culture, they offer a choice of theatre, musical and operatic entertainment, and a range of galleries. The works of local artists can be seen at **Maine Coast Artists' Gallery** on Russell Avenue, Rockport. Traditional boat construction can be seen at the **Artisans' College** on Sea Street.

Camden lies below the Camden Hills State Park. From the top of the 900ft (277m) **Mount Battie** in the park, there is a magnificent view of Camden Harbor and Penobscot Bay. Camden Snowball Ski Area is on Hosmer Pond Road.

Downeast/Acadia Region

Route 1 curves round the northern end of Penobscot Bay, then heads east for Ellsworth, where Route 3 heads south over a causeway to Mount Desert Island.

Acadia National Park

Most of Mount Desert Island constitutes Acadia National Park. Information about the park and a free map can be collected at the Hulls Cove Visitor Center, reached soon after crossing the causeway. A 15-minute video presentation, 'The Search for Acadia', provides useful background and an introduction to the mountains-meet-the-sea character of the park.

The visitor centre, open from 1 May to 31 October, has schedules of naturalist activities in the park, though these are not usually available before early June and cannot be obtained by post. In winter, when the centre is closed, information may be available from Park Headquarters, 3 miles (4.8km) west of Bar Harbor on Highway 233. Between June and October

More than 120 miles (190 km) of walking trails criss-cross Acadia National Park. There are also 50 miles (80 km) of gravel roads for those on foot, horseback, bicycle or horse-drawn carriage.

a free newspaper, '*Acadia Beaver Log*' gives news of ranger-led tours, sea trips, mountain hikes and tide charts.

Unspoilt Acadia has 17 mountain peaks, craggy granite rocks, woodland, salt-marshes and lakes, most of it accessible to the energetic. More than 120 miles (190km) of walking trails criss-cross the park and there are 50 miles (80km) of gravel carriage roads closed to motor traffic but ideal for those on foot, horseback, bicycle or carriages drawn by powerful Percheron or Belgian horses. These trips operate six times a day from Wildwood Stables (Tel. 207 276-3622).

The carriage roads, most of which are reserved for skiers and people on show-shoes in winter, were laid down by wealthy families who had summer homes on Mount Desert Island (pronounced as in dessert) – the Rockefellers, Morgans, Fords, Vanderbilts, Astors and Pulitzers. It was people like these who donated land to create Acadia, and created a trust in 1901 to protect the island from uncontrolled development. Textile tycoon George Bucknam Dorr, who became the trust's director, worked for more than 40 years to ensure that Acadia would be preserved for public use. It eventually gained National Park status in 1916, with Dorr its first superintendent until he died in 1944.

The walking and hiking trails are good for a gentle stroll, a brisk walk, or a strenuous hike, such as the five-hour ascent of the South Ridge Trail up Acadia's highest mountain, the 1,530ft (470m) **Cadillac**. Here, climbers are rewarded on a clear day by a wonderful view of all Acadia and its surrounding bays, and a lot of the rest of Maine. (Motorists who drive up the **Park Loop Road** to the bare granite summit are similarly rewarded.) Visibility is usually best in Fall and winter. There is a special magic about standing atop Cadillac at dawn, because this is one of the first parts of the United States on which the sun rises. It is the highest coastal point north of Rio de Janeiro.

Entrances to the Park Loop Road are at Hulls Cove, Cadillac Mountain (Route 233 near Bar Harbor) and Stanley Brook (Route 3 at Seal Harbor). A ranger collects the entrance fee, which is valid for seven consecutive days.

Allow at least half a day if you can for the loop road. The 20-mile (32km) two-lane route takes in Acadia's only sand beach, called, predictably, **Sand Beach**. The sand is coarse. People swim from here, but the water is cold. The route also gives access to exciting **Thunder Hole**, at Ocean Drive, where people congregate at high tide to have their ears assaulted by Atlantic waves, forced into a narrow channel between cliffs, trapping air which gets released with a noise like gunfire. Nearby, to the south, at **Otter Cliffs**, pink granite buttresses 100ft (31m) high, stand with their feet in the sea.

The Park Loop Road has a number of lookout points where cars can park. Vistas include glacier-carved valleys and lakes, steep granite cliffs and areas of thick, coniferous forest. Guided nature walks are available on woodland, seashore and mountain terrains. Self-guided driving tours along a 56-mile (90km) route covering the entire Park Loop Road and Sargent Drive can be made with the aid of a cassette tape prepared by the Eastern National Parks and Monuments Association.

Activities in the park include freshwater and saltwater fishing (ice-fishing in season), cross-country skiing, snowmobiling, kayaking and cycling. Try Acadia Bike and Canoe Rentals, 48 Cottage Street, Bar Harbor (Tel. 207 288-5483) or

Bar Harbor Cycle Shop, 141 Cottage Street, Bar Harbor (Tel. 207 288-3886). Other options include gliding (Island Soaring Glider Rides, Route 3 Bar Harbor Road, Bar Harbor Airport, Tel. 207 667-7627), and there are plenty of cruises to choose from with historical, whale-watching, birdwatching, fishing or sightseeing themes. Family-owned Maine windjammers – hand-built schooners with capacity for about 20 persons – can sidle into places that are inaccessible to cars, and this makes them perfect for ornithological sorties.

Hundreds of plant species are found in the National Park's 40,000 acres (16,200 hectares). A conveniently condensed way of seeing more than 400 of them is provided in one acre (0.4 hectare) at **Wild Gardens of Acadia**, 5½ miles (8.8km) along the Park Loop Road from Hulls Cove Visitor Center. Twelve sections cover different types of habitat. The wildflowers and plants, all of which are labelled, are looked after by members of Bar Harbor Garden Club.

The wild blueberries which grow profusely in Acadia, some flourishing in almost bare stone, bloom in June, and the fruit usually ripens in mid-August. Visitors can pick them for their own consumption only.

Birdwatching is a popular pastime in the park and its offshore islands. As well as seabirds, shore birds and waterfowl, there are bald eagles, horned owls, scoters and warblers, and in 1991 a pair of peregrine falcons returned to the island and reared three chicks. Peregrines had been absent from Acadia for 35 years, their numbers reduced by mainland use of chemical pesticides, and other factors. Mammals include the cheerful-looking harbor seals that lie out on the rocks, porpoises and whales, white-tailed deer, eastern coyotes, snowshoe hares and red foxes.

There is no shortage of places to visit within the park and at Bar Harbor and nearby villages. The one part of Acadia on the mainland is the 2,000-acre (810-hectare) **Schoodic Peninsula**, about 90 minutes' drive from Bar Harbor. It has a one-way 6-mile (9.6km) loop road and a gravel road to the top of Schoodic Mountain. The sea puts on a dramatic show at Schoodic Point.

Bar Harbor

Bar Harbor, with a population of about 4,150, is the main resort community on Mount Desert Island. Here and at other small townships and communities there is plenty of comfortable accommodation, though reservations are advised in summer, especially July and August. Two woodland campgrounds offer the only

ISLE AU HAUT

Those who like really remote wilderness places should go to Isle au Haut (High Island), 15 miles (24km) south west of Mount Desert Island. The resident community numbers about 50.

You have to leave the car behind and take the mailboat (Tel. 207 367-5193) from Stonington on the mainland. Stonington is 40 miles (64km) south west of Ellsworth on Route 15.

Isle au Haut has 17 miles (27km) of hiking trails, pebble beaches, birdwatching and terrific sea views. Make a day trip, or stay overnight. There are a few cottages to rent, and Keepers House, a bed and breakfast inn which used to be the island's lighthouse, has some accommodation. There is also Duck Harbor campground.

For information on Isle Au Haut accommodation call 207 367-2261.

Bar Harbor is a lively community, providing accommodation for those exploring Acadia National Park.

accommodation within the National Park, apart from the Isle au Haut site. Recreational vehicles up to 35ft (10.7m) can be accommodated, but there are no electricity hook-ups. In summer, comfort stations, picnic tables, fire rings and cold running water are provided. Facilities dwindle to pit toilets and drinking water by handpump the rest of the year. In winter, some of the park's road network is closed.

The history of Mount Desert Island's Abnaki Indian residents, who were there when the white man arrived in the 1500s, is told at **Abbe Museum**, off the Park Loop Road, near Sieur de Monts Spring. Jewellery made from porcupine quills, and a canoe and wigwam made from tough birch bark are displayed. There are also stone tools, pottery and bone items from prehistoric times. The nearby nature centre opens from mid-June until the end of September.

Bar Harbor Historical Museum, at 34 Mount Desert Street, tells of the town's history as a fishing and shipbuilding town in the 17th and 18th centuries. The more recent development of its resort era is depicted in a fine collection of photographs. The museum (no charge for admission) is open Monday to Saturday, 1-4pm, from mid-June to October. The island's tourism goes back to the mid-19th century when a noted painter set a trend and others followed. Some of America's wealthiest families took summer homes here. Some 60 homes were wiped out during the terrible fire of October 1947, along with 17,000 acres (6,880 hectares) of the park. Natural reafforestation has taken place to a considerable extent.

More than 50 creatures indigenous to Mount Desert Island are exhibited in life-like poses at the **Natural History Museum** at the College of the Atlantic on Route 3 in Bar Harbor. Summer field studies are held (Tel. 207 288-5015).

Other Attractions in Acadia

On the west side of the island, at Southwest Harbor on Route 102, is the **Wendell Gilley Museum**, where beautifully handmade bird carvings by Gilley, a local man who gained nationwide recognition, are displayed. Ospreys, bald eagles, mallards and about 300 other species are mounted on driftwood. The museum is open from May to December (Tel. 207 244-7555). Also at Southwest Harbor, at Clark Point Road, is **Mount Desert Oceanarium** (admission fee), with curious marine occupants in numerous tanks, including moon snails and sea cucumbers.

People taking a boat trip to Cranberry Island have a chance to find out about New England's maritime history and the island's seafaring and fishing heritage at the **Islesford Historical Museum**, open daily from mid-June to early September (Tel. 207 244-9224).

As well as sea bathing at Sand Beach, reached by a long 'staircase', there is **Echo Lake Beach**, west of Somes Sound, which is accessible to people in wheelchairs. The picnic area, water fountains and restrooms are also wheelchair accessible. People swim in the freshwater lake.

The weather can be changeable in Acadia, even in summer. Fog sometimes strikes in the morning. Be prepared for everything. Dress in layers and have rainwear – and sun cream – handy. Campers are advised to be prepared for cold nights. A free booklet about the national park, available at the Hulls Cove entrance, warns hikers planning more than a short trek to equip themselves with a trail map, watch, knife, matches, flashlight, water, food, insect repellent, wet weather gear and a first aid kit. They should hike with a companion, and leave their itinerary with someone or displayed in their car windscreen. Every year there are more than 20 search and rescue emergencies.

For information about the park write to the Superintendent's Office, Acadia

MAINE'S FAR EAST

Some travellers may want to go as far east as Lubec, in Sunrise County, a community of just over 2,000 people. About the same size is nearby Eastport, where a ferry goes to the Quoddy Bay Islands. Sunrise County region, comprising Washington County, was once a lumber and granite quarrying centre. It has many quiet, attractive little towns, salmon rivers, and commercially-grown blueberries.

The east coast has two state parks, **Quoddy Head** and **Cobscook Bay**, both attracting cross-country skiers and snowshoers. Still on Route 1, on the wide St Croix River, is Calais. On the opposite bank is the Canadian province of New Brunswick. Below Calais, in the river, is **Dochet's Island National Historic Site**. Samuel de Champlain tried to set up a trading post and form a settlement here in 1604.

Most of the inland and northern part of Washington County is privately-owned paper company land. Cross-country skiers and snowmobilers take to the logging roads in winter.

National Park, Bar Harbor, Maine 04609 (Tel. 207 288-3338).

Inland Maine

Some 45 miles (72km) north of Acadia National Park, at the head of the tidewater on Penobscot River is Bangor (population 32,000), an industrial, commercial and banking city.

Bangor

Business boomed in Bangor in the 19th century when logs were exported to many parts of the world. The restored 1845 Greek Revival **Isaac Farrar Mansion**, on Union Street, was the home of one of the lumber tycoons of that time. It features richly covered woodwork, with stained glass and mahogany panelling demonstrating some of the ways in which Farrar invested part of his wealth.

The men who conveyed logs along the Penobscot River to Bangor's lumber mills have a tribute to them in the form of a large bronze statue on Harlow Street.

Augusta

I-95 connects Bangor with Maine's capital, Augusta, in the Kennebec/Moose River Valley Region. Augusta (population 21,500) sits astride the Kennebec River. The Governor's Residence, **Blaine House** (1833), and **Maine State Museum,** both on State Street, are worth a visit. On the opposite bank of the Kennebec is **Old Fort Weston** on Cony Street, built in 1754 as a defence against the Indians.

Augusta, formerly called Cushnoc by the Abnaki Indians, was the site of a Plymouth Colony trading post as early as 1628.

The Katahdin/ Moosehead Region

West of Moosehead Lake, Maine's largest inland stretch of water, are the active recreational areas of **The Forks** and **Jackman**, where whitewater rafting, canoeing, hunting and fishing are available. This wilderness country also has an extensive network of ski-towing and snowmobiling trails. It is an area of lumbering and pulp-hauling operations, with public

This huge statue at Bangor pays tribute to the town's lumbermen.

access permissible where commercial interests are not disturbed. Just east of The Forks a woodland walk leads to the thundering 90ft (28m) Moxie Falls.

Within the northern half of the Katahdin/Moosehead region is the huge **Baxter State Park**, 200,000 acres (80,940 hectares) of wilderness bought and donated by former state governor Percival Baxter on condition that it should be 'forever left in its natural state'. This directive has been observed. Roads in the park are very narrow and twisty, with gravel surfaces. Travelling by car has to be undertaken with the greatest care, and at a very leisurely speed. Those contemplating a tour are strongly advised to find out what to expect before they set out.

The state capitol at Augusta. The city was the site of a Plymouth Colony trading post as early as 1628.

MOOSEHEAD LAKE

Moosehead Lake, in the Katahdin/Moosehead region, is more than 40 miles (64km) long and some 10 miles (16km) wide. It has a 420-mile (670km) shoreline, sparsely populated, but a popular summer recreation area.

Greenville (population under 2,000) is the largest town on Moosehead Lake. Located at the lake's southernmost point, it offers a choice of canoe rentals and campsites.

Moosehead Marine Museum, on North Main Street (Tel. 207 695-2716) records with exhibits, documents and photographs the heyday of the steamship, and the history of the logging industry around the lake. To experience the steamship age, visitors in July and August can sail on the *SS Katahdin*, built in 1914. Known locally as 'the Kate', it is operated in association with the museum.

Several companies operate scenic flights over the lake or the wilderness.

For a few days' self-skippered cruising on the lake you can rent a modern six-berth houseboat from Socateen Boat Cruises (Tel. 207 534-8827) or Old Mills Campground Marina (Tel. 207 534-7333). The companies are based at **Rockwood**, on the west shore, a noted hunting, fishing and camping area at the base of the startlingly beautiful **Mount Kineo**, which rises to more than 1,800ft (550m). You can also take a water taxi from Rockwood across the lake to the base of Mount Kineo, once a thriving resort area. The trail to the top of Mount Kineo is a popular half-day hike.

Lily Bay State Park on the eastern shore has a swimming beach and facilities for boating, fishing, picnicking and camping.

Maps, park regulations and other information are obtainable from Park Headquarters, 64 Balsom Drive, Millinocket, Maine 04462 (Tel. 207 723-5140). Reservations for camping should be made by mail well in advance. Motorists on day visits, as well as overnighters, need a travel permit in the park. There are no trailer hook-ups on the campgrounds.

The highest of the park's 45 ridges and peaks is Maine's tallest mountain, 5,267ft (1,605m) Mount Katahdin. Eighteen of the peaks are more than 3,000ft (914m) high. The park offers 75 miles (120km) of hiking and climbing trails. The 2,000-mile-long (3,200km) **Appalachian Trail**, more than 200 miles (320km) of which go through Maine, has its northern terminal at Mount Katahdin.

Winter sports are an important part of the economy around the state park. Although snowmobiling is restricted to the perimeter road inside the park, there are good trails outside, from Millinocket in the south to Oxbow in the north.

About 10 miles (16km) east of the park, on Route 159, is Patten, the small gateway town for the park's northern entrance. Farming, lumbering and wood products are its main industries. On Route 159 is Patten **Lumberman's Museum**, with more than 3,500 artefacts relating to the industry and its history displayed in nine buildings (Tel. 207 528-2650 or 2547).

The Aroostook Region

To the north west of Baxter State Park is the **Allagash Wilderness Waterway**, leading into the enormous Aroostook region. Known as 'the County', this region is bigger than the combined size of Connecticut and Rhode Island. Only about 100,000 people live here. This is potato-growing and pulp and paper mill country.

MAINE

Sebago Lake, the state's second largest stretch of inland water, draws boaters and anglers to south-west Maine (see previous page).

Four million acres (1.62 million hectares) are forested, another million acres (404,700 hectares) are cultivated. Rugged travellers camp here and enjoy the canoeing, hiking, hunting and fishing.

Madawaska, a paper-making centre on Route 1 and the St John River, is the northernmost town in Maine, bordering with Canada. Much of this northern region was settled by Acadian refugees expelled from Nova Scotia in the mid-18th century. In late June an annual week-long festival presents Acadian arts and crafts, sports, traditional music and dance performances, and Acadian food.

South-Western Maine

Maine's second largest lake, Sebago, lies in the south-west of the state, very much a four-season destination. Planted either side of the wide Androscoggin River, just off I-495 south west of Augusta, the cities of **Lewiston** (population 40,000) and **Auburn** (population 23,000) form a southern gateway to the region. They offer good shopping and accommodation. **Lost Valley Ski Area** is just north of Auburn. West of the twin cities is the Oxford Hills area, its apple orchards rich in blossom in springtime. All this area is a fruitful hunting ground for rockhounds – avid seekers of quartz, tourmaline, feldspar and other stones.

Off the north-west shore of Sebago Lake is **Sebago**, a village where tourism has joined the farming and lumbering industries. A local road leads almost to the top of Douglas Mountain (1,415ft – 431m). On a clear day you can see the Atlantic Ocean, the highest of New Hampshire's White Mountains and, below, Sebago Lake and neighbouring smaller lakes.

Sebago Lake State Park is on the north shore of the lake. Also here is the only remaining lock on the **Cumberland and Oxford Canal**. It dates back to 1830 and is still used by boats cruising between Sebago Lake and Long Lake.

One of the oldest Shaker settlements in the US, founded in the 1790s, and the only one situated in Maine, is on Route 26, to the north west of Sebago Lake at New Gloucester. The **Sabbathday Lake Shaker Museum** (admission fee) has a meeting house and about a dozen rooms with Shaker furniture, folk art and crafts dating from the 18th and 19th centuries. Sabbathday is more than a museum. A nucleus of the Shaker community still grows farm produce and herbs. The museum (Tel. 207 926-4597) is open daily, except Sunday, 10am to 4.30pm from late May to early October.

On Route 11 to the south west of Sebago Lake is Newfield, where there is a restored 19th-century village called **Willowbrook** (Tel. 207 793-2784). More than 11,000 items are exhibited in nearly 40 buildings.

Bethel, at the north-eastern flank of the White Mountain National Forest, is a picture postcard town with mountain views and well-maintained white clapboard homes set around a green. The **Moses Mason House and Museum** at 15 Broad Street, dating from 1813, has eight rooms decorated and furnished in Federal period style. Rufus Porter painted the murals in the hallway and up the staircase. The house (admission fee) is open July and August, Tuesday to Sunday, 1-4pm, and also by appointment.

To the west of Bethel, off Route 2, is the **Sunday River Ski Resort**, a four-season recreational area with good fishing and canoeing in its numerous rivers and lakes. North of Bethel, Route 26 runs through **Grafton Notch State Park** – the notch is cut between Old Speck and Baldpate mountains – and crosses the Appalachian Trail. This stretch is designated a Maine Scenic Highway.

More and more people are finding their way to the lovely **Rangeley Lakes** area, renting boats and canoes at Rangeley to explore some 40 lakes and connecting streams set among the mountains. Between Rangeley and the village of Oquossoc, at Dodge Pond Road, Rangeley (Tel. 207 864-3443) is the **Wilhelm Reich Museum**, which contains the library, scientific equipment and some personal effects of the well-known natural scientist.

Near Rangeley is one of Maine's largest winter sports slopes, the **Saddleback Ski Area**. Several companies in the area operate scenic flights over the lakes, mountains and forests.

Route 16 east from Rangeley reaches Stratton on Flagstaff Lake, a logging community at the turn of the century. The town is still involved in forest products, but has diversified into tourism, with year-round outdoor sports and activities. It is also a good area for sighting moose, deer, eagles, loons and other birds.

One of Maine's leading ski resorts, the **Sugarloaf**, is in the Carrabassett Valley area, south of Stratton. Sugarloaf is busy all year, with a wide choice of activities. Hiking is offered on the Appalachian Trail. There are dog-cart rides, whitewater rafting and art events in summer and Fall, downhill and cross-country skiing, ice skating and other sports in winter.

Immediately south of the Sugarloaf is the town of **Kingfield**, where the economy is again based on farming, lumbering and wood products. It is also a hunting and fishing area.

Kingfield is the birthplace of the gifted Stanley family, and the **Stanley Museum** on School Street is famous for its collection of Stanley Steamer cars – steam-driven vehicles invented by the Stanley brothers, Francis and Freelan. It also has thought-provoking photographs by their sister, Chansonetta, depicting American rural life at the turn of the century. The family talents embraced painting and music, too. In August the Stanley Museum (donation suggested) opens from Monday to Saturday from 10-4pm. From October to July it opens on Tuesday, Thursday and Friday from 9am to 5pm. Seven miles (11km) south of Kingfield is the Wire Bridge, the oldest suspension bridge in the country. It was built in the mid-1800s.

Route 142 from just south of Kingfield leads to Phillips (Route 4 from Rangeley), home base of the Sandy River and Rangeley Lakes Railroad. Today, one-mile (1.6km) rides through woodland in a vintage train drawn by a replica locomotive are operated by the **Sandy Railroad Park** over a section of the original narrow-gauge track. The railroad (admission fee) is open on the first and third Monday of the month from May to November, with departures at 11am, 1pm and 3pm.

Gold-panning day trips are available in **Mount Blue State Park** to the south west on Route 142. There's a campground beside Lake Webb. There are conservation education programmes, fishing, hiking, skiing, mountain climbing and other pursuits (Tel. 207 585-2347).

A Place for All Tastes

Two things are likely to spring to most people's minds when they think about New England: the rainbow of colours that comes with the Fall; and the diverse history of the region. Nature certainly endowed the region richly when presenting such a wonderful buffer between summer and winter. And few places on earth can have such visible roots; so many historic buildings, sites and landmarks. New England is a place of culture, with many art galleries, libraries, theatres and concert halls. It also has the great outdoors. Truly, there is something to suit all tastes.

New England is a very compact region. It is easy, though something of a rush, to visit all six states in the space of a two-week holiday, but discriminating travellers take their time, planning an itinerary that will enable them to savour the things that interest them most, yet leave time to enjoy the unexpected. During their stay they will be taking note of places and experiences they can investigate further, the next time they come to New England.

September sees Providence, Rhode Island, launching into its Waterfront Festival – a celebration of music, art, craft and food.

Hiking and Cycling

Shoe leather and pedal power are two of the best means of obtaining the most from outdoor New England, and there is lots of terrain to tramp over or cycle across.

The **Appalachian Trail**, which crosses much of the eastern seaboard area of the US, runs through New England and can be joined at a number of locations. Vermont has its **Long Trail** running some 225 miles (360km) through the centre of the state, and in New Hampshire there are trails in the White Mountain National Forest, as well as others maintained by the Audubon Society of New Hampshire (Box 528B, Concord, NH 03302, Tel. 603 224-9909). Massachusetts maintains trails in most of its state parks.

THESE BOOTS WERE MADE FOR MUSIC

Husband-and-wife hiking enthusiasts Rich Woller and Nancy Stoll combine hiking with history and culture in a range of walking holidays they organize in various parts of New England.

One of their most popular tours, called 'Birds, Beethoven, Berries Or Bach', coincides with the Boston Symphony Orchestra's season at Tanglewood, in the Berkshires, and offers hiking by day and concerts at night.

The couple also combine walking with other festivals, visits to historic locations and canoeing. 'Straight' hiking tours are also available. Brochures can be obtained from Rich and Nancy at Berkshire Hiking Holidays, PO Box 2231, Lenox, MA 01240 (Tel. 413 499-9648).

Cyclists can have a great time throughout New England, on trails in state and national parks. One of the most popular areas is the **Cape Cod National Seashore,** and there are many other trails in Massachusetts. New Hampshire offers good cycling in the coastal area, as well as in central and western parts of the state. **Franconia Notch State Park**, in the White Mountains, has a cycling path. Maine has scenic routes in the **Acadia National Park** and in some coastal areas, especially around Kennebunkport.

Bicycle rental agencies are to be found throughout the region.

Camping

Camping covers everything from roughing it in the wilderness to fairly sophisticated living standards on locations with laundromats, shops, and even cinemas. Between the extremes there's a wealth of campsites in beautiful spots in state parks and forests. Some states prohibit camping outside designated areas, but others issue permits for wilderness camping. Maine and New Hampshire allow camping in wilderness areas without a permit. In Vermont a permit is needed if a group of more than ten people wants to camp in a wilderness area.

Information on campsites and trailer-parks in each state can be obtained from the following addresses.

- US Forest Service, RR 1, Box 1940, Manchester Center, VT 05255 (Tel. 802 362-2307) – for camping in the Green Mountain National Forest, Vermont; Vermont Dept of Forests, Parks and Recreation, Agency of Natural Resources, 103 South Main Street, Waterbury, VT 05676 (Tel. 802 241-3650).
- Bureau of Parks and Forests, Dept of Environmental Protection, 165 Capitol Avenue, Room 265, Hartford, CT 06106 (Tel. 203 566-2304).
- White Mountain National Forest, 19 North Main Street, Laconia, NH 03246 (Tel. 603 528-8721); New Hampshire Campground Owners Association, PO Box 320, Twin Mountain, NH 03595 (Tel. 603 846-5511).
- Acadia National Park, PO Box 177, Bar Harbor, ME 04609 (Tel. 207 288-3338); Maine Forest Service, State House Station 22, Augusta, ME 04333 (Tel. 207 287-4980); The Maine Campground Owners Association, 655 Main Street, Lewiston ME 04240 (Tel. 207 782-5874).
- Massachusetts Division of Forests and Parks, 100 Cambridge Street, Boston MA 02202 (Tel. 617 727-3180); Massachusetts Office of Travel and Tourism, 100 Cambridge Street, 13th Floor, Boston MA 02202 (Tel. 617 727-3201).

• Rhode Island Tourism Division, Dept of Economic Development, 7 Jackson Walkway, Providence, RI 02903 (Tel. 401 277-2601).

Boating and Sailing

Boating in all its forms – everything from windjammers to surfboards, canoes to cruisers – is one of the most popular pursuits in New England, and the region's waters are as varied as the craft. If you fancy something less expensive than chartering a classic J-class craft at Newport, Rhode Island, there's everything from dinghy sailing upwards along the whole stretch of coast from Connecticut to Maine, and there are thousands of lakes and rivers for canoeists of all standards. The Connecticut River Watershed Council, 312 First New Hampshire Bank Building, Lebanon, NH 03766 (Tel. 603 448-2792) has canoeing information about the Connecticut River, which courses through much of New England.

New England has thousands of lakes and rivers for canoeists of all standards. Boating in all its forms is one of the most popular pursuits.

Fishing

New England's coastal waters are rich in flounder, mackerel, haddock, striped bass, cod and bluefish, with bluefin tuna and shark waiting in deep waters to tempt the big game anglers. Charter fishing boats are numerous all along the coast.

Fisherfolk with more modest ambitions – and an eye to supper rather than the trophy room – can gain a goodly catch of mussels, scallops or clams almost anywhere along the coast.

Inland, the streams, lakes and ponds teem with trout, largemouth bass, northern pike, perch, sunfish, catfish and pickerel, while the colder northern lakes are filled with lake trout, landlocked salmon, smelt, yellow perch and many other species.

A licence is required for freshwater fishing in all six of the New England states. Although a few restrictions may apply to certain types of catch, a licence is not required, in general, for saltwater fishing. Licensing and other information about fishing may be obtained from the following organizations:

- Fisheries Division, Dept of Environmental Protection, 79 Elm Street, Hartford, CT 06106 (Tel. 860 424-3474).
- Dept of Environmental Management, Division of Fish and Wildlife, 22 Hayes Street, Providence, RI 02908 (Tel. 401 277-3576).
- Massachusetts Division of Fisheries and Wildlife, 100 Cambridge Street, Boston, MA 02202 (Tel. 617 727-3151).

Coastal and inland waters provide good sport for enthusiastic anglers.

- New Hampshire Dept of Fish and Game, 2 Hazen Drive, Concord, NH 03301 (Tel. 603 271-3422).
- Vermont Dept of Fish and Wildlife, Agency of Natural Resources, 103 South Main Street, Building 10 South, Waterbury, VT 05676 (Tel. 802 241-3700).
- Maine Dept of Inland Fisheries and Wildlife, 284 State Street, Augusta, ME 04333 (Tel. 207 287-8003).

Events and Festivals

New England's calendar is filled with events and festivals of all kinds, from small country craft shows and flower festivals to huge state fairs; from weekend performances by local bands to international festivals of folk, jazz and classical music. There are re-enactments of historic events, parades and rallies of all kinds.

March introduces spring, with a host of daffodil and other spring bloom shows in the southern part of the region. The biggest event at this time – as it has been for more than a century – is the **New England Spring Flower Show** in Boston, whose citizens really let their hair down on 17 March with one of America's biggest St Patrick's Day parades.

The northern states say their hello to spring in April when sugar-houses in

GET YOUR SKATES ON

Skiing, of course, is New England's prime winter sport, and facilities are excellent and widespread. But skiing is a comparatively new pursuit, and many of the old, traditional winter activities are still popular.

Skating arenas are found in many communities, frequently owned by colleges, clubs or recreation departments and usually accessible to the public for a modest charge. Many inns and resorts also have their own rinks.

Sledding and tobogganing lives on, and again many inns have sleds, and slopes, which guests can use. For those with a rather more romantic turn of mind there are horse-drawn sleigh rides (sometimes with hot cider or a glass of punch).

Vermont was the birthplace of America's latest winter activity – snowboarding. This is like surfboarding, except that it's performed on snow. The sport first took off at Stratton Mountain in the early 1980s, and snowboarding programmes are now featured at ski areas throughout the state, with board rentals and instruction available.

If you would like to try snowmobiling, tours and rentals are available at many resort areas. Tours usually take place over private trails in the company of an experienced guide.

A popular spectator sport when snow is on the ground is dog-sled racing in which teams of 4, 8 or 12 compete over distances ranging from 4 to 12 miles (6.4 to 19.2km). Teams are usually made up of Siberian or Alaskan Huskies, Alaskan Malamutes or Samoyeds, but Ann Diamond, president of the New England Sled Dog Club says a dog of any breed can be trained for sled-racing if it loves to run. West Highland Terriers, here's your chance!

Snowshoes are still a popular way to explore the back country, with the advantage that snowshoes let you get to places inaccessible to those on skis. Summer hiking trails often make good snowshoe routes.

If all else fails you can always make a snowman, or sit in front of a roaring log fire with a hot, relaxing drink...

New England's calendar is filled with festivals of all kinds. This is the gay community's event at Provincetown on Cape Cod.

Maine, New Hampshire and Vermont open their doors to show the public how maple syrup gets from the tree to the breakfast table. Mid-April sees runners slogging it out in the gruelling Boston Marathon, and re-enactments of Paul Revere's Ride and the Battle of Concord and Lexington.

Throughout Rhode Island, May Breakfasts of jonnycakes and other traditional dishes are served at schools, churches, clubs and other public places.

Teams from the two oldest universities in the US bend their backs in the **Yale-Harvard Regatta** on the Thames River at New Haven, Connecticut, in early June. Of course, 4 July sees parades and celebrations everywhere, but the grand-daddy of them all – certainly in terms of being the oldest – is the parade at Bristol, Rhode Island. The state was the first to declare independence from Britain, two months before the Declaration of Independence was signed.

Also in Rhode Island, Newport livens up July with music to suit all manner of tastes. First comes the **Newport Music Festival**, with performances staged in some of the Mansions, followed by the famous **Newport Folk Festival**. The following month Newport is stomping again with the **JVC Jazz Festival**.

New England has many fascinating museums. This giant locust is an exhibit in Boston's Science Museum.

Over in Massachusetts the Boston Symphony Orchestra moves from Boston to Lenox to spend July and August with international performers at the **Tanglewood Music Festival**. Maine celebrates a month of classical and popular music at the **Bar Harbor Music Festival**, which begins in mid-July. At the same time, Maine puts country life on show at the **Bangor State Fair**.

The oldest, and one of the largest, antique shows in New England is staged in New Haven, Connecticut, in mid-September, and in the same month Providence, Rhode Island, breaks into a weekend of music, art, craft and food in its **Waterfront Festival**.

Mid-September also sees the **Eastern States Exposition**, the largest agricultural show and fair in the region, being held at Springfield, Massachusetts, while pipe bands and kilted dancers and athletes gather for the Highland Games at Lincoln, New Hampshire. Towards the end of the month, folk musicians get together at Barre, Vermont, for the **National Traditional Old Time Fiddlers' Contest**.

Winter opens up a treasure chest of carnivals, ice festivals, dog-sled races, hockey matches and cross-country skiing rallies. Christmas and New England, of course, were made for each other, with

FALL FOLIAGE

Why does New England get such a brilliant show of Fall foliage? The only other place in the world where autumn colours are as vibrant is Japan.

As far as the yellows and oranges are concerned, these are usually masked by the green, which fades in autumn as shorter periods of daylight and cooler temperatures cause a breakdown of chlorophyll. Other chemical processes produce the bright reds, purples and bronzes. The sugar content in maple leaves, for example, builds up in the warmth of the sun in the Fall, and is trapped by the cold of the night. The higher the accumulation of sugar, the redder the leaves. Those exposed to the sun may turn more red than those in the shade.

There is no way of predicting the exact moment when Fall foliage will be at its peak. In any case, it varies within New England, and the dedicated 'leaf peeper' can start in late September in the north and follow the foliage southward through the six states until early November.

In New Hampshire's White Mountains, nearly 20 tree species contribute to the show of colour, several presenting their particular hue at the same time. They include sugar maple, red maple, striped maple, sumac, pin cherry, beech, witch hazel, mountain ash, speckled alder, red oak, and white and yellow birches.

torchlight processions and carol singing taking place everywhere. The classic celebrations at this time are held at Mystic Seaport, Connecticut.

The Fall brings a range of colours – and lots of visitors – to New England, especially to the northern states.

The Right Place at the Right Price

Hotels

The price range given for the following hotels should be regarded as a general guide. Room rates can vary greatly for the different seasons and there may also be a wide divergence in rates between properties offering similar standards. It is always worth asking whether any special discounts are operating. Be assured that any accommodation you choose, however inexpensive, will be clean and wholesome. Key:

▮ up to $75
▮▮ $75-$125
▮▮▮ Over $125

Greater Boston

Beacon Hill B & B ▮▮
27 Brimmer Street
Boston
MA 02108
Tel: (617) 523-7376
In the historic district overlooking Charles River, within walking distance of downtown Boston.

Boston Harbor Hotel ▮▮▮
70 Rowes Wharf on Atlantic Avenue
Boston
MA 02110
Tel: (617) 439-7000
Fine harbour views to be had from this prestigious 230-room hotel.

Boston Marriott Long Wharf Hotel ▮▮▮
296 State Street
Boston
MA 02116
Tel: (617) 227-0800
One of seven Marriott hotels in Greater Boston, this well-appointed 400-room hotel offers extensive views of the harbour.

Copley Plaza Hotel ▮▮▮
138 St James Avenue
Boston
MA 02116
Tel: (617) 267-5300
Part of Boston's history, this classic grand hotel is one of the city's social focal points.

Tremont House ▮▮▮
275 Tremont Street
Boston
MA 02116
Tel: (617) 426-1400
In the heart of the theatre district and night life, Tremont House has very reasonable rates which just creep into the ▮▮▮ category.

Cambridge

Harvard Square Hotel ▮▮
110 Mt Auburn Street
Cambridge
MA 02138
Tel: (617) 864-5200
This 72-room hotel, only a block away from the subway, overlooks historic Harvard Square.

Brookline

The Bertram Inn ▮
92 Sewall Avenue
Brookline
MA 02146
Tel: (617) 566-2234
A Victorian home with antique furniture. One block from subway station, then 10 minutes to Boston.

1087 Beacon Street ▮
1087 Beacon Street
Brookline
MA 02146
Tel: (617) 566-0088
Inexpensive bed and breakfast in a Victorian house. 11 rooms, some with private bathroom. Streetcar stop outside – 10 minutes to Boston.

Massachusetts

Barnstable

Ashley Manor ▮▮▮
Box 856
3660 Olde King's Highway
Barnstable, MA 02630
Tel: (508) 362-8044
The large rooms in this country inn have open fireplaces and four-poster beds with canopies.

Chatham

Chatham Bars Inn ▮▮▮
Shore Road
Chatham
MA 02633
Tel: (508) 945-0096
A splendid 152-room resort hotel in extensive grounds facing the ocean, with its own private beach.

Haverhill

Best Western Merrimack Valley Lodge
401 Lowell Avenue
Haverhill
MA 01832
Tel: (508) 373-1511
This 130-room hotel has an exercise room and outdoor pool. Some of the rooms are reserved for non-smokers.

Lenox

Blantyre
Lenox
MA 01240
Tel: (413) 298-1661
Turreted mansion with Tudor façade in 85 acres (35 hectares) in the foothills of the Berkshires. Croquet, tennis, pool and spa.

Martha's Vineyard

David's Island House
120 Circuit Avenue
Oak Bluffs
MA 02557
Tel: (508) 693-4516
Eighteen rooms, some with private baths, others with shared baths, in a location close to ferries.

Nantucket

Anchor Inn
66 Centre Street
Nantucket
MA 02554
Tel: (508) 228-0072
In the historic district, this 1806 inn is close to the ferries, beaches and museums.

The Wauwinet Inn
120 Wauwinet Road
Nantucket
MA 02584
Tel: (508) 228-0145
An ultra-luxurious 19th-century inn set on a narrow peninsula, with a number of cottage suites and 36 guest rooms. Tennis, various watersports and harbour cruises are available.

Plymouth

Sheraton Inn
180 Water Street
Plymouth
MA 02360
Tel: (508) 747-4900
One block from the sea, and close to major attractions, the hotel has 175 rooms in a three-storey building round the swimming pool.

Salem

Amelia Payson Guest House
16 Winter Street
Salem
MA 01970
Tel: (508) 744-8304
This bright and beautiful bed and breakfast has four large guest rooms with private bathrooms. Situated beside the Common, it is within walking distance of all Salem's attractions.

Sturbridge

Publick House Historic Resort
On the Common
Route 131
Sturbridge
MA 01566
Tel: (508) 347-3313
Near Old Sturbridge Village, the property has provided food and lodging since 1771.

Westminster

Westminster Village Inn
9 Village Inn Road
Westminster
MA 01473
Tel: (508) 874-5351
Facilities include a health club, pool and tennis at this 73-room inn.

Williamstown

Field Farm B & B
554 Sloan Road
Williamstown
MA 01267
Tel: (413) 458-3135
Country estate on 254 acres (105 hectares) of land. Scenic walking and skiing.

Rhode Island

Johnston

Hi-Way Motor Inn
1880 Hartford Avenue
Johnston
RI 02919
Tel: (401) 351-7810
A serviceable 35-room motel which provides a good night's rest at very reasonable cost.

Newport

Admiral Fitzroy Inn
398 Thames Street
Newport
RI 02840
Tel: (401) 846-4256
A well-appointed 1854 inn with 18 rooms. Fitzroy, commander of the Beagle *on which Darwin sailed to research for* Origin of the Species, *also developed the barometer. Some examples in the entry hall.*

Best Western Mainstay Inn
151 Admiral Kalbfus Road
Newport
RI 02840
Tel: (401) 849-9880
Next to the Jai Alai Centre and handy for the harbourfront and downtown historical area.

Marshall Slocum Guest House
29 Kay Street
Newport
RI 02840
Tel: (401) 841-5120
A much-acclaimed 1855 inn where guests get a full Yankee breakfast. Those on a three-day mid-week visit may qualify for a complimentary lobster dinner.

The Melville House
39 Clarke Street
Newport
RI 02840
Tel: (401) 847-0640
This 1750 colonial inn is two blocks from the harbour. A substantial breakfast is served.

Newport Islander Doubletree Hotel
Goat Island
Newport
RI 02840
Tel: (401) 849-2600
On a private island in Newport Harbor, this hotel is still close to downtown Newport. Indoor and outdoor pools, health club, sauna, racquetball and tennis courts.

Oceancliff I & II
Ocean Drive
Newport
RI 02840
Tel: (401) 846-6667
In extensive grounds overlooking Narragansett Bay, each waterfront suite with a balcony or patio has two bathrooms and two colour TVs. Among the amenities are an indoor swimming pool and tennis courts.

Providence

Grand Heritage Hotel ▮▮▮
Kennedy Plaza
Providence
RI 02903
Tel: (401) 421-0700
In the heart of Providence, close to the historic East Side, this turn-of-the-century hotel has 217 guest rooms and a rooftop ballroom with a panoramic view of the city.

Holiday Inn Downtown ▮▮
21 Atwells Avenue
Providence
RI 02903
Tel: (401) 831-3900
A fourteen-floor hotel with 274 rooms and suites, a heated pool and whirlpool.

Connecticut

Hartford

The Goodwin Hotel ▮▮▮
Goodwin Square
One Haynes Street
Hartford
CT 06103
Tel: (203) 246-7500
Opposite the Civic Center, the hotel offers garage valet parking and room service until 1am. The 124 units include 11 suites.

Susse Chalet Inn ▮
185 Brainard Road
Hartford
CT 06114
Tel: (203) 525-9306
All 130 units have TV. Continental breakfast is served. There is an outdoor pool.

Ivoryton

Copper Beech Inn ▮▮▮
46 Main Street
Ivoryton
CT 06442
Tel: (203) 767-0330
An 1800s 13-guestroom inn with 9 de luxe rooms, each with a Jacuzzi, in the converted carriage house. Some have cathedral ceilings with exposed beams. Other rooms in main house, excellent restaurant.

New Haven

Regal Inn ▮
1605 Whalley Avenue
New Haven
CT 06515
Tel: (203) 389-9504
Basic but comfortable rooms with TV. Special rates for senior citizens.

Residence Inn by Marriott ▮▮
3 Long Wharf Drive
New Haven
CT 06511
Tel: (203) 777-5337
Over 100 suites with kitchens and TV, some with fireplaces. Outdoor pool.

Mystic

Mystic Hilton ▮▮▮
20 Coogan Boulevard
Mystic
CT 06335
Tel: (203) 572-0731
Friendly 184-room hotel close to Mystic's factory outlet stores and Aquarium. Restaurant, lounge, exercise room and indoor pool.

Norwalk

Garden Park Motel ▮
351 Westport Avenue (Route 1)
Norwalk
CT 06851
Tel: (203) 847-7303
In the south-west corner of the state, near the sea, this 21-unit motel provides the basics reasonably (no meals) and allows pets.

Norwich

Norwich Inn & Spa ▮▮▮
607 West Thomas Street (Route 32)
Norwich
CT 06360
Tel: (203) 886-2401
A luxury turn-of-the-century inn with attractive villas as well as rooms. Full health club and spa facilities, sauna, indoor and outdoor pools, tennis and jogging trails.

Washington

The Mayflower Inn ▮▮▮
118 Woodbury Road
Washington
CT 06793
Tel: (203) 868-9466
Former country house in English-style gardens. 25 rooms, most with king-size canopied beds, fireplaces and mahogany and marble baths.

Vermont

Arlington

Arlington Inn ▮▮
Historic Route 7A
Arlington
VT 05250
Tel: (802) 375-6532
Elegant Greek Revival mansion with tennis courts, close to local attractions.

Brandon

The Brandon Inn ▮▮▮
20 Park Street
Brandon
VT 05733
Tel: (802) 247-5766
Located on the village green, the 1786 inn is on the National Historic Register. It has a terrace and outdoor pool.

Burlington

Holiday Inn ▮▮
1068 Williston Road
South Burlington
VT 05403
Tel: (802) 863-6361
Live entertainment and dancing Tuesday to Saturday. Indoor and outdoor pool.

Charlotte

The Inn at Charlotte ▮
RR1
Charlotte
VT 05445
Tel: (802) 425-2934
Charming no-smoking rooms set around a courtyard. Handy for visits to Shelburn Museum, Lake Champlain and the Wild-flower Farm.

Essex Junction

The Inn at Essex ▮▮
70 Essex Way
Essex Junction
VT 05452
Tel: (802) 878-1100
Midway between Lake Champlain and the Green Mountains, the Inn at Essex has 97 rooms, each one different. More expensive suites have fireplaces. The service is excellent.

Killington

Mountain Green Ski & Golf Resort
Killington Road
Killington
VT 05751
Tel: (802) 422-3000
Condominium suites from studio to four-bedroom units. Amenities include health club, massage, weight room, sauna, mineral spa, clubhouse, golf course, racquetball and volleyball.

Middlebury

October Pumpkin B & B
East Middlebury
Middlebury
VT 05740
Tel (802) 388-9525
'Polite Pets Welcome' at this 1850 home in the Greek Revival style in Robert Frost country.

Stowe

Butternut Inn at Stowe
2309 Mountain Road
Stowe
VT 05672
Tel: (802) 253-4277
Texas hospitality in non-smoking country home. Heated pool by mountain stream.

St Johnsbury

Holiday Motel
25 Hasting Street
St Johnsbury
VT 05819
Tel: (802) 748-8192
In the North-east Kingdom, within 15 minutes' drive of Burke Mountain, the motel has a heated pool.

Underhill

Rolling Meadow Farm Guestrooms
Underhill
VT 05489
Tel: (802) 899-4062
The farmhouse is in good walking and cross-country skiing terrain, between Burlington and Smugglers Notch ski area. The farm has livestock and maple sugaring.

Woodstock

The Woodstock Inn and Resort
14 The Green
Woodstock
VT 05091
Tel: (802) 457-1100.
Warmly hospitable staff look after guests in 146 luxurious rooms and suites. Sporting pursuits at the resort include golf, tennis (indoor and outdoor), squash, croquet, racquetball, downhill and cross-country skiing and a fully equipped sports centre.

New Hampshire

Exeter

Exeter Elms Campground
188 Court Street
Exeter
NH 03833
Tel: (603) 778-7631
On-site trailer rental on well-spaced riverside sites in the Sea-coast Region. A family of four can stay for under $20 a day. Canoe and boat rentals, pool, restrooms.

Hanover

The Hanover Inn
Main and Wheelock Streets
Hanover
NH 03755
Tel: (toll-free) 800-443-7024
Overlooking the campus of Dartmouth College, the Hanover Inn has guestrooms with colonial-style décor.

Jackson

The Wentworth Resort Hotel
Jackson Village
NH 03846
Tel: (603) 383-9700
This 60-room Victorian inn has an 18-hole golf course, outdoor pool, tennis courts, hayrides through the village, an illuminated skating rink and, within a 15-minute drive, downhill and cross-country skiing.

Meredith

The Inn at Mill Falls
Route 3
Meredith
NH 03253-9423
Tel: (603) 279-7006
The hotel section of the Mill Falls complex, with shops, restaurants and galleries, close to Lake Winnipesaukee. Through windows in an indoor bridge you can watch the millrace. The hotel has 54 guestrooms with en suite bathrooms.

North Conway

Eastern Slope Inn Resort
Routes 16 and Main Street
North Conway
NH 03860
Tel: (603) 356-6321
A National Historic Site, the resort has spa facilities and tennis courts. Four major ski mountains in the vicinity. There is a restaurant in a glass-enclosed courtyard.

North Woodstock

The Woodstock Inn
Route 3
Main Street
North Woodstock
NH 03262
Tel: (603) 745-3951
A few minutes' drive from Franconia Notch and many other attractions, this friendly four seasons inn has another property across the street overlooking the Pemigiwasset River. One room there has a Jacuzzi at the foot of the king-size canopy bed.

Portsmouth

Sise Inn
40 Court Street
Portsmouth
NH 03801
Tel: (603) 433-1200
No expense spared in the Victorian-style furnishings and fittings of this Queen Anne-style inn. It is handy for the waterfront, entertainment, shops and dining out.

Troy

The Inn at East Hill Farm
Monadnock Street
Troy
NH 03465
Tel: (603) 242-6495
Great value. This year-round farm resort near Keene offers hay or sleigh rides, hiking, water-skiing, cross-country skiing, sledding and skating. Three hearty meals a day are included in the lodging price. Pets allowed.

Maine

Bar Harbor

Bar Harbor Holiday Inn Sunspree Resort ▮▮▮
123 Eden Street
Bar Harbor
ME 04609
Tel: (207) 288-9723
With extensive ocean frontage, the hotel has a marina, with a lobster pound. It has tennis courts, fitness room and outdoor pool. It is close to Acadia National Park.

Damariscotta

Lake Pemaquid Camping ▮
Damariscotta
ME 04543
Tel: (207) 563-5202
Pitch your tent, trailer or recreational vehicle here. A group of up to six people can occupy a site with hook-ups on the 7-mile (11km) lakeside. Boats and canoes for rent, pool, sauna, ball game courts and organized fun. Pine cabin rentals also available.

Hulls Cove

Inn at Canoe Point ▮▮▮
Hulls Cove
ME 04644
Tel: (207) 288-9511
The inn, on Mt Desert Island, is 2 miles (3km) from Bar Harbor and is reached by causeway. The five guestrooms include a top-floor suite. A fortifying breakfast is served.

Kennebunkport

Captain Lord Mansion ▮▮▮
Kennebunkport
ME 04046
Tel: (207) 967-3141
Built for a sea captain in the early 1800s, this elegant mansion has an octagonal cupola from which he could observe vessels on the river. The 16 guestrooms are sumptuously furnished with antiques – one room has an 1820 English four-poster bed.

Newcastle

The Newcastle Inn ▮▮▮
River Road
Newcastle
ME 04553
Tel: (207) 563-5685
The inn, beside the Damariscotta River, has lovely old furniture and a reputation for epicurean food. Breakfast – a multi-course gourmet event – is included in the room rate. Dinner is optional.

Ogunquit

Milestone Motor Inn ▮▮▮
Route 1
Ogunquit
ME 03907
Tel: (207) 646-4562
If you don't want to drive, take a vintage trolley. This AAA Three-Diamond inn has some rooms overlooking the ocean, and a large outdoor heated pool.

Portland

The Pomegranate Inn ▮▮▮
49 Neal Street
Portland
ME 04102
Tel: (207) 772-1006
In the historic residential Western Promenade part of Portland, handy for downtown. The walls in this inn's guestrooms have been regarded as huge canvases on which professional artists have painted designs.

Radisson Eastland Hotel ▮▮
157 High Street
Portland
ME 04101
Tel: (207) 775-5411
In the historic and arts district near the Old Port, the price at this hotel includes breakfast.

Restaurants

Places to eat, at various price levels, are easily found in the small towns and villages of New England, as well as in the cities and mountain resorts. However, it is possible to drive long distances in wilderness areas without encountering developed communities. Many restaurants open for dinner as early as 5pm, but by 9pm, especially in more rural regions, you may not find anywhere open. The price categories given are for a three-course meal without drinks, tax or gratuities. Most menus cover a wide range of prices, with some moderate and some more expensive dishes. Key:

▮▮▮	$30 and over
▮▮	$20-30
▮	up to $20

Greater Boston

Anthony's Pier 4 ▮▮▮
140 Northern Avenue
Boston
MA
Tel: (617) 482-6262
Surrounded on three sides by water, Anthony's huge seafood restaurant has superb harbour and city views. It's popular with tourists, locals and celebrities.

The Bay Tower Room ▮▮▮
60 State Street
Boston
MA 02109
Tel: (617) 723-1666
Creative American fare 33 floors above Faneuil Hall Marketplace, with harbour and city views.

The Border Cafe ▮
32 Church Street
Harvard Square
Cambridge
MA
Tel: (617) 864-6100
A loud, widly popular restaurant serving spectacular Mexican dishes at very low prices. On Saturdays the wait is 2 hours: leave your name early and browse the local shops.

Commonwealth Brewing Company ▮
138 Portland Street
Boston
MA
Tel: (617) 523-8383
More than a dozen beers are made in the basement. The décor includes gleaming copper piping and vats. The food is equally good and varied.

Durgin-Park ▮
340 N. Market Street
Boston
MA
Tel: (617) 227-2038
Long-established diner serving traditional Yankee food. No-nonsense staff bring platters of fried seafood and boiled dinners to long tables of diners. Busy in season.

Nick's Comedy Stop
100 Warrenton Street
Boston
MA 02116
Tel: (617) 482-0930
Dinner show package – Italian food at Giancarlo's at Nick's, and tickets for one of the best comedy clubs.

Jimmy's Harborside Restaurant
242 Northern Avenue
Boston
MA.
Tel: (617) 423-1000
A traditional place to meet and eat overlooking Boston Harbor.

Massachusetts

Deerfield

The Deerfield Inn
The Street
Historic Deerfield
MA 01342
Tel: (413) 774-5587
The inn, at the heart of Historic Deerfield, bases some of its excellent traditional meals on cookbooks in the village museum. Superb surroundings.

Edgartown

Navigator Restaurant and Boathouse Bar
Two Main Street
Edgartown
MA 02539
Tel: (508) 627-5420
Colonial/Yankee fare on Martha's Vineyard island.

Gloucester

Evie's Rudder
73 Rocky Neck Avenue
Gloucester
MA 02930
Tel: (508) 283-7967
Long-established eating place in a 160-year-old waterside building.

Lenox

Seven Hills Inn
100 Pluncket Street
Lenox
MA 01240
Tel: (413) 637-4457
70-seat restaurant in the Berkshires serving continental cuisine.

Nantucket

21 Federal
21 Federal Street
Nantucket
MA 02554
Tel: (508) 228-2121
Some of the best American food on the island is served here.

Newburyport

David's Restaurant
11 Brown Square
Newburyport
MA 01950
Tel: (508) 465-0910
Three restaurants in one: upstairs is formal and more expensive; ***Downstairs at David's*** *has excellent steak, burgers and seafood; a children's room serves pizza and ice cream for kids, with toys and videos.*

Plymouth

Hearth 'n' Kettle (John Carver Inn)
25 Summer Street
Plymouth
MA 02360
Tel: (508) 746-7100
Traditional American family fare at one of a chain of restaurants.

Uxbridge

Cocke 'n' Kettle Restaurant
South Main Street
Route 123
Uxbridge
MA 01569
Tel (508) 278-5517
Large, popular restaurant on a colonial estate. Continental menu.

West Dennis

Lighthouse Inn
One Lighthouse Inn Road
West Dennis
MA 02670
Tel: (508) 398-2244
One of Cape Cod's well-patronized seafood restaurants, with seating for 200.

Worcester

Sweetheart
270 Shrewsbury Street
Worcester
MA
Tel: (508) 752-3700
Classic Indian cuisine.

Rhode Island

Block Island

Manisses
Spring Street
Block Island
RI 02807
Tel: (401) 466-2421
The best restaurant on Block Island. Try the seafood or dishes from the inn's smokehouse. Romantic candlelight atmosphere.

Newport

The Boathouse Restaurant
636 Thames Street
Newport
RI 02840
Tel: (401) 846-7700
Owned by native Newporters, this restaurant has nautical décor. It offers seafood, steaks and Cajun dishes.

The Cooke House
Bannister's Wharf
Newport
RI 02840
Tel: (401) 849-2900
Formal dining in an 18th-century setting, overlooking the harbour. Fresh ingredients, including produce from the restaurant's farm.

The Mooring
Sayers Wharf
Newport
RI 02840
Tel: (401) 846-2260
The place to be to see the harbour and yachts and to enjoy creatively presented lunches and dinners.

Providence

Angelo's Civita Farnese
141 Atwell's Avenue
Providence
RI
Tel: (401) 621-8171
A family-run, no-frills restaurant in the middle of the Italian district. Inexpensive pasta and pizza dishes amid lots of bustle.

Hemenway's Seafood Grill
One Old Stone Square
Providence
RI
Tel: (401) 351-8570
Fresh seafood flown in from around the world.

Connecticut

Farmington

The Whitman
1125 Farmington Avenue
Farmington
CT
Tel: (203) 678-9217
Sunday brunch at $15.95 includes a complimentary Bloody Mary or House Champagne. After the savouries, let yourself loose at the chocolate bar.

Ivoryton

Copper Beech Inn
46 Main Street
Ivoryton
CT 06442
Tel: (203) 767-0330
An exquisite menu at this French country restaurant and inn. A place to celebrate – or if an excuse is needed just celebrate being there.

Litchfield

Toll Gate Hill Inn and Restaurant
Route 202
Litchfield
CT
Tel: (203) 567-4545
Innovative dishes at reasonable cost – unless you want to splash out $110 for a bottle of wine! That's the top bracket: wine prices start at $9.

Mystic

Flood Tide Restaurant
The Inn at Mystic
Route 1
Mystic
CT 06335
Tel: (203) 536-8140
Don't eat here if you're in a rush – each course deserves to be savoured. Try to reserve a table overlooking the harbour.

The Steak Loft
Olde Mystick Village
Mystic
CT 06335
Tel: (203) 536-2661
Fresh seafood and salad bar open daily for lunch, dinner and 'quick bites'. The locals have voted the steaks the best in New London County for the past 10 years.

Stamford

Amadeus
201 Summer Street
Stamford
CT
Tel: (203) 348-7775
Cafe, bar and grill where cosmopolitan cooking has a Viennese accent.

Stonington

Randall's Ordinary
Route 2
North Stonington
CT 06359
Tel: (203) 599-4540
Nothing ordinary here – the term is an 18th-century one for a tavern. The cuisine is 18th century, too. Hearth cooking, using recipes of the time, is practised at the open fireplaces in each of the three dining rooms. An historic experience with every meal.

Vermont

Burlington

Carber's Restaurant and Lounge
115 St Paul Street
Burlington
VT 05401
Tel: (802) 862-4106
'Vermontabilia' surroundings. A test in decision-making – 100 'grandwich' combinations. American, Mexican, Italian and Caribbean dishes, and a long beer list.

Sakura Japanese Restaurant
2 Church Street
Burlington
VT 05401
Tel: (802) 863-1988
Popular downtown location with relaxed atmosphere and all-Japanese cuisine. Take-out available.

Essex Junction

Butler's Restaurant
The Inn at Essex
70 Essex Way
Essex Junction
VT 05452
Tel: (802) 878-1100).
Top-of-the-range outlet of New England Culinary Institute.

Killington

Hemingway's Restaurant
Route 4
Killington
VT 05751
Tel: (802) 422-3886
For dining in the grand style, in an atmospheric stone-walled wine cellar or beneath a vaulted ceiling, this much-acclaimed restaurant offers fine food superbly presented.

Manchester

The Village Country Inn
Manchester Village
Manchester
VT 05254
Tel: (802) 362-1792
Wholesome but sophisticated country menus are offered here. The cuisine has a French touch.

Montpelier

Main Street Grill and Bar
118 Main Street
Montpelier, VT
Tel: (802) 223-3188
One of the training establishments of the New England Culinary Institute – first class innovative fare.

Quechee

Rosalita's
Waterman Place
Quechee
VT 05059
Tel: (802) 295-1600
Mexican food in cheerful Mexican atmosphere.

Rutland

Sirloin Saloon
200 South Main Street
Rutland
VT 05701
Tel: (802) 773-7900
Steaks, prime rib, wood-grilled seafood, heart-healthy dishes, home-made desserts and children's menu. At various Vermont locations.

Stowe

Whiskers Restaurant
1652 Mountain Road
Stowe
VT 05672
Tel: (802) 253-8996
Lobster, steaks, chicken and pasta dishes served with all-you-can-eat from salad bar.

Woodstock

The Woodstock Inn
14 The Green
Woodstock
VT 05091
Tel: (802) 457-1100
The inn celebrated its bicentenary in 1993. The cuisine in the spacious formal restaurant delights business and leisure visitors. The inn's Eagle Cafe is a less expensive option.

New Hampshire

Gilford

The Tavern, Gunstock Inn
Route 11A
Gilford
NH 03246
Tel: (603) 293-2021
Country dining with gourmet specials in the shadow of Gunstock Mountain, overlooking Lake Winnipesaukee.

Glen

The Bernerhof Inn
Route 302
Glen
NH 03838
Tel: (603) 383-4414
A Taste of the Mountains Cooking School is based in this Mount Washington Valley hotel. Choose from the Middle European menu – Schnitzel Cordon Bleu, Fondue Bernese – or the seasonal specialities.

Keene

One Seventy Six Main
176 Main Street
Keene
NH
Tel: (603) 357-3100
Pub-style restaurant serving a wide range of international beers as well as burgers, Italian dishes, snacks and sandwiches.

North Woodstock

The Woodstock Inn
Route 3
Main Street
North Woodstock
NH 03262
Tel: (603) 745-3951
A wide choice of creative dishes. One of the specials is Venison Sauté served with a sauce of wild mushrooms and juniper berries.

Portsmouth

1853 Schoolhouse Restaurant
Woodbury Avenue
Portsmouth
NH
Tel: (603) 431-4650
Former one-room schoolhouse with casual friendly atmosphere, and varied menus. Folk-singing from 9pm on Fridays and Saturdays.

Sandwich

The Corner House Inn
Routes 109/103
Center Sandwich
NH
Tel: (603) 284-6219
Good value eating, and from November to May a story-telling session comes with dinner and entertainment for $9.95. It starts at 6.30pm – reservations suggested.

Maine

Bar Harbor

Jordan Pond House
Park Loop Road
Bar Harbor
ME 04609
Tel: (207) 276-3316
They've been serving teatime popovers straight from the oven, with strawberry jam, for 100 years at this former farmhouse. Book well in advance for lunch or dinner – this is the only restaurant in Acadia National Park. Closed in winter.

Camden

Waterfront Restaurant
Bay View Street
Camden
ME
Tel: (207) 236-3747
Seafood, with lobster and bouillabaisse specials, dominate at this restaurant. It has outdoor dining area and fine views of Camden harbour.

Cape Elizabeth

Two Lights Lobster Shack
225 Two Lights Road
Cape Elizabeth
ME
Tel: (207) 799-1677
Not only lobsters, but also clams, shrimps and hamburgers are served here. Closed in winter.

Kennebunkport

White Barn Inn
Beach Street
Kennebunkport
ME
Tel: (207) 967-2321
The inn restaurant is famed among locals and visitors alike for its superb seafood and New England regional menu.

Portland

Bay Harbour Restaurant
231 Front Street
South Portland
ME
Tel: (207) 799-5552
A view of the busy waterfront, inside or on the outdoor deck.

The Great Lost Bear
540 Forest Avenue
Portland
ME
Tel: (207) 772-0300
A popular rendezvous in the former Cameo Theatre. Lively bar/restaurant serving steaks, burgers, hot and spicy dishes and salads.

Index

Where there is more than one reference to text, the main entry is in **bold**. References to illustrations are in *italic*, those to maps are marked by an asterisk.

INDEX

INDEX